8/09

The Integration of
Major League Baseball

The Integration of Major League Baseball

A Team by Team History

RICK SWAINE

McFarland & Company, Inc., Publishers
Jefferson, North Carolina, and London

The author thanks SABR colleagues Mark Armour, George English, Rollie Hemond, Larry Lester, George Nicholson, Jim Sandoval, Steve Weingarden, and recently deceased Jules Tygiel for research information and guidance, and Connie Betterley for editorial assistance.

Topps and Bowman baseball cards are reproduced courtesy of the Topps Company, Inc. Fleer baseball cards are reproduced courtesy of Upper Deck.

LIBRARY OF CONGRESS CATALOGUING-IN-PUBLICATION DATA

Swaine, Rick, 1950–
The integration of Major League Baseball : a team by team history / Rick Swaine.
p.   cm.
Includes bibliographical references and index.

ISBN 978-0-7864-3903-4
illustrated case binding: 50# alkaline paper ∞

1. Baseball—United States—History.   2. Baseball—Records—United States.   3. Major League Baseball (Organization)—History. 4. Racism in sports—United States—History.   5. Discrimination in sports—United States—History.   I. Title.
GV863.A1S95   2009
796.357093—dc22   2009003183

British Library cataloguing data are available

On the cover: New York Yankees catcher Elston Howard in March of 1955 (Associated Press).

Manufactured in the United States of America

McFarland & Company, Inc., Publishers
Box 611, Jefferson, North Carolina 28640
www.mcfarlandpub.com

TABLE OF CONTENTS

PREFACE

The Integration of Major League Baseball is not another nostalgic trip through Negro League history or a re-telling of the Jackie Robinson–Branch Rickey saga.

This book focuses on the teams themselves, and the owners, front-office executives, and managers who were the heroes, villains, or fainthearted spectators of integration. In these pages some of the most respected and revered names in baseball will be disparaged by the record of what was actually accomplished under their watch. By the same token, unsung heroes of the day will be identified. In each case, the acquisition, deployment and, where possible, the treatment and support of black players is evaluated; the effect of integration or the failure to integrate on team performance is determined; and the persons who made the critical decisions are identified.

Although a few people came close, nobody went on record to say, "I won't have any [blacks] on my team because I hate them." Likewise, acts of courage and sensitivity were often hidden or denied because of the attitude of the times. But the men who welcomed black players to improve their teams, as well as the grand old game, established a different track record from those who shunned them to the detriment of the franchises they represented and the sport itself.

Of course, the question that begs to be asked is: "Why besmirch the reputations of a bunch of dead guys by dredging up ancient history?" One answer is that we need perspective. In other words, the records of men like Lou Boudreau or John Quinn can only be properly appreciated when compared with those of contemporaries like Al Lopez or George Weiss.

But more important, there's something to be said about learning from our past. For instance, going into the 2008 season only 50 percent of the sixteen franchises that were around when the color line was broken had employed a black manager, while almost 80 percent of the fourteen teams that came into existence after 1960 have had a black manager. Furthermore, the list of original teams that have never hired a black manager is eerily similar to a compilation of the more notorious resisters of integration more than 50 years ago. How much of this is coincidence? Can any of it be attributed to outside influences, to demographics or geographic location, for instance? Have candidate qualifications played a part? Or does the bulk of the blame lie with a self-perpetuating organizational culture?

You make the call.

INTEGRATION TIMELINE

1845	*September 13.* Alexander Cartwright publishes the first set of baseball rules
1857	*March 10.* Organized Baseball is born, with the formation of the National Association of Base Ball Players
1865	*April 9.* The Civil War ends
1865	*December 18.* Slavery is officially abolished with ratification of the Thirteenth Amendment
1867	*October 18.* A petition by the black Pythians of Philadelphia to enter Organized Baseball is denied
1869	*May 4.* The Cincinnati Red Stockings make their debut as baseball's first openly professional team
1876	*February 2.* The National League, baseball's first major league, is formed
1878	*The season.* Bud Fowler becomes the first black player in Organized Baseball (minor leagues)
1884	*May 1.* Moses Walker becomes the first black player in Major League Baseball
1884	*September 4.* Moses Walker makes his last major league appearance
1887	*July.* Chicago manager Cap Anson forces Newark to bench black players for an exhibition game
1887	*July.* The International League, of which Newark is a member, moves to ban black players
Pre-1901	The American League gains major league status, creating the present-day two-league format
Pre-1901	John McGraw's attempt to pass black player Charlie Grant off as an American Indian fails
1911	*The season.* The Cincinnati Reds employ two dark-skinned Cuban players claiming "Castillian" ancestry
Post-1920	Fritz Pollard becomes the first black professional football player
1936	*August.* Black track star Jesse Owens wins four gold medals in the Summer Olympics in Berlin
1937	*June 22.* Black boxer Joe Louis wins the heavyweight championship of the world

1944	*November 25*. Commissioner Judge Kenesaw Mountain Landis dies
1945	*September 2*. World War II ends
1945	*October 23*. The Brooklyn Dodgers sign Jackie Robinson to play for their Montreal Royals (IL) farm team
1946	*April 18*. Robinson debuts with Montreal — the first black player in the International League since 1889
1946	*August 27*. The Race Question report is issued
1946	*October*. The American and National Football Leagues re-integrate after a decade of segregation
1947	*April 15*. The Dodgers become the first major league team to integrate, with the debut of Robinson
1947	*July 5*. The Cleveland Indians become the second team to integrate, with the signing and debut of Larry Doby
1947	*July 17*. The St. Louis Browns become the third to integrate, with the signing and debut of Hank Thompson
1947	*July 19*. The Browns become the first team with two black players, with the debut of Willard Brown
1947	*August 23*. The Browns release Thompson and Brown but minor leaguer Chuck Harmon stays in the system
1947	*August 26*. Dan Bankhead debuts with the Brooklyn Dodgers — the first black major league pitcher
1948	*April 20*. Roy Campanella debuts with the Brooklyn Dodgers — the sixth black major leaguer
1948	*July 9*. Satchel Paige debuts with the Cleveland Indians — the seventh black major leaguer
1948	*December*. The Boston Braves sign their first black player — career minor leaguer Waldon Williams
1949	*January*. The New York Giants sign their first black players — Monte Irvin, Hank Thompson, and Ford Smith
1949	*February*. The New York Yankees sign their first black player — Luis Marquez
1949	*April 19*. The Cleveland Indians become the first team with three black players, with the debut of Minnie Minoso
1949	*May 20*. Don Newcombe debuts with the Brooklyn Dodgers — the ninth black major leaguer
1949	*June*. The Chicago White Sox hire John Donaldson — the first black major league scout
1949	*June*. The Chicago Cubs sign their first black player — career minor leaguer Robert Burns
1949	*July 8*. The New York Giants become the fourth team to integrate, with the debut of Hank Thompson and Monte Irvin

Post-1949	Jackie Robinson becomes the first black player to win the Most Valuable Player Award
1950	*April.* The Boston Red Sox sign their first black player — Negro League veteran Piper Davis
1950	*April 18.* The Brooklyn Dodgers become the first team with four black players, with the recall of Dan Bankhead
1950	*April 18.* The Boston Braves become the fifth team to integrate, with the debut of Sam Jethroe
1950	*April 25.* Chuck Cooper (Boston Celtics) becomes the first black basketball player drafted by the NBA
1950	*May.* The Red Sox release Piper Davis after a 30-day trial with Eastern League Scranton (Class A)
1950	*July.* The Chicago White Sox sign their first black players — Bob Boyd and Sam Hairston
1950	*September 1.* Chuck Cooper and Earl Lloyd become the first black players in the NBA
1950	*October.* The New York Yankees and Philadelphia Phillies meet in the last all-white World Series
Pre-1951	The Pittsburgh Pirates hire Rickey and sign their first black players — several minor leaguers
1951	*March.* The Philadelphia Athletics sign their first black player — career minor leaguer Marion Scott
1951	*May 1.* The White Sox become the sixth team to integrate, with the acquisition of Cuban Minnie Minoso
1951	*May 25.* Willie Mays debuts with the New York Giants — the seventeenth black major leaguer
1951	*July 18.* Satchel Paige re-integrates the St. Louis Browns
1951	*July 21.* Sam Hairston becomes the first African American to play for the Chicago White Sox
1951	*September.* Don Newcombe becomes the first black pitcher to win 20 games
1952	*February.* The Cincinnati Reds sign their first black players — several minor leaguers
1952	*March.* The Washington Senators sign their first black players — Juan Delis and minor leaguer Luis Morales
1952	*The season.* Sam Bankhead becomes the first black manager, with Provincial League Farnham (Class C)
1952	*The season.* Johnny Britton and Jimmy Newberry become the first black players to play professional baseball in Japan
1952	*April 13.* Dave Hoskins becomes the first black player to play in the Texas League (Class AA)
1953	*April 22.* The Pirates become the seventh team to integrate, with the debut of Puerto Rican Carlos Bernier

1953	*The season.* The Boston Red Sox re-integrate their minor league organization, with the signing of Earl Wilson
1953	*May.* The St. Louis Cardinals sign their first black player, career minor leaguer Len Tucker
1953	*August.* The Detroit Tigers sign their first black player, career minor leaguer Claude Agee
1953	*September 13.* The Philadelphia Athletics become the eighth team to integrate, with the debut of Bob Trice
1953	*September 17.* The Chicago Cubs become the ninth team to integrate, with the debut of Ernie Banks
1953	*September.* The New York Yankees are the last major league team to win a pennant with a segregated roster
1954	*April 13.* Hank Aaron debuts with the Milwaukee Braves — the thirty-ninth black major leaguer
1954	*April 13.* Curt Roberts becomes the first African American to play for the Pittsburgh Pirates
1954	*April 13.* The St. Louis Cardinals become the tenth team to integrate, with the debut of Tom Alston
1954	*April 17.* The Cincinnati Reds become the eleventh team to integrate with the debut of Puerto Rican Nino Escalera and African American Chuck Harmon
1954	*April.* Nate Peeples gets two at-bats as the only black player in Southern Association (Class AA) history
1954	*July 17.* The Brooklyn Dodgers become the first team to have five black players in their lineup
1954	*September 6.* The Washington Senators become the twelfth team to integrate with the debut of Cuban Carlos Paula
Post-1954	The Philadelphia Phillies sign their first black player — career minor leaguer Charlie Randall
1955	*April 14.* The New York Yankees become the thirteenth team to integrate, with the debut of Elston Howard
1957	*January 22.* Jackie Robinson announces his retirement from Major League Baseball
1957	*April 16.* The Philadelphia Phillies become the fourteenth team to integrate, with the debut of Cuban Chico Fernandez
1957	*April 22.* John Irving Kennedy becomes the first African American to play for the Philadelphia Phillies
1957	*August 13.* Joe Black becomes the first African American to play for the Washington Senators
1958	*June 6.* The Detroit Tigers become the fifteenth team to integrate, with the debut of Dominican Ozzie Virgil

Pre-1959	The Detroit Tigers return Maury Wills, acquired on a conditional basis, to the Los Angeles Dodgers
1959	*April 10.* Larry Doby becomes the first African American to play for the Detroit Tigers
1959	*July 21.* The Boston Red Sox become the sixteenth and last team to integrate, with the debut of Pumpsie Green
1960	*The season.* The Kansas City Athletics become the last team to employ an all-white roster for an entire season
1961	*April 10.* Willie Tasby becomes the first black player to play for the expansion Washington Senators
1961	*April 11.* Julio Becquer and Lou Johnson become the first black players to play for the Los Angeles Angels
1961	*June 19.* Gene Baker (Pittsburgh) becomes the first black manager of a major-league farm club
Post-1961	The Southern Association (Class AA) disbands without ever accepting integration
1962	*January 24.* Jackie Robinson becomes the first black player elected to the Baseball Hall of Fame
1962	*May 10.* Buck O'Neill (Chicago Cubs) becomes the first black coach in the major leagues
1962	*May 10.* Roman Mejias and Jim Pendleton become the first black players to play for the Houston Colts
1962	*May 11.* Felix Mantilla and Charlie Neal become the first black players to play for the New York Mets
1962	*The season.* The Baltimore Orioles become the last team to employ an all-white roster for an extended period
1966	*April.* Emmett Ashford becomes the first black umpire in the major leagues
1969	*April 7.* Elston Howard (New York Yankees) becomes the first black coach in the American League
1971	*February 9.* Satchel Paige becomes the first black player selected to the Hall of Fame as a Negro Leaguer
1971	*September 1.* The Pittsburgh Pirates field a lineup of nine black players against the Philadelphia Phillies
1971	*October 9.* The Pittsburgh Pirates start eight black players in the first game of the World Series
1974	*November.* Frank Robinson (Cleveland Indians) becomes the first black major league manager
1976	*September 19.* Bill Lucas (Atlanta Braves) becomes the first black major league director of player personnel
1989	*February.* Bill White becomes president of the American League — the first African American in such a high position

1989   *September.* Cito Gaston (Toronto Blue Jays) becomes the first black manager
            to capture a pennant

1993   *September.* Bob Watson (Houston Astros) becomes the first black major-
            league general manager

INTRODUCTION: BASEBALL'S IGNOBLE HISTORY OF SEGREGATION

In October 1867, less than two years after the Thirteenth Amendment to the Constitution abolished slavery in the United States, the first attempt by black players to enter white baseball was rebuffed. The black players were members of the Pythians of Philadelphia, which like many of the top white teams of the era had evolved from a men's social club. The Pythians applied for admission to the Pennsylvania Base Ball Association, the governing body of baseball in that state. On the eve of the vote, the Pythians were persuaded to withdraw their application when it became clear that they had no chance to prevail. A few months later, the Pennsylvania Association issued a statement that it was "against the admission of any club which may be composed of one or more colored persons." This position was justified with the extraordinary explanation, "If colored clubs were admitted there would in all probability be some division of feelings, whereas, by excluding them no injury could result to anyone." Apparently this sounded an alarm within the 10-year-old National Association of Base Ball Players, and its rules were promptly amended to formally bar "colored" players. After the National Association of Base Ball Players disbanded several years later, its successor organizations generally relied upon peer pressure and an informal, but effective, gentlemen's agreement among the league owners and executives to exclude black players.[1]

The Evolution of "Organized Baseball"

Professional baseball can trace its inception to July 20, 1858, when admission was charged for the first time for a game between all-star teams from Brooklyn and New York.[2] By 1871 the National Association of *Professional* Base Ball Players supplanted the National Association of Base Ball Players, as all pretense of maintaining an amateur organization was abandoned. The new association formed baseball's first professional league and dictated the game's playing and organizational rules, including the continued exclusion of black players.

The National Association of Professional Base Ball Players was actually run by baseball players, an intolerable situation when there was a buck to be made, and in 1876 it was usurped by the National League of Professional Baseball Clubs, which was controlled by the team owners. The National League is generally considered the first "major league," although it initially faced challenges from other circuits. After its closest rival, the International Association, was vanquished in 1879, the general framework for "Organized Baseball" was formed with the development of the National Agreement, a pact among most of the top leagues in existence to mutually respect player contracts and cease raiding the rosters of member teams. The National League then contracted to eight teams and instituted a reserve clause to further limit the players' ability to offer their skills to the highest bidder in an open market.

The reserve clause and other conditions that the players considered onerous led to the formation of the American Association in 1882; it enticed many dissatisfied National Leaguers to jump teams. A truce was declared in 1883 when the American Association was recognized as an official major league on par with the National League.

Baseball's First Black Players

Both free and enslaved black men played baseball during the first half of the 19th century as baseball evolved from informal bat and ball games like rounders and town ball and rapidly gained popularity as a club sport. In fact, the first recorded baseball game between two black teams, the Henson Baseball Club of Jamaica, now the borough of Queens, and the Unknowns of Weeksville, an African American neighborhood in the heart of Brooklyn, took place on November 15, 1859.[3] A decade later, the first known contest between organized black and white teams, the aforementioned Pythians versus the Olympic Club, would be played in Philadelphia. The Olympic Club prevailed in that first match, but two weeks later the Pythians notched the first recorded victory of a black team over white competitors, the City Items.[4]

On May 1, 1884, Moses Fleetwood Walker, a 27-year-old black catcher, opened the season behind the plate for the Toledo Blue Stockings of the American Association. Walker is generally considered to be the first acknowledged black major leaguer. He would also be the last until Jackie Robinson of the Brooklyn Dodgers broke the color barrier in 1947.

Amidst the confusion of the era, the baseball establishment's resolve to keep black players out at all levels had faltered. In 1878, 20-year-old John "Bud" Fowler broke in as a pitcher with the Lynn, Massachusetts, entry in the ill-fated International Association and reportedly bested the pennant-winning Boston National League squad in an exhibition contest by a score of 2 to 1. Against all odds, Fowler's professional career in white baseball would span almost two decades, and for 50 years he would hold the remarkable distinction of being one of the last, as well as the first, known black players in professional baseball.[5]

Recent research into his career indicates that Fowler played in 13 different professional minor leagues over an 18-year period with numerous forays into semipro and black baseball. Many of the white professional teams he played for were in desperate straits and failed to finish the season. Though he began as a pitcher and could play anywhere, he is best remembered as a speedy, sure-handed second baseman. The best information available indicates that he played a total of 465 games in ten different seasons from 1878 through 1895 and managed a composite .308 lifetime average in predominantly white professional baseball. Interestingly, Fowler seldom played for the top all-black teams of his time, though he was certainly one of the top black performers, apparently preferring life on the fringes of white baseball despite the discrimination he faced. But in 1895, the 37-year-old veteran teamed with the great Grant "Home Run" Johnson to form the Page Fence Giants, a club that would develop into a legendary independent black baseball powerhouse. The footloose Fowler, however, left the club during the season to make one last appearance in white minor league baseball with Adrian in the Michigan State League.[6]

Moses Walker may have been the second black player in Organized Baseball after Fowler, but he was the first black major leaguer. In 1883, he signed with Toledo, then a minor league

Bud Fowler, in the middle of the top row, in an 1894 Keokuk (Western League) team photograph, was the first known black player in Organized Baseball when he debuted 16 years earlier with Lynn, Massachusetts, of the International Association (Larry Lester).

team in the Northwestern League, after starring for Oberlin College. When the American Association expanded from eight to twelve teams, the Toledo franchise was admitted into the new league, and they brought their star catcher along. During the season, Moses' younger brother Welday, an outfielder, briefly joined him on the Toledo roster. Evidence indicates that the only other acknowledged black player to appear in Organized Baseball before 1886, aside from Fowler and the Walker brothers, was first baseman Jack Frye, who played with Reading of the Interstate Association in 1883.[7] A few years ago, researchers discovered William White, a 19-year-old Brown University student who filled in at first base for one game for the National League Providence Grays in 1879. White may actually have been the first black major leaguer. Evidence seems to indicate that he was the son of a white plantation owner and his black slave, but whether he was acknowledged to be a black man by the standards of the time is in doubt.[8]

Walker was a major league talent. Toledo's ace pitcher Tony Mullane remembered, "[Walker] was the best catcher I ever worked with, but I disliked a Negro and whenever I had to pitch to him I used to pitch anything I wanted without looking at his signals."[9] This lack of teamwork no doubt contributed to Walker's mediocre fielding stats, but his .263 batting mark was well above the league norm and ranked third highest on the squad, a highly unusual achievement for a catcher in that era. Walker shared Toledo's catching duties with another freshman, Deacon McGuire, who registered a paltry .185 in 1884. But Walker was back in the minor leagues when the 1885 season rolled around while McGuire would go on to play 26 major league seasons. The fraternity of major league club owners had moved quickly to mend the breach in the gentleman's agreement that kept black players out of the highest level of professional baseball. After Walker made his last appearance of the 1884 season on September 4, the major leagues would not see another acknowledged black player for 63 years, though Walker and several others would continue to ply their trade in the minor leagues for another decade.

Modern research indicates that at least 33 acknowledged black players appeared on predominantly white teams in the minor leagues between 1878 and the close of the century.[10] The high point was the 1887 season when seven acknowledged black players performed in the International League. At the time, the International League was considered just a step below the major leagues, and five of the circuit's black players were bona fide stars. Bud Fowler played second base for Binghamton, Moses Walker and pitcher George Stovey formed an all-star battery for Newark, Bob Higgins won 20 games for Syracuse, and future Hall of Famer Frank Grant, generally considered the top black player of the 19th century, starred at second base for Buffalo.[11]

The Re-Segregation of the Game

But during the 1887 season growing anti-black sentiment began to make things increasingly difficult for black players. In late June, nine of Bud Fowler's white teammates on the eighth-place Binghamton squad formally protested his presence on the club with a telegram to the front office. They threatened to strike "if the colored players, who have been the cause of all our trouble, are not released at once." A few days later, Fowler and his .350 batting average that had caused so much trouble were gone. In Bob Higgins' first appearance for Syracuse, his white teammates allowed 21 unearned runs, and his catcher was fined and suspended for his deliberately poor play. However, the most damaging event of the season occurred when Cap Anson, player-manager of the Chicago Nationals, refused to let his team take the field for a scheduled exhibition game against Newark if Stovey and Walker were permitted to play. Understandably reluctant to forfeit the receipts from such a lucrative match, the Newark club capitulated. Almost immediately thereafter the league's board of directors addressed the issue by instructing the league secretary not to approve any more contracts involving black players. Those already under contract would be allowed to finish out the season, but no new pacts would be issued.[12]

The Syracuse and Buffalo franchises stood up for their black stars and fought the ban, forging an agreement whereby Higgins and Grant were allowed to return in 1888. The Newark club, however, abandoned its black players. Stovey, winner of 34 games in 1887, went to play in the less competitive but more enlightened New England League while Walker caught on with Syracuse. Due to continued hostility, Higgins and Grant didn't return the next year, leaving the intrepid Moses Walker as the sole black player in the International League for the 1889 campaign. He was not invited back the next season.[13] For the next few years, a handful of black teams and individual players struggled on in lesser circuits until the racial barrier was firmly entrenched. Fowler and future Negro League Hall of Famer Sol White, who spent part of the 1895 season with Fort Wayne in the Western Interstate League, are among the last acknowledged black players to appear in Organized Baseball before the turn of the century.[14]

Much blame for the re-segregation of Organized Baseball has been assigned to Cap Anson, player-manager of the Chicago National League squad and one of baseball's all-time greats. In 1884, Anson threatened to take his team off the field if Toledo permitted the Walker brothers to play against his squad in an exhibition game. He was forced to back down that time. But when the management of the Newark team caved in to his objections to Walker and Stovey in 1887, the move to re-establish racial barriers in Organized Baseball gained strength until every known black player was purged from the ranks of Organized Baseball.[15] In addition to being one the great black players of the 19th century, Sol White was also the first black baseball historian. In 1907, he published *Sol White's Official Baseball Guide* in which he identified Anson as someone "with repugnant feeling, shown at every opportunity, toward colored ball players."[16] White also claimed that Anson thwarted an attempt by the National League's New York Giants to sign George Stovey after the 1886 season.[17]

Banned from organized ball, the best black players gravitated to independent teams that gradually coa-

All-time great Cap Anson helped derail a 19th century movement to integrate baseball by refusing to allow his team to take the field against black players (1961 Fleer card).

lesced into organized leagues. In 1906, the International League of Colored Baseball Clubs in America and Cuba was formed. The Roaring Twenties would be the heyday of black baseball, but the boon times came to an end with the onset of the Great Depression. As the financial hardships of the 1930s took a tremendous toll on the weakly administered Negro Leagues, black baseball fell to its lowest point in 1932. But Franklin Delano Roosevelt's New Deal soon began to turn the economy around. Beginning in 1933, the annual East-West Negro League All-Star Game became a major attraction, and by the 1940s, the Negro National League representing the East and the Negro American League representing the South and the Midwest were thriving enterprises.

"Passing" Attempts

During Organized Baseball's self-imposed segregation era, there were isolated attempts to slip black players into the lineup by claiming heritage other than American Negro. The most well-known effort was John McGraw's 1901 attempt to pass second baseman Charlie Grant off as a Cherokee Indian named Charlie Tokohama. McGraw, who would go on to manage the New York Giants for more than 30 years before stepping down as the winningest manager in the history of the National League, was at the helm of the Baltimore Orioles at the time. He spotted the rather light-skinned Grant playing for a black team and reportedly picked the name Tokohama off of a map. Unfortunately, the ruse was exposed by the discriminating eye of White Sox owner Charles Comiskey, who recognized Grant/Tokohama as a member of a Chicago-area black team and publicly exposed him as a Negro. Comiskey showed his own true colors as well as Grant's, managing to denigrate three minority groups in one sitting with the threat, "If McGraw keeps this 'Indian' I will put a Chinaman on third base. This Cherokee is really Grant fixed up with war paint and feathers. His father is a well-known Negro in Cincinnati where he trains horses."[18] Despite an impressive spring performance, Grant was released before getting a chance to play in a regular-season game.[19]

This wasn't the first time the Indian ruse had been unsuccessfully attempted. Some publications identify mulatto southpaw Bert Jones as the last black 19th-century major leaguer. Jones, who was called "The Yellow Kid" after a popular cartoon character of the era, pitched in the Kansas State League in 1898.[20] But according to *The Cooperstown Symposium on Baseball and American Culture*, an attempt to pass Jones off as an Indian was exposed before it got off the ground.[21]

Another well-known incident involved Jimmy Claxton, who pitched briefly for the Oakland Oaks of the Pacific Coast League in 1916. Following his May 28 debut, newspaper accounts reported that Claxton hailed from an Indian reservation back east and gave mildly encouraging reviews of his performance. But Claxton never got another chance to take the mound before drawing his release on June 3, 1916. *San Francisco Chronicle* sports editor Harry B. Smith wrote, "Claxton pitched last year, according to reports, with the Oakland Giants [a black team], but Manager Rowdy [Elliott] declared that he had appeared at the Oakland headquarters with an affidavit signed before a notary showing him to be from one of the reservations in North Dakota." In interviews conducted long after his playing days were over, Claxton blamed Elliott for not giving him a fair chance and said that a friend betrayed him by divulging his racial heritage to the Oaks.[22]

It was eventually learned that Claxton was born at Wellington, a British Columbia mining town on Vancouver Island, to American parents. According to his parents' wedding certificate, "The bridegroom is a coloured man; the bride a white woman." But Claxton's heritage was more complex than that. Later in life, he described his ethnic heritage as Negro, French and Indian on his father's side, and Irish and English on his mother's. The 1910 census designated Claxton as mulatto, but ten years later he would be listed as black. The Indian tribe connection came when he was recommended to the Oaks as a fellow tribesman by an Oakland Giants fan who was part-Indian.[23]

After his release by the Oaks, Claxton resumed life as a baseball vagabond, pitching for barnstorming and semiprofessional teams well into his 40s. He claimed to have pitched in all but two of the contiguous 48 states (missing Maine and having the good sense to avoid Texas). In 1932, at the age of 39, Claxton made his Negro League debut with the Cuban Stars, whose pitching staff was led by Luis (Lefty) Tiant, father of the future major league star hurler. He was still playing competitive baseball at age 52 and was still spry enough to pitch in an old-timer's game at age 63.[24] As fortune would have it, Claxton 's brief stint with the Oaks coincided with a visit by a photographer from the Collins-McCarthy Candy Company. The company was producing Zeenuts baseball cards depicting Pacific Coast League players. Claxton's likeness was included in the 1916 Zeenut set, making him the first known African American baseball player to be depicted on a baseball card, one of which sold for $7,200 in a 2005 Sotheby's auction.

Despite these documented failures, there's little doubt that some black players were able to pass as whites, especially in remote minor league outposts. In 1910, Dick Brookins, a third baseman with Regina in the Class D Western Canada League, was banned when it was somehow determined that he was black after a protest from a rival club. Brookins, whose 1910 statistics were expunged from league records, was a four-year veteran of Organized Baseball at the time.[25]

Latinos Cross the Line

A year after the Brookins episode, the Cincinnati Reds hit upon a formula for qualifying Hispanic players with suspiciously dusky skin tones for major league duty. Third baseman Rafael Almeida and outfielder Armando Marsans were veterans of Cuban baseball who had played for a Negro League barnstorming team, the All-Cubans, in 1905. In *A History of Cuban Baseball: 1864–2006*, Peter Bjarkman describes Almeida as "a light-colored mulatto" and Marsans as "displaying skin tones a full shade darker than a significant portion of [African-American Negro Leaguers]." The pair debuted together on July 4, 1911, and their appearance occasioned a furor in Cincinnati. But public pressure abated when the Reds produced documentation in the form of a letter from "a Cuban baseball official in Havana" that both men were of Castilian rather than Negro heritage.[26] Almeida spent three seasons as a part-timer with the Reds, but Marsans' major league career lasted eight years as he played for the St. Louis Browns and the New York Yankees after a successful three-and-one-half-year stint in Cincinnati.

According to *A History of Cuban Baseball*, 38 Cuban players appeared in the major leagues before Jackie Robinson's 1947 debut, and about a third of them are known to have played in the Negro Leagues.[27] Most had brief big league careers, but a few Hispanic former Negro Leaguers overcame suspicions about their racial heritage to enjoy significant big league careers. The most noteworthy of these brave souls were Dolf Luque, Mike Gonzalez, Bobby Estalella, and Tommy de la Cruz.[28]

But Cubans weren't the only Latino group to come under suspicion of having "a Senegambian in the bat pile"— to use a phrase written by famed correspondent Red Smith.[29] Puerto Rican hurler Hiram Bithorn, Venezuelan right-hander Alex Carrasquel, and Mexican outfielder Mel Almada were Hispanic players who suffered racist taunts due to their "swarthy" complexions.[30]

During the 1945 campaign, Organized Baseball's final season of official segregation, at least 15 Latino players performed in the major leagues. While it's commonly accepted that Latinos with various degrees of black ancestry were permitted to play major league baseball while the game was segregated, the color barrier remained rigidly in place for American-born blacks. For example, the father of star Negro League catcher Roy Campanella was white and Roy's skin was several shades lighter than many Latino big leaguers, but he was forced to ply his trade in the Negro Leagues rather than the majors. In fact, one would be hard-pressed to name an African American who managed to pass. American-born players with darker-than-average skin or traces of traditional "Negroid features" were invariably challenged. The harassment of 19th-century catcher Sandy Nava and outfielder George Treadway supposedly drove them out of the league.[31] Chief Meyers, a Native American, also heard the catcalls, and outfielder Bing Miller was sometimes called Booker T. Miller due to his dark skin tone.[32] Even Babe Ruth was rumored to have some Negro blood coursing through his veins, hence the nickname "Jidge" that he was tagged with in his early years in the league.[33]

Pressure to Integrate Builds

The revival of the Negro Leagues as the country pulled out of the depths of the Great Depression made it extremely difficult to ignore the talents of black ballplayers. The charismatic Satchel Paige rose to stardom, and via a blend of extraordinary ability and even more remarkable showmanship became the first black player to capture the attention of white baseball fans everywhere. Josh Gibson and Buck Leonard emerged as the Babe Ruth and Lou Gehrig of black baseball. "Cool Papa" Bell ran the bases like Ty Cobb. Ray "Hooks" Dandridge and Willie Wells, known as "El Diablo," reinvented infield defensive play, and Cuban great Martin Dihigo starred on the mound, at the plate, and in the field. Sluggers like Willard "Home Run" Brown, "Turkey" Stearnes, "Mule" Suttles, and Monte Irvin rivaled Gibson as the league's foremost power hitter, and Leon Day, Ray Brown, and Hilton Smith battled Paige for top-hurler recognition.

Exhibition contests pitting Negro League stars against major leaguers drew huge crowds that raised the national awareness of black baseball. Cardinal pitching great Dizzy Dean, at the time the biggest name in baseball after Babe Ruth, became a one-man publicity machine as he unabashedly extolled the talents of Paige and others. "It's too bad those colored boys don't play in the big league because they sure got some great players,"[34] crowed Diz.

The performances of blacks in other sports helped to remove lingering questions regarding athletic ability and improved the image of all black performers. Like Organized Baseball, professional basketball was not open to black players. The fledgling National Football League fielded about a dozen black players, including notables Fritz Pollard, Duke Slater, and Paul Robeson, before slamming its doors shut in 1933. But Joe Louis, the Brown Bomber, captured the World Heavyweight Championship on his way to gaining recognition as the greatest boxer of all-time. Jesse Owens captured four gold medals during the 1936 Olympic Games in Berlin to the consternation of Adolf Hitler. The second-place finisher in the 200-meter dash was Mack Robinson, whose little brother Jackie was starring in four sports for Muir Technical High School in Pasadena at the time. In 1940, the Harlem Globetrotters, at the time a competitive team who only clowned around for the audience after establishing a safe lead, beat the Chicago Bruins to capture the World Professional Basketball Tournament.

Though the country's mood and laws still embraced segregation, the decade leading up to the breaching of Organized Baseball's color barrier was marked by significant progress in efforts to gain equal rights for minorities in all facets of life. In 1936, President Franklin Delano Roosevelt established the Office of Minority Affairs. In 1940, Benjamin O. Davis became the first black general in the United States Armed Forces, and in 1941, just before the bombing of Pearl Harbor, Roosevelt issued an executive order prohibiting discrimination in the military. In 1944, Adam Clayton Powell became the first black U.S. Congressman, and the Supreme Court ruled that minorities could not be denied the right to vote in primary elections. *Ebony* magazine was first published in 1945, and that same year New York enacted legislation to establish a Fair Employment Practices Commission and became the first state to make it an "unlawful employment practice to discriminate because of race, creed, color, or national origin."

Fueled by the migration of blacks from the rural south to northern urban areas, the voice of the black press became more strident and influential in demanding fairer treatment if not outright equality for African Americans. Black sports columnists, led by Wendell Smith of the *Pittsburgh Courier*, Joe Bostic of Harlem's *People's Voice*, Fay Young of the *Chicago Defender*, and Sam Lacy of the *Baltimore Afro American* and *Washington Tribune*, spearheaded a drive to force Major League Baseball to accept Negroes that began in earnest during the 1930s. Under pressure from these crusading black writers, the first cracks in Organized Baseball's resolve to keep the color barrier intact began appearing in the last years of the decade.

Sensitivity to the plight of black citizens received an unexpected boost from within the ranks of Organized Baseball in 1938 when New York Yankee outfielder Jake Powell told a radio audience that he enjoyed "cracking niggers over the head" as a cop in the off-season.[35] The Yankees slapped the reserve outfielder on the wrist with a suspension, but the incident provided the national press with an invitation to weigh in on the subject of race relations in baseball. Respected columnist Westbrook Pegler's accusation that Organized Baseball dealt with "Negroes as Adolf Hitler treats the Jews," may have been an overstatement, but the point was made.[36]

That same year, Washington Senators owner Clark Griffith opined, "There are few baseball magnates who are not aware of the fact that the time is not far off when colored players will take their places beside those of other races in the major leagues."[37] National League president Ford Frick and Chicago Cubs owner Phil Wrigley chimed in with similar sentiments.[38]

In 1940 Pittsburgh Pirates president William Benswanger said, "If it came to an issue, I'd vote for Negro players. There's no reason why they should be denied the same chance that Negro fighters and musicians are given." A few years later, Benswanger spoke again of integrating baseball with the comment, "I know there are many problems connected with the question, but after all, somebody has to make the first move."[39]

The implementation of the draft in anticipation of the country's entry into World War II further increased pressure on anti-integration forces as black men were called to duty along with whites. In 1942, Brooklyn Dodger manager Leo Durocher drew national attention when he told the *Daily Worker* he "knew of several capable Negro players that he would be willing to sign if Negroes were permitted to play in the major leagues."[40] Durocher's remarks drew a reprimand from the Commissioner of Baseball, Judge Kenesaw Mountain Landis, who was moved to proclaim, "Negroes are not barred from organized baseball — and never have been in the 21 years I have served," a comment that Dodger president Larry MacPhail deemed "100% hypocrisy."[41]

Phantom Tryouts

Meanwhile the black press began pushing for tryouts of Negro League stars under the theory that once their talents were put on display they couldn't be denied. But even that seemingly innocuous request would not be met.

On March 18, 1942, Herman Hill, the West Coast correspondent for the *Pittsburgh Courier,* showed up at the Chicago White Sox spring training facility in Pasadena, California, accompanied by two local black players, Jackie Robinson and Nate Moreland. The trio approached Sox manager Jimmy Dykes asking for a tryout. The request was denied. Dykes is alleged to have said, "Personally I would welcome Negro players on the White Sox. The matter is out of the hands of us managers. We are powerless to act and it's strictly up to the club owners and Judge Landis to get the ball-a-rolling. Go after them!"[42] More than a decade later, Dykes would be in charge when the Philadelphia Athletics integrated, and he would ultimately manage four other integrated teams before his 21-year managing career came to a close.

Later that year, Pittsburgh Pirates president William Benswanger agreed to extend a tryout to four Negro League stars, Josh Gibson and Sam Bankhead of the Grays and Willie Wells and Leon Day of the Newark Eagles, who were selected in a poll conducted by the *Pittsburgh Courier*.[43] But the promised audition never materialized. The next year, Benswanger, again under pressure from the press — this time *The Daily Worker*— agreed to take a look at Roy Campanella of the Baltimore Elite Giants and two other black stars, pitcher Dave Barnhill and second baseman Sammy Hughes.[44] According to Campanella, he actually received a written invitation.[45] But peer pressure from the lords of baseball trumped the press and the workout was cancelled.

On September 1, 1942, the Cleveland Indians reportedly announced that they would hold a tryout for Sam Jethroe, Parnell Woods, and Eugene Bremmer, members of the Negro League Cleveland Buckeyes, but it never materialized.[46]

That same year, Pants Rowland, president of the Pacific Coast League Los Angeles Angels, announced tryouts for a trio of black players, but was forced to back down under pressure from other league owners. Later, Vince Devincenzi, owner of the Oakland Oaks, ordered manager Johnny Vergez to take a look at two black players. Vergez refused and the trial never occurred.[47]

In the spring of 1945 at the Dodgers' Bear Mountain training camp, Joe Bostic showed up with veteran Negro Leaguers Terris "The Great" McDuffie and Dave "Showboat" Thomas in tow and demanded a tryout. Brooklyn general manager and president Branch Rickey, who already had his own plans for integration, was not interested in either the 34-year-old pitcher McDuffie or the 39-year-old first baseman Thomas but allowed them to work out anyway.[48]

But the most infamous "phantom tryout" occurred in Fenway Park on April 16, 1945, when the Boston Red Sox agreed to audition three black players to placate a local politician.[49]

By prior agreement, leading black columnist Wendell Smith chose three players for the tryout: Sam Jethroe, Marvin Williams, and Jackie Robinson. Availability was certainly a key selection criterion, but in retrospect, the selection of Robinson marks Smith as a remarkable judge of baseball talent. Robinson was just beginning his first Negro League season with the Kansas City Monarchs. Since ending his collegiate career at UCLA four years earlier, he had played professional football and basketball, but little baseball except some service ball in the army during World War II. Even in college, Robinson had not been rated particularly high as a baseball player, yet Smith selected him ahead of many experienced Negro League stars.[50]

Red Sox coach Hugh Duffy supervised the tryout. After they worked out for about an hour, Duffy told the black players, "You boys look like pretty good players. Hope you enjoyed the workout," and promised someone would contact them. None of them ever heard from the Red Sox.[51]

Wartime Talent Shortage

Despite the fact that wartime manpower demands had significantly reduced the level of play in the major leagues and the fact that black soldiers were dying next to white ones defending the United States, Organized Baseball's tacit ban of black players would remain intact throughout World War II.

To fill their rosters, the St. Louis Browns employed one-armed center fielder Pete Gray, the Cincinnati Reds used Dick Sipek, who was deaf, as a spare outfielder, and the Washington Senators signed combat-wounded veteran Bert Shepard to pitch with an artificial leg. The Detroit Tigers signed 40-year-old semi-pro star Chuck Hostetler off the sandlots to patrol their outfield and New York City sanitation worker Ed Boland spent his vacation in the Senators outfield.[52] The average age of the 1945 Chicago White Sox starting lineup was more than 34 years of age except for 19-year-old shortstop Cass Michaels. The New York Yankees activated 42-year-old batting practice pitcher Paul Schreiber, who hadn't seen major league service in 22 years, and the Brooklyn Dodgers pressed 43-year-old scout Clyde Sukeforth, who had retired five years earlier, into duty behind the plate. Hod Lisenbee, who served up Babe Ruth's 58th homer in 1927 and had been out of the majors for nine years joined the Cincinnati Reds bullpen at age 46 in 1945.

Former stars like Babe Herman, Lloyd and Paul Waner, Al Simmons, and Guy Bush were lured out of retirement. Pepper Martin gave up the managerial reins at Rochester to rejoin the St. Louis Cardinals. Jimmie Foxx, who had been forced into early retirement by sinus problems, signed on with the Philadelphia Phillies for the 1945 season and added seven more homers to a final tally that would stand for two decades as second on the all-time list to Babe Ruth. Leo Durocher, manager of the Brooklyn Dodgers, made two ill-fated attempts to return to active duty, but his aging body couldn't take it. At the other end of the spectrum, lefty Joe Nuxhall took the mound for the Cincinnati Reds at the tender age of 15, and Carl Scheib toiled on the hill for the Philadelphia Athletics at age 16. The 1944 Brooklyn Dodgers shortstop corps included 16-year-old Tommy Brown, 17-year-old Eddie Miksis, and 18-year-old Gene Mauch.

Yet the moguls running Major League Baseball refused to bolster the depleted talent pool with the likes of Satchel Paige, Josh Gibson, Roy Campanella, Buck Leonard, or Ray Dandridge, all of whom were ready and available.

The Boston Red Sox finished the 1945 season in seventh place. Mike Ryba, a 42-year-old former catcher, was the third biggest winner on the beleaguered pitching staff, 38-year-old Bob Johnson was their big slugger, and 38-year-old National League slugger Dolph Camilli was lured out of retirement to share first base with the immortal Catfish Metkovich. Manager Joe Cronin, fat and nearly 40, was stationed at third base before a broken leg ended his active career. Yet the Red Sox had no room on their roster for Jackie Robinson.

The Role of *The Sporting News*

In contrast to the black press, *The Sporting News*, a strong defender of the status quo in Organized Baseball, was a staunch opponent to integration. The August 6, 1942, edition, for example, carried an editorial entitled "No Good From Raising Race Issue." The editorial's tone is set with the opening statement, "There is no law against Negroes playing with white teams, nor whites with colored clubs, but neither has invited the other for the obvious reason they prefer to draw their talent from their own ranks and do not care to run the risk of damaging their own game."[53]

The editors charged that white players did not participate in the Negro Leagues, choosing to ignore Latino players whose skin color was so light that they were able to play in the majors before and after participating in black baseball. The editorial went on to feign much concern for the future of the grand institution of Negro League Baseball, which the publication barely bothered to cover. Great anxiety was also expressed over exposing those poor black fellows to the hazing of white players and fans. The editors even worried that the legend of the great Satchel Paige might be tarnished if he took the mound to face major league hitters, apparently ignorant of the fact he'd been faring quite successfully against them for years in exhibition contests.

The editorial maintained that "agitators" were responsible for leading the uninformed black populace astray: "...there are agitators, ever ready to seize an issue that will redound to their profit of self aggrandizement, who have sought to force Negro players on the big leagues, not because it would help the game, but because it gives them a chance to thrust themselves into the limelight as great crusaders in the guise of democracy." "Colored people" were advised to "concede their own people are now protected and that nothing is served by allowing agitators to make an issue of a question on which both sides would prefer to be let alone."[54]

The editors ended the column with a "quite pertinent" anecdote about a Joe Louis interview in his home the day after he defeated Jim Braddock for the heavyweight championship. Louis set out a pork chop lunch for the writers before excusing himself with the explanation, "I'm gonna have lunch with some friends in the kitchen. When we get through we'll talk some more."[55]

Almost five years later, with Jackie Robinson firmly established in the Brooklyn Dodgers lineup, another editorial assured readers that "*The Sporting News* has not changed its view as expressed in 1942."[56] The Joe Louis/pork chop anecdote was even retold.

Commissioner Landis: The Last Barrier

The biases of *The Sporting News* and the magnates notwithstanding, the most formidable obstacle baseball integrationists had to overcome is generally considered to be Judge Kenesaw Mountain Landis, the long-time commissioner of Major League Baseball.

Judge Kenesaw Mountain Landis, the commissioner of Major League Baseball from 1920 through 1944, reputedly was adamantly opposed to integrating the game (1961 Fleer card).

Landis became Baseball's first commissioner on January 12, 1921, in the wake of the infamous Black Sox scandal. He didn't rise to power—he walked into it. Rumors that several key players on the Chicago White Sox had conspired with gamblers to throw the 1919 World Series to the underdog Cincinnati Reds had resulted in the convening of a grand jury in Chicago in the summer of 1920. As it became embarrassingly evident that something fishy was going on, the owners went into a public relations panic. The triumvirate of American League president Ban Johnson, National League president John Heydler, and Cincinnati Reds owner Garry Herrmann, who had been administering the game as the National Commission, didn't have the power or the fortitude to address the problem. Something had to be done to restore public confidence in the integrity of the game. A charismatic strongman was needed to take control of things, so Landis was offered the job and given almost unlimited powers, which he freely used and abused. One of his first acts as commissioner was to ban the eight suspected White Sox players from Organized Baseball for life within hours after they were acquitted in a jury trial.

Landis was a federal judge who gained his position at least in part because two of his brothers happened to be Indiana congressmen.[57] On the bench he was considered a grandstander, known for sensational and controversial rulings in high profile cases that were often overturned.[58] Jack Lait, editor of the *New York Daily Mirror*, who was a court reporter in Chicago when Landis ruled, wrote, "Landis was an irascible, tyrannical despot. His manner of handling witnesses, lawyers, and reporters was more arbitrary than the behavior of any jurist I have ever seen before or since."[59] Landis first caught the public's attention in 1907, his third year on the bench, when he fined Standard Oil $29 million for accepting kickbacks, a ruling that was eventually overturned. He ingratiated himself to the lords of baseball when he delayed rendering a decision on an anti-trust suit filed against Organized Baseball by the upstart Federal League until the newcomers were forced to settle.

Respected columnist Heywood Broun once wrote, "His [Landis'] career typifies the heights to which dramatic talent may carry a man in America if only he has the foresight not to go on the stage."[60] Former umpire George Moriarty wrote in a 1947 letter that "Judge Landis had convenient hiding places for his ideals. If the populace was not looking, he had little compunction [*sic*] about defending the underdog, but if the spotlight were turned on in full focus, he would defend anyone to the last camera."[61]

On the integration front, Landis is consistently portrayed as a champion of discrimination, a man who didn't hesitate to wield his considerable power to resist any attempt to integrate the game.

According to Bill Veeck in *Veeck—as in Wreck*, Landis orchestrated the sale of the Philadelphia Phillies out from under him in 1943 when he found out about Veeck's plan to purchase the downtrodden franchise and stock the roster with Negro League stars. The accuracy of Veeck's account has been the subject of intense debate in baseball circles over the years and is covered in more detail in a later chapter. The National League did, in fact, suddenly sell the Phillies to lumberman William Cox that year, but there's no documentation as to whether or not Veeck's plan had anything to do with it.

Another commonly cited incident occurred in December 1943, when Landis was pressured into letting noted entertainer and civil rights activist Paul Robeson address the owners at their annual meeting in Manhattan. In addition to being an accomplished singer and famous Broadway actor, the multi-talented Robeson was an attorney who had been both a 12-letter man and Phi Beta Kappa at Rutgers University. He had also been one of professional football's first black players in the early 1920s. Before Robeson was brought into the room, Landis cautioned the owners not to get into any discussion with him. Robeson made a 15-minute presentation arguing for the introduction of black players into Organized Baseball and was ushered out of the room when there were no questions or comments afterward. Landis then moved on to the next item on the agenda as if the eminent Robeson hadn't even been there.[62]

The program for the 2007 Society for American Baseball Research (SABR) Convention in St. Louis included a fascinating presentation by baseball historian Norman Macht entitled "Does Baseball Deserve Its Black Eye?" The gist of Macht's presentation was that the baseball establishment kept the color barrier intact primarily for economic reasons — as good businessmen protecting their investment — rather than prejudice or racism. He argued that the prewar attitude of the country was very conservative and strongly pro-segregation, and the owners were simply reflecting or accommodating that bias. Landis had no role in the owners' decision of which ballplayers to hire. His job was simply to enforce the rules of Major League Baseball, and since there was no rule regarding the employment of black players, there was nothing for him to adjudicate.

Whether Landis was acting out of personal prejudice or simply executing the will of the owners who hired him, he was an effective deterrent to integration. Few would have had the audacity to proclaim, "There is no rule, formal or informal, or any understanding — unwritten, subterranean, or sub-anything — against the hiring of Negro players by the teams of Organized Baseball," as Landis huffed in 1942, and even fewer could have gotten away with it.[63]

Judge Kenesaw Mountain Landis died of a heart attack at age 78 on November 25, 1944, only days after the major league owners recommended a long-term extension of his contract. His death removed a most formidable obstacle to the integration of the game.

We will probably never know for sure if Landis spearheaded Organized Baseball's resistance to integration or if he was merely doing his job extremely well. Likewise, we will probably never know exactly why the owners resisted. Uncertainty about the economic impact of integration on the business is not an unreasonable motivation. It's also possible that the Major League Baseball leadership really was so ignorant of the Negro Leagues that they truly had doubts about the ability of black players. Other explanations beside prejudice could be simple fear of the unknown or reflexive protection of the status quo.

For this reason, Landis and others whose careers in baseball ended prior to integration will be given the benefit of the doubt in these chapters. Such forbearance, however, cannot be extended to those who established or maintained a poor track record in the integration area long after the issues of economic viability and playing ability had been put to rest.

Chapter 1

THE DAWN OF BASEBALL'S
INTEGRATION ERA

On April 18, 1946, 27-year-old Jackie Robinson became the first acknowledged black player to take the field in Organized Baseball in the 20th century when he stepped into the batter's box for the Montreal Royals. It was nothing less than a smashing success. In front of a packed house, Robinson lashed out four hits and scored four times to lead the visiting Royals to a 14–1 victory over the Jersey City Giants.

But the first seeds of the movement to re-integrate Organized Baseball were sown in 1903 in the lobby of the Oliver Hotel in South Bend, Indiana, almost twenty years after Moses Walker had been driven from the major leagues. The Ohio Wesleyan University baseball squad, scheduled to begin a series against Notre Dame the next day, was checking in, but a problem had arisen. One of their star players, a 22-year-old black man named Charles Thomas, was being denied lodging due to the color of his skin. Thomas's coach and friend was Branch Rickey, who was only 21 years of age himself. Rickey finally persuaded the manager to allow Thomas to sleep on a cot in his room. Later that night, Rickey watched Thomas tear at his skin as he fought to control his sobs. As he tried in vain to console his friend, the young coach silently vowed to do everything in his power to stop racial injustice.

More than 40 years later, Rickey, who had become general manager and part owner of the Brooklyn Dodgers, would mastermind "The Great Experiment," as the plan that would enable Jackie Robinson to cross the color barrier would come to be called.

The uniting of Branch Rickey and Jackie Robinson together for the purpose of breaking baseball's color barrier was the final episode in a remarkable confluence of events, some engineered and some simply happenstance, that resulted in the breaching of Organized Baseball's color barrier.

Branch Rickey: The Mahatma

Wesley Branch Rickey was born December 20, 1881, and grew up on an Ohio farm. He was an outstanding football and baseball player at Ohio-Wesleyan before a summer semi-pro baseball job cost him his eligibility. Before the 1902 season, he became the school's baseball coach and two years later added the title of head football coach to his resume.[1]

The young man caught on as a catcher with Dallas of the Texas League following his graduation in 1904 and soon found himself in the major leagues when his contract was sold to the Cincinnati Reds of the National League. His stint in Cincinnati came to end before he

General Manager Branch Rickey of the Brooklyn Dodgers defied Organized Baseball's "gentlemen's agreement" by signing Jackie Robinson to a Montreal Royals contract in 1945 (Larry Lester).

made a big league appearance when the devout Methodist refused to play ball on Sundays. Eventually he ended up with the American League St. Louis Browns, where he played a single game in 1905 before returning home to tend to his ailing parents. In 1906, he shared catching duties with veteran Jack O'Connor and hit for the second-highest batting average in the league among regular catchers. By this time, Rickey was also pursuing a law degree which, along with his continued refusal to play on Sundays, was a problem. He was swapped to the New York Highlanders in the off-season, but an arm injury derailed his catching career, and he quit after a poor 1907 campaign.[2]

After dabbling in politics and overcoming tuberculosis, Rickey enrolled at the University of Michigan Law School in 1909 and soon took over the reins of the school baseball team as well. After obtaining his law degree, Rickey invested in a small practice in Boise, Idaho, but soon returned to coaching at Michigan when the law business didn't pan out. St. Louis Browns owner Robert Hedges, who had been deeply impressed with Rickey when he played for the Browns, offered him a job. By the end of the 1913 season, Rickey was serving as both general manager and field manager for the woeful American League cellar dwellers.[3]

In 1917, Rickey left the downtrodden Browns to take over the reins of the National League St. Louis Cardinals. With the Cardinals, Rickey pioneered the farm system, which enabled the team to acquire and develop young players through a network of agreements with various minor league teams. By the time Rickey moved on to Brooklyn in 1942, the Cardinals were a National League power with a farm system that included 33 teams and had hundreds of young players under contract.[4]

Like all men of accomplishment, Rickey had already attracted legions of admirers and an army of detractors before undertaking the desegregation of Organized Baseball. His worst critics considered him a duplicitous, sanctimonious, hypocritically religious moneygrubber, and even his allies admitted he could be pompous, overly pious, and tight with a buck. But he was also smart, resourceful, and hardworking — a visionary in both matters of business and social issues. He was a 64-year-old man in questionable health when he determined to break the color barrier. When his concerned wife asked why it was up to him, Rickey responded, "I'm doing it because I can't help it. I cannot face God much longer knowing that His black creatures are held separate and distinct from his white creatures in the game that has given me all that I can call my own."[5]

Jackie Robinson: The Trailblazer

Jackie Robinson was no stranger to the sports world before he was selected to break baseball's color barrier, but he was known more for his prowess in football, basketball, and track than in baseball. After attending junior college in Pasadena, he gained national fame at UCLA from 1939 through 1941, becoming the school's first four-letter man. Sportswriters called him "the Jim Thorpe of his race." On the football field, Jackie averaged over 11 yards per carry as a junior. Remembered as a Gayle Sayers/O.J. Simpson/Eric Dickerson–type running back, he sharing backfield duties with Kenny Washington, who would later become the first black man to play in the National Football League.[6] On the basketball court, Robinson led the Pacific Coast Conference in scoring as a junior and as a senior. Already the holder of the national junior college long-jump record, he captured the NCAA broad-jump title and probably would have gone to the 1940 Olympics had they not been cancelled by the war in Europe. In addi-

tion, he was the Bruins regular shortstop in baseball. Ironically, baseball was Jackie's weakest sport at UCLA although he had been voted the most valuable player in Southern California junior college baseball.[7]

Robinson's father deserted the family shortly after his birth, and Jackie grew up in a poor single parent home in Pasadena, California. His older brother Mack would become a world-class track star, but he was unable to find gainful employment in segregated Pasadena after starring in the 1936 Olympics.[8] Due to financial pressures at home, Jackie had to drop out of college in 1941, a few classes

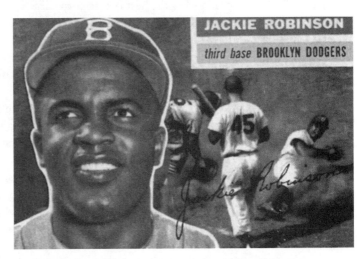

Jackie Robinson became the first acknowledged black player in Organized Baseball in the 20th century, as well as the game's first black MVP, batting champ, and Hall of Famer (1956 Topps card).

short of a degree. He took a job as an athletic coach for the National Youth Administration and played some semipro football. In the fall of 1941, he signed on to play professional football with the Honolulu Bears.[9]

Returning home from Hawaii shortly after Pearl Harbor, Robinson was drafted into the army in 1942. He was denied entry into Officers Candidate School (OCS) despite his college background before fellow soldier and boxing great Joe Louis intervened on his behalf. After OCS, Robinson was appointed morale officer for the black troops at Fort Riley and won concessions for them that predictably angered a few higher-ups in command. Reassigned to Fort Hood, he defied a white bus driver's orders to move to the back of the bus and was subject to court martial. Facing the possibility of a dishonorable discharge, Robinson prevailed at his hearing, but the army had had enough of the controversial young black lieutenant and quickly mustered him out with an honorable discharge.[10]

Needing a job, Robinson hooked up with the Kansas City Monarchs and hit .387 as the powerful Negro American League team's shortstop in 1945, his only Negro League season.

The Search for "The First"

Shortly after coming to Brooklyn in 1942, Branch Rickey had quietly obtained necessary backing from within the organization to pursue integration. With the end of World War II already in sight, the death of Commissioner Kenesaw Mountain Landis in November 1944 gave Rickey the freedom to begin putting his plan into action. Surprisingly, he found an unexpected ally in Landis' successor, Albert "Happy" Chandler, a former governor and state senator from Kentucky.

Rickey directed his top scouts, Clyde Sukeforth, George Sisler, Wid Matthews, and Tom Greenwade, to follow the Negro Leagues. Ostensibly they were looking for prospects for the Brown Dodgers, a new black team that Rickey was forming. In actuality, the Brown Dodgers were a subterfuge to allow Rickey to scout Negro talent without arousing suspicion. Gradually, Jackie Robinson emerged as the best prospect to carry the integration banner. His educational background, strength of character, morals, and experience in the spotlight had as much to do with his selection as his baseball ability. And the fact that he was available for Rickey's scouts to examine during the 1945 Negro League season while most of the other top candidates were still in the service was of no small consideration. It's particularly ironic that Robinson's difficulties with white authority in the military helped him rise to the top of Branch Rickey's list.

Interestingly, Jackie Robinson apparently wasn't Rickey's first choice to break the color barrier. The enterprising executive had been trying to figure out a way to tap Negro baseball talent for some time. Legend has it that Rickey didn't begin the hunt for black talent for the Dodgers until 1945, but he had actually intended to break the color barrier two years earlier. According to correspondence in the possession of former scout Tom Greenwade's heirs, Rickey charged Greenwade with scouting black talent for the organization in the spring of 1943. Furthermore, the effort focused on a dark-skinned Cuban shortstop named Silvio Garcia, who was considered the top player in the Mexican League at the time. There's evidence that Rickey dispatched Walter O'Malley, then a junior partner on the Dodgers ownership team, to Cuba with instructions to sign Garcia, but the shortstop had been drafted into the Cuban army.[11]

The quest to find a black player for the Dodgers organization stalled temporarily after the Garcia attempt. One story has it that the effort was abandoned after Garcia was asked how he would react to an opponent's racial slurs. His response, "I would kill him," supposedly scared Rickey off. In all probability, the project was put on hold because the most likely prospects were either in military service or subject to be drafted and no one knew how much longer the war would last.[12]

When Rickey again deployed his top scouts to cover the Negro Leagues, Greenwade was assigned to scout Jackie Robinson. Later, the New York Yankees would lure Greenwade away, and he would gain fame for putting Mickey Mantle in pinstripes.

The Announcement of Robinson's Signing

On October 23, 1945, it was announced to the world that Jackie Robinson, star shortstop of the Negro League Kansas City Monarchs, had signed a contract to play baseball for the Montreal Royals of the International League, the top minor league team in the Brooklyn Dodgers organization. Robinson had actually signed with the Dodgers organization a few months earlier. In that now-legendary first meeting, Rickey extracted a promise that Robinson would hold his sharp tongue and quick fists in exchange for the opportunity to break Organized Baseball's color barrier. The news was heralded in the black press and was generally received positively in national publications despite the predictable objections.

Many players of dubious racial ancestry had managed to slip past the guardians of baseball's racial barrier down through history, but there could no doubt about the heritage of Branch Rickey's choice to break the color barrier. Columnist John Crosby called Robinson, "the blackest black man, as well as the handsomest, I ever saw."[13]

After the initial furor died down, the baseball world began a campaign to downplay the threat to their empire. Influential *New York Daily News* columnist Jimmy Powers rated Robinson's chances of making the grade as 1,000 to one.[14] An editorial in *The Sporting News* characterized Robinson as player of Class B ability "if he were six years younger" and predicted that "the waters of competition in the International League will flood far over his head."[15] Star hurler Bob Feller of the Cleveland Indians proved to be an equally poor judge of talent, opining that Robinson had "football shoulders and couldn't hit an inside pitch to save his neck."[16] Feller would later embellish his scouting reputation by promising that Clint "Hondo" Hartung, one of the most notorious flops in major league history, was "a cinch to develop into one of the best hitters in the National League."[17] And Southern-born outfielder Dixie Walker of the Dodgers dismissed the news with the shortsighted comment, "As long as he isn't with the Dodgers, I'm not worried."[18]

"*The Sporting News* believes that the attention which the signing of Robinson elicited in the press around the country was out of proportion to the actual vitality of the story," the editors of the publication intoned.[19]

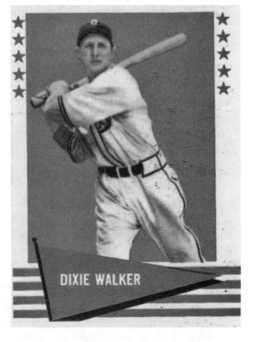

Popular Brooklyn outfielder Dixie Walker circulated an anti–Robinson petition and requested a trade prior to Jackie's rookie season, but later softened his stance (1961 Fleer card).

Robinson's Debut with Montreal

Plagued by a sore arm, Robinson performed poorly during the Royals' 1946 pre-season training camp. But when Montreal opened the season against the Jersey City Giants at Roosevelt Stadium, he was playing second base and hitting in the number-two spot in the batting order.

After grounding out in his first at-bat, Robinson blasted a three-run homer over the left field wall in the third inning. In the fifth inning, he bunted for a hit, stole second, and made a daring play to take third on a grounder to the third baseman. From third base, he danced far off the bag, darting back and forth and bluffing a steal until the harried pitcher balked him home. Two innings later, he singled sharply to right field and immediately proceeded to steal second base again before scoring on a triple. In the eighth, Robinson again bunted safely. He once again took an extra base, advancing from first to third on an infield single and scored by provoking a balk from the Jersey City hurler.

The next day, the headline in *The Pittsburgh Courier* read, "Jackie Stole the Show." According to Joe Bostic of the *Amsterdam News*, "He did everything but help the ushers seat the crowd."[20]

"The Race Question"

By July 8, 1946, Robinson was hitting .354 and had scored 57 runs in 59 games for Montreal. But while Robinson was tearing up the International League, powerful forces in Organized Baseball were working diligently to preserve the whiteness of the grand old game. That same day at a meeting of club owners and league executives, Larry MacPhail, general manager and part-owner of the New York Yankees, was named to chair a special steering committee "to consider and test all matters of Major League interest and report its conclusions and recommendations." In addition to MacPhail, the committee was comprised of league presidents Ford Frick of the National League and Will Harridge of the American League, owners Sam Breadon of the St. Louis Cardinals, Tom Yawkey of the Boston Red Sox, and Phil Wrigley of the Chicago Cubs.

Working with fervor and speed rarely seen in the executive circle of professional baseball, the committee prepared a report, drafted by MacPhail, for the owners' August meeting. The report, dated for submission on August 27, 1946, dealt with matters dear to the owners' hearts such as preserving baseball's monopoly against the Mexican League threat, fending off "outsider's" attempts to organize the players, and exploring ways to minimize bonuses being doled out for untried amateur prospects. Another section of the report was entitled "The Race Question."[21]

"The Race Question" ended up being a rehash of the same excuses that Organized Baseball had been using for decades. Concern was feigned for the continued financial health of the Negro Leagues if the major leagues acquired their best players. But the real problem, according to the report, was the poor quality of the black players who had never been properly coached. After taking a few potshots at "political and social drum beaters" who "know little about baseball," the study bemoaned the scarcity of talent in black baseball. It didn't come out directly against integration of the game, but cautioned against moving too fast and urged that no further action be taken until all the problems could be worked out. According to Rickey, the entire report was adopted by a 15–1 vote with the Dodgers representing the minority.[22]

The only thing that made the "The Race Question" study remarkable was that at the time it was undertaken, Robinson and four other black players had been acquitting themselves quite well in Organized Baseball and drawing record crowds for months.

MacPhail's report didn't see the light of day for years. Copies were passed out during the meeting and quickly collected at the end. The report was unknown to the public until Rickey mentioned it in a speech at Wilberforce College, an African American school, on February 16, 1948. Initially, the owners vigorously denied the very existence of the document until MacPhail admitted he had the only remaining copy. A copy for public consumption miraculously surfaced a few years later. It seems Commissioner Happy Chandler had kept a copy for his files too.[23]

Before Jackie Robinson's debut, the baseball establishment's defense for keeping the game segregated generally hinged on two arguments. The first was the contention was that there just weren't any black players who were good enough to merit a shot at the majors. The second rationale centered on financial concerns — the fear that white fans wouldn't pay to watch black players and didn't want to sit in the stands with Negro fans.

Robinson's first year in Organized Baseball emphatically dispelled both of those tired excuses. He quickly proved to be a big league talent. At the end of the year, he boasted the highest batting average in the International League at .349, led the circuit in runs scored with 113 in 124 games, placed second with 40 stolen bases, and posted the highest fielding average at second base. In addition, the Royals romped to the International League pennant and went on to capture the Little World Series Championship.

On the financial front, Robinson made the turnstiles hum. The Royals established a new attendance record in Montreal, but Robinson's impact on the road was even greater. Attendance at Royals games in other International League cities almost tripled over the previous year. More than a million people came to watch Robinson and the Royals perform that year, an amazing figure for the minor leagues.

There were four other black players in Organized Baseball in 1946, all in the Brooklyn organization, and they didn't do so bad either. Catcher Roy Campanella and pitcher Don Newcombe, who Rickey signed away from the Baltimore Elite Giants and Newark Eagles respectively, led Nashua to the New England League championship. Johnny Wright, late of the Homestead Grays, began the season at Montreal with Robinson. Wright became the first black pitcher to take the mound in Organized Baseball, but early in the season he was sent to Three Rivers of the Canadian American League after only two appearances with Montreal. He was replaced by 34-year-old lefthander Roy Partlow, who would get a ten-game trial before also being dispatched to Three Rivers.[24] Wright and Partlow would subsequently pitch Three Rivers to the Canadian American League championship. Two other Negro League stars were also reported to be in line for opportunities in Organized Baseball that year. A few weeks after the announcement of Robinson's signing, Bakersfield of the California League received permission from the National Association to sign pitcher Chet Brewer, who was closing in on 40 years of age.[25] It would be six years, however, before Brewer would make an appearance in Organized Baseball. A few months later, while Robinson was training with Montreal, *The Sporting News* published a rumor that "A third Negro player is reportedly on way to Montreal," identifying Monte Irvin as that player.[26] But Irvin would have to wait three seasons for his opportunity in Organized Baseball.

Though it contained nothing new, "The Race Question" did represent a shift in the baseball establishment's traditional position. The financial issue had become a tough sell in light of the International League attendance boom. The owners could still express anxiety over the plight of the Negro Leagues, but nobody really cared. The only thing left was the contention that black players weren't good enough for the major leagues, which couldn't be disproved as long as none of them got a chance.

Shortly after the owner's meeting in which "The Race Question" was presented, Rickey met with Commissioner Chandler to seek his support for bringing Robinson up in 1947. "I'm going to have to meet my maker someday. If he asks me why I didn't let this boy play and I say it's because he is black, that might not be a sufficient answer," Chandler subsequently claimed to have told Rickey.[27] Backed by Chandler, Rickey defied his fellow owners and gave Jackie Robinson that chance.

Robinson Breaks the Major League Color Barrier

In preparation for the 1947 campaign, the Brooklyn Dodgers and their top farm clubs set up spring training camp in Havana, Cuba. Based on his performance at Montreal, it seemed a foregone conclusion that Robinson would get a chance with the parent team, but he was still listed on the Royals roster when the workouts started. Rickey chose Havana to avoid the racial attitudes of the spring training sites in the south. His plan was to allow the Dodgers veterans to gradually get used to having Robinson around and to see for themselves what an asset he would be to their pennant prospects. Three other black players, Campanella, Newcombe, and Partlow, were also on hand. Rickey scheduled a seven-game exhibition series between the Dodgers and the Royals to showcase Robinson's skills, and he dominated the contests with a .625 batting average.

One problem that Rickey and Robinson had to overcome was that the Dodgers had Eddie "The Brat" Stanky at second base, which was clearly Robinson's best position. A favorite of manager Leo Durocher, Stanky was a leadoff man extraordinaire who had worried pitchers for a league-high 137 walks the previous year. Therefore, it was determined that Robinson would make his major league debut at first base.

During training camp, a crisis arose when a core of southerners on the team, reportedly led by Dixie Walker, began to circulate a petition against Robinson. Rickey and Durocher promptly quashed the mini-rebellion. Shortly thereafter, Durocher, an avid Robinson supporter, received a one-year suspension from the commissioner's office for associating with gamblers, actors, politicians, and other unsavory characters. Rickey deftly took advantage of the cover provided by the resulting clamor to quietly transfer Robinson to the Brooklyn roster.

Robinson broke the major league color barrier on April 15, 1947, opening day of the season. Robinson had played in a few pre-season games in Brooklyn, so his April 15 debut at Ebbets Field was somewhat anticlimactic with less than 27,000 fans showing up for the historic occasion. But a few days later, Robinson's first appearance outside of Brooklyn drew more than 37,000 fans to the Polo Grounds. In contrast to his first minor league game, Robinson started slowly in the majors, but he electrified the big crowd with his first major league home run. The next day, a Saturday, he rapped out three hits in front of a record crowd of 52,000 at the Polo Grounds.

Contrary to dire predictions, Robinson's first season in the major leagues went fairly smoothly as the rookie steadfastly stuck by his promise to Rickey to turn the other cheek. He was the target of flashing spikes, beanballs, insults, and death threats. He placed second in the majors in being hit by pitches, avoiding first because a deformed right arm forced leader

Whitey Kurowski to stand almost on top of the plate.[28] Later, a threatened strike by the St. Louis Cardinals was short-circuited by Rickey and National League president Ford Frick.

For his rookie campaign, Robinson hit .297, led the league with 29 stolen bases, and finished second in the loop with 125 runs scored. In 151 games, he lashed out 175 hits, including 12 homers. Usually hitting from the second spot in the batting order, he walked 74 times and led the league in sacrifice hits. On defense, his 16 errors at first base were the second-highest total in the league, but his fielding was generally considered at least adequate. The 1947 season was the first in which the Baseball Writers Association of America selected a Rookie of the Year, and Robinson beat out 21-game-winner Larry Jansen of the New York Giants for the award. In National League Most Valuable Player voting, he finished fifth behind third baseman Bob Elliott of the Braves, Cincinnati ace Ewell Blackwell, Giants first baseman Johnny Mize, and teammate Bruce Edwards, the Dodgers' catcher.

At season's end, his old adversary Dixie Walker grudgingly admitted, "No other player on this club, with the possible exception of Bruce Edwards, has done more to put the Dodgers up in the race than Robinson has. He is everything that Branch Rickey said he was when he came up from Montreal."[29]

In fact, baseball's great experiment was a huge success. Despite the continued concerns of the owners, integration proved to be a financial windfall for Major League Baseball. Robinson and the Dodgers eclipsed the home attendance record they had set the previous year. They also broke single-game attendance records in every National League stadium they played in during the 1947 season, with the exception of Cincinnati's Crosley Field where the attendance record for the first night game held up. Reported attendance for Major League Baseball that year was almost 20 million fans, an all-time record.

Other black players soon followed in Robinson's wake. On July 5, 1947, Larry Doby pinch-hit for the Cleveland Indians to become the first black player in the American League. Later, Hank Thompson and Willard Brown got trials with the St. Louis Browns, and pitcher Dan Bankhead joined Robinson in Brooklyn. In addition, 12 black players performed in the minor leagues. In the Dodgers organization, Campanella caught for Montreal, Newcombe had another fine season with Nashua where catcher Ramon Rodriguez also got a trial, and shortstop Sammy Gee played for Three Rivers. Chuck Harmon also played in the Canadian League with the St. Louis Browns' Gloversville franchise. The Samford Bombers of the Colonial League featured six black players, including five from the Negro Leagues.[30] And Robinson's former Pasadena neighbor Nate Moreland won 20 games for El Centro in the independent Sunset League.

The Sporting News Weighs in Again

Meanwhile, *The Sporting News* steadfastly continued to question the wisdom and viability of integration. In reaction to a threatened early-season strike against Robinson by the Cardinals and intense abuse directed his way by the Phillies, the publication renewed its objection to "mixed teams" and made another pitch for separate black and white teams in Organized Baseball.[31]

Two months later, following the debut of Larry Doby, a *Sporting News* editorial entitled "Once Again, That Negro Question" reminded readers, "There never has been a regulation barring Negro players." The editorial went on to quote an unidentified all-star complaining about the 28-year-old Robinson, who put in only one minor league season, and four-year

Negro League and two-year Navy veteran Doby getting major league chances without the same "previous schooling in white baseball" that he had endured. "If we are to have Negroes in the majors, let them go through the long preparation the white player is forced to undergo. Let us not discriminate against the white player because he is white," demanded the player. "*The Sporting News* believes that this summation is worthy of consideration," was the editorial opinion.[32]

In August, *The Sporting News* almost jubilantly reported in bold print, "Browns' Negro Players Bat Only .194 and .178," and a week later, under the banner "Negro Issue Fizzling Out," Dan Daniel's column predicted "Little by little, the Negro players will slide into the background."[33]

Then in February 1948, another *Sporting News* editorial condemned Rickey for bringing the report containing "The Race Question" to the public forum. "...the Brooklyn president's speech rendered the game a distinct disservice," criticized the editorial, characterizing Rickey's words as, "Just a bit of ancient history which thoughtful citizens of all races agreed would be left unsaid."[34]

Midway through the 1948 season, a *Sporting News* editorial skewering Bill Veeck for bringing Satchel Paige to the major leagues assured readers that its criticism of signing the veteran hurler, "obviously is not based on Paige's color."

"Certainly, no man at all familiar with the editorial policy of *The Sporting News*, and its reactions to the striving of the Negro to gain a place in the major leagues, will question the motives of this paper," the editorial sanctimoniously intoned.[35]

Just to prove how slowly some things change, in 1961 the following editorial entitled "Games Shining Record on Racial Issue" appeared in *The Sporting News*:

> Baseball has done its part. It has not sidestepped any issue and, in fact, has been a leader in the fight to end segregation.
>
> At the same time we don't believe that baseball is under any obligation to be a crusader or martyr in this issue. That it seems is the role some people think baseball should play in the racial issue in Florida.
>
> There have been demands (not requests, but demands) that baseball find better housing for its Negro players in Florida. Virtually all general managers have said they will do what they can, but they do not believe it is their place to rewrite the laws of Florida.
>
> The housing issue in Florida, like many others in this vein cannot be solved overnight by ranting, raving, or flag waving. Calm and patient approach is the better answer. That is what most baseball men believe want to do and we feel they should not be stampeded by private agencies or individuals who are trying to exploit baseball for their own personal gain.[36]

Five years later, the game polished its "shining record" with the hiring of its first black major league umpire, Emmett Ashford.

The Forgotten Generation

In modern times, the perception persists that the walls of prejudice came tumbling down when Jackie Robinson crossed baseball's color barrier in 1947. But the reality is that large segments of the barrier remained intact as much of Organized Baseball continued to resist the intrusion of "coloreds" long after Robinson's historic debut. Five years after Robinson first took the field for the Brooklyn Dodgers, only six of baseball's sixteen major league franchises had allowed a black player to don their uniform, despite the fact that the first teams to commit to integration enjoyed phenomenal success. By the time Robinson's sensational 10-year career ended, black major leaguers had captured six Most Valuable Player awards and won Rookie of the Year honors seven times. But three teams still hadn't been able to find a black player worthy of gracing their lineup. In fact, more than a dozen years passed between the debut of Jackie Robinson and that of Pumpsie Green, the first black man to take the field in the uniform of baseball's last holdout, the Boston Red Sox.

The black players who immediately followed the trail blazed by Jackie Robinson also had to overcome tremendous obstacles to get a chance to succeed in Major League Baseball. Like Robinson, they too felt the hostility of teammates and fans; endured flashing spikes aimed at their shins and beanballs aimed at their heads; suffered the indignities of Jim Crow laws, racial slurs, and threats against their lives; and knew the pressure to succeed against daunting odds with no second chance in the offing. They too bore "the hopes, aspirations and ambitions of thirteen million black Americans on [their] broad, sturdy shoulders." But most failed to receive the recognition they deserved.

Many of these men are mentioned in the following pages. But the names of hundreds more, especially those who toiled in the minor leagues without ever getting a chance at the big time, are lost to history.

Chapter 2

THE BROOKLYN/LOS ANGELES DODGERS

The Brooklyn Dodgers realized an immediate windfall profit from Branch Rickey's courageous, far-sighted decision to break baseball's color barrier. In 1947, Jackie Robinson was the only significant addition to the everyday lineup, while the pitching staff was depleted by the trade of ace hurler Kirby Higbe to the Pittsburgh Pirates for a bunch of fringe players because he objected to Robinson's presence. Yet the Dodgers captured the National League pennant by a margin of five games over the defending World Champion St. Louis Cardinals, establishing a new all-time franchise attendance record in the process. Furthermore, the Dodgers continued to reap huge dividends for decades thereafter as Rickey laid the foundation that enabled them to become the most successful team in the National League over the next 20 years. After winning only a single pennant from 1921 through 1946, they captured ten pennants from 1947 through 1966 and also won four world championships.

Rickey's innovative action gave Brooklyn a tremendous head start over the competition in the acquisition of black talent. The Dodgers signed the first five black players to enter Organized Baseball in the 20th century without having to conceal their racial identity. Shortly after the announcement of Robinson's signing, Rickey signed star catcher Roy Campanella of the Baltimore Elite Giants and young fireballer Don Newcombe of the Newark Eagles. During the first decade of integrated major league baseball, Robinson, Campanella, and Newcombe would capture five National League Most Valuable Player Awards among them. The Dodgers also signed veteran Negro League hurlers Johnny Wright and Roy Partlow in 1946, neither of whom would make the majors.

With Robinson's remarkable success, the Dodgers became *the team* for the Negro population of the country. Playing for "Jackie Robinson's Brooklyn Dodgers" became the dream of every young black ballplayer, and the club was in a position to sign virtually any black free agent they wanted.

The Dodgers' Failure to Sign More Black Players

But the Dodgers failed to take full advantage of their position. In fact, Robinson, Campanella, and Newcombe would be the only black players signed during Rickey's tenure who would go on to lasting stardom with the Dodgers. From 1947 until he left to take over the Pittsburgh Pirates after the 1950 season, Rickey recruited only three veteran Negro Leaguers of note: pitcher Dan Bankhead of the Memphis Red Sox, speedy outfielder Sam Jethroe of the Cleveland Buckeyes, and shortstop Jim Pendleton of the Chicago American Giants. All three would enjoy modest success in the majors, but Jethroe and Pendleton would never wear a Brooklyn uniform, while Bankhead would underachieve in Dodger flannels. Moreover, the only young black prospect signed during that period who would make a significant contribution to the Dodgers was infielder Charlie Neal, who would enjoy several good seasons with the club after it relocated to Los Angeles.

Rickey's failure to sign more black stars for the Dodgers is a mystery not in keeping with his reputation as a shrewd businessman and judge of baseball talent or his humanitarian track record.

It's been speculated that one of the reasons the Dodgers didn't recruit more black stars is that Negro League club owners were reluctant to deal with Rickey because he didn't pay them for the rights to Robinson and Campanella.[1] Kansas City Monarchs owner Tom Baird publicly criticized Rickey for signing Robinson away from his club. "I have been informed that Mr. Rickey is a very religious man," said Baird, "If such is true, it appears that his religion runs towards the all mighty dollar." Baird threatened to take the Dodgers to court but was quickly pressured to back down by those interested in facilitating integration.[2] Many years later, Effa Manley, owner of the Newark Eagles, said, "Rickey raped us. We were in no position to protest, and he knew it."[3]

For his part, Rickey contended, "I failed to find a single player under uniform contract and I learned that players of all teams become free agents at the end of each season, with no written guarantee or consideration."[4] In 1948, Commissioner Happy Chandler validated Rickey's position. The Chicago American Giants complained that the San Diego Padres of the Pacific Coast League owed them compensation for signing catcher John "Hoss" Ritchey, the 1947 Negro American League batting champ. Chandler denied the complaint when Chicago couldn't produce a signed contract.[5]

It's easy to be critical of Rickey for these actions, but the Negro League owners were experienced businessmen. Rickey considered the Negro Leagues "a front for a monopolistic game, controlled by booking agents in Chicago, Philadelphia, and New York," according to biographer Andrew O'Toole.[6] Whether this was an exaggeration or not, there was a legitimate reason the Negro League magnates didn't have their players under ironclad contracts, and it certainly wasn't in the players' interests. Unlike their Organized Baseball brethren, they weren't protected by the reserve clause that bound a player to a franchise in perpetuity. Therefore, they didn't want to risk having contracts that obligated them to pay a player who was injured or under-performing when they stood the risk of losing him when his contract was up. As Jackie Robinson put it, "I wasn't signed to a contract because Kansas City didn't know whether I would make good, so they didn't want to have trouble getting rid of me."[7] Tom Baird, of course, saw it from an owner's perspective, insisting, "According to the rules and regulations of the two Negro Leagues any player accepting terms by letter or telegram or playing with a club becomes the property of that club."[8] Interestingly, after the signing of Robinson and other integration pioneers established a market for black talent, Negro League franchises quickly decided that more formal contracts were a good business practice after all.[9]

Rickey reportedly did lay out $15,000 for Dan Bankhead during the 1947 season, which was thought to be the highest price for a black player up to that time.[10] The Bankhead deal, in fact, may have discouraged Rickey from purchasing more established Negro League stars. He personally scouted Bankhead and acquired him in hopes that he would give the Dodger staff a boost down the stretch, but the right hander suffered from stage fright in his big league debut. He was of no help to the Dodgers that season and spent the next two years in the minors.

Another reason Rickey didn't acquire more black players for the Dodgers might have been concern about a player revolt. In general, the white Dodger players accepted, if not embraced, integration, and things had actually gone more smoothly on the field than in the executive suites. But Rickey knew that could change quickly. The players, first and foremost, were concerned about their jobs. A sudden large influx of black players at either the major or minor league level could be perceived as a threat and galvanize opposition against them. The Dodgers did, in fact, seem to employ a quota system during the Rickey era.

Roger Kahn, acclaimed author of *The Boys of Summer* wrote, "by 1949 the Dodgers were backing away from further good black prospects. With Robinson, Campanella, and Newcombe already signed, Rickey elected to slow down integration, even if it meant losing good ballplayers. He thought three blacks in a starting lineup of nine was a good balance. 'It would not have been prudent,' he remarked privately years later, 'to have had too many Negroes on any one club.'"[11]

But a sincere desire on Rickey's part to see integration succeed rapidly may have been the greatest factor contributing to Brooklyn's failure to land more black stars. The Dodgers apparently had dibs on future Hall of Famers Larry Doby[12] and Monte Irvin,[13] but let them go to the Cleveland Indians and New York Giants respectively to support the integration effort. Rickey also claimed such munificence in his decision to peddle Jethroe to the Boston Braves before the 1950 season, although a cynic might suspect that the $100,000 sales price was a contributing factor.[14] Concerned about Jethroe having to go it alone in Boston, Rickey also offered Dan Bankhead's services as a pitcher/companion to the Braves, but was declined.[15]

The Integration Era

All five of the black players in the Organized Baseball during the 1946 season experienced some degree of success in the Brooklyn minor league system. Yet the Dodgers sent Wright and Partlow back to the Negro Leagues and brought in only two more black minor leaguers to start the 1947 season, 18-year-old Detroit schoolboy phenom Sammy Gee and Cuban catcher Ramon Rodriguez. Neither lasted. Gee hit only .184 for Three Rivers, and Rodriguez, assigned to Nashua, missed most of the season with injuries.

Late in the 1947 season, Dan Bankhead became the second black Brooklyn Dodger and fifth black major leaguer behind Robinson, Larry Doby, who debuted with the Cleveland Indians in early July, and Hank Thompson and Willard Brown, who got 30-day trials with the St. Louis Browns shortly thereafter. Immediately brought to the majors after his acquisition, Bankhead became the first black pitcher to take the mound in the major leagues on August 26, getting pounded by the Pittsburgh Pirates in a little more than three innings of relief duty. His hitting was much better, however, as he also became the first black man to homer in his first big league at-bat. Bankhead's only significant contribution to the 1947 pennant race was a scoreless four-inning stint on Jackie Robinson Day to earn the first save ever garnered by a black reliever.

Despite Robinson's outstanding rookie performance, the Dodgers and Cleveland Indians were the only major league teams to start the 1948 season with black players on their major league rosters. Larry Doby was in Cleveland's opening day lineup, and Campanella joined Robinson on the Brooklyn squad. Campy had replaced Robinson in Montreal in 1947 and, in one respect, outdid him by capturing the International League Most Valuable Player Award. At age 26, Campanella had already been playing professional baseball for more than a decade and was clearly ready for the major leagues. But Rickey had other plans. The racial barrier had fallen in the International League, and the San Diego Padres of the Pacific Coast League had catcher John Ritchey for the 1948 campaign. That left the American Association as the only segregated Triple A circuit. Rickey's plan was for Campanella to start the season on the Dodger bench before reporting to their St. Paul farm club after big league rosters were reduced in mid–May to become the American Association's first black player. Legend has it that Rickey forbade manager Leo Durocher from playing Campanella behind the plate lest the fans and

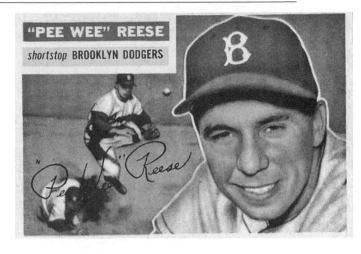

Star shortstop Pee Wee Reese, a southerner, was an early Jackie Robinson supporter on the Dodgers (1956 Topps card).

writers become overly enthused about the squatty catcher and protest his demotion when the time arrived.[16] In fact, the Dodgers brought Campanella to camp as an outfielder and even tried him out at third base in an attempt to hide his talents.[17] Aside from a few transgressions by Durocher, things proceeded as planned. Campanella was demoted to St. Paul after only two appearances with the Dodgers and slammed 13 homers in 39 American Association contests before being brought back to take over the regular catching chores in Brooklyn.

Rickey's maneuvering may have cost the Dodgers the 1948 pennant. The Dodgers' regular catcher Bruce Edwards, who had enjoyed a banner season in 1947, had a bad arm, and the club struggled to a 27–34 record before Campanella rejoined them on July 2. After he took over behind the plate, the club played at a .613 pace, which would have been good enough for the pennant. But they had fallen too far behind to catch the Boston Braves and finished in third place.

At the beginning of the 1949 campaign, Newcombe was also required to undergo additional seasoning before being promoted to the Dodgers in late May. Despite spending the first six weeks of the season with Montreal, Big Newk won 17 games and the National League Rookie of the Year Award as the Dodgers captured another National League pennant.

Rickey and the Dodgers were presented with a dilemma for the 1950 season. The previous year, the Dodgers had three black players after Newcombe was recalled. Meanwhile, the American League Indians started and ended the 1949 season with three black players, although only Doby and Satchel Paige were with them most of the year. Therefore, the idea of a three-blacks-per-team limit had crept into the media consciousness, doubtlessly encouraged by some mathematically inclined sportswriter who figured that four blacks on a 25-man roster resulted in a significantly higher ratio of blacks to whites than the national average at that time.

But the Dodgers had two top-notch black prospects pounding at their door. Dan Bankhead had overcome his nervousness to win 20 games for Montreal the previous year and was ready to claim a spot on the Dodger staff. Outfielder Sam Jethroe was also ready for the big time after hitting .326 for Montreal and establishing a new International League record with 89 stolen bases. The problem was partially alleviated when Jethroe's contract was sold to the Boston Braves, but there was still much pre-season debate in the press over the ramifications of having four black players on the team. The speculation was that either Bankhead or Newcombe would have to be traded. *The New York Age*, a black publication, bluntly posed the question: "Will Bankhead be retained by the Brooklyn Dodgers or will he be peddled elsewhere to keep the Negro 'quota' at the right number in Ebbets Field?"[18] When the 1950 season began, both black hurlers were in the Dodger rotation with Campanella behind the plate and Robinson at second base. Four black players on the Dodgers roster didn't create a problem as feared. Though the Dodgers lost the pennant to the Phillies on the last day of the season, Robinson, Campy, and Newk enjoyed excellent seasons, and Bankhead turned in a decent rookie performance.

While Rickey was patiently putting the finishing touches on a Dodger dynasty, however, he was losing a bitter internal battle for control of the organization. Eventually Rickey was squeezed out, and he departed after the 1950 season to run the Pirates, taking his most loyal scouts and front office staff with him.

The O'Malley Era

Walter O'Malley was a politically connected corporate attorney who became chief counsel for the Dodgers about the same time Rickey came over from St. Louis. O'Malley, whom Roger Kahn called "The Great Manipulator," quickly recognized that there was a buck to be made in the grand old game, and in 1943 he went in with Rickey and John Smith, president of the Pfizer Chemical Corporation, to purchase controlling interest in the club.[19] Soon O'Malley set his sights on the presidency of the Dodgers, the position occupied by Rickey. He resented the credit Rickey received for the club's success and began questioning the older man's decisions and openly battling him for day-to-day control of the club. When Rickey's contract as president was up in 1950, O'Malley successfully argued against renewal in spite of the franchise's amazing success.[20]

Before the 1951 season, the Dodgers went on a recruiting spree, signing several black prospects. They purchased veteran pitcher Joe Black and promising young infielder Jim Gilliam from the Baltimore Elite Giants and grabbed dark-skinned Cubans Hector Rodriguez and Sandy Amoros from the Mexican and Dominican leagues respectively. Fancy-fielding Cuban shortstop Chico Fernandez was signed as a free agent, and the nation's sandlots yielded a couple of African American youngsters named Maury Wills and John Roseboro. All of these players eventually reached the big leagues and played regularly with the Dodgers or other teams. But for the first season since the color line was crossed no new black players were added to the parent roster by the new Rickey-less regime in Brooklyn.

In fact, 1951, O'Malley first season as the president of the club, marked the Dodgers' loss of status as baseball's top employer of black major leaguers. Despite a promising 1950 campaign, Bankhead was dispatched to the minor leagues early in the season, leaving the club with only three black players — Robinson, Campanella, and Newcombe. After leading by 13½ games in mid–August, they lost the pennant to the New York Giants on Bobby Thomson's game-winning homer, the famous "shot heard around the world," in the bottom of the ninth inning of the final game of the season. The fact that the Giants had four black players shouldn't have been lost on the Dodgers brass.

But the Dodgers again held the limit at three black players in 1952. Newcombe was drafted into the army, and Joe Black took his place as the club's top pitcher. Used primarily out of the bullpen, the 28-year-old Black pitched the club to the pennant, winning 15 games and National League Rookie of the Year honors. Later in the season, the club numbered four black players on the roster again when young Sandy Amoros was briefly promoted to fill in for injured Carl Furillo.

The Dodgers didn't return to the number of black players they had when Rickey left until 1953. Furthermore, they seemed to re-adopt the old "one-a-year" strategy although the need for the quota no longer existed. Remembering the mid–1950s, long-time Dodger Ed Roebuck recalled, "We were very cognizant of the quota system, which meant that only a certain number of blacks could make it to the majors, and that no team could have more than a few blacks, and that some teams didn't have any blacks at all yet."[21]

In 1953, Dodger Manager Charlie Dressen had fallen in love with the speedy Jim "Junior" Gilliam's second baseman's glove and leadoff skills and was determined to get him in the lineup. Of course, that necessitated the shift of Jackie Robinson, who had led National League second baseman in fielding in 1952, to another position. Robinson graciously agreed to make room for Gilliam, but dissention arose from another source. The original plan was for Robinson to move to third base, where he had prior experience. That didn't sit too well with feisty veteran third sacker Billy Cox or his close friend pitcher Preacher Roe, who hailed from Ashflat, Arkansas. Manager Charlie Dressen and the Dodger brass moved quickly to quell the mini-revolt by giving in. Instead of moving to third base, Robinson was stationed in left field most of the season, displacing promising young Sandy Amoros rather than a white Dodger.[22] Robinson enjoyed his last really good year in 1953 while Gilliam scored 125 runs to give the club the leadoff man they had sorely lacked for years. Gilliam also gave Brooklyn their fourth black Rookie of the Year since 1947. Although the Dodgers again took the National League flag, they succumbed to the Yankees in the World Series for a fifth time.

In the spring of 1954, 24-year-old Sandy Amoros was back to contend for the Dodgers left field job after leading the International League with a .353 batting average for Montreal the previous year. The speedy left-handed hitter had also slammed 23 homers and was an excellent defensive outfielder. But the racial situation was reaching critical mass, at least in the eyes of the front office where the Cox/Gilliam controversy was still fresh in the corporate memory. Stationing Amoros in left field would mean moving Robinson to third base full-time; and with Campanella behind the plate, Gilliam at second, and Newcombe or Joe Black on the mound, there would be more black faces than white ones on the field. The situation that many white baseball men feared — the black players taking over — seemed to be coming to pass, and the O'Malley-led Dodger front office didn't have the stomach for it.

Despite hitting a sensational .421 during the exhibition season, Amoros was returned to Montreal for another year of "seasoning." He forced a mid-season recall by pounding the ball at a .352 clip with 14 homers in 68 games. On July 17, the young Cuban outfielder appeared in the starting lineup along with Newcombe, Robinson, Campanella, and Gilliam for the first time — and nothing happened! The event that had occasioned so much concern was anticlimactic, meriting only a brief mention in *The Sporting News*.[23] That year, the Dodgers forfeited their National League title to the New York Giants, who featured black stars Willie Mays, Monte Irvin, and Hank Thompson in their lineup, and dark-skinned Puerto Rican Ruben Gomez as their number-two starter.

Before spring training got underway in 1955, Jackie Robinson confronted O'Malley about the existence of a black player quota. O'Malley rashly responded by indicating, "The club wouldn't hesitate to put nine Negroes on the field if they were the best available players." Evidently, columnist Dick Young, who had gained something of a reputation as an O'Malley sycophant, felt compelled to cover for the Dodger boss, by explaining the economic risks inherent in such an action in a *Sporting News* column that ran under the banner, "What's 'Saturation' Point for Negroes on a Club? Eight in Dodgers Camp."[24] After the obligatory fawning over O'Malley, Young wrote of the desirability of gradual rather than abrupt change, predicting that top prospect Charlie Neal, for whom the club had reportedly refused a $125,000 offer, would be judiciously returned to the minors rather than upset the team's delicate racial balance.[25]

Sure enough, accompanied by shortstop prospect Chico Fernandez, the 24-year-old Neal, after an excellent 1954 season in Triple A, was sent to Montreal for the ubiquitous "additional seasoning," and Joe Black was dispatched to Cincinnati in an early season trade. The 1955 Dodgers won their first World Championship with five black players on the roster. Campanella, Robinson, Gilliam, and Amoros were in the lineup regularly, and Newcombe, who had become the first black player to participate in the annual Baseball Players Golf Tournament in Miami that spring, led the pitching staff.[26]

The club's suspension of its "one new Negro a year" program would cost them dearly. The Dodgers left future star Roberto Clemente exposed in the minor league draft when they couldn't find room for him on the roster, and Branch Rickey and the Pittsburgh Pirates quickly scooped him up. Ironically, Clemente is the only black Hall of Famer signed by the Dodgers during the O'Malley family's ownership reign of nearly 50 years.

The Dodgers captured the National League crown once again in 1956, slipping past the Braves and the surprising Cincinnati Reds to win by one game. Newcombe was the man of the hour, winning 27 games and the National League Most Valuable Player Award. That year, the Dodgers finally added Charlie Neal to their parent roster. Neal fit nicely into a three-way platoon arrangement. With a right-hander on the mound, Gilliam played second with Amoros in left. When a lefty started, Gilliam shifted to left and Neal moved in to second. In July, shortstop prospect Chico Fernandez was brought up to give the Dodgers seven black players, the most they had ever had and the most in the big leagues at that time.

The 1957 season was the beginning of a transition period for the Dodgers as they fell to third place behind Milwaukee and St. Louis amid rumors of an impending move to Los Angeles. The nucleus of black players that the 1950s dynasty had been built around was breaking down. Robinson retired after the club's 1956 World Series loss to the Yankees; Campanella seemed to be about finished; Newcombe suffered through his first losing season; and Amoros had lost playing time in left field. Gilliam was still manning second base, and Neal had taken over for Pee Wee Reese at shortstop with Fernandez being swapped to the Philadelphia Phillies. The only new addition to the ranks of black Dodgers was John Roseboro, who arrived during the year to back up Campanella behind the plate.

The Move to Los Angeles

Before the 1958 season, the Dodgers pulled up stakes in Brooklyn and made their much anticipated move to California. More than 1.8 million Los Angeles fans paid to see the Dodgers limp home in seventh place. In their last season in Brooklyn, they had only attracted a little more than one million fans while contending for the pennant.

The Dodgers new home was one of the whitest cities in baseball. According to the 1960 census, the Los Angeles metropolitan area boasted a population of more than 6.7 million people of which less than 9 percent were black. It may have been coincidental that the number of black players in Dodger uniforms took a dive during their first year in the "City of Angels."

Campanella was paralyzed in an automobile accident just before the beginning of spring training. Then Amoros was mysteriously demoted to Montreal, and Newcombe was traded to Cincinnati after starting the campaign with six straight losses. By the middle of their first season in Los Angeles, only three black players remained on the Dodgers roster: Gilliam shuttled between the outfield and third base, Neal took over at second, and Roseboro replaced Campy behind the plate. In a year when more than 60 black players appeared in the major leagues, about 35 of them as regulars, the Dodgers plunged to their lowest minority representation since 1949, the third year of integration. The Giants, Braves, Indians, and Reds all had more black players, and integration laggards, like the Athletics, Orioles, and Pirates, had as many.

The decade came to a fitting conclusion as the Dodgers surprised everyone by capturing the 1959 National League pennant and the World Series. The veteran Gilliam settled in at third base full time, Roseboro continued to establish himself as one of the top catchers in baseball, and second baseman Neal finished among the league leaders in Most Valuable Player balloting. In mid-season, Maury Wills replaced disappointing Don Zimmer at shortstop, providing a needed spark as the club charged from fourth place to the pennant. Wills, who spent 8½ years in the minors before getting his chance, would go on to become the best black Dodger signed during the post–Rickey era.

The move to Los Angeles turned the Dodgers into the most prosperous and stable franchise in baseball and made their owner one of the most influential figures in the game. After Walter O'Malley's death in 1979, the torch was passed to his son Peter, who ran the franchise through the 1997 campaign. An indication of the franchise's stability is that only four men managed the Dodgers during the 47 years of O'Malley leadership: Charley Dressen, Walter Alston, Tommy Lasorda, and Bill Russell.

O'Malley's Track Record

Due to the signing of Jackie Robinson the Dodgers held an unquestioned status as the champion of equal opportunity in baseball. But their track record since the Rickey era brings that reputation into question. Interestingly, Jackie Robinson and Roy Campanella, the first two black players elected to the Baseball Hall of Fame, are the only black players commonly associated with the Dodgers to make it to Cooperstown. Frank Robinson, Juan Marichal, and Eddie Murray are other black Hall of Famers who briefly wore Dodger blue, but they signed and spent their best years with other teams.

Under Rickey, the Dodgers didn't coddle their black athletes, but they did evince some sensitivity. When Robinson was breaking in, Rickey shifted the Dodgers' spring training site to Havana, Cuba, to lessen the racial tension. The aforementioned Kirby Higbe was quickly dispatched to the Pittsburgh Pirates when he indicated he would have trouble overcoming an aversion to playing with black players. Popular Dixie Walker, the "The People's Choice" in Brooklyn, also made his prejudice known and also found himself in Pittsburgh after the 1947 campaign.[27]

But under O'Malley, the club's relationship with its black players seemed to deteriorate. With the exception of the agreeable Campanella, who Robinson considered something of an "Uncle Tom," and company man Jim Gilliam, black players invariably seemed to have trouble with the Dodger brass.[28] Friction ensued between Robinson and the O'Malley front office,[29] especially in the latter stages of Jackie's career. Bankhead, Amoros, Newcombe, Neal, and later Wills, Roseboro, Tommy Davis, and Willie Davis all departed on less than amicable terms.

Spring training was an ordeal for black players in the Dodgers system. In 1950, the Dodgers purchased an old military base in Vero Beach, re-christened it "Dodgertown," and set up spring training operations there. Within the facility, both black and white players, from raw recruits to established stars, were housed together in the old barracks according to their status achieved by their performance on the field. But the town of Vero Beach didn't welcome African Americans. The black players were forced to go to Gifford, a tiny neighboring berg, for limited off-campus recreational activities as well as basic necessities like haircuts.[30] Some black players felt that O'Malley should have used his considerable economic clout more freely to encourage some local attitude adjustment.[31]

Treatment of Black Prospects

In addition, the club's treatment of young black prospects was somewhat callous. In the early 1950s, the Dodgers stockpiled talented black prospects who were easily lured into signing with "Jackie Robinson's team." Too often, these young players were allowed to wither on the vine, consigned to waste their careers in the vast Dodger farm system without getting a decent chance to gain a spot on the parent club or go to another team.

Jim Pendleton, for example, sacrificed his prime starring for St. Paul and Montreal, while waiting in vain for Pee Wee Reese to grow old. Pendleton was already 25 years old and one of the best shortstops in the Negro Leagues when the Dodgers acquired his contract before the 1949 season. Pendleton's manager, Clay Hopper, who managed Robinson in his rookie season at Montreal, promised early in the 1950 campaign, "I'll have Pendleton in the majors before this year is out."[32] But it didn't happen that year — or the next. Pendleton was one of the most sought-after players in the minor leagues, but the Dodgers repeatedly rejected attractive offers for his services, including a reported six-figure bid from the Braves after the 1951 campaign.[33] Yet he couldn't oust Reese at shortstop, and the Dodgers wouldn't give the speedy, versatile right-handed hitter a crack at their troublesome left field job though he was also a fine outfielder. When Don Zimmer emerged as a worthy heir to Reese, the Dodgers finally swapped Pendleton to the Braves before the 1953 season without ever giving him a major league at-bat. It's conceivable that the only reason the club finally let Pendleton go is that they didn't want him further complicating their delicate racial balance by contending for the left field spot.

Other examples abound. Outfielder/third baseman Robert Wilson was signed off the Houston Eagles roster in 1950 at the age of 25 and spent almost nine years hitting over .300 in the organization before getting a quick three-game trial in 1958. Twenty-seven-year-old Cuban Rene Valdez was the sensation of the Dodgers' 1957 training camp after winning 22 games for Portland the previous year, but he was farmed out after a 13-inning trial and spent the next five years winning 62 games for the Dodgers top farm teams without getting another opportunity. Fancy-fielding Panamanian third baseman Clyde Parris, signed out of the Provincial League at the age of 25, never got a big league shot although he led the International League in hitting in 1956 and starred for Dodger farm clubs for eight years. Shortstop Lacy Curry hit .382 in his 1951 debut in the Dodger system but in 10 years never played above Class AAA. Charlie Neal eventually did become a Dodger, but only after completing a six-year minor league apprenticeship. Even Maury Wills, winner of the 1962 Most Valuable Player Award and the Dodgers first captain since Pee Wee Reese, had to spend more than eight years in the Dodgers minor league system before finally getting a shot with the parent club in 1959 at the age of 28.

Early Burnouts

Another indication of an underlying racial problem in O'Malley's Dodgerland was the alarming number of established black players who experienced mysterious early burnouts during the 1950s.

Dan Bankhead, Major League Baseball's first black pitcher, posted a fine 9–4 won-lost record in 1950, his first full season in the big leagues, and finished in the top ten in the league in both saves and games pitched. The next year, he lost his effectiveness, and a year later, he was out of Organized Baseball.

Joe Black was a rookie sensation in 1952, winning 15 games. After making only two starts all year, manager Charley Dressen started him three times in one week in the World Series. He was never the same again, posting only 15 more major league victories in the next five years before retiring.

At the age of 31, Don Newcombe's won-lost record dropped from 27–7 in 1956 to 11–12 in 1957. The next year, he found himself with the Cincinnati Reds, and by 1961, he was in the minor leagues. Newcombe eventually admitted to a serious alcohol problem that started while he was with the Dodgers.[34]

Charlie Neal also faded quickly. As a 28-year-old in 1959, he was the best second baseman in the National League, hitting .287 with power and leading the league's second sackers in fielding. But over the next two years, his batting average plummeted more than 50 points. Furthermore, the man who teammate John Roseboro once described as having jets on his legs was mysteriously transformed from one of the surest glove men in the majors to a tentative, error-prone defensive liability.[35] Neal experienced a slight resurgence after a trade to the New York Mets in 1962, but he was out of professional baseball after the 1963 season. Maury Wills claimed that "...Neal became ill, psychologically and emotionally. Before you knew it, he was through."[36] Years after his career ended, Neal admitted that something had happened to him, although he couldn't put his finger on what it was. "All of a sudden I was missing ground balls before they got to me," he said.[37]

The Dodgers' treatment of outfielder Sandy Amoros also raises questions about the team's commitment to equitable treatment of black players at that time. Though his great clutch play in the final game of the 1955 World Series preserved the Dodgers victory, Amoros never developed into the dominant player he was expected to become. He was thrown at often and developed problems handling left-handed pitching. But from 1954 through 1957, he was a valuable platoon player for Dodgers. In 1957, he posted a career-best .277 batting average, but he refused to sign when offered a 1958 contract for the same money. The Dodgers punished their 28-year-old former World Series hero by selling his contract outright to Montreal, reportedly reaching a "gentlemen's agreement" with other clubs to clear him through waivers.[38] Amoros spent the next two seasons in exile with Montreal before being traded to Detroit in 1960.

Marginality

The Amoros situation was not unique. In the early years of integration, there was only room for black front-liners on major league rosters. Bench spots were generally reserved for whites. This tendency to employ whites of marginal or average ability over similarly talented black players has been termed "marginality."[39] During the 1950 season, for example, all of the nine black players who appeared in the big leagues were front-line players. The seven position players were Jackie Robinson, Larry Doby, Roy Campanella, Monte Irvin, Luke Easter, Sam Jethroe, and Hank Thompson, who hit a collective .296 and averaged almost 22 homers and 85 runs batted in apiece. The two hurlers, Don Newcombe and Dan Bankhead, posted a combined 28–15 won-lost mark. As late as 1959, there were almost as many future Hall of Famers as full-time benchwarmers among the black players who appeared on big league rosters.

The Dodgers were faithful adherents of the "starters-only" policy. From 1947 through 1959, the only black players to spend a full-season in a second-line role were Joe Black and young Charlie Neal. Black spent the 1953 season in the Dodgers bullpen trying to regain his 1952 Rookie of the Year form, and Neal rode the pines in 1956 as heir apparent to a regular infield spot. The multi-talented Jim Pendleton couldn't win a spot on the Dodger bench as his path to the majors was blocked by the immortal Rocky Bridges. The Dodgers kept Rex Barney around for six years, waiting for him to find the strike zone, but released Dan Bankhead a year after his promising rookie season. Carl Erskine spent three years on the Dodgers roster trying to rehabilitate his sore arm while Joe Black had to do his rehabbing in the minor leagues. White Brooklyn favorites like Duke Snider, Gil Hodges, Pee Wee Reese, and Clem Labine, were allowed to age gracefully as role players in Dodger blue, while Newcombe and Amoros were jettisoned at the first sign of slippage. O'Malley even tried to ship Robinson to the New York Giants at the end of his career before Robinson foiled the trade by retiring.

The 1960s and Beyond

Though the Dodgers would never regain their early status as the undisputed leader in the employment of black players, they experienced another black talent boon in the 1960s. Wills developed into the most prolific base-stealer in history, and Gilliam and Roseboro continued to be valuable contributors. Future outfield stars Tommy and Willie Davis joined the club in 1960. The 1963 team that vanquished the New York Yankees in four straight games for the World Championship fielded a starting lineup that featured five black players: Wills, Gilliam, Roseboro, and the Davises. In fact, during the regular season second baseman Nate Oliver often gave them six black starters in the lineup.

In 1965, the Dodgers captured another world championship with the same nucleus of black players. The only change was the replacement of injured Tommy Davis in left field with Lou Johnson, one of the last Negro Leaguers to graduate to the majors. The same cast captured the National League pennant again in 1966, but dispersed after being swept by the Baltimore Orioles in the Series.

But the practices established in the 1950s continued through the next decade. The only black Dodgers to occupy bench seats for an entire season in the 1960s were infielder Nate Oliver and developing young outfielder Willie Crawford. Larry Sherry, the 1959 World Series hero, languished in the Dodger bullpen for years afterward trying to recapture the glory, but series co-star Charlie Neal was promptly shuffled off to the expansion New York Mets when his productivity declined. A few years later, two-time batting champ Tommy Davis was also swapped to the lowly Mets when he was slow recovering from a broken leg, yet Johnny Podres was given every opportunity to revive his ailing arm. John Roseboro and Maury Wills were traded when they began to show signs of wear and tear while the Dodgers hung on to fading white veterans like Wally Moon, Ron Fairly, and Jim Lefebvre. Among the black players, only

Gilliam was allowed to grow old and retire gracefully. By 1968, the Dodgers were a second-division club with Willie Davis the only black player left in their regular lineup.

The pattern repeated itself in the 1970s and into the future. Wills, who rejoined the Dodgers for a second tour of duty after a two-year sojourn to Pittsburgh, was unceremoniously released in 1972 when Bill Russell developed into an adequate replacement. On the other hand, Russell was retained for years after his days as a regular shortstop were over while his long-time black keystone partner Davey Lopes was quickly traded after an injury-plagued campaign. Dusty Baker enjoyed eight productive years in the Dodger outfield but was immediately let go when his performance dipped at age 34. Meanwhile, his less accomplished white outfield mate, Rick Monday, stuck around for six years as a backup outfielder after his days as a first-stringer were over.

During that time, the Dodgers also made deals to acquire high-profile black stars who passed through Los Angles all too quickly. Richie Allen spent one year in Dodger blue before going to Chicago to win the American League Most Valuable Player Award for the White Sox. Frank Robinson tied for the club lead in homers in 1972, his only year with the Dodgers. Jimmy Wynn led the club to the 1974 pennant and was traded after he tailed off the next season. Fortunately, Reggie Smith and Dusty Baker were allowed to stay longer and spark the Dodgers to successive pennants in the late 1970s as steady, conservative Walter Alston yielded the managerial reins to Tommy Lasorda.

The Dodger Image

The Dodgers carefully maintained their image as a leader in race relations. The organization had always been charitable with retired black stars in publicly conspicuously ways. Gilliam became one of the first black coaches. The franchise was extremely generous with the stricken Campanella and helped his old battery mate Newcombe get back on his feet after alcohol almost ruined his life.

But that image took a big hit in the spring of 1987. Shortly after their opening game of the season, Dodgers vice president Al Campanis appeared on ABC's "Nightline," hosted by Ted Koppel. The show was intended to be a tribute to Jackie Robinson, marking the 40th anniversary of his history-making major league debut. But it ended up being an embarrassing racial incident. Campanis was a Dodger-lifer, the last of the old executive guard who moved from Brooklyn to Los Angeles. He began as minor league infielder in the Brooklyn system in 1940 and managed to make the big leagues for a seven-game trial during the war before entering the service. After his discharge, he was second baseman Jackie Robinson's double-play partner with Montreal in 1946. Shortly thereafter, Campanis, who had earned a master's degree from New York University, made the move from the field to the executive side of the game. He served as a scout, manager, and instructor before taking over as scouting director in 1957. By 1968, he had worked his way up to vice president in charge of player personnel.

According to an account in *The Cultural Encyclopedia of Baseball*, Campanis responded to a question from Koppel as to whether prejudice was responsible for the lack of blacks in executive positions in baseball. Campanis answered, "No, I don't believe it's prejudice. I truly believe that they may not have some of the necessities to be, let's say, a field manager, or perhaps a general manager." The Dodger vice president went on to opine that "[Black people] are gifted with great musculature and various other things. They're fleet of foot, and this is why there are a lot of black major league baseball players. Now, as far as having the background to become club presidents, or presidents of banks, I don't know."[40]

Dodger management, led by Walter's son Peter O'Malley, initially tried to rally around the seventy-year-old Campanis and minimize the damage, but the media ran with the story and Campanis' resignation was requested.

Ironically, until the Koppel interview, Campanis seemed to enjoy a good reputation among black players. Robinson is quoted as having once said, "Al Campanis is a good guy. He was very good on integration when it counted."[41] In fact, Campanis was one of three white players recruited by the Jackie Robinson All-Stars back in the fall of 1946 for a series against major league opponents.[42] Pedro Guerrero, one of the most prominent black players on the Dodgers during the 1980s, expressed unhappiness over Campanis' ouster, saying, "...he's always treated me, all the Latin players, very well." Four-time batting champ Bill Madlock, who had joined the Dodgers late during the previous campaign was angry about Campanis' statements but admitted, "The guys who know him better ... the whites, the Blacks, the Latins ... all speak very highly of him."[43]

Unfortunately, many in the Dodger hierarchy must have secretly shared Campanis' opinions. Roger Kahn wrote that the O'Malley clan was a "staunchly Irish Catholic family" and that "[Walter] O'Malley was burningly aware of ethnicity and in time created in Dodger management an entirely Roman Catholic hierarchy."[44] Kahn also recalled columnist Dick Young insisting that O'Malley told him he wanted to leave Ebbets Field "because the area is getting full of blacks and spics," a statement O'Malley denied making.[45] At the time of the Campanis gaff, 13 of the 66 franchise staffers listed in the club's media guide were minorities, but three — Campanella, Newcombe, and Lou Johnson — were attached to the speaker's bureau, and eight — seven of them Latinos — were scouts.[46]

The Dodgers survived with their precious reputation bruised but intact. Yet to this day they have never had a black manager, putting them in the minority of big league teams. They did enjoy something of a revival as baseball's premier Equal Opportunity Employer in the latter part of the 20th century, but it wasn't due to a renewed commitment to African American players.

PARADE SPORTIVE
PAUL STUART
LE PREMIER PROGRAMME DU GENRE
Interviews des Célébrités de tous les Sports   Correspondance: 4314 St-André, Montréal, 34
SPORTez-vous bien !

PHOTO PARADE SPORTIVE

Al CAMPANIS

A 1987 television interview with then–Dodgers vice-president Al Campanis, who had been a Robinson teammate at Montreal in 1946, showed that bias still existed in baseball 40 years after the color line was crossed (Cuban card).

Interestingly, the Dodgers had never been leaders in the recruitment of players from the Caribbean. Other than Dolf Luque, who spent a few years in Brooklyn in the early 1930s, wartime Puerto Rican recruit Luis Olmo and Sandy Amoros were the only Latino Dodgers of note until Manny Mota was acquired in 1969. They let a good Latino player, Clemente, slip through their fingers, yet they were trailblazers in introducing players of other nationalities. The Dodgers were the first team to extensively mine Mexican talent and were rewarded in 1981 when Fernando Valenzuela burst into stardom and "Fernandomania" swept Los Angeles. In 1994, the Dodgers acquired Chan Ho Park, who became the first Korean to pitch in the big leagues, and a year later, they imported the first major star from Japan, pitcher Hideo Nomo.

The 1997 squad featured a multi-national starting rotation that included Nomo from Japan, Park from South Korea, Ismael Valdez from Mexico, Ramon Martinez from the Dominican Republic, and Tom Candiotti, a Caucasian from California. But the only dark-skinned position players to make a significant contribution that year were Dominicans Raul Mondesi and Wilton Guerrero.

Not another Jackie Robinson in the bunch!

Chapter 3

THE CLEVELAND INDIANS

Cleveland Indians owner Bill Veeck followed Rickey's "Great Experiment" with considerable interest and perhaps a tinge of jealousy. The 33-year-old Veeck, who reveled in his reputation as a baseball maverick, was always on the lookout for anything new and innovative that would improve his ball club and aggravate the baseball establishment in the process.

Veeck's father had been the president of the Chicago Cubs for 15 years until his death in 1933 when Bill Jr. was 19 years old. Since young Bill had grown up hanging around Wrigley Field, Cubs owner Phil Wrigley hired him to help out in the front office after his father died. Though not a wealthy man, Veeck managed to buy the struggling Milwaukee Brewers American Association franchise eight years later, with Wrigley's blessing.[1] Only 27 at the time, Veeck quickly gained notoriety for his wild promotions and unconventional style of running a franchise. He also directed the Brewers to three pennants while setting new attendance records and sold his interest for a tidy profit in late 1945.[2] In the meantime, he'd enlisted in the Marines and was wounded in action at Bougainville in the South Pacific, an injury that would result in the loss of a portion of his right foot within a few years and eventually the whole leg.[3]

After selling the Brewers, Veeck began shopping around for a major league franchise to call his own and soon set his sights on the Indians. He put together a group of investors that included comedian Bob Hope and acquired controlling interest in the club during the 1946 campaign.

Franchise History

Since winning the world championship under the fabled Tris Speaker in 1920, the Indians had been an also-ran club, usually finishing around the bottom of the first division. The 1946 squad was buried in the second division when Veeck arrived, and despite 26 wins and a major league record 348 strikeouts from the great Bob Feller, they would end up in sixth place with a 68–86 won-lost record.

In 1947, Veeck's first full season in charge, the Indians climbed to fourth place. Moreover, attendance, which improved immediately after he took over the previous year, rose another 50 percent for the year thanks to his bold, innovative, and sometimes outrageous ways of luring fans to the ballpark. Without a source of income outside of baseball, Veeck's financial lifeblood was paid attendance, and he loved coming up with new promotions and gimmicks to keep the turnstiles humming.

Veeck's Background

Veeck was an excellent baseball man, as well as a marketing genius, and that side of him was impressed by the success of Robinson and the Dodgers on the field. He insisted that the opportunity to acquire quality talent at bargain-basement prices was his primary consideration, but as "promoter extraordinaire," he also had to be greatly impressed by the impact Robinson was having on National League attendance.[4]

Long an avid fan of black baseball, Veeck often took in games when Negro League stars barnstormed through Chicago. He was said to have been in the stands for the infamous 1934 exhibition contest when Satchel Paige out-dueled Dizzy Dean and his major league all-stars 1–0 in 13 innings.[5]

Although its veracity is disputed, Veeck claimed to have had a plan to integrate the major leagues years before Rickey accomplished the feat. During the war years, the hapless and penniless Philadelphia Phillies had essentially become a ward of the National League. The story goes that Veeck was interested in buying the club and had a plan to stock it with top

Under maverick owner Bill Veeck the Cleveland Indians organization became a leader in the recruitment of black players in the late 1940s (National Baseball Hall of Fame Library, Cooperstown, N.Y.).

Negro League stars — a scheme that was shot down by Commissioner Landis and National League president Ford Frick, who quickly came up with another buyer for the Phils. This account was first reported in Veeck's 1962 autobiography *Veeck — As in Wreck* and eventually became a part of the lore of baseball's integration era.

In 1998, more than a decade after Veeck's death, an article appeared in the Society for American Baseball Research's *National Pastime* that labeled the story a fabrication. The article, entitled "A Baseball Myth Exploded," suggested that the story was probably invented by Veeck in the early 1960s to embellish his own reputation and steal some of Rickey's thunder.[6] But evidence subsequently surfaced indicating that Veeck had talked of the plan as early as 1946 — well before there were kudos to bestow for anti-segregationist activities.[7]

Whether Veeck really came close to preceding Rickey to the "Great Emancipator" throne is questionable, but there's little doubt that he was always well ahead of the field when it came to the integration of baseball.

The First Black American Leaguer

A month into Jackie Robinson's rookie season, Veeck announced that the Indians had "engaged the services of Abe Saperstein's organization for the purpose of scouting Negro talent on an international scale."[8] On a local scale, he directed his scouts to find the best black player around.

The top recommendation was 23-year-old second baseman Larry Doby of the Newark Eagles. Actually, Doby must have been relatively easy to "discover," since he was hitting well over .400 for Newark and leading the Negro National League in homers and runs batted in. Veeck negotiated a $15,000 purchase price with Eagles owner Effa Manley on July 3, 1947 (although lesser amounts have been cited elsewhere).[9] Shortly thereafter, Doby was on a train to join the Indians on the road in Chicago. He signed his Cleveland contract the morning of July 5 in borrowed White Sox office space, and that afternoon he became the first black man to play in the American League, striking out in a pinch-hitting appearance.

The day following his pinch-hit debut, Veeck ordered Doby's insertion into the lineup for the second game of a Sunday doubleheader. The problem was that Doby was an infielder, primarily a second baseman, and the Indians infield featured veteran stars Joe Gordon at second base, Ken Keltner at third, and player-manager Lou Boudreau at shortstop. There-fore, Doby got his initial start before a big Sunday afternoon crowd at first base, a position he hadn't played since high school. Of course, he didn't have a first baseman's mitt so he had to borrow the incumbent's. Doby had only a scratch single to show for five trips to the plate. Not surprisingly, he looked awkward in the field, though he wasn't charged with an error. Doby didn't start another game for the Indians that year. His first taste of the big leagues was a disaster as he batted only .156 and struck out 11 times in 32 at-bats, mostly as a pinch-hit-ter.[10]

The Indians had Doby slated for the minor leagues in 1948 to gain experience and to learn how to play the outfield. The scouting report on him was that he possessed good speed and a strong arm, but had small hands that would handicap him as an infielder.[11] Plus, the Indians had Gordon returning at second base after leading the club in homers the previous year. So the decision was made to transform Doby into an outfielder where the team needed help. In the spring of 1948, Veeck brought Cleveland icon Tris Speaker, regarded as the best center fielder of all-time, to camp to teach Doby the finer points of outfield play.[12] Either Speaker was a great tutor or Doby was a stellar student — or both. Doby learned his lessons so well that the club tore up his ticket to the minors and put him in right field on opening day. He hit .301 for the year and mastered fly-chasing techniques so well that he was shifted to the all-important center field post halfway through the campaign.

Satchel Paige and the 1948 Pennant

With the Indians battling for first place in mid-season, Veeck made another bold move. On July 9, 1948, the great Satchel Paige ambled to the mound to relieve for the Indians against the Washington Senators. Paige was already a legend. His was one of the most recognized names in baseball — black or white. But with estimates of his age ranging from a self-pro-claimed 39 to nearly 50, he was considered far too old for major league baseball. Most of baseball saw Paige's signing as another of Veeck's grandstand stunts to bolster gate receipts. The Indians owner was roundly chastised in the press for making a mockery of the game and jeopardizing his team's pennant chances for the sake of a quick buck. *The Sporting News*, after exaggerating the publication's own efforts in promoting integration, followed with a scathing indictment of Veeck. "Veeck's gone too far in his quest of publicity and he has done his league's position absolutely no good insofar as public reaction is concerned," the editors railed. "To bring in a pitching rookie of Paige's age casts a reflection on the entire scheme of operation in the major leagues. To sign a hurler of Paige's age is to demean the standards of baseball in the big circuits. Further complicating the situation is the suspicion that if Satchel was white, he would not have drawn a second thought from Veeck."[13]

Paige made the editors of *The Sporting News* eat their words, with a generous helping of "crow" heaped on. Satch was a huge box-office hit, but it was his sensational pitching as much as his famous name that drew big crowds whenever he started. He won several clutch games down the stretch and finished his freshman season with a 6–1 won-lost record and stingy 2.48 earned run average. When he got word that *The Sporting News* had nominated him American League Rookie of the Year, the old showboat joked, "I declined the position. I wasn't sure which year the gentlemen had in mind."[14]

With Doby starring in the outfield and Paige contributing key victories on the mound, the Indians raced to their first pennant in 28 years and capped off their season with a World Series triumph over the Boston Braves. They also established new all-time attendance records by luring more than 2.6 million fans to Municipal Stadium and drawing unsurpassed crowds on the road as well.

Full Speed Ahead

Emboldened by the spectacular success of Doby and Paige, the Indians dove headlong into the Negro League player market, acquiring black ballplayers of all ages by the bushel. Unlike Rickey, who preferred promising young black prospects, Veeck wasn't opposed to signing established Negro League veterans. During the 1948 season, the Indians acquired future major leaguers Minnie Minoso and Jose Santiago from the New York Cubans, and Al Smith from the Cleveland Buckeyes. The Indians also signed Fred Thomas, a renowned basketball star at Assumption College in Quebec.[15] Thomas was the first black player in the Eastern League but didn't last long in the Indians system. He also gave professional football a try with the Toronto Argonauts before settling on a basketball career with the Harlem Globetrotters. Thomas was eventually inducted into the Canadian Basketball Hall of Fame as well as the Afro-American Hall of Fame.[16]

At the beginning of the 1949 season, the Indians reportedly had 14 black players in their organization.[17] Before the season, they had acquired veteran slugger Luke Easter, shortstop Artie Wilson, and outfielder Harry Simpson from the Homestead Grays, Birmingham Black Barons, and Philadelphia Stars respectively. They also obtained contract rights to catcher John Ritchey when they picked up San Diego as a minor league affiliate, and they signed former Negro League pitching star Roy Welmaker. Among the younger black prospects they signed were first baseman Nat "Sweetwater" Clifton and pitchers Brooks Lawrence and Cleo Lewright. Lawrence would eventually develop into a National League star while Clifton would play two years in the Cleveland organization, hitting a promising .311 before forsaking baseball for basketball when the National Basketball Association opened its doors to black players.[18] The Indians ended up losing Wilson in a dispute with the New York Yankees over which team owned rights to his contract, but Veeck got former Negro League batting champ Luis Marquez from the Yankees when he filed a counter-complaint (see chapter 15).

After acquiring first baseman Mickey Vernon and starting pitcher Early Wynn in a big trade with Washington, the Indians were expected to repeat in 1949, but they ended up in third place. Age suddenly caught up with Boudreau, Gordon, and Keltner, rookie pitching star Gene Bearden lost his effectiveness, and a heart condition forced relief ace Russ Christopher into retirement. Doby had another fine season, but Paige failed to duplicate his rookie success. Cuban outfielder Minnie Minoso began the season with the Indians, earning the club the distinction of being the first major league team with three black players on their roster at once. He was farmed out after a nine-game trial, but in August Luke Easter made his much-ballyhooed debut with the Indians.

Big Luke

Easter's introduction to the big leagues may have been handled even more poorly than Doby's. Big Luke, who succeeded legendary slugger Josh Gibson as the cleanup hitter for the Homestead Grays, began his first season in Organized Baseball in 1949 with San Diego in the Pacific Coast League and developed into a tremendous gate attraction with his mammoth home runs. But he was performing in excruciating pain, having cracked his kneecap early in the year. In June, Easter's terrorization of Pacific Coast League pitchers came to an end when Veeck brought the big slugger to Cleveland for surgery. Six weeks later, Easter was in the Indians' lineup.

Seldom has a player been asked to perform under more difficult conditions, but the Indians were going nowhere, and Veeck sorely needed Easter to boost sagging attendance. Big Luke gave it a valiant effort, but he wasn't ready, and the results were disastrous. The old publicity pump had been well primed, and Cleveland fans were expecting a Ruthian-type performance from Easter. When all they got was a hulking, ancient first baseman awkwardly playing right field on a bad leg while trying to shake off six weeks of rust, their attitude turned surly. According to *The Sporting News*, Easter became "the most booed player in the history of Cleveland stadium."[19] The fans' animosity carried over into the next season until Easter was finally able to turn things around with a barrage of tape-measure homers. But by the time Easter got the fans on his side, Bill Veeck was no longer on the Cleveland scene. A combination of financial and personal problems had forced him to sell the franchise in November 1949.

Veeck vs. Rickey

Some baseball historians insist on trying to diminish Branch Rickey's contribution to the integration of Organized Baseball. They argue that the mood of the country had changed and baseball was ready to change. Someone else would have integrated the game if Rickey hadn't is the gist of their argument, and Veeck is usually identified as the most likely to have initiated the move.

It is difficult to imagine that baseball would have remained segregated much longer after the advances made by minorities during the war years. But then again it's incredible that the racial barrier remained in place as long as it did. Whether Veeck would have spearheaded baseball's integration, how long he or someone else would have taken to initiate it, and how successfully it would have been accomplished are all intriguing questions.

Veeck is the most likely candidate other than Rickey primarily because the field is so weak. It seems unlikely that owners like Stoneham of the Giants, Perini of the Braves, or Comiskey of the White Sox, whose teams were among the first to follow the Dodgers and Indians, would have ventured into the integration arena before success was first achieved by someone else.

As to timing, Veeck waited almost a year and a half after Robinson's sensational debut with Montreal before he signed Doby. As a newcomer to major league ownership, Veeck didn't have the respect of the baseball establishment and the public that Rickey enjoyed. In addition, the city of Cleveland could hardly be considered as hospitable a venue as New York for the debut of baseball's first black player, despite the integration of the Cleveland Browns' All-American Football Conference squad in 1946. One of the smaller cities in the majors, Cleveland was a conservative blue-collar town without a particularly large or politically active minority contingent. Nor did the franchise have a culture that would foment leadership in the integration area. Commenting on the news of Jackie Robinson's signing, Veeck's predecessor Alva Bradley ingenuously stated, "Colored players have never been discriminated against in the major leagues. They have simply never been able to get into the minor leagues to get the proper training for major league competition."[20]

Cleveland was also one of the last franchises to employ a Hispanic player. The Cuban-born Minoso was the first Latino to get into a regular-season game with the Indians — barely beating out Mexican Roberto "Bobby" Avila, who came into the Cleveland organization before Minoso. Avila, a second baseman who would play ten seasons in Cleveland and capture the 1954 American League batting championship, is usually not considered one of the early black players. But he was described by reporters as one of the "swarthier Mexicans," and he is a player who may not have been able to find employment in Organized Baseball before the color line was broken. In fact, Avila auditioned for the Dodgers in their 1947 training camp while Robinson was still on the Montreal roster, a move that black writers Sam Lacy and Wendell Smith interpreted as management's attempt to provide a "barometer" of the reaction of white Dodgers toward a dark-skinned teammate.[21] The Dodgers didn't sign Avila, who was 23 years old and already an established Mexican League star at the time. He returned to Mexico to win the 1947 Mexican League batting crown before signing with the Cleveland organization the next season.

In retrospect, it's doubtful that anyone but Rickey would have attempted integration before 1948. But the more critical question is whether integration would have been achieved as successfully as it was under anyone but Rickey.

Veeck's frenetic approach to integrating the Indians was the antithesis of the calculated, conservative strategy used by Rickey to introduce Robinson. Rickey studied several prospects and personally chose Robinson to break the color barrier based on character as much as ability. After a lengthy interview, a contract was signed several months before it was publicly announced. Before his big league debut, Robinson spent an entire season with Montreal while Rickey prepared his team, the press, and the general public for the advent of a black player in the big leagues. In addition, the Dodgers recruited other black players to accompany Robinson in his first year with Montreal and in his first spring training with the parent club.

In contrast, Veeck met and signed Doby, introduced him to the press and his stunned teammates, and got him into his first big league contest in a matter of hours.

The fact that Veeck's helter-skelter maneuvering in regard to integration actually worked serves to show the wealth of ready-made talent available in Negro League baseball at the time. His selection of Doby to break the American League color barrier was a curious one. If Veeck's primary motive was to increase attendance, as his critics suspected, Doby was a poor choice. There's no argument that he was one of the Negro League's top talents, but he was a virtual unknown outside of the Negro Leagues and had no place to play on the Cleveland squad. The Indians could, however, have used some help in the outfield in 1947 when the garden corps of Dale Mitchell, George "Catfish" Metkovich, Hank Edwards, Hal Peck, and Pat Seerey contributed only 40 homers to the Indians' attack. Under the circumstances, it would have made more sense for the Indians to sign an experienced Negro League outfielder. Among those who were available at the time were Monte Irvin, Sam Jethroe, Willard Brown, Henry Kimbro, and Claro Duaney. In fact, Irvin had reportedly been offered to the Indians along with Doby, but Veeck declined.[22] And Jethroe, who had starred for the Cleveland Buckeyes for years, would have been a tremendous gate attraction in Cleveland.

Then there's the matter of Doby's personality. Rickey had chosen Robinson for his intensity and mental toughness as much as his physical talent. Doby, on the other hand, was sensitive and introverted. Veeck himself later admitted, "[Doby] was not the best man we could have picked for the first Negro player in the league ... his inner turmoil was such a constant drain on him that he was never able to realize his full potential."[23]

Uncharacteristically, Veeck barely publicized Doby's debut. He held a press conference just before Doby's first game, too late to attract curious fans or those who wanted to witness history in the making. In addition, Doby broke in on the road rather than in front a hometown crowd. It's possible that Veeck just wanted a black player to secure his own place in baseball history and Doby was the first to come to his rather short-spanned attention.

In summary, it seems doubtful that Veeck or anybody else would have been able break down the baseball color barrier as deftly as Rickey. Doby initially met with failure in Cleveland, as would Hank Thompson and Willard Brown in St. Louis, but Robinson's early success in Brooklyn kept the door open for others to receive opportunities.

Whatever his motivation and regardless of his methodology, Veeck deserves credit for having the courage and foresight to stick to his decision to integrate the Indians, especially in light of Doby's dismal debut. An editorial in the May 1949 edition of *Ebony* magazine read, "Although Robinson pioneered in the majors, probably Doby has been a more important factor in sending club owners into the chase for Negro talent."[24]

Veeck also deserves credit for recognizing that Doby's future lay in a move to the outfield. Even if Doby had been able to break in with the Indians at second base, he would have had to contend with runners taking out racist aggressions or simply trying to intimidate him. In light of future problems in his career, it's doubtful that Doby would have handled it as well as the fiery Robinson. Veeck also showed good judgment in hiring a black public relations man, Lou Jones, to lay the groundwork for introducing a black player in Cleveland and to serve as Doby's road companion and mentor.[25] Veeck even shifted the franchise's Triple A affiliation from Baltimore to San Diego before the 1949 campaign in order to create a more hospitable path for black prospects to reach the Indians.

But the signing of Paige, something that only Veeck had the audacity to do, may have actually been his greatest contribution to the integration movement. When Satchel joined the Indians midway through the 1948 campaign, the baseball establishment was still clinging to the excuse that there simply weren't many top-notch black players to be had, despite the success of Robinson and Doby (Campanella had just rejoined the Dodgers from St. Paul). But Paige's sensational performance immediately exposed the absurdity of that contention and gave the Negro Leagues legitimacy in the eyes of many baseball insiders and fans.[26] After all, if old Satch could still make major league hitters look foolish at his advanced age, maybe the talent level in black baseball wasn't that much lower than the majors after all. People began wondering how many other black all-stars were out there.

New Ownership

Sadly, the Veeck era in Cleveland came to a premature end shortly after he directed the Indians to their first world championship. Divorce proceedings forced him to begin negotiations to sell the club, and the transfer was competed after the close of the 1949 season. The new ownership group, headed by insurance executive Ellis Ryan, was more "hands-off" in its approach. Former slugger Hank Greenberg, who Veeck had hired the previous year, was elevated to general manager at Veeck's recommendation, and Boudreau remained in the manager's job. Both were considered to be supporters of black players and were expected to continue Veeck's recruitment policy.

As the game's first Jewish superstar, Greenberg had personally felt the arrows of prejudice and undoubtedly sympathized with black trailblazers. While still a player with the Pittsburgh Pirates during Jackie Robinson's first year in the majors, Greenberg had been one of the first white players on an opposing club to offer encouragement to the Dodger rookie.[27]

Boudreau is one of the unsung heroes of baseball's integration movement. He was never a Veeck favorite. In fact, before the 1948 campaign when Boudreau indicated that he wasn't interested in remaining with the Indians as a player if stripped of his management duties. Veeck asked for his resignation as manager and sought to trade him to the St. Louis Browns. Veeck's trade negotiations were thwarted by the virulent objections of the Cleveland fans, and he was forced to offer his manager-shortstop a contract extension.[28] Therefore, Boudreau had no incentive to go along with the integration program just to make Veeck look good. Although he may not have believed the acquisition of Doby to be the best personnel move for the team, he didn't fight it. In fact, he seemed to do everything he could to make the youngster feel welcome, individually introducing him to the other players and warming up with him before the game. Shortly after Doby's debut, Boudreau grumbled, "They've got to get me a guy to go with him. I won't stand for a good ballplayer having to go through the kind of hell that kid will get all by himself. He's got to have a roommate. Veeck's got to get me another Negro player. I won't let that kid take it alone. That's the only squawk I have."[29] When initially approached about bringing in Satchel Paige, Boudreau hesitated due to the pitcher's age. According to legend, however, his mind was quickly changed after a few swings against the veteran in an informal workout.[30]

As a manager, Boudreau generally got along well with the black players under his command. He helped Doby develop into a star and showed patience when Easter got off to a slow start in the big leagues. In fact, he was said to have developed a reputation for favoring black players, which in the context of times probably meant that he treated them fairly.[31] Controversial black star Vic Power,

LOU BOUDREAU

Lou Boudreau, Cleveland player-manager from 1942 through 1950, was an unsung hero in baseball's integration movement (1961 Fleer card).

who Boudreau later managed in Kansas City, called him "a beautiful man."[32] Boudreau was even able to handle the unique and enigmatic Paige, who seemed to have an aversion to rules.

Under Greenberg and Boudreau, former Negro League stars and future major leaguers Sam Jones, Dave Pope, and Dave Hoskins were added to the Indians' impressive stable of black prospects in 1950 as the Indians finished their first post–Veeck season in fourth place despite winning 92 games. Paige wasn't retained by the new ownership and Minoso spent the entire season in San Diego, so Doby and Easter were the only two black players to perform in a Cleveland uniform during the 1950 season. In fact, they were the only black players in the entire American League as the Indians reigned as the sole integrated team in the league for the third straight year. Boudreau, finishing out his three-year contract, was clearly a lame duck manager. In November, former catcher Al Lopez was tapped to replace him as the manager, and a few days later Boudreau's player contract was transferred to the Boston Red Sox.

The Lopez Era

Al Lopez managed the Indians from 1951 through 1956 before moving to the Chicago White Sox, where he managed another nine years. In Cleveland, he finished in second place behind the New York Yankees each year except 1954, when he led the Indians to 111 victories

The Indians' track record in the promotion and retention of black players took a downward turn under the management of highly respected Al Lopez from 1951 through 1956 (1965 Topps card).

and the pennant. With the White Sox, he continued in the runner-up role for two more years before leading them to the 1959 flag. In fact, Lopez managed the only two teams to break the Yankee reign over the American League from 1949 to 1964. He was widely considered a genius in handling a pitching staff and earned a place in the Baseball Hall of Fame for his managing.

Lopez, however, did not earn a reputation as a friend of black players. Doby claimed that his performance was affected by Lopez's "racism."[33] After Doby was sent packing a second time by Lopez late in his career, he said, "I can't have any respect for a man who lacks regard for a man because he's in a minority [group].... I just don't care to play for him."[34] Unfortunately for Doby, Lopez would get yet another crack at him before the outfielder's career was over. Minoso was traded or released four different times by Lopez-managed teams and claimed, "[Paul] Richards was a 100% better manager than Al Lopez."[35] Even Al Smith, who was sometimes referred to by teammates as "Little Bobo" because he was perceived as a Lopez favorite, said Lopez was a difficult person to get along with.[36] "I was hopeful about making the Indians [in the spring of 1952], but Al Lopez wouldn't play me. I assume he knew who I was, but we didn't talk," Smith recalled.

"He didn't give any encouragement to young players or talk about the Indians' tradition or way of doing things. He was a quiet guy whose attitude was that you had to show him what you could do. But he didn't give me a fair shot to show him anything."[37] Despite a fine 1952 campaign at Indianapolis, Smith didn't get a chance with the Indians until midway through the 1953 season. Vic Power never played for Lopez but had problems with him nevertheless. Power said that Lopez instructed his pitchers to throw at black hitters' legs because their quick reflexes allowed them to avoid beanballs. He also claimed that Lopez didn't like Latin players and had nixed an attempt by Veeck to acquire him for the White Sox.[38]

The reputation Lopez developed in regard to his relationship with black players is so suspect that Wes Singletary devoted an entire chapter to the subject in his Lopez biography. Singletary notes that most of the criticism against Lopez emanates from interviews with Larry Doby. He also points to many comments to the contrary by other players — black and white — before concluding that questions about Lopez's treatment of black players result more from the distant relationship he maintained with all his players rather than racism or prejudice. Singletary acknowledges, however, that "Lopez is less than tactful when expressing his perception of the treatment afforded those first black players in Organized Baseball. He [Lopez] insists that the news media made more out of it than there actually was and that all players suffered verbal abuse in some form or another, not simply blacks or minorities," a sentiment the biographer concedes to be "patently untrue."[39]

But Lopez's poor track record with black players under his command speaks for itself. When he assumed the managerial reins in 1951, the Indians seemed on the threshold of a magnificent dynasty fueled by the infusion of top-notch young black talent that Veeck and Greenberg had amassed. Doby and Easter were among the brightest stars in the American League, and the farm system was loaded with black prospects. Harry Simpson and Minnie Minoso had enjoyed sensational seasons with San Diego in 1950 and were considered top prospects, as were teammate Al Smith and Portland star Luis Marquez. Further down in the system, Sam Jones, Dave Pope, Dave Hoskins, Jose Santiago, and Brooks Lawrence were also showing great promise. Unfortunately, Smith would be the only member of the group who would achieve significant success with the Indians under Lopez, although Minoso, Jones, Lawrence, and Simpson would eventually develop into stars for other organizations.

Abbreviated Careers of Black Indians

One of the first moves the Indians made after Lopez took over would end up being the most damaging. With Minoso and Simpson exhibiting too much talent to be farmed out again, the Indians began the 1951 season with the only four black players in the American League on their roster. Everybody knew this was too many. Since Doby and Easter were entrenched stars, either Simpson or Minoso had to go. Lopez wanted lefty hurler Lou Brissie of the Philadelphia Athletics for his bullpen, so the Indians acquired him in a complicated three-way deal that sent Minoso to the Chicago White Sox while southpaw reliever Sam Zoldak and reserve catcher Ray Murray went to the Athletics.

Minoso, of course, became a major star with the White Sox, immediately vaulting them from the second division into contention for the American League pennant. Brissie pitched fairly well for the Indians, ranking third in the league in saves, but Zoldak posted a better earned run average while pitching more innings for the Athletics. Three years later, Minoso's star was shining brighter than ever in Chicago while Brissie was heading up the American Legion youth baseball program, a chronic condition caused by a war injury having prematurely ended his pitching career.

In 1952, Lopez and the Indians made their first attempt to get rid of Easter, who had grown immensely popular in Cleveland. Like Satchel Paige, Easter's age was always a source of debate. He was at least 34 years old when he came up in late 1949, although he'd claimed to be 27 when he signed with the Indians. Although Big Luke was one of the premier power hitters in the game, he was never really Lopez's type of player. Lopez liked fast, good defensive players backing up his prized pitchers, something that the gimpy-kneed Easter was not by that point in his career. The previous year, Easter had placed fourth in the league and led the Indians in both homers and runs batted in, despite missing about 30 games with injuries. When he got off to a slow start in 1952, he found himself back in the minor leagues in midseason, an indignity that a white player of his accomplishments would never have had to endure. Easter's hot bat, however, forced his recall a couple of weeks later and he rallied from his horrible first half to finish the season with 31 homers, the second highest total in the league behind Doby. His performance won him *The Sporting News* nomination as the Outstanding Player in the American League for 1952.

The 1953 Indians roster included five black players after Al Smith came up in July to join Doby, Easter, Simpson, and pitcher Dave Hoskins. That year, the only black American Leaguers outside of Cleveland to spend the full season in the majors were former Indians Minnie Minoso with Chicago and Satchel Paige with the St. Louis Browns. Some critics attributed the Indians' failure to capture the pennant that year (they finished eight and one-half games behind the Yankees) to their relative abundance of black players.[40] Manager Lopez may have been listening.

Early the next season, a little more than a year after Easter had been named the Outstanding Player in the American League, the Indians jettisoned him to the minors. Plagued by injuries, Easter had been able to play only 56 games in the field in 1953, although he hit a career high .303. After six 1954 pinch-hitting appearances, he was optioned back to the minor leagues again. Easter reluctantly reported to Ottawa of the International League, intent on slugging his way back to the big leagues as he had two years earlier. He did belt the ball at a .348 clip while slamming 15 homers in less than half a season, but the Indians acquired outfielder Vic Wertz from the lowly St. Louis Browns to play first base after Easter's initial replacements failed. Splitting the season between Ottawa and San Diego, Easter batted .315 and hit 28 homers in the minors while Wertz finished the year with a mediocre .257 batting average and 15 homers in the big leagues. Yet after the season, the Indians cut ties with Easter, who went on to play Triple A ball for another ten years and become a minor league legend.

Harry Simpson was demoted to the minors along with Easter early in the 1954 season, leaving the pennant-bound squad with four black players. Doby finished second to the Yankees' Yogi Berra in Most Valuable Player balloting, and Al Smith, in his first year as a regular, was the left fielder and leadoff man. In addition, Dave Pope served as a valuable outfield reserve, and Dave Hoskins spent most of the season buried in the bullpen. The Tribe's success that year was largely due to tremendous performances from no less than eight top-notch hurlers. In addition to the big three of 23-game-winners Bob Lemon and Early Wynn and 19-game-winner Mike Garcia, 35-year-old Bob Feller posted a 13–3 won-lost record, and Tiger retread Art Houtteman won 15 games. The bullpen featured former Most Valuable Player Hal Newhouser and rookie standouts Don Mossi and Ray Narleski, all of whom posted below-3.00 earned run averages.

With young phenom Herb Score ready to join their already well-stocked pitching staff, the Indians, who had already allowed Brooks Lawrence to drift out of their farm system, obligingly traded Sam Jones to the Chicago Cubs. Then the club sold disappointing Harry Simpson to the Kansas City Athletics early in the 1955 season. That year, the Indians fell back to their familiar second-place position behind the Yankees. After the campaign, Doby, the 1954 American League home run champ and runs batted in leader, was shipped to the Chicago White Sox in exchange for shortstop Chico Carrasquel and outfielder Jim Busby.

When Lopez left the Indians after the 1956 season, they were down to a single black player of note. In fact, Al Smith was the only black player on the Indians roster for most of Lopez's last season at the Cleveland helm. That year, Doby starred alongside Minnie Minoso in the White Sox outfield, Cleveland rejects Harry Simpson, Sam Jones, and Brooks Lawrence also starred in Kansas City, Chicago and Cincinnati respectively, and ageless Luke Easter rejuvenated the Buffalo International League franchise by blasting 35 homers for the Bisons.

It can be argued in Lopez's defense that managers don't make trades, which are the province of the general manager. But managers with the presence of Al Lopez can certainly influence deals. Lopez can be given a bye on the Minoso trade, since the Indians were loaded with outfielders at the time. But Lopez clearly engineered the disposal of Easter by refusing to play him. Then Sam Jones, who had wasted two seasons at Indianapolis, was included in a deal with the Cubs that brought in Ralph Kiner to bolster the Cleveland offense. Ironically, Kiner was the same type of player as the freshly discarded Easter — a defensively challenged veteran slugger with health issues. Lopez could only find 26 innings of mound work for Dave Hoskins in 1954 after he posted a 9–3 won-lost record as a rookie the previous year, and he was soon returned to the minors. Lopez couldn't get promising Harry Simpson to produce in Cleveland, although he blossomed after being shipped to Kansas City where he performed for Lou Boudreau.

But the worst example of Lopez's failure to fully utilize black players is the case of outfielder Dave Pope. During the club's pennant-winning 1954 campaign, the speedy Pope hit a solid .294 while backing up Dave Philley, who compiled a meager .226 batting mark. The next year, Pope, who was good enough defensively to handle center field, batted .298 and slugged the ball at a .519 clip through mid–June. But Lopez continued to stick with Philley in right field. Consequently, Pope was sent to the Baltimore Orioles at the June 15 trading deadline in a deal that brought veteran outfielder Gene Woodling to Cleveland. For the season, Woodling hit 20 points lower and smacked fewer homers for the Indians than Pope did in less than half as many at-bats.

Lopez had moved on to the Chicago White Sox when the Indians really began to pay the price for squandering their wealth of black talent. Under Kirby Farrell, they tumbled to sixth place in 1957 with Al Smith and rookie infielder Larry Raines the only black players in significant roles.

The Arrival of "Frantic Frank" Lane

Greenberg was fired before the 1958 season, and he joined Lopez in Chicago, while former White Sox and Cardinal general manager Frank Lane took over in Cleveland. Lane, who was a confirmed trade-aholic, promptly acquired Minoso from Lopez's White Sox in exchange for pitcher Early Wynn and Al Smith. Larry Doby also ended up back with the Indians after taking a more circuitous route through Baltimore. Raines was returned to the minors, but righthander Jim "Mudcat" Grant, who would later win 20 games for the Minnesota Twins, and longtime farmhand Billy Harrell were brought up from the minor leagues. In June, Lane engineered a trade with Kansas City for Vic Power, and the contingent of black players on the Indians roster was back up to five, the most in the American League.

With old favorite Joe Gordon at the helm in 1959, the Indians battled the White Sox down to the wire for the American League pennant before ending up in second place. Minoso, Power, and Grant starred, and Doby paid a final dividend when Lane swapped him to the Tigers in a lopsided exchange for young Tito Francona. Francona would register a .363 batting mark in 1959 and continue to be a solid contributor for another five seasons with the Indians.

But the irrepressible Lane's days were numbered in Cleveland when he first traded Minoso back to Chicago for a bevy of prospects and then sent popular home-run king Rocky Colavito to Detroit for boring singles-hitting batting champ Harvey Kuenn just before the start of the 1960 campaign. Halfway through the season, Lane outdid himself by trading managers, sending popular Joe Gordon to Detroit for aging Jimmy Dykes. Amid the controversy and confusion, the Tribe slipped to fourth place.

After finishing second or better seven times in the 1950s, the Indians would never be serious contenders throughout the 1960s. Their highest finish of the decade would be a distant third place in 1968, 17 games off the pace.

Lane is generally assigned the brunt of the blame for the Indians' collapse. When the club finished fifth in 1961, Roger Maris, Rocky Colavito, and Norm Cash, three players who had been traded away during Lane's brief tenure, slammed 147 homers among them — three less than the entire Cleveland squad.

But the loss of racially enlightened Joe Gordon as manager may have weighed just as heavily as the loss of the sluggers. As a player, Gordon had been supportive of black teammates, especially young Larry Doby.[41] An unconfirmed story that Gordon followed an early Doby strikeout by intentionally fanning himself to make the rookie feel better has become part of integration lore.[42] Ironically, in Gordon's last game managing the Indians he started veteran Don Newcombe, who had recently been picked up on waivers. Under Gordon's successor Jimmy Dykes, Newcombe would have to wait more than three weeks for another starting opportunity — his last in the major leagues.

The 1960s and Beyond

During the 1960s, the Indians seemed to have a singular lack of success with black players. The only black players to spend the entire 1960 campaign on the Cleveland roster were Power and Grant. Young Walt Bond, one of the last Kansas City Monarchs, was initially designated to fill Colavito's right field spot as well as the power void Rocky left behind. But Bond failed in his first attempt and would never make it in Cleveland, although he would eventually enjoy some big league success with the Houston Colt 45s. Tommie Agee would flunk three trials with the Indians from 1962 through 1964 before capturing 1966 Rookie of the Year honors following a trade to the Chicago White Sox.

Power was swapped to Minnesota after a sub-par 1961 campaign and regained his .290 batting form with the Twins. Grant was also a relative disappointment in Cleveland, though the 67 American League victories he recorded prior to being traded by the Indians were the most by a black hurler in league history at the time. Grant caught his stride in Minnesota, and his 21 victories in 1965 led the Twins to the pennant. Willie Kirkland arrived from San

Francisco in 1961 with huge power-hitting expectations, but he departed three years later without fulfilling them. Leon Wagner, acquired from the Los Angeles Angels in 1964, had some good years with the Indians but left bickering with Cleveland management. Tommy Harper and Chuck Hinton are other black stars who failed to live up to advance billings in an Indian uniform.

Popular and respected Gabe Paul, who had overseen the surprisingly successful integration of the Cincinnati Reds in the mid–1950s, replaced Lane as Cleveland general manager before the 1961 season. But a downward spiral caused by the faltering attendance that accompanied the club's poor performance was in effect. Paul even brought in former Cincinnati manager Birdie Tebbetts in 1963, but it didn't help. In 1968, the club hired Alvin Dark to fill the managerial seat. Dark was considered a genius when he led the San Francisco Giants to the 1962 National League pennant, but less than two years later remarks disparaging black and Hispanic players cost him his job. In Dark's first year at the helm, the Indians won 86 games and rose to third place. Cuban hurler Luis Tiant led the way, winning 21 games and leading the league with a sensational 1.60 earned run average, but in the off-season Dark forbade his ace to pitch winter league ball. The action severely strained their relationship, and Tiant wound up losing 20 games in 1969 as the Indians fell to sixth place in the new six-team Eastern Division alignment.

Major League Baseball's First Black Manager

The 1970s would be no better. In fact, the Indians would only finish above .500 four times from 1970 through 1993. But less than three years after the death of Jackie Robinson in October 1972, another black man named Robinson would make baseball integration history, this time in the uniform of the Cleveland Indians. The 1975 season marked the first time a black man would be the manager of a major league baseball team, as future Hall of Fame slugger Frank Robinson became player-manager of the Indians. Ironically, one of Robinson's first moves was to get rid of Larry Doby, then an Indians coach who had been considered a leading candidate for the managerial slot. Doby left amidst accusations that he was a racially divisive influence in the Cleveland clubhouse.[43]

In Robinson's first season at the helm, the Indians won more games than they had the previous campaign, and the next year they finished with their first winning record in eight years. Robinson wouldn't make it through a third campaign in Cleveland, but he would receive additional opportunities and would go on to manage 14 full seasons and portions of two others for four major league organizations.

With the exception of the New York Yankees, Cleveland had been the most successful franchise in the American League from 1947 through 1959, claiming two pennants and finishing second six times. Under Veeck's leadership, the franchise got a tremendous jump in signing the best black players available. It's too bad for Cleveland fans that circumstances forced Veeck to sell the club. Under less enlightened leadership, the team squandered much of its huge advantage. If the Indians had been able to blend more of their outstanding black talent into their lineup and continue their recruitment of top black players, at least a few of those second-place squads of the 1950s might have been winners. And the misfortunes of future decades may have been averted.

Chapter 4

THE ST. LOUIS BROWNS

In the early years of Organized Baseball's integration process, the St. Louis Browns were the Jekyll and Hyde of the major leagues. Actually, this was an improvement, since the Browns more closely resembled the monstrous Mr. Hyde in terms of performance on the diamond. Unfortunately, this condition would continue even after the franchise's reincarnation as the Baltimore Orioles in 1954.

Technically, the Browns were the third team in Major League Baseball to integrate, trailing the Cleveland Indians by about two weeks. But the door only stayed open for about a month, as they quickly became the only major league team to fail dismally in their initial attempt to integrate and the first team to re-segregate. It would be almost four years before they extended another opportunity to a black player.

Franchise History

The original St. Louis Browns enjoyed a proud history in the old American Association back in the 1880s. But the second edition of the Browns had little to boast about. After joining the newly formed American League as the Milwaukee Brewers in 1901, the franchise moved to St. Louis. From 1902 until they fled St. Louis after the 1953 campaign, they won a lone, tainted pennant in 1944 when the best players in the country were off doing their patriotic duty. Prior to World War II, they hadn't had a winning season since 1930, averaging more than 93 losses a year during that span. The St. Louis retort to Washington's famous chant "First in War, First in Peace, and Last in the American League" was "First in Shoes, First in Booze, and Last in the American League."

Wartime baseball offered the Browns a welcome break from their losing ways. The club's brief revival stemmed from the fact that many of their best players were found unfit for military service. But after the boys in uniform came home the Browns quickly returned to familiar territory near the bottom of the American League standings. By July 1947, they were firmly entrenched in the cellar, and the turnstiles were clicking at a pace that would only fill a little more than 320,000 seats for the season. That total was by far the worst among the 16 major league teams and less than 40 percent of the 15th-ranked Washington Senators' gate count.

The Browns Attempt Integration

On July 16, 1947, 11 days after Doby broke the color line in the American League, Dan Daniel wrote, "In St. Louis they say the fans would never stand for Negroes on the Cardinals or the Browns. St. Louis, they insist, 'is too much of a Southern city.'"[1]

The next day, Hank Thompson, recently of the Negro League's Kansas City Monarchs, started at second base for the Browns and went hitless in a 16–2 drubbing by the Philadelphia Athletics. Two days later, Willard Brown, who came from Kansas City along with Thompson, banged into a couple of rally-ending double plays in his big league debut to cement a 1–0 loss to the Boston Red Sox.

Daniel's words proved to be somewhat prophetic, however. Contrary to expectations, there were no incidents of violence, but St. Louis baseball fans never warmed up to the two black players.

Ironically, the Browns may have had a black player in uniform more than 30 years earlier. In 1916, Cuban-born Armando Marsans, whose debut with Cincinnati five years earlier had alarmed segregationists, was acquired from the Federal League St. Louis Blues by none other than Branch Rickey, then general manager of the Browns. Marsans, the Browns' regular center fielder that year, was the club's first Latino player. A quarter of a century later, the Browns would employ another dark-skinned Cuban, Bobby Estalella.

The Browns acquired the services of Brown and Thompson in 1947 under an option whereby the Monarchs were paid $5,000 down with an additional payment of $5,000 apiece due if the club elected to keep them. When the option period was due to expire, Brown had done little to distinguish himself, but Thompson had overcome a bad start to settle in at second base and hit for an average considerably higher than the overall team mark. Unfortunately, the financially-strapped Browns were still losing big and drawing little, so they opted to let the pair return to Kansas City rather than ante up the precious additional funds required to keep them.[2]

The entire Thompson/Brown affair was handled in a typically (for the Browns) ineffectual manner that inevitably doomed it to failure. The front office hadn't even bothered to consult with manager Muddy Ruel, who was strongly opposed to their acquisition.[3] Management only half-heartedly attempted to deny that economics rather than pure old fashioned baseball sense was the determining factor in their decision, while simultaneously conceding that the large crowds drawn by Jackie Robinson wherever the Dodgers played may have influenced the decision to acquire Thompson and Brown in the first place.[4] No one was confused. Columnist J. Roy Stockton of the St. Louis *Post-Dispatch* set the tone when he wrote, "Players should be brought up to the majors because they can help the club on the field, not as a shot in the arm for the box office."[5]

The Browns also failed to appreciate the attitude of the local African American population toward the franchise. Sportsman's Park, which the Browns owned and rented to the National League St. Louis Cardinals, had been the last big league stadium to maintain officially segregated seating. They finally capitulated during the war, but "unofficial" discriminatory seating practices still existed in 1947.[6] Therefore, black fans felt no particular loyalty to the Browns and weren't inclined to support them in what they suspected was little more than a token commitment to integration. Furthermore, black baseball fans in St. Louis had the option of waiting until the Dodgers came to town and watching Jackie Robinson play against the Cardinals, without having to stomach the wretched Browns.

Though the general population of St. Louis didn't seem to care who played for the Browns, the Brownie players certainly did. At least one threatened to quit rather than play with the two black men, and others doubtlessly would have if there had been any chance that another team would be interested in their services. Outfielder Paul Lehner reportedly "popped off" in the clubhouse when he heard about it. Two days later, when he failed to show until five minutes before game time, it was rumored that he had walked out.[7] It was later revealed that his tardiness was because he had gone to management to demand either his immediate release or a big raise to make the situation more palatable.[8] With a few exceptions, notably star short-stop Vern Stephens, Brown and Thompson were treated as outcasts — ignored by their team-mates, save for an occasional disparaging remark. Before games the two black players always had to warm up with each other because no one else would play catch with them, and dur-ing the games they were subjected to the brush-back pitches and racist taunts from the oppo-sition without support from their teammates. Brown reportedly used a teammate's bat to slam his lone homer, the first by a black player in American League history. The owner is said to have intentionally cracked it on the dugout steps rather than have Brown use it again.[9]

In addition, the failure of the Browns' management to do their homework hurt both the team and the two players. The Brooklyn Dodgers had carefully scouted and recruited Jackie Robinson in the winter of 1945, and he spent his first year with their top farm club in Mon-treal before his major league debut. In contrast, the Browns had not scouted the Negro Leagues. It appeared that they'd just rang up the nearby Kansas City Monarch franchise, ordered "a couple of colored players to go," and slapped them in the lineup.

Had they bothered to investigate, the Browns would have discovered that neither Brown nor Thompson possessed the personal attributes or background that would have made them good candidates for such a pressure-filled assignment. The club thought Brown was only 26 years old, but he was really in his mid–30s and had been playing professionally for at least 14 years. He was one of the top performers in the Negro Leagues, but was considered lazy and stubborn. He had a reputation for being a guy who would rise to the occasion in front of big crowds — which he wouldn't find in St. Louis — but otherwise saved his energy by playing hard only when necessary.[10] Brown would never get another big league chance after the Browns let him go, although he later returned to Organized Baseball and starred in the Texas League until he was well past 40 years old.

The talented and versatile Hank Thompson claimed to be only 21 years old when he debuted with the Browns, but he was already a veteran of the U.S. Army and reform school, in addition to four seasons in the Negro American League. He was considered something of a "hoodlum" and reportedly carried a gun.[11] Thompson would later get another chance with the New York Giants and enjoy eight productive years in the National League. After leaving the game, however, he would experience trouble with the law and spend significant time in jail.[12]

The Thompson/Brown experiment was an act of sheer desperation on the part of the Browns. Richard Muckerman had first bought into the Browns in 1943 and purchased decrepit Sportsman's Park from former owner Phil Ball's estate in 1947. He sank most of his assets into refurbishing the old stadium and soon found himself in dire financial straits when attendance at Browns' games continued to decline. The situation reached its nadir on July 14, two days before the rights to Brown and Thompson were purchased from the Monarchs, when only 478 fans paid their way into Sportsman's Park to see the hapless Browns do battle with the slightly less inept Washington Senators.

The DeWitt brothers, Bill and Charlie, who ran the front office, also held stock in the club, and they were also suffering. Bill DeWitt was a Branch Rickey protégé, and Charlie had also worked for Rickey. In fact, Bill DeWitt got his start in baseball as a 17-year-old office boy in the Browns' front office under Rickey. When Rickey moved to the Cardinals, young Bill went with him. Later, Bill moved back to the Browns with Rickey's encouragement, and in 1936 he helped put together an ownership group led by Donald Barnes to purchase the club from the estate of Phil Ball. Bill was vice president of the club under Barnes, and Charlie, who had made a small fortune in the insurance business, joined him in the Browns front office.

"Apart from other considerations, it seems in order that this large Negro population should have some representation on their city's ball team," Charlie DeWitt said in announcing the acquisition of Brown and Thompson.[13] St. Louis did in fact have one of the highest non-white populations among major league cities.[14]

For more than strictly financial reasons, the DeWitts were undoubtedly sincere in their desire to see a black player succeed in St. Louis. They just didn't have the wherewithal to accomplish it. The Browns have been maligned for their initial misguided stab at integration, but they did make an honest attempt to recruit black players, and they made inroads in the area before most of their contemporaries.

The Browns also negotiated an option on Negro League star Piper Davis of the Birmingham Black Barons at the same time they acquired the rights to Brown and Thompson. Although he was 30 years old at the time, Davis was probably a better candidate to succeed under the difficult circumstances than either Brown or Thompson. He was a talented and versatile performer, a speedy line-drive hitter who could play either the infield or outfield. He was also a leader and, unlike Brown and Thompson, there were no questions about his character. In 1948, he would take over as player-manager of the Barons and lead them to the Negro American League pennant. But the Browns wanted Davis to prove himself in the minors. With his Barons still fighting for the pennant, he declined the minor league opportunity, and the Browns let his option lapse.

Around the same time they purchased the rights to Thompson and Brown, the Browns also signed Chuck Harmon, a collegiate basketball star for the University of Toledo.[15] Harmon was assigned to the Browns' Gloversville-Johnstown affiliate in the Canadian-American League, where Dodger farmhands Roy Partlow and Johnny Wright had broken the color barrier the previous year. They would be the only big league franchise besides the Dodgers to have a black player in their farm system in 1947.

The DeWitt brothers purchased controlling interest of the franchise from Muckerman in 1949, but little changed for the grievously under-funded operation. They had to sell off their few quality players just to stay in business. In 1948, they had moved up to sixth place with the same record as the previous year and then ended up seventh in both 1949 and 1950.

Veeck and Paige Re-Integrate the Browns

Midway through the 1949 campaign, nearly two years after inaugurating the Browns' ill-fated integration experiment, Hank Thompson became the first black player to take the field for the New York Giants. The next spring, the Boston Braves joined the ranks of teams who'd abandoned their color barrier. But despite the success of black players on all four of these teams, no other franchises seemed ready to join their ranks. The outlook seemed to brighten considerably when Branch Rickey took over the operation of the Pittsburgh Pirates after the 1950 season, although it would be several years before his efforts to integrate bore fruit. Then the

Chicago White Sox pulled off a stunning trade to acquire Minnie Minoso from the Cleveland Indians, bringing membership in the exclusive club to five. In the middle of the 1951 season, Bill Veeck assumed ownership of the Browns and immediately sent for the venerable Satchel Paige.

With the taste of humble pie still lingering on their palates from their first bashing of Paige three years earlier, critics were relatively silent about bringing the ancient hurler back to the majors. But few really expected him to have much of an impact. Old Satch was thought to be a least 43 years old (actually he was 45) and had made his living barnstorming since the Indians let him go after the 1949 season. Veeck had reportedly advised Satch against signing with another club after his release by Cleveland, saying he would be getting another club and wanted the veteran to pitch for him.[16] True to his word, Veeck inked Paige to a St. Louis contract, and on July 18, almost four years to the day after Brown and Thompson debuted with the Browns, the veteran took the mound in a 7–1 loss to the Washington Senators.

Although Paige attracted much needed publicity for the Browns and surprised everyone by proving to be one of the American League's top relief pitchers, Veeck failed to add another black player to the Browns' roster during his brief ownership. Contrary to popular perception, the Browns already had a few black players in their organization when Veeck took over the club. Though they had backed away from the forefront of the integration battle after the ill-fated Thompson/Brown episode, their interest in black players had remained. Harmon drifted out of the system after the 1949 season when the Browns were forced to cut back their minor league operations, but they had signed a few young black prospects, including pitcher Harry Wilson and outfielder Willie Tasby.[17] Wilson would never get a shot at the majors despite winning 59 games in four years in the Browns farm system, and Tasby would spend nine years in the minors before graduating to the big leagues.

Negro League legend Satchel Paige was the only black St. Louis Brown from 1951 until the franchise moved to Baltimore after the 1953 season (1949 Bowman card).

Efforts to Recruit Other Black Players

Veeck reportedly tried to persuade Negro League icons Buck Leonard and "Cool Papa" Bell, who were both in their mid-to-late 40s, to join Paige on the Browns, but the two proud veterans refused to buy into the gimmick.[18] The Browns did, however, manage to attract another Negro League legend. Shortly after the Browns inked Paige, their Toronto farm club acquired pitcher Leon Day from the Winnepeg Buffaloes of the independent Mandak (Manitoba/Dakota) League. Revealing an embarrassing lack of knowledge of the Negro Leagues, *The Sporting News* described Day as a 27-year-old prospect — which would have made him about 11 years old when he was starring for the Brooklyn Eagles in the Negro National League back in 1935.[19] Though Day recorded an excellent 1.58 earned run average in 14 International League games in 1951 and followed with a fine 13–9 won-lost record for the Browns' Scranton squad in the Eastern League in 1952, he was never summoned to join Paige on the Browns staff.

The St. Louis Browns are the only major league franchise able to list two Negro League Hall of Famers on their alumni roster. Paige, of course, was the first Negro Leaguer voted in when the Hall of Fame established criteria for considering Negro League stars in 1971, and Willard Brown joined him in 2006 via nomination of a special committee established to reevaluate Negro League stars. Leon Day, who was tapped for the Hall of Fame in 1995, would have made three if the Browns had only given him a chance to help out their dreadful pitching staff.

Veeck made other unsuccessful attempts to stock the Browns with former Negro League talent. Along with Day, he acquired former Negro League catcher/third baseman Charlie White, who later served as a backup catcher for the Milwaukee Braves. Late in the season, he purchased former Kansas City Monarch pitcher Frank Barnes, who would later get trials with the Cardinals, from the Yankees organization. He also signed outfielder Lomax "Butch" Davis and infielder John Irvin Kennedy, who finished the 1951 season with Albany in the Eastern League. In September, the Browns announced the signing of former Negro League veterans Jehosie Heard, Jesse Douglas, and Curley Williams along with youngster James Sheehan.[20]

Heard was one of the aces of the Birmingham Barons in the 1940s. He was 32 when he joined the Browns organization, although he claimed to be five years younger. In his first taste of Organized Baseball, he won 20 games for Victoria in the Western International League and earned a big league trial with 16 victories for Pacific Coast League Portland in 1953, but he wouldn't stick in the majors. Kennedy was cut loose by the Browns system before the 1952 season, but he later got a brief major league trial with the Philadelphia Phillies.[21] Douglas, whose Negro League career dated back to 1937, was more than 30 years old. He played for Western League Colorado Springs in the Chicago White Sox organization in 1951, but he never advanced beyond Class A. Young Sheehan would never make a mark in Organized Baseball.

Curley Williams and Lomax Davis seemed like legitimate big league prospects. Williams was a shortstop with some pop in his bat who enjoyed several fine seasons with Newark, Houston, and New Orleans in the Negro Leagues. He was 28 when he joined Douglas with Colorado Springs late in the 1951 campaign. Though he performed well, the Sox had no place for him in their system,

Leon Day, a future Negro League Hall of Fame hurler, toiled in the Browns' farm system without getting a big league opportunity (Larry Lester).

and he was released along with Douglas. In St. Louis, Marty Marion, who was making a come-back with the Browns after starring with the Cardinals for 10 years, blocked his path at short-stop, so Williams began the 1952 season with the Triple A Toledo Mud Hens. Davis, who first appeared in the Negro Leagues in 1946, hit .456 and .406 in the Mandak League before blasting the ball at a .350 clip for Eastern League in his first taste of white Organized Base-ball. He began the 1952 campaign back in the Eastern League with Leon Day at Scranton but swapped places with Williams in June.[22] The next spring, Williams went to training camp with the Browns but didn't get a chance to play and jumped to the Dominican League.[23] Davis also dropped out of Organized Baseball after his contract was sold to Edmonton of the Class A Western International League before the 1953 season.[24] His .319 average for Toledo the pre-vious season had been highest on the team.

The next spring, Joe Durham, a speedy young outfielder, was signed at a tryout camp in Thomasville, Georgia.[25] Durham made it to the majors with the franchise before military duty waylaid his promising career. But by then the Browns had become the Baltimore Ori-oles and Veeck was long gone from the scene.

It's something of a mystery that Veeck wasn't more successful introducing black players during his term as owner of the Browns. The team was terrible, losing an average of slightly more than 97 games a season, finishing in the cellar twice and grabbing seventh place once during the Veeck years. They could have used an injection of talent from any source, and Veeck had the connections and loyalty of the black baseball community. The old saying that it's hard to drain the swamp when you're busy fighting alligators is probably applicable.

Promotional genius that he was, Veeck met his match in St. Louis. Even the drawing power of Satchel Paige and fabulous stunts like sending midget Eddie Gaedel up to "pinch-walk" in an official major league contest couldn't offset the Browns' lack of talent. Also work-ing against Veeck was the fact that the Browns had to share St. Louis, one of the smallest major league cities, with the infinitely more popular and successful St. Louis Cardinals. Veeck, who was actually a pretty fair judge of baseball talent, simply couldn't afford to buy top-flight black players and didn't have time to wait for young prospects to mature. For instance, he reportedly had first crack at Ernie Banks of the Kansas City Monarchs. But knowing he couldn't afford the young shortstop, he directed him toward the Chicago Cubs.[26]

The Reign of Rogers Hornsby

Another problem was Veeck's ill-advised selection of Rogers Hornsby to take over as man-ager of the Browns in 1952. Hornsby, one of the greatest hitters in the history of the game, was a St. Louis institution who had played for and previously managed both the Browns and Cardinals. But his last major league managerial assignment had ended in 1937, though he had enjoyed some success in the minors since then. Veeck brought him back in hopes of attract-ing a few sentimental fans to the ballpark.

Hornsby, however, was not known for sensitivity or as a great admirer of black players. Satchel Paige, who supposedly fanned the old slugger five times in one game back in the day, reportedly called Veeck when he heard the news of Hornsby's appointment. "Mr. Veeck, I'm not sure I should sign to play for this man, because in his eyes I'm nothing more or less than a no-good nigger son of a bitch," complained Paige.[27] Veeck was able to placate the veteran hurler, but problems soon arose when Hornsby fined him for arriving late for an exhibition game because he couldn't get a cab to pick him up at his rooming house in the poor section of town.[28] Hornsby was well aware of his reputation and had even brought up the thorny subject of working with black players himself in his job interview with Veeck. "If they're good players, they'd be welcome to play for me," he vowed.[29]

Of course, other than Paige, the Browns had precious few good players of any description, but Hornsby evidently wouldn't have been able to see past skin color anyway. After watching Larry Doby play one time in 1947, Hornsby told H.G. Salinger of the *Detroit News*, "Bill Veeck did the Negro race no favor when he signed Larry Doby to a Cleveland contract. If Veeck wanted to demonstrate that the Negro has no place in major league baseball, he could have used no subtler means to establish the point. If he were white he wouldn't be considered good enough to play with a semi-pro club. He is fast on his feet but that lets him out. He hasn't any other quality that could possibly recommend him."[30]

It's probably no coincidence that the Seattle club Hornsby managed in 1951 was the only team in the Pacific Coast League without a black player that year, especially given that the Rainiers promptly integrated after he left.[31] Many years later, former Brownie shortstop Joe DeMaestri would recall, "He [Hornsby] was the worst man-

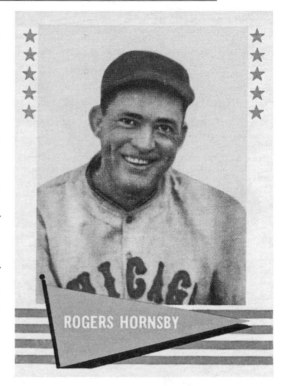

Former slugging star Rogers Hornsby slowed the progress of integration as manager of the St. Louis Browns and later the Cincinnati Reds (1961 Fleer card).

ager and worst person I ever played for. Everyone hated him." DeMaestri added, "the only time that I saw Satchel Paige upset was when Hornsby got after him in spring training in Burbank. Hornsby didn't like Satch, and I think it was simply because he was black."[32]

Hornsby's stint with Browns lasted only 51 games, but it came at a key time — the start of Veeck's first full year as owner of the club. The presence of the old "Rajah" undoubtedly discouraged many Negro League veterans who might have been considering joining Veeck's merry band. Upon his departure, Hornsby's former charges celebrated "Emancipation Day."[33]

Ironically Joe Gordon, whose major league playing career had ended the previous year, was rumored to be in line to manage the Browns when Veeck took over in 1951.[34] Apparently Gordon, who was managing Sacramento in the Pacific Coast League and leading the league in homers at the time, couldn't be had. With the Indians, Gordon had befriended Larry Doby when he joined the club, and he would subsequently enjoy some success as a big league manager who seemed to be able to get good production out of the black players under his command. If he had been available to help Veeck, the franchise's fortunes may have been significantly altered.

The Last Days of the St. Louis Browns

Veeck replaced Hornsby with former Cardinals star Marty Marion, who had retired as a player to manage the Cards in 1951. Dismissed after one season, he returned to the active ranks with the Browns and had been handling shortstop duties. The slight decline in the team's already poor performance under Marion's leadership was probably due more to his absence from the regular lineup to handle managerial chores than his managerial skills.

As the Browns continued to starve at the box office, Veeck sought permission to move the franchise to Baltimore for the 1953 campaign, but his colleagues rebuffed him in a transparent, but ultimately successful, attempt to force him out of the game. After an enforced stay in St. Louis for another financially ruinous last place season, Veeck sold out. The new ownership group quickly received the permission to move that the outsider Veeck had been denied.

Chapter 5

THE BALTIMORE ORIOLES

The shift of the St. Louis Browns franchise to Baltimore before the 1954 season was one of six made by the original sixteen major league teams between 1953 and 1961, after more than half of a decade of stability. In none of the other shifts, however, was the club's former identity so completely obliterated. When the St. Louis Browns became the Baltimore Orioles, they changed cities, team names, owners, general managers, managers, coaches, mascots, and logos. They also almost completely revamped their roster.

Predictably among the missing when the team assembled in Baltimore for the beginning of the new season was old St. Louis favorite Marty Marion. Another Brownie who didn't get a bus ticket to Baltimore was Satchel Paige. As had happened in Cleveland four years earlier, Paige was summarily dismissed from Organized Baseball on the heels of Veeck's departure, despite having been the Browns representative on the 1953 American League All-Star Team. The new regime had to know they were giving up a great drawing card as well as a capable pitcher, but Paige had proved tough for his St. Louis field bosses to handle, and once again Veeck had exacerbated the situation by letting the old-timer get away with it.[1]

The New Regime in Baltimore

The franchise might have moved a little further north, but it was still located south of the Mason-Dixon line. The Baltimore Orioles were an International League club affiliated with the Cleveland Indians when Jackie Robinson signed with Montreal in 1946, and the city welcomed him with the worst abuse he faced that season.[2] After one game, a hostile crowd reportedly kept him trapped in the clubhouse until after midnight.[3] After the 1948 campaign, Bill Veeck, then in charge of the Cleveland Indians, terminated the club's working agreement with the Orioles in favor of San Diego, where black prospects could be more comfortably introduced. The Orioles affiliated with the Browns for the next two years before entering into an agreement with the Philadelphia Phillies, where they wouldn't have to worry about black players.

In 1954, Baltimore civic leaders and the new franchise owners, led by attorney Charles Miles, were anxious to show that they wouldn't be a hindrance to the continued integration of the game. But they immediately got off on the wrong foot by cutting Paige loose. A replacement had to be found, but the system was virtually barren of good ballplayers, especially black ones. Charles Harmon and Charlie White had moved to other organizations, for which they would perform in the big leagues during the 1954 season, and youngsters like Joe Durham and Willie Tasby weren't ready. Therefore the onus fell on the slight shoulders of 34-year-old rookie lefthander Jehosie Heard, the first black Baltimore Oriole. But Heard would make only two brief appearances for the Orioles before being dispatched to the minors amid rumors of drinking and domestic problems.[4] For most of the new team's first season in Baltimore, the roster remained all white until young outfielder Joe Durham was called up for a September trial.

The new ownership group had brought in former Philadelphia Athletics manager Jimmy Dykes to replace Marty Marion as field manager. Bill DeWitt's career continued on an unusual downward path. The former club owner had stayed on as the Browns' president through Veeck's reign and was originally appointed acting general manager by the new regime. Soon he was forced out of that spot when another Athletics refugee, Art Ehlers, arrived in Baltimore. DeWitt finally ended up in New York as assistant to Yankee general manager George Weiss. It's certainly hard to imagine any current baseball moguls taking a job as assistant general manager after selling their franchise.

The first edition of the new Baltimore Orioles posted the exact same record as the last edition of the old Browns, 54

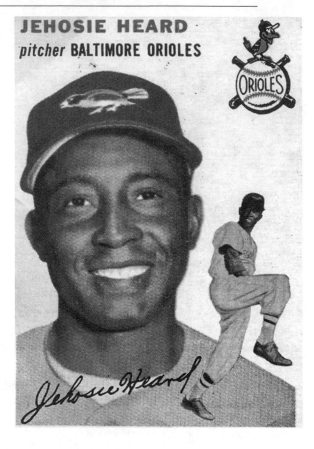

Pitcher Jehosie Heard, whose major league career lasted less than four innings, was the first black player to perform for the Baltimore Orioles (1954 Topps card).

wins against 100 losses, but attendance topped one million, and the franchise showed a profit for the first time in years. Ownership employed their newfound wealth judiciously to beef up the farm system and lure Paul Richards away from the Chicago White Sox to assume the dual role of general manager and field manager.

The Paul Richards Era

Richards had been considered a miracle worker as manager of the Sox and given much of the credit for the club's rapid ascension from doormat to contender. He'd been at the helm when Minnie Minoso debuted as the first black player to play for the Sox and was greatly admired by the star outfielder.

As general manager of the Orioles, he quickly completed the house cleaning begun by his immediate predecessors. The Orioles began the 1955 campaign with only four players who had accompanied the team from St. Louis on the roster: Vern Stephens, Les Moss, Bobby Young, and Duane Pillette. They also began their second season with no black players on their roster. In a blinding swirl of deals, Richards soon rid the Orioles of all Brownie holdovers, but the transactions netted only one black player — outfielder Dave Pope who was acquired from Cleveland. Pope, a productive fourth outfielder on the Indians' 1954 pennant-winning squad, had power and good speed. The former Homestead Gray was thought to be 29 at the time of the trade, but it is now known that he lost track of four years when he entered Organized Baseball. He'd hit close to .300 and showed power with Cleveland during the 1954 campaign and the first third of the 1955 season, but given regular duty with the Orioles, he lost his batting prowess in Baltimore's spacious Memorial Stadium.[5]

By 1956, the wheels of change were fully engaged. Former Negro League star first baseman Bob Boyd was drafted from the Cardinal's system and joined Pope on the Orioles opening-day roster. Pope was swapped back to Cleveland in May, but a few days later the Orioles acquired pitcher Connie Johnson, another former Negro League star. Both Boyd (age 36) and Johnson (age 33) had begun their Organized Baseball careers in the White Sox system and played for Richards in Chicago, but they had been unable to establish themselves in the big leagues. Though both players had been found wanting in Chicago, they were more than good enough for Richards' Baltimore club. Both turned in solid performances, and the Orioles improved by 12 games and jumped to sixth place. When young right-hander Charlie Beamon came up for a September trial, it was first time in franchise history that they had three black players on the major league roster.

In 1957, the franchise finished with its first .500 mark since World War II and inched up another notch in the standings to fifth place with Johnson leading the pitching staff and Boyd pacing the hitters. During the season, the team employed a franchise-to-date high of five black players, but the younger guys from the farm system didn't contribute much. Joe Durham returned from two years of military duty to hit only .185 in 77 games. Beamon was also a disappointment, and Lenny Green, who would eventually develop into a solid big leaguer, only got a late-season look.

Before the 1958 season began, Larry Doby passed through the Orioles' hands without playing a game in a Baltimore uniform. Before the season, Durham was sent to Vancouver and subsequently lost to the Cardinals in the minor league draft. Charlie Beamon also found himself back in the minor leagues later that year, but he left a big impression by plunking six American League hitters to finish among the league's leading headhunters despite a mere 50 innings of work. Lenny Green stuck around for most of the campaign, but couldn't find regular work as aging veterans and utility types monopolized playing time in the Baltimore outfield. Bob Boyd hit over .300 again, but Connie Johnson's record slipped, although he maintained a decent earned run average. After a disappointing sixth-place finish, Paul Richards stepped down as general manager to concentrate on his field duties, and the Orioles tapped Lee MacPhail to fill the general manager's chair.

Lee MacPhail as General Manager

Lee MacPhail is the son of Larry MacPhail, the Yankee executive who fought to keep Jackie Robinson out of the major leagues. The younger MacPhail would go on to become one of the most powerful executives in Major League Baseball, serving a decade as American League president from 1974 through 1984. Before coming to Baltimore, he was the director of player personnel for the New York Yankees from 1948 through 1958, part of an administration that stoutly resisted putting a black player in Yankee pinstripes. In short, Lee MacPhail did not arrive in Baltimore with an impressive pedigree in the equal opportunity area.

Never exactly a leader in the integration department, the Orioles became the whitest team in baseball under MacPhail's direction. Early in the 1959 campaign, MacPhail swapped Lenny Green to Washington, where he would emerge as first-rate center fielder and leadoff man. Boyd was reduced to platoon duty, and Johnson found himself back in the minor leagues as the Orioles began turning their pitching chores over to a group of bright hurlers who came to be known as Paul Richards' "Kiddie Corps."

On the bright side, 26-year-old Willie Tasby, who had been in the organization since the pre–Veeck era, won the regular center field job. He became the first black player from within the system to make a substantial contribution as he led the team in runs scored while playing a center field that drew comparisons to Willie Mays. Early in the 1960 season, however, Tasby was shipped to the Boston Red Sox in exchange for journeyman outfielder Gene Stephens. The trade left Bob Boyd, almost exclusively a pinch-hitter by that time, as the only black player on the roster. Under Richards' leadership, the youthful 1960 edition of the Orioles, with three rookies in the infield and two in the starting rotation, threatened the Yankees and managed to finish in second place with 89 victories. But the unfortunate trade of Tasby cost them dearly. Tasby hit .281 in a Boston uniform, while Stephens posted an anemic .238 average for the Orioles.

The promising young Orioles never quite fulfilled their potential. They remained a predominately white team, as well as a non-pennant winner, throughout the first half of the 1960s. They finished third in 1961 with rookie outfielder Earl Robinson the only black player to spend the whole year on the roster. Richards departed late in the campaign to take over as general manager for the new Houston Colt 45s franchise. Under Alabama-born Billy Hitchcock, a member of the 1947 Browns squad that rejected integration, the Orioles dropped to seventh place in 1962. Earl Robinson spent most of the season on the disabled list, and Ozzie Virgil and Nate Smith made only token appearances, giving the Orioles an entirely Caucasian roster for a good portion of the year — probably the last all-white roster in major league history.

In 1963, Baltimore acquired veteran outfielders Al Smith and Joe Gaines from the White Sox and Reds respectively. During the 1964 season, at least nine black players appeared in an Orioles uniform, although rookie outfielder Sam Bowens was the only one to spend the whole year with the club. The next year, the Orioles were down to a pair of black players with center fielder Paul Blair, who would remain with the Orioles for 12 years, joining Bowens. The speedy, strong-armed Bowens had also looked like a future star after hitting .263 with 22 homers and 71 runs batted in as a rookie right fielder in 1964. But in 1965 he lost his regular job to Curt Blefary, a white player who would put up rookie numbers (.260, 22, 70) that were almost identical to Bowens' freshman marks while earning the nickname "Clank" for his less-than-stellar glove work.

The Turning Point — Frank Robinson

The 1966 campaign would be a turning point for the Baltimore Orioles. Lee MacPhail resigned as general manager to take a position in the Commissioner's Office, and Frank Robinson arrived from Cincinnati to take the American League by storm. Discussions that culminated in the deal that brought Robinson to Baltimore in exchange for pitcher Milt Pappas and two second-line players began during the annual Major League winter meetings while MacPhail was still in office, but it was his successor Harry Dalton who finally pulled the trigger.

Robinson, only 31 years old, was one of the premier players in the game. In ten years with Cincinnati, he had averaged more than 32 homers and 100 runs batted in per year while compiling a .303 batting mark. In 1961, he led the Reds to the pennant and captured National League Most Valuable Player honors. In announcing the acquisition of their first "Grade A Negro player," the Orioles acknowledged that they were trying to change their image. They hoped Robinson's presence would "win friends in the Negro community" that comprised 30 percent of the city's population at that time. It was even admitted that the Orioles had been accused of prejudice, but club management intended to erase that "erroneous impression" with a plan to "add ticket outlets in the Negro community and to hire some Negro employees."[6]

The rest is history. Robinson captured the American League Triple Crown and led the Orioles to the 1966 American League pennant. In the World Series, they swept the defending-champion Los Angeles Dodgers who were led by some guys named Koufax, Drysdale, and Wills. Robinson was overwhelmingly voted the American League Most Valuable Player and became the first player in history, black or white, to capture the MVP award in both leagues. Ironically, the individual who made the Robinson transaction possible was Cincinnati owner Bill DeWitt, the former face of the old St. Louis Browns.

The Orioles only employed three black players at the major league level in 1966: Robinson, Blair, and Bowens — the fewest of the 20 big league teams in existence at the time. But that would change quickly under Dalton's leadership. By 1969, the Baltimore roster included nine black performers for most of the year as the Orioles ended the decade with another American League pennant. Robinson, Paul Blair, and Don Buford manned the outfield, and 23-game-winner Mike Cuellar became the American League's first black Cy Young Award honoree. Amazingly, five other black players (Elrod Hendricks, Chico Salmon, Dave May, Curt Motton, and Marcelino Lopez) filled sup-

porting roles — a sure sign of progress from the early days of integration when there was no room for black players who weren't stars.

The Orioles' nucleus of black stars led them to another pennant in 1970, followed by a World Series victory over Robinson's former Cincinnati team. By 1973, Robinson had moved on, but Harry Dalton was still in place, guiding the club to an American League Eastern Division flag with a cast of black players that included holdovers Cuellar and Blair fortified by Don Baylor, Tommy Davis, Earl Williams, Grant Jackson, Frank Coggins, and Al Bumbry. The Orioles repeated in 1974 and remained one of the most successful teams in baseball for the next ten years.

After 89 and 95 loss seasons in 1986 and 1987, the Orioles dipped into their past and hired

The 1966 acquisition of Frank Robinson, the first black superstar to play for the Orioles, led to the organization's first World Championship (1969 Topps Game card).

Frank Robinson to turn things around as manager six games into the 1988 season. The immediate result was the worst season in Baltimore history, but the next year Robinson drove the squad up to second place, two games off the pace, and was named American League Manager of the Year for the 1989 campaign.

Ironically, manager Robinson's best player was Cal Ripken Jr., whose nickname was "Mr. Milk." Ripken would eventually replace Robinson as the greatest Oriole of all time in the hearts of Baltimore fans.

Chapter 6

THE NEW YORK/SAN FRANCISCO GIANTS

On July 8, 1949, the New York Giants became the fourth major league team to put a black player on the field when Hank Thompson started at second base and Monte Irvin later pinch hit in a 4–3 loss to the Brooklyn Dodgers.

By any conceivable measure, the integration of the Brooklyn Dodgers in the National League and the Cleveland Indians in the American League had to be considered a smashing success. The first two teams to field a black player had captured surprise pennants in the first two years of integration, and the first two black major leaguers, Jackie Robinson and Larry Doby, played major roles. In addition, attendance records had been shattered in each city, additional black stars had been added to the rosters, and promising black prospects were starring in both farm systems. Furthermore, there had been no major incidents of violence and remarkably few protests or overt displays of racism.

Reason dictated that the race would be on to snap up the Negro League's remaining black stars and put them in major league flannels. But incredibly, Major League Baseball still hesitated. On opening day of the final year of the turbulent decade of the 1940s, the Dodgers and Indians were still the only two teams with black players on their roster. Even more disappointing was the fact that only one new black player, Cleveland's Minnie Minoso, had joined Jackie Robinson, Larry Doby, Roy Campanella, and Satchel Paige, who had all starred in the majors in 1948.

In 1949, the major league All-Star Game, fittingly played at Brooklyn's Ebbets Field, hosted its first black participants. Robinson, Campanella, and freshman hurler Don Newcombe, who was called up to the Dodgers in late May, made the National League squad, and Larry Doby was named to the American League team. Yet at the end of the third full season of integration at the big league level, the number of black performers who'd been given a shot at the majors stood at a mere eleven. Furthermore, only the four all-stars could be considered established major leaguers. Of the other seven, only Hank Thompson, with a .280 batting average in 75 games for the Giants in 1949, had shown enough promise to be counted on in 1950. Monte Irvin of the Giants, Minnie Minoso and Luke Easter of Cleveland, and the Dodgers' Dan Bankhead had all shown promise in the minors, but had disappointed in big league trials. Veteran Willard Brown had returned to Negro League stardom after his release by the Browns in 1947, and the venerable Satchel Paige was headed in the same direction after a disappointing sophomore season with the Indians. Evidently the moguls who guarded the gates of Major League Baseball still weren't convinced that black players were good business.

But a few more teams had begun hedging their bets. The New York Yankees, Boston Braves, and New York Giants all recruited established Negro League stars for the 1949 season. Of course, these accomplished veterans would be required to prove themselves in the minor leagues before they could be fitted for major league uniforms. The Giants were by far the most prolific new entry into the ranks of integrated teams, signing no less than six distinguished Negro League veterans that year.

Leo the Lip

The introduction of black players to the rosters of the Dodgers, Indians, and Browns were all "top-down" actions initiated by the team owners. Much of the credit for the Giants' decision to sign black players, although probably not as much as he claimed, goes to manager Leo "The Lip" Durocher. Durocher was a peppery, good-field/no-hit shortstop for the St. Louis Cardinals' Gas House Gang in the mid–1930s. He was traded to the Dodgers in 1938 and took over the managerial reins in 1939. By 1941, he had cemented his Brooklyn legacy by leading the club to its first National League pennant in more than 20 years.

A sharp, combative manager on the field and a dapper, man-about-town off it, Durocher was tremendously popular in Brooklyn and commanded the respect, if not the admiration, of his players. In 1942, before the arrival Branch Rickey in Brooklyn, Durocher had drawn a rebuke from Commissioner Landis for admitting a willingness to have black players in his lineup.[1] Later, he enthusiastically embraced Rickey's plan to integrate the Dodgers and was supposed to play a key role in smoothing the way for Jackie Robinson's debut. But shortly before the 1947 campaign began, Durocher was suspended by Commissioner Happy Chandler for the entire season for consorting with unsavory characters, pirating the affections of actress Laraine Day from her husband, and generally setting a poor example for the impressionable youth of America. Though Durocher's suspension was a blow to Rickey's plans, the ensuing turmoil did provide a convenient diversion which Rickey alertly used as cover to quietly transfer Jackie Robinson's contract from Montreal to Brooklyn. To fill in for Durocher, 62-year-old scout Burt Shotton was summoned, and he proceeded to lead the Dodgers to the National League pennant.

Durocher returned to the Brooklyn helm for the 1948 season, but by midseason the club was floundering in fifth place. In his absence, the Dodgers had found out they could win without him and also got a glimpse of how much more relaxing life could be. Meanwhile, the neighboring Giants weren't doing too well themselves under Polo Grounds legend Mel Ott. On July 16, the impossible happened — arch-rival Leo Durocher moved across the river to take over the reins of the Giants.

Franchise History

In the first half of the 20th century, the New York Giants were the most successful team in the National League. Under the field leadership of John McGraw from 1902 through 1932 they captured ten pennants and hoisted three world championship banners. Star first baseman Bill Terry took over for an ailing McGraw during the 1932 season and led the Giants to the 1933 pennant and a World Series victory in his first full year at the helm.

In 1936, at the age of 32, Horace Stoneham inherited the franchise from his father Charles C. Stoneham. The senior Stoneham had made his fortune in the securities market, earning a somewhat less than "squeaky-clean" reputation in his financial dealings.[2] After the club captured pennants in 1936 and 1937 under Terry's command, young Horace presided over a gradual ten-year decline in the team's fortunes. According to Durocher, Stoneham had only two occupations in life, "He owns the Giants and he takes a drink every now and then," a sentiment that's also been attributed to Bill Veeck.[3] "Horace shunned publicity.... He traveled in his own narrow circles. He was not only uncomfortable with strangers, he was suspicious of them," said Durocher.[4] The Giants owner was, however, a true baseball fan who, unlike most of his colleagues, genuinely liked baseball players. He populated the front office with former Giants like "King Carl" Hubbell and "Prince Hal" Schumacher. He also employed his nephew Chub Feeney as general manager and maintained a clannish front office heavily staffed by loyal fellow Irishmen like Tom Sheehan and Eddie Brannick.[5] When Terry stepped down as manager after the 1941 season, Stoneham moved him upstairs and prevailed upon popular veteran slugger Mel Ott to take over as manager.

Ott's Giants were a nice bunch of nice guys. At least that's what then-Brooklyn-manager Durocher said in 1946 just before tagging on his famous punch line, "Nice guys finish last"—an utterance that eventually made it into *Bartlett's Quotations.*[6] The Giants did, in fact, finish the 1946 season in the National League basement—their fourth straight second-division finish. They climbed to fourth place in 1947 on the strength of 221 homers, a new major league team record. But changes were needed. Ott, who had played more than 20 seasons for the Giants and blasted 511 homers himself, really was too nice a guy to be a top manager. When the Giants played only .500 ball for the first half of the 1948 season, Ott offered his resignation, which Stoneham accepted with relief.

Casting about for a new manager, Stoneham asked Rickey about the availability of Burt Shotton, who had returned to civilian life when Durocher came back from his suspension. But Branch Rickey was looking for a way to ease Leo out the door, and an incredible plan came together—one that solved the problems of both teams by filling the Giants' void and creating a desired vacancy on the Dodgers' bench for the return of Shotton. It also turned the entire city of New York on its ear. Durocher was public enemy number one among the Giant faithful. Nobody was hated more—by the Giants or the rest of the league—than the cocky, loud-mouthed Dodger manager was. The idea of "The Lip" succeeding McGraw, Terry, and Ott, the revered line of Giants legends who had filled the manager's chair since 1902, drove Giants fans crazy. And Dodger fans weren't too happy about it either.

Eventually the furor died down, but the Giants finished in fifth place in 1948, playing only slightly better under Durocher's leadership than they had under Ott. The Dodgers, however, played markedly better under Shotton and climbed up to third place by the end of the campaign.

The Decision to Integrate

The Giants squad that Durocher took over wasn't his type of team. While setting a new major league home run record in 1947, they stole only 29 bases—the same number Jackie Robinson swiped that year all by himself. Durocher began lobbying Stoneham to sacrifice some power for faster, better defensive players. The Giants owner didn't want to part with his power-hitting, if somewhat slow-moving, sluggers, but Durocher eventually wore him down. When Stoneham asked him for a detailed written recommendation for personnel changes, Durocher responded with a four-word report: "Back up the truck."[7]

Reluctantly, Stoneham agreed to begin replacing his favorite bashers with quicker men and bolster the team's pitching staff. Another point Durocher fought for was signing a few players from the wealth of fine Negro League talent waiting to be tapped by Major League Baseball. It took some fast-talking, but he convinced Stoneham that the Giants needed an immediate infusion of black talent to catch up with their cross-town neighbors, who already had Robinson and Campanella in their lineup.[8] This argument struck a responsive chord with Stoneham. The Dodgers and Giants were the only teams in the 20th century to go head-to-head with a competitor in the same league in the same city. The Giants enjoyed a distinct advantage for the first 30 years or so of the rivalry, but the worm had turned in the 1940s — coinciding with Durocher's arrival in Brooklyn. While the Dodgers had developed into winners, the Giants had devolved into also-rans. They couldn't afford to wait around. They needed "major league-ready" talent.[9]

Before the 1949 season, the Giants acquired Monte Irvin from the Newark Eagles, and Hank Thompson and Ford Smith from the Kansas City Monarchs, all of whom were well known to Organized Baseball. Irvin was one of the premier players in Negro League baseball and had been considered by many as the best choice to break the color barrier before Robinson.[10] He was 30 years of age and had been playing professionally since 1937. Thompson had been part of the St. Louis Browns' abortive attempt to cash in on the "Negro player craze"

Leo "The Lip" Durocher lobbied for the integration of the Giants and was rewarded with a National League pennant in 1951 and a World Championship in 1954 (1952 Bowman card).

two years earlier. He was only 23 years old but had already spent four years with the Monarchs and served two years in the military. In 1948, he led the Negro American League in stolen bases while playing both the infield and outfield. Two problems involving Thompson had to be worked out, however. First, the player demanded a share of his purchase price, which he received.[11] Then there was the matter of the gentleman Thompson had killed in a barroom altercation the previous year, which required the help of the Giants' front office to smooth over.[12] The 30-year-old Smith, a fireballing right-hander, may have been considered the top prospect of the three. He worked out with the Giants at their spring training camp in Phoenix and is credited with the distinction of being the first black player in history to don a Giants uniform.[13]

Irvin, Thompson, and Smith were assigned to the Giants' International League Jersey City farm club at the beginning of the 1949 season, and veteran Negro League catcher Ray Noble joined them during the campaign. The Giants also reinforced their American Association farm club in Minneapolis early in the season with the acquisition of 35-year-old hurler Dave Barnhill and 36-year-old third baseman Ray Dandridge from New York of the Negro American League.

Irvin was a sensation with Jersey City, and Thompson also played well. In mid-season, they were called up to the parent club, where Durocher welcomed them with open arms. He immediately called a team meeting and laid it on the line. "About race, I'm going to say this," Leo announced, "If you're green or purple or whatever color, you can play for me if I think you can help this ballclub. That's all I'm going to say about race." Irvin later said, "I know that Jackie had some trouble with the Dodgers, but we [he and Thompson] never had any problem on the Giants.... I think Leo Durocher was responsible because of the way he handled it."[14]

Thompson faced Don Newcombe in his first at-bat for the Giants, becoming the first black hitter to face a black pitcher at the big league level.[15] Though Irvin had been the brighter star in the Negro Leagues, Thompson initially enjoyed more success. He quickly took over as the Giants' regular second baseman while Irvin had trouble finding playing time and failed to hit as expected.

The integration of the Giants didn't have the same immediate impact as integration had in Brooklyn and Cleveland. While the Dodgers captured another pennant in 1949, the Giants finished fifth again, with a worse record than they had managed the previous year. But Durocher had started to break up Mel Ott's old gang. During the 1949 season, the Giants got rid of slugging first baseman Johnny Mize and hard-hitting catcher Walker Cooper, two of the biggest names in the National League. Then in the off-season outfielder-third baseman Sid Gordon, right fielder Willard Marshall, shortstop Buddy Kerr, and pitcher Red Webb were swapped to the Boston Braves for the brilliant keystone combination of Eddie Stanky and Al Dark.

In the spring of 1950, the Giants shifted Thompson to third base to make room for Stanky at second, but Irvin returned to Jersey City. The club also extended a trial to Kenny Washington, Jackie Robinson's former backfield partner at UCLA, but the 31-year-old prospect failed to impress.[16] To keep Thompson company, the club signed 19-year-old Jose Fernandez as a bullpen catcher.[17] But Irvin won a quick return trip to the parent club by batting an amazing .510, blasting 10 homers, and driving in 33 runs in 18 International League games. After rejoining the Giants, he hit a solid .299 to establish himself as a big leaguer. Thompson, meanwhile, got acclimated at third base and had an excellent year at the plate. After a sputtering start, the Giants' version of the "Great Experiment" seemed to be working, as they climbed to third place behind Philadelphia and Brooklyn, only five games off the pace.

Meanwhile, down on the farm, Ray Noble was transferred to Oakland of the Pacific Coast League, and Ford Smith, who won 10 games for Jersey City in 1949, came down with pneumonia and won only 2 contests in 1950.[18] But veterans Dandridge and Barnhill starred for Minneapolis again. The big pay-off came, however, when the Giants plucked 19-year-old Willie Mays off the roster of the Birmingham Black Barons during the season.[19]

The 1951 Pennant

The 1951 season was probably the most satisfying in the history of the New York Giants. They were 13½ games behind the Dodgers in mid–August, but surged to a first-place tie before winning a one-game playoff for the pennant on Bobby Thomson's famous home run. The Giants began and ended the unforgettable campaign with four black players on their roster, making them the most prolific employer of black talent in the major leagues at the time. Irvin, the National League leader in runs batted in that year, Thompson, and backup catcher Ray Noble were there at the beginning and the end, although Thompson spent a few weeks with Minneapolis. The fourth black player on the Giants' roster at the beginning of the season was 30-year-old Artie Wilson, a superb defensive shortstop who led the Negro American

League in batting in 1948. Wilson debuted in Organized Baseball in 1949 with San Diego in the Cleveland Indians organization, but he was subsequently awarded to the New York Yankees when a dispute arose over his signing. He was re-assigned to Oakland, where he mentored young Billy Martin, his double-play partner. The next year, he led the Pacific Coast League in hits, but Yankee shortstop Phil Rizzuto, the 1950 American League Most Valuable Player, stood in his way to promotion. In the off-season, Wilson was swapped to the Giants, where he won a utility infield job by batting .480 average in spring exhibition games.[20]

Legend has it that Wilson's major league career was doomed because Dodger skipper Charlie Dressen, who had been his manager at Oakland, introduced a defensive alignment that rendered the speedster helpless at the plate. Dressen bunched his defense short and on the left side, challenging the slap-hitting lefty batter to pull the ball to right field.[21] The truth is that Wilson had stymied that defensive setup in both the Negro and minor leagues and would probably have been able to deal with it in the major leagues if given a decent chance.[22] San Francisco Seals' manager Lefty O'Doul employed the "Wilson shift" for the first time during the 1949 season, and Wilson ended the campaign with a .348 mark.[23] The next year, he slapped out a Pacific Coast League leading 264 hits facing the shift all season. The real reason Wilson's big league career was limited to 22 at-bats was an informal quota on the number of black players a team could employ.[24]

Wilson's days in New York were numbered when Durocher first laid eyes on 19-year-old Willie Mays in spring training prior to the 1951 campaign. Mays began the season at Minneapolis, where teammate and former Negro League great Ray Dandridge took him under his wing. When the Giants got off to a slow start, Durocher began badgering Stoneham to bring him up, but the Giants owner refused to add a fifth black player to the roster. "No, we've got too many already," he complained.[25] But Durocher kept up the pressure and ultimately an opening for Mays was created with Artie Wilson being sent down to the minors, sacrificed to preserve the quota. Wilson went on the play regularly in Triple A through 1957, banging out more than 200 hits three more times and fielding brilliantly without getting another shot at the big time.[26]

Ray Dandridge, however, never made it up to the major leagues for a single day. Known for his sensational glove work, Dandridge was already a grizzled veteran of 16 seasons in the Negro and Mexican leagues when he signed with the Giants in 1949, yet he finished the campaign with the second-highest batting average in the American Association. The next year, he was selected the league's Most Valuable Player as he led Minneapolis to the pennant. Yet he remained in the minors.

Long after his career ended, Dandridge met Stoneham at an old-timers' game. "I cussed him out," Dandridge said. "I asked him, 'Gee, couldn't you have brought me up even for one week, just so I could say I've actually put my foot in a major league park.'" Another former Negro League third base great, Judy Johnson, who was a confident and advisor to Connie Mack in Philadelphia, claimed that he tried to get Mack to acquire Dandridge, but the Giants wouldn't sell him.[27] When the Negro League Committee selected Dandridge for the Hall of Fame in 1987, Commissioner Peter Ueberroth introduced him in induction ceremonies as "the greatest third baseman who never played in the major leagues."[28]

The Giants' infield personnel selections during the 1951 campaign demonstrate how difficult it was for black players to make it in organized baseball in that era, even with an "enlightened" team. The club's primary backup infielders that year were washed-up veteran Bill Rigney, dead-armed former Dodger Spider Jorgensen, rookie Davey Williams, and Jack "Lucky" Lohrke, whose claim to fame was surviving a bus crash that killed several of his minor league teammates. None of these guys belonged in the same league with Artie Wilson or Ray Dandridge — much less a higher one. In addition, the club farmed Hank Thompson out for a couple of weeks during the pennant race. The previous year, he had been regarded as one of the top third in baseball and had proven versatile enough to play second base and shortstop in his Negro League days.

On May 25, 1951, the Willie Mays era officially got underway in New York. Durocher patiently nursed his young prodigy through a slow start and was rewarded when Mays sparked their sensational pennant drive and was voted National League Rookie of the Year. Mays, of course, went on to develop into one of the greatest players in Major League Baseball history. When he left the Giants during the 1972 season, he stood in second place on the all-time home run list behind Babe Ruth, despite missing two prime years while in military service. Shortly thereafter, Mays was surpassed by Hank Aaron, another former Negro Leaguer, but he held third place for more than 30 years until his godson Barry Bonds passed him in 2004.

In the Giants' World Series loss to the Yankees that year, fans got to see the first all-black outfield to appear in a major league contest as Hank Thompson joined Willie Mays and Monte Irvin in the Giants' garden. Thompson was filling in for injured Don Mueller in right field, his first outfield duty of the year.

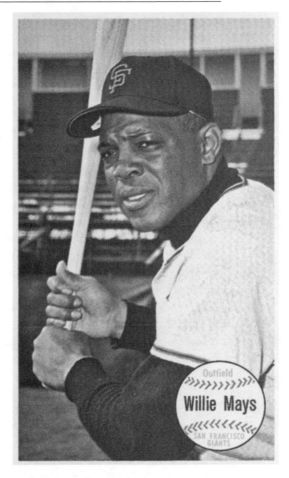

Willie Mays, a Durocher protégé, became one of the greatest players of all time with the Giants and godfather to future home run king Barry Bonds (1964 Topps Giant Issue card).

In 1952, Irvin spent the first two-thirds of the season on the disabled list, Mays was inducted into the service, and backup catcher Ray Noble was demoted to the minor leagues. This left Hank Thompson as the only black player on the roster for part of the campaign. But both Irvin and Noble were back full time in 1953, and pitcher Ruben Gomez, who was signed as a free agent after obtaining his release from the Yankees' organization, debuted with 13 victories. Though the colorful Gomez would be the last prominent black player added to the Giants' parent roster for several years, the club signed several black prospects that year who would eventually make it to the major leagues, including Bill White, Willie Kirkland, Tony Taylor, Ozzie Virgil, Marshall Bridges, Sherman Jones, John Kennedy, and Bob Perry.

The 1954 World Champions

In 1954, the Giants recaptured the National League pennant after two years of Brooklyn rule. The World Series that year was a dream come true for black baseball players and fans. Since the Yankees had been dethroned by the Cleveland Indians, for the first time ever, two teams featuring top-flight black players would meet on the biggest stage in professional sports. Both the Giants and Indians were front runners in the recruitment of black baseball players at the minor league level and employment at the top level. Center fielder Willie Mays, fresh from two years in the military, was the National League batting champ and Most Valuable Player, while Monte Irvin flanked him in left field, Hank Thompson was stationed at third, and Ruben Gomez was in the starting rotation. They swept the highly favored Cleveland Indians, who featured Larry Doby, Al Smith, and supersub Dave Pope, in four straight games.

The Series victory propelled the Giants into the forefront in the minds of young black prospects. Unlike the Dodgers and Indians, however, the Giants fully pressed their advantage. From 1955 through 1959, they added future black stars Orlando Cepeda, Willie McCovey, Juan Marichal, the Alou brothers — Felipe, Matty, and Jesus — Manny Mota, Jose Pagan, and Jim Ray Hart to a farm system that was already loaded with talented black phenoms.

The Giants slipped to third place in 1955, and Durocher stepped down as manager at the close of the season. The decline continued under Durocher's replacement Bill Rigney, who led the club to consecutive sixth-place finishes the next two seasons. In 1957, five of the 35 black players who appeared in the National League wore Giant uniforms, only slightly better than par for the league. Willie Mays was still performing at his peak, and Ruben Gomez made a comeback to lead the staff with 15 games victories after two down seasons, but the other three black players were rookies whose performance was mediocre. The rookies all had some claim to fame, however. Shortstop Andre Rodgers, a former cricket player, was the first major leaguer from the Bahamas. Catcher Valmy Thomas became the first Virgin Islander to appear in the big leagues. Thomas was from St. Croix, although his parents traveled to Puerto Rico so that he would be born in better medical facilities.[29] And infielder Ozzie Virgil, who the next year would become the first black player to play for the Detroit Tigers, was the first major leaguer from the Dominican Republic.[30] Also carried on the roster was Bill White, who had debuted with 20 homers as the Giants' regular first baseman in 1956 before being inducted into military service. White would go on to become a star with the St. Louis Cardinals after his discharge and would eventually be named president of the National League — the first black man in the game to hold such a high executive office.

The Move to San Francisco

But while the parent club had been floundering, the farm system had been flourishing. In 1958, the franchise's first year in San Francisco, the Giants climbed to a surprising third place in the final standings. Furthermore, they

An unhappy minor leaguer in the Yankees' system, pitcher Ruben Gomez obtained his release to join the Giants rotation (1956 Topps card).

placed three young black players on the Rookie All-Star Team: first baseman Orlando Cepeda, who won Rookie of the Years honors, and outfielders Willie Kirkland and Leon Wagner. Another productive black rookie, Felipe Alou, was also among the nine black players who performed for the Giants that year — the most in the major leagues. Cepeda would enjoy a Hall of Fame career, and Wagner and Alou would also develop into all-stars. Kirkland would slam an impressive total of 91 homers over the next four years, but would never quite fulfill his potential.

Unlike the Dodgers whose move to Los Angeles gave them a distinctly whiter fan base, the San Francisco/Oakland metropolitan area hosted a large non-white population. Ironically, Bay Area fans didn't embrace Mays, a situation that was probably exacerbated by his cool relationship with manager Rigney. But the locals fell in love with Orlando Cepeda. Fans of the new Giants wanted their own hero, not a second-hand New York idol. Gradually, Mays' exploits warmed up the hometown crowd, though he never experienced the adulation he had received in New York.

Another black veteran who didn't fare as well on the West Coast was Ruben Gomez. Gomez holds the dual distinction of being the last pitcher to win a game in a New York Giants' uniform as well as the first to pitch the San Francisco Giants to victory. But after he fell to 10 victories in 1958, he was sent to Philadelphia along with Valmy Thomas in a trade that added Jack Sanford to the Giants' rotation. It was one of the best deals in franchise history.

In 1959, the Giants challenged for the National League pennant before fading in the final days of the campaign. First baseman Willie McCovey, another future black Hall of Famer, captured the Giants' second straight Rookie of the Year Award, temporarily shoving Cepeda into the outfield. In addition, former Negro League hurler Sam Jones came over from the Cardinals to post the lowest earned run average in the National League and tie for the league lead in victories. His efforts earned him *The Sporting News* Pitcher of the Year Award although the Baseball Writers Association gave the Cy Young Award to Earl Wynn. The team's shortstop of the future, Jose Pagan, also got a brief taste of the big leagues.

The 1960s and Beyond

For the third straight season, the Giants debuted a future black Hall of Famer in 1960 when Juan Marichal, the Dominican Dandy, hurled a one-hit shutout of the Philadelphia Phillies in his first big league appearance. Marichal would retire in 1975 with 243 major league victories, a total that would stand as the highest for a Latin American pitcher until it was topped by Nicaragua's Dennis Martinez in 1998.

The 1961 campaign began with former Giants shortstop Alvin Dark in the managerial slot. Dark had been a star quarterback at Louisiana State University and was considered something of a zealot when it came to religion, a reputation that would last throughout his 30-year career as a player and manager. Dark appointed his ex-teammate Mays as team captain, the first black player in history to hold that informal but widely respected title.

The Giants' 1962 pennant-winning squad featured black superstars Mays, Cepeda, McCovey, and Marichal. In addition, Jose Pagan capably handled shortstop, Felipe Alou hit .316 and developed into one of the best right fielders in the game, and his younger brother Matty batted .292 as a valuable outfield spare. Also on the roster for most of the campaign was young Manny Mota, who contributed little to the pennant cause but would end a 20-year big league career with a .304 lifetime average.

Although the Giants only captured one pennant during the 1960s, they were usually strong contenders. During the decade, they were also the dominant team in the major leagues in terms of black talent, especially Latinos. In the fall of 1961, ten of the players listed on the Giants' 40-man roster were Latinos—five from the Dominican Republic, three from Puerto Rico, and two Cubans.[31] Credit for the huge influx of Caribbean talent goes primarily to Giants scout Alex Pompez. A Cuban-American native of Key West who spent most of his adult life in New York, Pompez had been primarily responsible for introducing Latinos into the Negro Leagues in the early part of the 20th century. He used his extensive contacts in African American and Latin American baseball to sign scores of dark-skinned players for the Giants.

The Giants manager from 1961 through 1964, Al Dark, had never enjoyed a particularly harmonious relationship with the Hispanic congregation on the Giants, particularly Orlando Cepeda. The problem seemed to stem primarily from the manager's strong aversion to Latino player's participation in winter leagues. But a full-scale racial incident erupted in 1964 when Dark was quoted in a *Newsday* magazine article as saying, "We [The Giants] have trouble because we have so many Negro and Spanish-speaking player on this team. They are just not able to perform up to the white player when it comes to mental alertness. You can't make most Negroes and Spanish players have the pride in their team that you can get from white players. You couldn't name three colored players in our league who are always mentally alert to take advantage of situations."[32]

Dark, of course, claimed he was misquoted, and *The Sporting News* predictably tried to help sweep the issue under the rug. Under the banner "Giant Skipper Given Pat on Back by Frick and Stoneham," the publication reported, "Beleaguered Alvin Dark, manager of the Giants, was exonerated of racism implications and given a vote of confidence by club president Horace Stoneham to bring to a quiet and dignified end what had threatened to become a very distressing situation."[33] But the man who really saved Dark's hide was Willie Mays, who publicly came to his manager's defense and "talked his black teammates out of rebellion."[34] Nevertheless, Dark was fired after the season as the Giants ended up in fourth place, only three games off the pace. The controversy may well have cost the team the 1964 pennant.

Throughout the remainder of the decade, the Giants battled the Pittsburgh Pirates for supremacy as equal opportunity employers. In 1964, third baseman Jim Ray Hart enjoyed a tremendous rookie year, and Jesus Alou came up to team with brother Manny to replace their other brother Felipe in right field. Infielder Tito Fuentes and outfielder Ollie Brown joined the lineup in 1966, and Bobby Bonds came up midway through the 1968 season. Failing to find a spot in the Giants outfield, George Foster was traded to Cincinnati where he would develop into a star slugger for the Big Red Machine of the 1970s.

The Giants captured a surprise National League Western Division title in 1971. Outfielder Bobby Bonds was their best player, but 40-year-old Willie Mays enjoyed a fine season, and veterans Marichal and McCovey also made significant contributions.

The Giants maintained a strong black player presence through the decade of the 1970s as the farm system produced Garry Maddox, Gary Matthews, Elia Sosa, and Larry Herndon. Willie McCovey made a stirring comeback for the Giants in 1977 after an absence of three years, and other black stars Bill Madlock, Willie Montanez, Von Joshua, Terry Whitfield, and Vida Blue were acquired through trades.

The Impact of Black Players on the Franchise

With all due respect to the Dodgers, the Giants were the franchise most impacted by the addition of black players to their organization. One need look no further than Hall of Fame membership rolls to appreciate the Giant franchise's contribution to the full integration of baseball. Five black Hall of Famers — Irvin, Mays, Cepeda, McCovey, and Marichal — rose to stardom with the Giants, more than any other big league franchise. In fact, for much of the 1960s the Giants had four black Hall of Famers together on their roster, more than any other team has ever had at any one time.

It's difficult for many baseball people to accept Leo Durocher as a hero for his role in the integration of baseball. His many critics regard him as an abrasive, loud-mouthed braggart with a certain baseball genius. In addition, "The Lip" has never been one to shy away from taking credit, whether it's due or not. In his biography, he claims to have short-circuited the petition against Robinson in the spring of 1947, though Rickey's threat to send the instigators packing probably had a bigger impact.[35] Durocher also takes full credit for engineering the trade that brought Eddie Stanky and Alvin Dark — and subsequently the 1951 pennant — to the Giants.[36]

But other than Durocher, the Giants' administration during the early years of integration seemed less than sensitive and sympathetic to the plight of black players. According to Happy Chandler, when the owners were discussing the prospect of Robinson joining the Dodgers, Stoneham "got up and said that if Robinson played for the Dodgers that the Negroes in Harlem, which was where the Polo Grounds were, would riot and burn down the Polo Grounds."[37] Shortly before Durocher joined the Giants, Stoneham fibbed, "We have tried out Negroes for several years, but as yet haven't found anyone who would fit in our plans."[38]

When the Giants signed Mays in 1950, they initially planned to send the unworldly 19-year-old to Sioux City in the Western League until a racial incident in that city rearranged the itinerary. Instead, the youngster was assigned to Trenton, where he would be the Inter-State League's first black player.[39] Likewise, young Bill White spent his rookie season with Danville as the only black player in the Carolina League, a circuit that forced out its first black player, Percy Miller, only two years earlier.[40] Willie McCovey had the dubious honor of integrating the Georgia State League with Sandersville as a 17-year-old. Two years later, he was assigned to Dallas in the Texas League, where he and other black players had to stay behind when their clubs visited the Shreveport Sports in Louisiana.[41] In 1954, Cuban-born 18-year-old Tony Taylor helped break the color barrier with Texas City in the Evangeline League, and the next year 17-year-old Orlando Cepeda, who didn't speak English, was sent to the Appalachian League, where he was the only black player in the circuit.

Looking back on the integration era years later, former general manager Chub Feeney remembered, "Of course we knew segregation was wrong. My uncle [Stoneham] knew it and I knew it, but pure idealists we were not. Competing in New York against the Yankees and the Dodgers, the resource we needed most was talent. Whatever Durocher told you, Leo's brain alone was not enough. In 1949, the Negro leagues were the most logical place in the world to look for ballplayers."[42] There's even some evidence that the Giants were trying to sign black Cuban star Silvio Garcia about the same time the Dodgers were interested in him back in 1943.[43]

Durocher, however, probably does deserve most of the credit for prodding the Giants to integrate and no small amount for his role in mentoring Willie Mays. These events are directly responsible for the franchise's greatest successes through the second half of the twentieth century up to the present.

In 1993, Barry Bonds left the Pittsburgh Pirates to join a San Francisco squad that had lost 90 games the previous year in large part because he wanted to follow in the footsteps of his godfather Willie Mays. It's fitting that Bonds would establish the all-time single-season major league home run record in 2001 and subsequently break Hank Aaron's career homer record in 2007 in a San Francisco Giant uniform. Unfortunately, his accomplishments are tainted in the eyes of many in the baseball world by allegations of steroid use, though it's suspected in some quarters that the color of his skin may also be working against him.

Chapter 7

THE BOSTON/MILWAUKEE/ATLANTA BRAVES

Although their numbers were small, 1949 was a great year for black major leaguers. Jackie Robinson led the National League in batting and stolen bases and was named the league's Most Valuable Player. Don Newcombe was named the National League Rookie of the Year after tying for the league lead in shutouts and finishing among the league leaders in winning percentage, strikeouts, and complete games. Robinson, Newcombe, and Roy Campanella were named to the National League All-Star Team, and Larry Doby was selected to the American League squad. And the Dodgers, led by their three black stars, captured the National League pennant.

The next year, 1950, would be a big year for blacks in other sports. On the national scene, Althea Gibson became the first black tennis player to compete in the national championships of the United States Lawn Tennis Association at Forrest Hills. Chuck Cooper of the Boston Celtics, Earl Lloyd of the Washington Capitals, and former Cleveland Indian farmhand Nat "Sweetwater" Clifton of the New York Knicks became the first black players in the National Basketball Association. And Marion Motley paced the National Football League in rushing while leading the Cleveland Browns to the title.

Yet the Boston Braves were the only new major league team to join the ranks of those with integrated rosters during the 1950 season, though a few more clubs decided to initiate their own "Great Experiments" at the minor league level.

Cynics have often questioned the purity of Branch Rickey's motives in taking action to break the color barrier.[1] The skeptics wondered whether the good deed was done primarily for altruistic purposes or for profit. There was no such confusion, however, when it came to the reasons for the Boston Braves' decision to integrate. It was strictly business.

Franchise History

In 1943, contractor Lou Perini along with two business associates in the construction industry, Joe Maney and Guido Rugo, acquired majority interest in the Boston National League franchise. The trio was immediately dubbed the "Three Little Steam Shovels." The "Shovels" tackled running the Braves as businessmen intent on making a profit. Their plan was simple — improve the product, thereby increasing sales. Speaking for the group, Perini said, "We don't know much about baseball, but we know plenty about business. We're going to build the best organization of baseball men we can and lend them our business judgement."[2]

The franchise that Perini and his pals took over had a lengthy losing tradition. From the beginning of World War I through the end of World War II, the Braves waged a ferocious battle with the Philadelphia Phillies for control of the National League cellar. In those 28 years (1918 through 1945), the Braves finished in the second division 25 times, crawling up to the dizzying heights of fourth place the other three seasons. Only the superior inferiority of the Phillies kept them from being the worst team in Major League Baseball.

Way back in 1914, the Braves had made a surprising run to capture the National League pennant and stunned the baseball world by winning the World Championship in four straight games over the highly favored Philadelphia Athletics. But thereafter their fortunes dropped steadily until they found themselves firmly ensconced in the depths of the National League standings only three years after ruling the baseball world. By that time, they had also lost the interest of the city of Boston to the Red Sox, who captured consecutive American League flags in 1915 and 1916, and would win the pennant again in 1918 before sinking into the doldrums themselves.

Bob Quinn, a longtime executive for a series of under-funded, losing teams, took over as general manager and team president after the 1935 season at the behest of the National League. By 1941, he had managed to add majority owner to his title when he headed up a syndicate that acquired the franchise, but the Braves (then called the "Bees") remained in dire financial straits. Quinn was retained as general manager after Perini and company assumed control, but manager Casey Stengel was fired almost immediately after he suggested to the new owners, "You guys run your steam shovels. I'll run the ballplayers."[3]

Early in the 1945 season, the Braves flexed their new financial muscle with the purchase of star pitcher Mort Cooper from the St. Louis Cardinals for $60,000 and pitcher Red Barrett. On hearing of the deal, Barrett quipped that the wrong club gave up the cash and backed up his words by leading the National League with 23 victories that year. Meanwhile Cooper developed a sore arm and won only 23 more games the rest of his professional career.

But the new owners also did some things right. They renovated Braves Field, began aggressively promoting the club, and brought night baseball to the city.

They promoted John Quinn to succeed his father as general manager in 1945 and lured hired highly respected, successful, and businesslike manager Billy Southworth away from the Cards. Fortunately, the acquisition of Southworth worked out much better than the Mort Cooper deal. In 1946, the Braves finished fourth, the first time in 12 years they'd managed a first division finish.

In 1948, the Perini group's investment yielded a National League pennant as Southworth brilliantly directed an eclectic assortment of has-beens and might-have-beens to a surprise first-place finish. The team featured ace pitchers Warren Spahn and Johnny Sain, the outstanding double-play combination of second baseman Eddie Stanky and rookie shortstop Al Dark, and slugging third baseman and 1947 MVP Bob Elliott. In addition, Southworth got remarkable mileage out of old Boston favorite Tommy Holmes as well as shopworn veterans Bill Voiselle, Nelson Potter, Jeff Heath, Mike McCormick, Jim Russell, and the re-acquired Red Barrett.

The Decision to Integrate

By 1948, Perini had emerged as the principal owner of the team. He still knew business, and he had also learned a thing or two about baseball. Shortly after Larry Doby's heroics against the Braves in the World Series, they signed their first black prospect, a 19-year-old infielder from New York named Waldon Williams. According to *The Sporting News*, young Williams had to be persuaded to forgo a boxing career that Joe Louis was urging him to pursue.[4] Maybe Waldon should have stuck to the ring because he never rose above Class B, despite hitting over .290 in five of six seasons in Organized Baseball. Scout Dutch Dorman scoured the Puerto Rican leagues and was reported to be particularly interested in Vic Power, who was known as Vic Pellot in Puerto Rico, and pitcher Gene Collins.[5] The Braves also signed pitcher Johnny Taylor, a Hartford native and veteran Negro League star who began his pro career in 1935, to become the first black player to appear with their Hartford Eastern League farm club.[6] Early in the 1949 season, they added George Crowe, formerly of the New York Black Yankees, to the Hartford roster after he impressed at a tryout camp, and later they purchased the contract of hard-hitting former Negro League second baseman George Handy from Bridgeport of the Colonial League.[7] Perini went so far as to promise that there would be "a delegation of Negro players" at his team's training camp the next spring.[8]

In 1949, the Braves dropped to fourth place and attendance slipped. The fact that it was the Dodgers, with their trio of black stars, who had taken the pennant away from his club was not lost on the Perini. The Braves' owner had also noted the effects of integration on the turnstiles and determined that black players were a valuable commodity. They could certainly play major league ball, and people would pay to see them do it. Like any good businessman, the scent of money had increased his flexibility. For the sake of profit, the Braves were anxious to join the ranks of Major League Baseball's integrated franchises.

The role played by John Quinn in the transformation of racial policy that occurred in the Braves' executive suite is not clear, but it was probably substantial. Perini reportedly wouldn't allow Jackie Robinson, Sam Jethroe, and Marvin Williams to audition for the Braves in 1945, even though the Red Sox had granted them a Fenway Park workout.[9] And according to former Commissioner Chandler, Perini had been against bringing Robinson into the National League.[10]

John Quinn, on the other hand, grew up in a more open environment. Black journalist Mabray "Doc" Kountze recounted a 1938 meeting with Quinn's father where the (then) Braves president suggested that the integration of baseball should start in the "Cradle of Liberty" and discussed ways in which it could be fostered. "Bob Quinn, Sr. left no doubt in my mind that he would have voted to remove the Major League color line in 1938," recalled Kountze, "But he told me, at the time, the other club owners would have voted him down."[11] It's highly likely that Bob Quinn's son and chief assistant shared the same views.

During World War II, John Quinn managed Patton's Third Army baseball squad, a service team made up predominantly of major leaguers. In the European Theater of Operations championship, they were defeated by a team from Oise Base that featured veteran Negro League stars Leon Day and Willard Brown, so he undoubtedly developed a keen appreciation for the talents of black players.[12] Quinn's daughter, Mrs. Roland Hemond, recalls that her father was upset that the first black Braves couldn't stay with their white teammates during spring training camp in Bradenton, Florida.[13] In addition, the Braves' front office under Quinn showed sensitivity toward the personal problems of black athletes after the team integrated. During Sam Jethroe's rookie season, there was much concern that the team's first black player had no one to room with on the road.[14] The front office listened to an offer of Dan Bankhead's services from the ever-accommodating Branch Rickey (see Dodgers chapter) and also evinced interest in acquiring Artie Wilson to keep Jethroe company early in the 1950 campaign,[15] although no deal was consummated. Quinn would go on to oversee the smooth transition of the Braves from a segregated team to an integrated powerhouse in the late 1950s before moving to Philadelphia to complete the dismantling of the Phillies' racial barrier.

The Purchase of Jethroe

Before the 1950 season, Perini and Quinn decided that the Braves needed a major league-ready black star — their own Jackie Robinson — to remain competitive in the integrated National League. However, most of the low-hanging fruit had already been picked by that time. Teams could no longer simply send a scout to take in a Negro League game and bring back a Robinson, Doby, or Campanella. But the player who had come closest to replacing Robinson was available for the right price. Sam Jethroe had signed with the Brooklyn Dodgers and joined their Montreal farm team midway through the 1948 campaign, a year and a half after the city hosted Robinson's debut in Organized Baseball. By 1949, Jethroe had come close to making Montreal fans forget Robinson with his own dangerous bat and daring exploits on the bases. Though Branch Rickey had always maintained that for the good of the cause he often stepped aside to allow other willing owners to sign Negro players, he stuck the Braves for full price in the Jethroe deal. Though a few fringe players were involved, the Braves essentially paid $100,000 for Jethroe's contract,

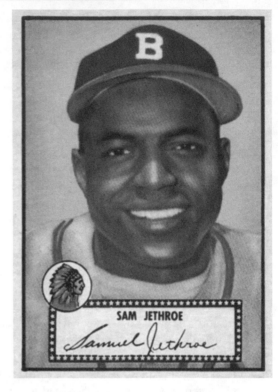

Sam "The Jet" Jethroe, the first black Boston Brave, is the oldest player in history to capture Rookie of the Year honors (1952 Topps card).

which Rickey had purchased from the Cleveland Buckeyes less than two years earlier for $5,000.

Jethroe wasn't exactly thrilled about coming to Boston. The 1945 tryout fiasco was still fresh on his mind, and the city had a long history of racial and ethnic animosity. Though Jethroe put on a good face and said all the right things, the city did not welcome him with open arms. He was crucified by the Boston press, who seemed to resent him personally for the amount of money the Braves had paid for his contract, even though he didn't get any of it. Jethroe was labeled a lemon before he played in his first major league game.[16] Nevertheless, he had a fine first season. He led the majors in stolen bases, swiping more than twice as many as his nearest competitor, and captured Rookie of the Year honors. But Jethroe's presence didn't seem to have the desired impact at the gate or in the won-lost column. The 1950 edition of the Braves repeated their fourth-place finish of the previous campaign, and the fans never really warmed up to their black star. In fact, attendance actually fell, though not as much as might have been expected, since the 1949 club was coming off a pennant-winning season.

Other Early Black Braves

Despite concern about Jethroe's loneliness, he remained the only black player on the Braves roster in 1950. The companionship issue was addressed before the 1951 campaign when

Braves drafted speedy Puerto Rican outfielder Luis Marquez from the Indians organization to keep Jethroe company on the road, while also providing a little competition for the center field job. Marquez, who was called "Heater" because of his great speed, was even tabbed as "another Sam Jethroe." But Marquez, who had batted over .400 to lead the Negro National League in 1947, didn't hit in Boston and was shuffled back to the Braves' Milwaukee farm club in the American Association after the season. Meanwhile Jethroe improved on his fine freshman season and was joined on the Braves' roster by former Negro League stars Buster Clarkson and George Crowe in 1952.

Clarkson, who played football at Wilberforce College, was a longtime Negro League star.[17] In his first season in Organized Baseball in 1948, he led the Provincial League in homers. Clarkson joined the Braves organization during the 1950 season, and after hitting .343 for Milwaukee in 1951, he got his got his first taste of the big leagues on April 30, 1952. The ever-supportive Boston press heralded his arrival by describing him as "a comparatively ancient colored shortstop."[18] Depending on the source, Clarkson was at least 36 and possibly as old as 39 in 1952 when he got a one-month, 25-at-bat trial before being returned to Milwaukee. Two years later, he would lead the Texas League with 42 homers.

Though Jethroe was the first black player to play for the Braves, first baseman George Crowe had signed with the franchise a year before his arrival. Like Clarkson, Crowe had an impressive background in another sport, having been selected hoop-crazy Indiana's first Mr. Basketball in 1939 before starring for the University of Indianapolis.[19] He later played a season in the National Basketball League before turning to baseball full time. Crowe spent his first three years in Organized Baseball tearing up the minor leagues without reaching the majors. It was bad enough that the Braves made Crowe, who was already in his late twenties, labor on the farm for so long without giving him a chance. But after he finally got an opportunity in 1952 and was out-hitting his first base competition, Earl Torgeson, the Braves sent him back to the minors to help their Milwaukee farm club capture the American Association pennant. *The Sporting News* announced, "Braves in Reverse Play, Bolster Farm Team with First Stringer." The article went on to make it clear that Crowe, the Braves third leading hitter at time, would not suffer a cut in pay for helping the Brewers out. It may have been the only time in baseball history that a first-string major leaguer was farmed out to bolster a minor league team.[20]

While the first black Braves were having their problems in Boston, the franchise was laying the foundation for a dynasty of which young black players were an integral part. Clarkson and veteran Negro League first baseman Len Pearson had been the first black players to perform for the Braves' Milwaukee farm club in 1950.[21] The Braves' Denver Bears farm club of the Class A Western League signed their first black players, infielder Pablo Bernard and pitcher Alberto Osorio, who were slotted to become the first black players in the Western League since Bud Fowler played with Topeka in the 1880s.[22] But they both ended up spending the 1950s season with the Braves' Ventura affiliate in the California League. Meanwhile the Eau Claire farm club of the Northern League became a starting point for young black prospects on their way up the organizational ladder. Outfielder Billy Bruton and pitcher Roy White became the first black players to play there in 1950, and the next year outfielder Horace Garner led the circuit in hitting.[23] Garner would never get a big league shot, despite impressive minor league numbers, while White would mysteriously disappear from Organized Baseball after posting a spectacular 16–3 record in the PONY League in 1954. Bruton, however, would go on to become the first black player to make the big leagues without prior Negro League experience.

The Braves hit the jackpot in 1952 when the contract of 18-year-old shortstop Hank Aaron was purchased from the legendary Negro League Indianapolis Clowns. Aaron, who would eventually break baseball's all-time career home run mark, and first-year outfielder Wes Covington, who would also make his mark as a big league slugger, ranked second and third in the Northern League in batting that year behind Joe Caffie, a young black outfielder in the Cleveland organization.

The Move to Milwaukee

Just weeks before the beginning of the 1953 season the Braves abandoned Boston for the greener pastures of Milwaukee. Bill Veeck, the city's former fair-haired boy, had set his sights on Milwaukee as a new home for his St. Louis Browns. But the Braves owned territorial rights to Milwaukee since the Brewers were one of their farm clubs, and Veeck's enemies in the exclusive fraternity of major league club owners urged Perini to beat the maverick club owner to the punch.

The new Milwaukee Braves were a spectacular success. They got off to a great start at the beginning of the 1953 season and gave the mighty Brooklyn Dodgers a surprising battle for the pennant before finishing in second place. They won 28 more games than they had in Boston the previous year and drew more than six times as many fans to new County Stadium. The first edition of the Milwaukee Braves team bore little resemblance to the last Boston Braves squad. Rookie Billy Bruton led the league in stolen bases, former Negro Leaguer Jim Pendleton enjoyed a fine rookie season as the club's fourth outfielder and backup shortstop, and freshmen hurlers Bob Buhl and Don Liddle shined. Bonus baby Johnny Antonelli, fresh from two years of military duty, moved into the number two spot in the starting rotation behind the great Warren Spahn, and another youthful returning service veteran, catcher Del Crandall, shoved Walker Cooper to the bench. Youngsters Lew Burdette and Johnny Logan came into their own, and sophomore third baseman Eddie Mathews developed into the top home run hitter in the major leagues. Joe Adcock and veteran outfielder Andy Pafko also proved to be valuable additions.

But Sam Jethroe, the club's "franchise saver" only three years earlier, was one of many who didn't make the trip to Milwaukee. He'd slumped in 1952, raising fresh suspicions about his age, and feuded with manager Charlie Grimm.[24] In the off-season, the Braves had acquired Jim Pendleton from the Dodgers to vie for the center field job. But rookie Billy Bruton beat both of them out, and Jethroe was sent to Toledo of the American Association. Like many Negro League veterans, Jethroe had neglected to count a few birthdays to enhance his value when a major league opportunity finally came knocking. Jethroe claimed to be 28 years old when he joined the Braves, but after he retired it was determined that he was actually at least 32 at the time, making him the oldest player in history to win the Rookie of the Year Award. But Jethroe didn't have anything on his center field successor in the age-falsification department. After Bruton completed a 12-year big league career, he also admitted to also having trimmed four years off his age when he signed with the Braves. Bruton, who was called the "Ebony Comet" in the minors, hit the first homer by a Milwaukee Brave in the club's opening game at County Stadium — a tenth inning game-winner. The blast was the only homer of Bruton's rookie season, but he led the league in stolen bases that year and would capture the base-stealing crown two more times before being swapped to the Detroit Tigers after the 1960 season.

The First Black Benchwarmers

All but forgotten in the jubilation of 1953 was George Crowe, the only black man to ever play for both the Boston and Milwaukee Braves. After being "demoted" to lead the Milwaukee Brewers to the American Association pennant in 1952, the Braves rewarded Crowe by turning the first base job over to newly acquired Joe Adcock the next spring. Crowe spent the unforgettable first Milwaukee Braves campaign warming the bench.

With Bruton, Crowe, and Jim Pendleton on the Braves' roster for the entire 1953 season, the franchise ranked fourth behind the Dodgers, Giants, and Indians in terms of black employment. More significantly, in an era when only the best black players got a shot at the big leagues and few who weren't top performers were kept around, none of the Braves black players could be considered stars. Bruton was the regular center fielder, but he hit only .250 as a rookie. Crowe was a pinch-hitter and backup first baseman. And Pendleton served primarily as a reserve outfielder and emergency shortstop. In fact, the 1953 edition of the Braves was the first team to keep two black benchwarmers for an entire season. Throughout the remainder of the 1950s, the Braves would continue to show a color blindness when it came to second stringers that was remarkable for the times.

For instance, former Negro League veteran Charlie White, was kept around to back up Del Crandall behind the plate. White was the Yogi Berra of the black ballplayer community. He was known as the "King of the Mullion Men," mullion being slang for a particularly ugly guy in the black player lingo of the era. Charlie White stories abounded, and outlandish or ridiculous comments invariably began with "As Chazz White used to say...." Alex Pompez always included White on the roster of barnstorming teams he organized for the comic relief he provided rather than his bat and glove.[25]

Hank Aaron and Other Black Prospects

In addition, the Braves' minor league system featured an abundance of talented black prospects. Hank Aaron advanced to Jacksonville of the Class A South Atlantic League and led the loop in hitting after moving to second base to accommodate shortstop prospect Felix Mantilla. Horace Garner was also stationed at Jacksonville and hit over .300 for the third year in a row. Covington spent the first part of the season with Evansville before being inducted into the service, and he was replaced by former Negro League star Nate Peeples. The ace of the Evansville staff was Panamanian hurler Humberto Robinson, a 17-game-winner. And infielder Ed Charles and pitcher Winston Brown starred for Ft. Lauderdale in the Florida International League.

The tremendous strides the franchise had made in the recruitment of black players after the expensive acquisition of Jethroe was just beginning to pay off however. In 1954, Aaron arrived on the big league scene ahead of schedule, replacing injured Bobby Thomson in left field. George Crowe was dispatched to the minors, but former St. Louis Brown farmhand Charlie White won the backup catcher job, joining Aaron and holdovers Bruton and Pendleton on the roster. That year, the club finished third, shattering the previous season's attendance record with a count of more than 2.1 million fans.

In 1955, seven black players spent at least a portion of the season with the Braves, the most on any big league team. Aaron blossomed into a star, and Bruton led the league in stolen bases for the third-straight year. Pendleton, White, rookie Humberto Robinson, and lefty newcomer Roberto Vargas did little to help the club, but George Crowe returned from the minors to make a significant contribution. Despite a spectacular 1954 campaign with Toledo, Crowe had been bypassed in the post-season big league draft and remained the property of the Braves. After spending the first half of the 1955 season on the bench, he took over at first base when regular Joe Adcock went down with an injury. Crowe actually put up better batting and fielding stats the last half of the season than Adcock had in the first half. But when the curtain rose on the 1956 campaign Adcock was holding down the Braves' first base spot, and Crowe was holding down a spot on the Cincinnati Reds' bench.

For the remainder of the 1950s and into the 1960s, the Braves remained one of the strongest franchises in baseball, helped greatly by a steady supply of top black talent. In 1957, Wes Covington joined Aaron and Bruton to form Major League Baseball's first all-black regular outfield and help lead the team to back-to-back pennants in 1957 and 1958. After the 1958 World Series, John Quinn returned to the East Coast, leaving Milwaukee for Philadelphia to take over as general manager of the hapless Philadelphia Phillies.

The Braves were getting long in the tooth as the 1950s drew to a close. In 1959, they ended the regular season tied for first place with the Los Angeles Dodgers but lost the best-of-three play-off for the flag. Fred Haney, who had succeeded Charlie Grimm as manager of the Braves in 1957, resigned after the playoff. In Hank Aaron's autobiography, Haney is assigned blame for the Braves'

As a member of the Atlanta Braves, Hank Aaron battled bigotry in his successful pursuit of Babe Ruth's career home run record and later became a high ranking front office executive (1964 Topps Giant Issue card).

subsequent decline. It's alleged that Haney was reluctant to have more than four black players on the field at a time, thus depriving talented young black players like Felix Mantilla and Juan Pizarro of the opportunity to develop because three "black slots" were monopolized by the club's regular outfielders. Mantilla is quoted as saying, "A lot of teams had an unwritten rule that you could have five white guys and four black guys on the field, but you crossed the line when you had five black and four white guys.... Fred Haney wouldn't put five black players on the field unless it was an emergency and there was nothing else he could do. If somebody was hurt and I had to fill in a shortstop or second base, that gave us four black guys, and Pizarro wouldn't pitch."[26]

The Early 1960s

Through the decade of the 1960s, the Braves would rank as one of Major League Baseball's leaders in acquiring and developing black talent. During the decade, the farm system cranked out young black stars like Lee Maye, Mack Jones, Rico Carty, Felix Millan, Ralph Garr, and Dusty Baker to join Aaron in the Braves' lineup. But others, like Felix Mantilla, Juan Pizarro, Ed Charles, John Wyatt, Manny Jiminez, Ellie Hendricks, Sandy Alomar Sr., Cito Gaston, Bill Robinson, and Diego Segui, would eventually have to move to other organizations to find success after maturing in the Braves' system.

Chuck Dressen, who had managed the Brooklyn Dodgers during the heyday of Robinson, Campanella, and Newcombe, took over the Milwaukee reins in 1960, and the club finished second, seven lengths behind the Pirates. From 1961 through 1964, they descended from fourth to fifth to sixth under Dressen, Birdie Tebbetts, and Bobby Bragan. Attendance plummeted, and rumors of another franchise move grew stronger. In 1962, Perini had sold out to Chicago insurance executive William Bartholomay, who wanted to shift the team to fast-growing Atlanta, Georgia. A fifth-place finish in 1964, accompanied by poor attendance, cemented the Braves' fate, although legal challenges forced them to remain in Milwaukee for another fifth-place showing in 1965.

The Move to the Deep South

The move to Atlanta in 1966 filled the Braves' black stars with apprehension. In Atlanta, they would be the first major league team located in the Deep South. Aaron, in fact, talked openly about not wanting to come to Atlanta.[27] Thankfully, the franchise chose to remain the Braves rather than adopt the name of the minor league team that had represented the city since 1902, the "Crackers."

From 1962 through 1965, the Atlanta Crackers were an integrated International League squad, but prior to that the Crackers belonged to the old Southern Association. The Southern Association had remained defiantly segregated until it ceased operations after the 1961 campaign, with one brief exception. In 1954, former Negro Leaguer Nate Peeples trained with the Crackers, a Braves Class AA farm club at the time. The 27-year-old outfielder, a former Dodger farmhand, had joined the Braves' organization the previous season and earned a promotional opportunity with an excellent season in the Class B Three I League.

Peeples was the sensation of the Crackers' training camp, topping off his performance with a home run off major league hurler Wilmer Mizell in a exhibition contest against Mizell's Fort McPherson squad, the only hit the Crackers managed that day.[28] Yet Peeples was dispatched to Jacksonville of the South Atlantic League after only four at-bats as the Crackers apparently succumbed to pressure from other clubs in the circuit.[29] Despite assertions by club officials that "the door was still open for Negroes in the league," Peeples would be the only black player in the league's history.[30] He would remain in the Braves' system for another five years, eventually reaching Triple A, but never getting a major league trial.

By the mid–1960s, Atlanta had become the hub of black political action, thanks to the presence of Dr. Martin Luther King's Southern Christian Leadership Conference. The city's black community was one of the brightest, most populous, and most influential in the country. Atlanta and the South in general had made big strides since Jackie Robinson's time, and many of the old Jim Crow laws had been struck down. Atlanta aspired to be the Capital of the New South, but it was still the Heart of Dixie. As the new Atlanta Braves opened the 1966 season, staunch segregationist Lester Maddox was running for governor of Georgia, an election he would win. Among the candidates he defeated for the Democratic nomination was future United States President Jimmy Carter. Maddox had risen to prominence when he refused to serve black customers in his Atlanta restaurant, barring the door armed with an axe handle that would become his trademark. Two years earlier, he had narrowly lost a bid to become the Mayor of Atlanta.

According to Aaron, "[In Atlanta] it was made perfectly clear to us from the very beginning that we weren't in Milwaukee anymore. There was often a hate mail letter or two in the mail, and I was always concerned about Barbara and the kids being abused when they went to the ballpark. If nothing else, they would hear me being called some of the same names that had burned my ears thirteen years before in the Sally League."[31]

The Braves' contingent of black stars, which included sluggers Felipe Alou, Rico Carty, and Mack Jones, in addition to Aaron, survived the southern migration and eventually came to appreciate the hitter-friendly confines of Atlanta's Fulton County Stadium, if not traditional southern hospitality. But the move made little difference in the standings for the Braves. They placed fifth again in 1966 as Paul Richards took over as general manager and Billy Hitchcock took charge of the dugout. In 1967, they fell to seventh place, the franchise's lowest finish since its last year in Boston.

In 1968, the Braves improved to fifth place under Richards' protégé Luman Harris, and Hank Aaron became the first black player to be honored with his own night in Atlanta.[32] That August, Satchel Paige, age 62 or so, was added to the roster so that he could accrue enough time to qualify for a big league pension. Paige's job title was advisor, and his duties primarily consisted of sitting in a rocker in the Braves' bullpen. But the old-timer grumbled incessantly about not getting a chance to pitch. Before the last game of the season, he finally took the mound for two exhibition innings to shut down a patchwork lineup that included Aaron.[33]

Paige was still around in 1969 and became something of a good luck charm for the Braves as they captured the National League Western Division title. But Paige was released late in the season after getting his pension time, and "The Miracle New York Mets" swept the Braves in the League Championship Series. The 1969 squad featured four hard-hitting black outfielders: Aaron, Carty, Felipe Alou, and Tony Gonzalez. In addition, former Giant and Cardinal Orlando Cepeda manned first base, and second baseman Felix Millan teamed with the shortstop tandem of Sonny Jackson and Gil Garrido in the middle. Future stars Ralph Garr and Dusty Baker and Hank's younger brother Tommie Aaron also found some playing time with the club. Although much bigger than Hank, Tommie failed to inherit the "batting gene," swatting 742 fewer career homers than his older sibling.

The All-Time Home Run King

The Braves were also-rans through the 1970s. The highlight of the decade was Aaron's pursuit of Babe Ruth's all-time career home run record, which he topped in 1974 amid numerous racial insults and threats against his life. It is somewhat ironic that the last remaining former Negro Leaguer bested the record of the former Yankee great in Major League Baseball's first southern outpost. After the 1975 season, Aaron returned to Milwaukee, where he would finish out his major league career as a designated hitter for the American League Milwaukee Brewers.

In 1976, communications mogul Ted Turner purchased control of the franchise and promptly appointed the Braves' Farm System Director and former farmhand Bill Lucas to the position of vice president of Player Personnel, the first black executive to hold such a key position. Lucas died suddenly of a massive stroke in 1979, but in 1982 Hank Aaron returned to the Braves' fold as vice president and director of player development, again giving the franchise one of the few minorities in a Major League Baseball upper-management position. That year, the club captured the Division Championship under Aaron's former teammate Joe Torre. As a top executive, Aaron helped lay the groundwork for an unparalleled Braves dynasty in Atlanta. From 1992 through 2005, the club finished first in their division each year with the exception of the strike-abbreviated 1994 campaign.

In 1999, baseball demonstrated how much official attitudes toward bigotry had changed when Braves' relief ace John Rocker popped off about gays and various ethnic groups in New York City, tossing in a few racial slurs about a black teammate in the process. Rocker was suspended for his comments and soon traded by the Braves when his presence resulted in clubhouse unrest. By the age of 28, the unrepentant lefthander's career was in ruins, and his mouth had run him out of baseball.[34]

Chapter 8

THE CHICAGO WHITE SOX

The first big league teams to give black players a legitimate chance benefited greatly from their actions, but none profited more than the Chicago White Sox did from their daring acquisition of Orestes "Minnie" Minoso from the Cleveland Indians. His arrival early in the 1951 season immediately transformed the Sox from American League doormats into serious contenders.

In 1950, the White Sox lost 94 games on their way to sixth place in the American League standings, their seventh-straight second-division finish. They were in fifth place the next year when they made a daring trade to acquire Minoso, a speedy outfielder-third baseman who hadn't been able to find regular work in Cleveland. The first black player to wear a White Sox uniform was an immediate sensation in Chicago. He debuted on May 1, 1951, with a home run against the New York Yankees at Comiskey Park. The Sox lost their first three games with Minoso in the lineup, but then reeled off 20 victories in their next 22 contests, vaulting into first place by the end of May. By mid–June, their lead over the second-place Yankees had grown to 4½ games, and the Cinderella team was the talk of the baseball world.

Despite being hopelessly outgunned, the scrappy, underdog squad remained in first place throughout the entire month of June and valiantly battled the powerful Bronx Bombers for the top spot into late July. Though the Sox faded to fourth place by the end of the season, new life had been injected into the moribund franchise. Furthermore, the groundwork had been laid for future success as attendance swelled to an all-time franchise high of 1,328,234 fans, almost 70 percent more than the previous season.

Franchise History

Charles Comiskey, often referred to as "the Old Roman," founded the White Sox in 1900 as an entry in Ban Johnson's Western League. They became a major league franchise the next year when the Western League morphed into the American League and promptly captured the first American League pennant. They won another pennant and beat the heavily-favored cross-town Cubs in the 1906 World Series with a squad that became famous as the "Hitless Wonders." By 1917, Comiskey had built another powerful championship team that bested the New Giants in the World Series. After falling to sixth in the war-shortened 1918 campaign, the Sox came roaring back to recapture the 1919 pennant. Heavily favored to beat the Cincinnati Reds for the World Championship, the Sox mysteriously lost amid persistent rumors of a gambling conspiracy to throw the Series to Cincinnati. In the last days of the 1920 season, with the Sox still in the pennant race, newly appointed Commissioner of Baseball Judge Kenesaw

Mountain Landis permanently banned eight "Black Sox" players from Organized Baseball for their roles in the fix.

Gutted by the loss of incomparable slugger Shoeless Joe Jackson, twenty-game winning pitchers Eddie Cicotte and Lefty Williams, standout third baseman Buck Weaver, power-hitting center fielder Happy Felsch, shortstop Swede Risberg, first baseman Chick Gandil, and utilityman Fred McMullin, the White Sox sank to seventh place in 1921. They remained near the bottom of the American League standings for the next 30 years, except for a few scattered fourth-place finishes and one third-place showing. Ill fortune continued to hound the franchise. Risberg's replacement at shortstop, Harvey McClellan, died of blood poisoning in mid-career. After the best season of his career, star center fielder Johnny Mostil attempted suicide and never fully recovered. Ace hurler Monty Stratton's career ended at age 26 when a hunting accident resulted in the loss of his right leg. And nifty fielding veteran second baseman Jackie Hayes suddenly went blind in one eye in spring training a few years later.

The Old Roman died in 1931, leaving the responsibility for day-to-day operation of the club to his son Louis, a rotund 46-year-old who had contracted scarlet fever in his mid-twenties and was forced to carry an oxygen mask with him at all times.[1] Louis Comiskey's greatest contribution to the franchise was hiring Jimmy Dykes, who managed the club from 1934 until he resigned early in the 1946 season. Dykes restored a measure of respectability in terms of performance, but his greatest contribution to the Sox cause may have been keeping the press distracted with his engaging personality and entertaining baseball tales.

A leadership void opened when Louis Comiskey died in 1939, leaving the club divided among his heirs. Though the Comiskey family still owned the club, it would be incorrect to say that they controlled it. Under the haphazard stewardship of Louis' widow, Grace Comiskey, the franchise became a stagnant operation with "confusion and chaos the order of the day."[2] On the field, the Sox reached rock bottom in 1948 when they lost 101 games and finished in the American League cellar. That year, wise guys in the press box tagged Chicago the "Basement Burg" as the cross-town Cubs also brought up the National League rear.[3] Furthermore, there seemed little hope for improvement. The Sox's best player was veteran Luke Appling, a living White Sox legend who had been born more than 40 years earlier and remained at shortstop despite having lost any semblance of normal middle-infielder range.

Frank Lane Takes Over as General Manager

But young Chuck Comiskey, who had been warming up as an executive in the Sox's minor league system, was finally ready to take over at age 22. Though inexperienced, young Comiskey wasn't afraid to shake things up — and things certainly needed it. After the disastrous 1948 campaign, his first major move was to bring in 52-year-old Frank Lane to serve as general manager. Lane had been a minor league player and ran a semipro league before he was hired by Larry MacPhail to work in the Cincinnati Reds' front office in 1933. Despite his age, he was the first baseball executive to enlist during World War II, and when he got out of the service MacPhail, who had moved to the Yankees, hired him to run their Kansas City franchise in the American Association. Lane had risen to the position of president of the American Association when the White Sox hired him to replace Leslie O'Connor.

Lane, who would soon come to be known as "Frantic Frank," started churning things up right away by trading old favorites like Taft Wright and Joe Haynes. In addition to the virtually stationary Appling at shortstop, Lane inherited an old-fashioned taskmaster named

Jack Onslow to whom young Comiskey had promised the Sox managerial job. He promptly set about trying to get rid of both of them. In Lane's first season, the Sox crept up to sixth place. They finished sixth again in 1950, but Lane replaced both Onslow and Appling while almost completely revamping the roster. He engineered fantastic deals that brought in left-hander Billy Pierce, who would rival Whitey Ford as the best lefthander in the American League throughout the 1950s, and under-sized second baseman Nellie Fox, a future Hall of Famer, for a couple of journeymen performers. He also managed to pry classy young shortstop Chico Carrasquel away from Branch Rickey and the Brooklyn Dodgers to supplant Appling.

The Arrival of Paul Richards and Minnie Minoso

Before the 1951 season, Lane made another brilliant move when he hired Paul Richards, a former big league catcher from Waxahachie, Texas, to take over the managerial reins. Along with Lane, Richards would be the co-architect of the White Sox stunning turnaround. Though he managed 12 years in the major leagues without winning a pennant, Richards earned a reputation as a brilliant and innovative strategist and an astute judge of talent. Despite his rural Texas roots, he seemed to keenly appreciate the talents of black players. While managing Buf-

falo of the International League Richards tabbed Montreal's Roy Campanella as "the best catcher in the business — major or minor leagues" and went on to say, "If (Rickey) doesn't bring that guy up, he may as well go out of the emancipation business."[4] Later, Richards invented the strategy of walking the pitcher batting ahead of Montreal leadoff hitter Sam Jethroe in order to bottle up the speedster on the bases.[5] Richards managed the Seattle Rainiers in 1950 and was very familiar with Minnie Minoso, who had spent the campaign tearing up the Pacific Coast League with San Diego. Convinced Minoso could be a major league star, Richards lobbied for his acquisition after he was hired to manage the White Sox.[6]

Richards' enthusiastic scouting report notwithstanding, the Minoso trade was a huge gamble on Lane's part. The deal was a three-way transaction involving the White Sox, Indians, and Philadelphia Athletics. The White Sox exchanged slugger Gus Zernial and hustling outfielder Dave Philley for Minoso and outfielder Paul Lehner. Philley for Lehner was basically a wash, so in essence the Sox swapped Zernial for Minoso even up. The popular Zernial had just set a new franchise home run record in 1950 while Minoso was an unproven rookie — and a relatively elderly one to boot. Although his true

Manager Paul Richards, the mastermind of the "Go-Go Sox" of the early 1950s, was instrumental in Minoso's acquisition (1952 Bowman card).

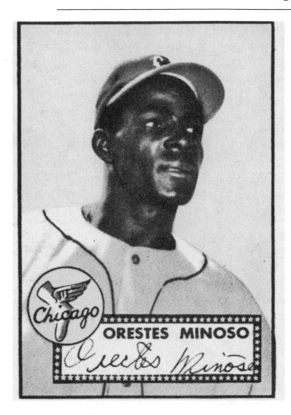

The daring 1951 acquisition of Minnie Minoso, the first black performer on the White Sox, immediately transformed the club from a lackluster second division outfit into a serious contender (1952 Topps card).

age remains a point of controversy to this day, Minoso was thought to be in his late twenties in 1951, about the same age as the more accomplished Zernial.

Minoso would be under intense pressure to succeed. In fact, he may have been placed under as much pressure as any player in the history of the game, including Jackie Robinson. When he debuted with the Sox, he was one of only four black players in the American League. Upon his acquisition, the White Sox became the only integrated team in the league besides Cleveland and only the fifth integrated squad in the major leagues. Replacing a popular star like Zernial would have been tough enough without the additional pressure of also being the first black player to represent Chicago — the second largest city in the country at the time and one that was deeply divided along both ethnic and racial lines.

The Integration Decision

In 1950, the Chicago metropolitan area had a non-white population in excess of 600,000 people, the second largest in the country.[7] Yet in the early 1950s most Chicago restaurants and hotels wouldn't accommodate black customers, and the city government seemed intent on containing the movement of black citizens to certain areas by using highways and other infrastructure to cordon off ghetto areas. The executive director of the Chicago Urban League called Chicago the most racially segregated city in the country, adding that it was a place where "a Negro dare not step out of the environs of his race."[8]

Nevertheless, the White Sox were rumored to be interested in signing hard-throwing Gentry "Jeep" Jessup of the Chicago American Giants back in 1947, but nothing came of it.[9] Shortly after arriving in Chicago, Lane indicated that he was interested in obtaining a "first class Negro player" and reportedly bid for Dodgers prospects Sam Jethroe and Don Newcombe.[10] Later, Lane also showed an interest in Monte Irvin, then with the Giants' Jersey City farm club.[11]

Apparently discouraged by the price tags other clubs were putting on their black prospects, Lane decided to find his own. He hired John Donaldson, a former Negro League star, to be the first black scout for a major league franchise.[12] The next year, Donaldson signed hard-hitting first baseman Bob Boyd of the Memphis Red Sox and Indianapolis Clowns catcher Sam Hairston after the conclusion of the Negro League season.

minor league apprenticeships were usually in order for the first black players in Organized Baseball. Even veteran superstars of black baseball like Robinson, Campanella, Newcombe,

Irvin, Easter, and Jethroe were required to prove themselves in the minor leagues before graduating to the majors. By the beginning of the 1950s, Organized Baseball was beginning to dig down into the second tier of Negro League stars. Furthermore, three years into the integration process, the novelty appeal of black players had worn off. Fans would willingly pay to see them for their baseball skills — not for the color of their skin. Therefore, this second wave of lesser-accomplished veterans could expect even more protracted minor league stints.

Boyd and Hairston were assigned to Colorado Springs in the Class A Western League for the last part of the 1950 season. From 1947 through 1950, Boyd had recorded batting marks of .339, .376, .375, and .356 for Memphis in the Negro American League while Hairston captured the league triple crown with Indianapolis in 1950. Both performed exceptionally for Colorado Springs, but it was determined that the 31-year-old Hairston and Boyd, who was also 31 although he was only thought to be 25 at the time, needed more "seasoning," and they were returned to the minors for the 1951 campaign.[13]

Boyd, who Bill James considers to have been the best player in the Negro League in 1949, hit .342 with Sacramento of the Pacific Coast League in 1951 and a league-leading .320 for Seattle in 1952 before getting an extended big league opportunity.[14] Though he was fast and considered a decent glove man, Boyd didn't have much power for a first baseman. Richards spent a few seasons trying to convert him into an outfielder, but Boyd was never able to crack the Sox regular lineup. He would appear in only 96 major league games for the White Sox in parts of three seasons before eventually finding success in Baltimore.

Sam Hairston found even less opportunity with the White Sox, at least as a player. Hairston started the 1951 season in Sacramento along with Boyd. In mid-season, he joined Minoso in Chicago, but got only five at-bats in more than a month with the club before being shipped back to the minors — apparently to make room for Boyd to get a late-season trial. Instead of being returned to Sacramento, however, Hairston was demoted all the way back down to Colorado Springs. Hairston would never get another big league opportunity, despite compiling impressive minor league statistics over the next decade. Instead, he went on to become one of baseball's first black "organization men," spending his career in the White Sox minor league system and staying with the organization as a scout and minor league coach after his career as an active player ended in 1960. Sam and his son John became the first black father/son combination to play in the major leagues when John came up to the Cubs in 1969. The next year, he signed another son, Jerry, to a White Sox contract. Jerry developed into a pinch-hitting specialist and played 14 seasons in the major leagues, all but one with the White Sox. In 1998, Jerry Jr. debuted with the Baltimore Orioles, making the Hairston family one of the major leagues' few three-generation families and its first black one.

Minoso also fell into the second tier of Negro League stars. Despite being a Negro League all-star before signing with the Cleveland Indians after the close of the 1948 Negro League season, he was initially assigned to Dayton in the Class A Central League. The next year, Minoso began the season with the Indians before being demoted to San Diego in the Pacific Coast League after only nine games. After starring for two seasons in San Diego without getting recalled, Minoso began the 1951 season with the Indians. Filling in for injured Luke Easter, he appeared in seven of the Indians' first ten games at first base before being traded to the White Sox.

Because Minoso is Cuban, Hairston is sometimes listed as the first black player to play for the White Sox. Ironically, the White Sox were one of the earliest team to recruit Latino players. In 1922, the White Sox extended a trial to Cuban-born Jose Acosta, who had played in Negro Leagues earlier in his career. In 1946, they traded for Venezuelan pitcher Alex Carrasquel, "whose skin was dark enough to stir debate about violations of the odious 'gentlemen's agreement.'"[15] Carrasquel jumped to the Mexican League before the 1946 campaign and didn't suit up for the White Sox until 1949. Early in the 1947 season, months before the Indians broke the American League color line with Larry Doby, the Sox auditioned former Cub hurler Hi Bithorn, a Puerto Rican. The club's first prominent Latino performer, however, was Venezuelan shortstop Chico Carrasquel, a nephew of Alex Carrasquel, who arrived a year before Minoso.

Minoso and the Go! Go! White Sox

With Minoso, Carrasquel, Nellie Fox, and rookie center fielder Jim Busby leading the charge, the heretofore plodding Pale Hose became known as the "Go! Go! Sox" for their dashing speed and daring base running. In 1951, they sent six players to the All-Star Game and established a new all-time franchise attendance record. Minoso led the league in steals, finished runner-up in batting, and placed fourth in Most Valuable Player balloting. Incredibly, the Baseball Writers Association selected Gil McDougald of the Yankees as Rookie of the Year despite the fact that Minoso had bested him in every major offensive category except homers.

But the White Sox failed to become a leader in the retention and development of black players, despite the success that Minoso brought to the franchise. During most of Minoso's initial seven-year tour of duty with the White Sox, he was the club's only black player of note. During that time, only six other black players joined him on the roster, mostly for short spells.

The problem was not reluctance on the part of Lane or Richards to bring in additional black players. The White Sox simply didn't have much of a farm system. Lane had built them into contenders by cunning trades rather than the development of young talent, and that methodology would sustain them throughout the decade of the 1950s. All of the key players on the 1951 squad, except for rookie center fielder Jim Busby, were acquired from other organizations. The 1959 pennant-winning squad was assembled in much the same manner, with shortstop Luis Aparicio and center fielder Jim Landis the only front-liners developed in the Sox system.

For several years in the 1950s, the franchise didn't even have a Triple A affiliate, and the situation was worse for black prospects because the Sox Double A farm club was the Memphis Chicks of the segregated Southern Association. In 1952, for instance, the Sox terminated their relationship with Sacramento of the Pacific Coast League and therefore had to loan Boyd to the independent Seattle Rainiers and send Hairston back Colorado Springs, well below his ability level. Three other former Negro League veterans who played for Colorado Springs in 1951, pitcher Willie Powell and infielders Curley Williams and Jesse Douglas, drifted into other organizations when there was no room for them to advance in the White Sox chain. During the 1951 season, the Sox also acquired 26-year-old Negro League ace Gene Collins and had to assign him to Waterloo in the Class B Three I League. The next year, the Sox signed 29-year-old former Kansas City Monarch ace Connie Johnson and 33-year-old former Homestead Gray hurler Bill Pope and started them out in Class A ball with Colorado Springs.

At the big league level, the Sox acquired veteran Mexican and Negro League star Hector "Hot Rod" Rodriguez from the Brooklyn Dodgers organization to handle third base in 1952. Rodriguez was almost 32 years old and had been playing professionally for more than ten years when he made his first major league appearance for the White Sox. A good gloveman,

Rodriguez got off to a sizzling start and was hitting well over .300 when he injured his foot. He refused to come out of the lineup and slumped over the second half of the season.[16] The next year, he was back in Triple A. Rodriguez's situation was typical of the pressure that black players were under to perform. Even hurt, he gave the club the best third base play they'd seen in years. Yet he was considered a failure and quickly returned to the minors, never to receive a second look.

Both Boyd and Johnson began the 1953 campaign with the White Sox, but early in the season they were sent down together to Charleston in the American Association where the Sox shared a working agreement with Washington Senators. Both were recalled by the Sox during the season and enjoyed moderately successful rookie campaigns. At the beginning of the 1954 season, Johnson was assigned to the independent Toronto Maple Leafs of the International League, while Boyd started the season in left field for the White Sox. Boyd enjoyed a sensational spring, but when his bat cooled off he was sold to Houston in the St. Louis Cardinals farm system. The sale of Boyd left Minoso as the only black player on the club again; a situation he would endure through the rest of the 1954 campaign and the first half of the 1955 campaign before Johnson was recalled.

Meanwhile, the organization was beginning to show some initiative in recruiting young black prospects. In 1953, they signed schoolboy catcher Earl Battey, who would become only the sixth black man to play for the White Sox when he debuted late in the 1955 season. Battey would eventually develop into an all-star receiver, but unfortunately (maybe predictably) it wouldn't be in Chicago. After wasting much of his youth backing up Sherm Lollar, Battey was swapped to the Washington Senators in 1960 just as Lollar's career went into decline. Battey became the first black star for the Washington Senators–Minnesota Twins franchise, while the White Sox struggled to find a replacement for Lollar throughout the 1960s.

Before the 1955 season, the White Sox made another notable foray into the black prospect market by signing Grover "Deacon" Jones, the first black player to be honored by the Baseball Hall of Fame. As a schoolboy, Jones was named the American Legion Player of the Year in 1951, thus becoming the first black player to have his name inscribed on a plaque in Cooperstown.[17] He hit over .400 in his second year in Organized Baseball, but an arm injury short-circuited his promising career.[18] Jones did make it to the big time for a couple of cups of coffee in the 1960s and subsequently became a respected major league batting coach.

The Departures of Richards and Lane

Richards departed late in the 1954 campaign to take over as manager and general manager of the Baltimore Orioles, and Lane followed him out of Chicago a year later to become general manager of the St. Louis Cardinals. His relationship with Chuck Comiskey, who desired a greater role in running the club, had become strained, and Lane was tired of the interference.[19]

Despite overseeing the wildly successful integration of the White Sox, both Richards and Lane had their detractors. Bob Boyd, whose career was stymied in Chicago but later revived in Baltimore under Richards, had conflicting emotions about him. "Strangely enough, one of the men who didn't like black players was Paul Richards," said Boyd. "Yet in some ways he was the greatest man I ever played for and the smartest manager. But he was prejudiced. He didn't like blacks. I was in enough team meetings where he would talk about the black players who were on the team coming in and he wouldn't say very nice things about them. Yet he wanted me playing for him when he went to the Orioles."[20]

On the other hand, Minnie Minoso, the black player who played the most under Richards, considered him "the best manager I would ever have in baseball."[21] Minoso was also a big fan of Frank Lane, who he often referred to as "Daddy Number Two."[22] But, other than Minoso, "Trader Lane" couldn't seem to get his hands on another first-rate black player for the White Sox. After he left the White Sox, Richards claimed that Lane had passed up the opportunity to get Ernie Banks before he signed with the Cubs.[23] But Lane did hire the first black scout and signed the first black players for the Sox system at a time when few other teams were integrating. And he certainly went out on a limb to acquire Minoso.

Ironically, when Chuck Comiskey and his brother-in-law Johnny Rigney, an ex–Sox hurler, assumed command after Lane departed, the White Sox finally came up with another top-flight black player. Following the conclusion of the 1955 World Series, they acquired veteran Larry Doby from Cleveland to flank Minoso in the outfield.

Marty Marion, long-time St. Louis Cardinal shortstop and former manager of both the Cardinals and St. Louis Browns, succeeded Richards in 1955. As a player with the Cards, Marion was suspected of being one of the ringleaders of the aborted strike attempt against Jackie Robinson,[24] but he subsequently seemed to have no problems managing black players. In his autobiography, Satchel Paige referred to Marion as a "fine guy," and Minoso considered him a good manager.[25] Larry Doby also thought highly of Marion. "He might have been ahead of his time in dealing with individuals as individuals and as human beings," opined Doby.[26] Both Minoso and Doby enjoyed fine 1956 seasons, but the Sox again finished third behind the Yankees and Indians for the fourth straight year.

Al Lopez Comes to Chicago

True to form, the Sox immediately took a step back from the integration forefront the next season. The front office had become disenchanted with Marion and, when Al Lopez left the Indians, they quickly persuaded him to take over as manager of the White Sox. Lopez had occupied the manager's seat in Cleveland when both Minoso and Doby were traded away, and within a year he oversaw the disposal of the pair again despite the club's improvement to second place in 1957. Before the 1958 season, Doby was traded to Baltimore, and Minoso was swapped back to Cleveland.

Though extremely unpopular with Chicago fans, the Minoso trade worked out well for the White Sox. In return for Minoso, they received future 300-game-winner Early Wynn and outfielder Al Smith, a hustling outfielder who lacked flash — an old Lopez favorite from their Cleveland days. The unfortunate Smith took the brunt of the fan's displeasure over the trade of their long-time favorite. He was booed mercilessly, and it affected his performance. It was especially difficult for him to hide since he replaced Minoso in left field and was conspicuous as the club's only black player that year besides backup catcher Battey.

Bill Veeck and the 1959 Pennant

The irrepressible Bill Veeck somehow wrested control of the White Sox from the Comiskey family shortly before the 1959 season, and the team promptly captured its first pennant since the Black Sox debacle 40 years earlier.

Veeck didn't have much chance to impact the opening day roster as Smith and Battey were again the only two black players on the squad. But when highly touted youngsters Johnny Callison and Norm Cash failed to provide much early season offense, it became clear that Lopez desperately needed a power hitter, preferably of the left-handed variety. At least Veeck knew better than to try to pick up Luke Easter or Dave Pope from the minors. Instead he brought in Harry Simpson, another bad memory from Lopez's days in Cleveland, who was immediately consigned to the bench while aging National League refugee Del Ennis got an extended shot in left field. Undaunted, Veeck then purchased Larry Doby, hardly an old Lopez favorite, who joined Simpson on the bench. Eventually, the painful Ennis experiment came to an end, and Doby got his chance. Over the next 21 games, he started ten times in right field before giving way to Simpson, who received an even shorter trial. Eventually, Doby was sent to the minors, and Simpson was traded to the Pittsburgh Pirates for Ted Kluszewski.

Based on their records the previous year, both Doby and Simpson deserved a longer look than Ennis. Plus they were sorely needed left-handed bats and better defensive outfielders than the right-handed hitting Ennis. Yet Ennis was given 24 games to try to prove he still had it — as many chances as Doby and Simpson combined. Lopez's handling of Doby and Simpson was reminiscent of the treatment certain black players received in Cleveland. He simply didn't play them, and eventually they were sent packing. It almost cost the White Sox the pennant, but Ted Kluszewski, acquired from Pittsburgh in exchange for Simpson, ended up providing the big left-handed bat the club needed to triumph over a surprise Cleveland contender and an injury-decimated Yankee squad.

During the season, Veeck had predictably tried to persuade Lopez that the Sox could use Satchel Paige's services, but the Sox manager adamantly refused.[27] Veeck also valiantly tried to re-acquire Minoso but was rebuffed by the Indians, who were chasing the Sox for the pennant.[28]

The 1960s and Beyond

Veeck succeeded in bringing Minnie Minoso back to Chicago in 1960, a deal that sent future batting champ Norm Cash packing. That year, Minoso and Smith were the only black players on the club until promising young outfielder Floyd Robinson was brought up late in the season. But Minoso's days were numbered when Veeck sold his interests to Arthur Allyn during the 1961 season. Despite two solid seasons in his second stint with the White Sox, he was swapped to the St. Louis Cardinals in the off-season.

The unfortunate deal to re-acquire Minoso before the 1960 season did not have the blessing of Al Lopez. Nor did another ill-fated trade the Sox made that off-season in which they dealt Earl Battey to the Senators for Roy Sievers.[29]

Veeck didn't stick around long enough to have much of an impact on the White Sox integration numbers. Farm system director Ed Short took over as general manager when he left, and for the decade of the 1960s, the Sox were below average in the American League in terms of number of black performers and well under the overall major league average.

Unlike the previous decade, however, the Sox farm system developed several promising young black players during the early 1960s, including Floyd Robinson, Don Buford, Tom McCraw, Buddy Bradford, Ed Stroud, and Jim Hicks, but all failed to produce as expected in Chicago. Robinson enjoyed several fine seasons before mysteriously tailing off at the age of 29. Buford's career didn't take off until he left Chicago for Baltimore, and McCraw, Bradford, Stroud and

Hicks never hit well enough to keep regular jobs. They also traded for lefty Juan Pizarro, who developed into a top hurler for the Sox before injuring his arm at the age of 28. Veteran Al Smith remained a solid contributor until he was swapped to the Orioles after the 1962 campaign. The White Sox even brought Minoso back into the organization in 1964, but he spent most of the season with Indianapolis before Lopez sent him away one last time. The year after Lopez retired, center fielder Tommie Agee, who had failed trials with the Sox the previous two years, became only the second black player to win the American League Rookie of the Year Award.

It's difficult to say just how much the White Sox were hurt by not acquiring or developing more black players during the integration era. They finished in second or third place every year from 1952 through 1958, but never narrowed the gap to within five games of the pennant winner and usually trailed by double-digit margins. After the 1959 pennant, the Sox remained contenders until Lopez stepped down following the 1965 season, but they only really came close in 1964 when they finished a single game behind the Yankees. That year, four black performers played key roles for the Sox, about average for the league.

Eddie Stanky, who grew up in Philadelphia but later found Alabama more to his liking, took over for Lopez in 1966. As a member of the 1947 Dodgers, Stanky was opposed to Robinson's presence and was thought by manager Leo Durocher to be one of instigators of an anti–Robinson petition.[30] Later with the Giants, Stanky took great pleasure in calling black backup catcher Ray Noble "Bushman," a practice that ceased when the husky receiver found out that the real "Bushman" was a circus ape.[31] Another time, Stanky unleashed a barrage of racial epithets at Jackie Robinson before he realized that teammate Monte Irvin was standing close by.[32] For three years in St. Louis, Stanky managed the team that columnist Wendell Smith considered the most prejudiced team in the majors.[33] It's not particularly surprising that Stanky never developed a reputation for working well with black players. He lasted two-and-one-half years in the White Sox managerial post and had no better luck with black players on the Sox than Lopez. Agee tailed off badly after his fine rookie season and was swapped to the New York Mets for two-time National League batting champ Tommy Davis after the 1967 campaign. After Stanky was fired midway through the 1968 season, Lopez was coaxed out of retirement to replace him, but his health soon forced him out of the dugout. The season ended with the Sox in ninth place. Davis finished the year 35 points below his lifetime average to date; yet, he led the club in hitting. In the off-season, he was left exposed in the expansion draft and quickly scooped up by the Seattle Pilots. Davis would rebound to enjoy several more fine seasons before he was through.

Lopez came back to give it another try in 1969, but he lasted only 17 games before giving way to Don Gutteridge. The club set another new low by finishing with the tenth worst record in the newly expanded 12-team league. During the campaign, Sandy Alomar, one of the club's few black players as well as one of the few bright spots of the previous campaign, was traded to the California Angels for aging Bobby Knoop. Then rookie star Carlos May, the team's best hitter, lost part of his right thumb in an accident while on military reserve training. The White Sox ended the decade of the 1960s with one of the whitest teams in the major leagues.

The White Sox wouldn't challenge for the pennant again until general manager Roland Hemond acquired black National League superstar Dick Allen in 1972. With manager Chuck Tanner coaxing a Most Valuable Player season out of the troubled slugger, the White Sox finished second behind Oakland in the American League Western Division. But the success was short-lived both for the White Sox and Allen.

The Return of Bill Veeck

Amazingly, Bill Veeck repurchased the White Sox in 1976 and talked 67-year-old Paul Richards into returning as manager after a 15-year absence from the dugout. The results were disappointing, but the next season the Sox challenged for the pennant under one of Veeck's old Cleveland favorites, Bob Lemon.

The White Sox had a chance to change the course of history in the early 1940s. In the spring of 1942, they had first crack at 23-year-old Jackie Robinson. Robinson, who lived in Pasadena where the White Sox trained, showed up at camp with pitcher Nate Moreland seeking a tryout. But manager Jimmy Dykes turned them away, explaining that it was out of his hands.[34] More than thirty years later, however, the White Sox would make black baseball history at last. During an otherwise forgettable 1976 season, Veeck activated coach Minnie Minoso to take a few swings as a designated hitter, making him the first four-decade black performer. And the old-timer actually lined out a hit to become the oldest man to do so at the major league level — depending, that is, on which of his ages is counted. Two years later, Veeck appointed Larry Doby to manage the club, giving Doby the distinction of being the second black big league manager as well as the second black big league player. Interestingly, Doby may have also been the second black player to break into white professional basketball, although he's often cited as the first. Doby played for the Paterson entry in the American Basketball League, a forerunner of the National Basketball Association in 1947, but future Harlem Globetrotter Bobby Knight performed for the Hartford Hurricanes that season.[35]

Bill Veeck managed to engineer one more black-player-first before he sold the White Sox for the last time.

In 1980, he brought Minoso back again for a couple of pinch-hitting appearances, making him Major League Baseball's only five-decade player as well as the last former Negro Leaguer to play in the major leagues.

Chapter 9

THE PITTSBURGH PIRATES

A decade before the baseball color barrier actually fell, the Pittsburgh Pirates looked like they would be among the leaders when/if integration came about. In the 1930s, Pittsburgh was home to both the Homestead Grays and the Pittsburgh Crawfords, two of the most popular and talented teams in the Negro Leagues. Most of the greatest players in the Negro Leagues, including Satchel Paige, Josh Gibson, Buck Leonard, Cool Papa Bell, Oscar Charleston, Judy Johnson, Smokey Joe Williams, Ted "Double Duty" Radcliffe, Ray Brown, Cannonball Redding, and Willie Wells, played for one or both clubs.

The city was also home to the *Pittsburgh Courier*, one of the top black newspapers in the country and a leader in pushing for the integration of Organized Baseball. In addition, Pirates president William Benswanger was sympathetic to integration. A mild-mannered gentleman and a classical pianist in his spare time, Benswanger came out strongly in favor of integration in 1940 and seemed on the verge of action a couple of years later.[1] He was reportedly involved in two attempts to conduct big league tryouts for Negro League stars at Pittsburgh's Forbes Field in the early 1940s. First, he promised to try out four Negro League stars, Josh Gibson and Sam Bankhead of the Grays and Willie Wells and Leon Day of the Newark Eagles, who were selected in a poll conducted by the *Pittsburgh Courier*.[2] That audition never materialized. Later, again under pressure from the press — this time *The Daily Worker* — he agreed to take a look at Roy Campanella of the Baltimore Elite Giants and two other black stars, pitcher Dave Barnhill and second baseman Sammy Hughes.[3] But peer pressure from the lords of baseball trumped the newspapers, and the workout was cancelled. Benswanger also claimed, "I tried more than once to buy Josh Gibson from the Homestead Grays but Cum Posey [Grays owner] always shook me off on the matter." Posey was said to be afraid that it might start a movement that would destroy the Negro Leagues.[4]

Instead of playing a key part in demolishing baseball's color barrier, the well intentioned, but irresolute, Benswanger became a mere footnote to the integration saga. He was out of baseball before Jackie Robinson played his first game for the Brooklyn Dodgers and almost five years would pass before the Pittsburgh organization would have a black player in uniform. Instead of catching the first wave of integration, the Pirates consigned themselves to more than a decade of mediocrity.

Franchise History

Benswanger was the son-in-law of Barney Dreyfus, who acquired controlling interest in the Pittsburgh franchise in 1900. Upon Dreyfus' death in 1932, ownership passed to his widow, and Benswanger left the insurance business to take over as club president.

In the early years, the Pirates were a National League power. With the great Honus Wagner manning shortstop and Fred Clarke at the helm, they captured the 1903 pennant, but subsequently lost the first World Series in history to the upstart American League's Boston Red Sox. Six years later, behind the spectacular pitching of Babe Adams, they exacted their revenge with a victory over Ty Cobb's heavily favored Detroit Tigers. The Pirates captured another World Championship in 1925 with a lineup that included Hall of Famers Pie Traynor and Kiki Cuyler. After adding the Waner brothers, Paul and Lloyd, they won another pennant in 1927 before being swept by the New York Yankees in the World Series. Under Benswanger's stewardship, the Pirates generally remained in contention through World War II. But they slumped badly immediately after the war, establishing a franchise record with 91 losses and finishing in seventh place in 1946.

In fairness, the city of Pittsburgh had a few things working against it as a leading integration site in the late 1940s and early 1950s. The city's black population didn't explode in the 1930s as it did in New York, Philadelphia, Baltimore, Washington, and other large East Coast cities. In 1940, Pittsburgh's black population was about a third of Washington's — a much smaller city.[5] By 1950, Pittsburgh's percentage of non-white residents was the smallest of all big league cities except Boston.[6] A rise in the ratio of non-whites to total population during the 1950s was due more to a decline in total population rather than a significant increase in minority numbers. This circumstance undoubtedly lessened the attractiveness of integration to the Pirates ownership during that era.

While Jackie Robinson was making baseball history in the International League during the 1946 season, the Dreyfus family sold the Pirates to a conglomerate headed by banker Frank McKinney, owner of the Indianapolis Indians of the American Association. Besides McKinney, the group included real estate tycoon John Galbreath, attorney Tom Johnson, and entertainer Bing Crosby. Under McKinney's leadership, the franchise's already dismal fortunes continued to decline. In addition to running the Pirates, McKinney had retained ownership of the Indianapolis American Association franchise, and his partners suspected that he sometimes used the major league Pirates as a farm team for his minor league Indians.[7] After a dismal last-place finish in 1950, McKinney's partners bought him out, and Galbreath was installed as club president. One of the new president's first moves was to hire 68-year-old Branch Rickey, a much-admired friend who was out of a job after losing a power struggle with Walter O'Malley for control of the Brooklyn Dodgers.

Branch Rickey in Pittsburgh

From 1947 through 1950, McKinney and general manager Roy Hamey had made no move to acquire black players for the under-talented Pirates. That figured to change drastically with the arrival of Rickey, the father of baseball's integration movement. The results, however, would be most disappointing.

Rickey took over as executive vice president and general manager of the Pirates under a generous five-year contract with promises of virtually carte-blanche authority and an open checkbook from Galbreath. Among the staff he brought along with him from Brooklyn were his brother Frank, his son Branch Jr. (nicknamed "the Twig"), and trusted scouts Clyde Sukeforth and Howie Haak. In Pittsburgh, he inherited a disgruntled team with few productive players. The star of the team was one-dimensional slugger Ralph Kiner, a weak-armed, lead-footed outfielder, who had paced the league in homers in 1950 — the fifth of seven consecutive seasons he would lead or tie for the lead. Kiner's home runs drew fans to the ballpark, but in Rickey's opinion he did little to help the team win games, and the prima donna treatment afforded him caused hard feelings among his teammates.[8]

In Pittsburgh, Rickey also had to face the consequences of some of his earlier actions. While with the Dodgers, the Pirates had been his favorite patsies when it came to trades. Since 1947, he had sent the Pirates a slew of not-ready-for-prime-time talent from the Dodgers' farm system, along with over-the-hill problems like Hugh Casey, Kirby Higbe, Vic Lombardi, and Dixie Walker. For good measure, he even threw in Gene Mauch, who would go on to establish several short- and long-term futility records as a big league manager after completing an undistinguished playing career.

While general manager of the Cardinals, the resourceful Rickey had gotten the jump on the opposition by organizing the first farm system, which allowed him to cheaply acquire and develop talented young players. When he took over the Dodgers in 1942, he repeated this process with some success, but his real success in Brooklyn didn't occur until he mined a fresh source of inexpensive talent — black baseball players. But by the time Rickey moved to Pittsburgh, however, extensive farm systems were the rule, and the Pirates' rivals had already snapped up most of the big league-ready Negro League talent. For the first time in his career, however, Rickey had money to work with thanks to the well-heeled Galbreath, so he decided to try another method to build a champion. In his first year with the Pirates, he reportedly laid out a half million dollars for young bonus players.[9] The most notorious was pitcher Paul Pettit, a $100,000 bonus baby who contributed a single major league victory to the Pirate cause.

Rickey's honeymoon with the Pirates was brief. By the end of his first year in Pittsburgh, the franchise had spent so much money that Galbreath was forced to put up additional funds to keep the team afloat. The other partners, who had never been that enamored with Rickey in the first place, became totally disenchanted and took steps to severely curb his authority and spending power. In addition, the fans and press quickly lost patience. Pittsburgh was (and is) a working man's town, befitting its nickname "The Steel City," and its denizens never really warmed up to the scholarly, long-winded Rickey. He would spend the next four years fending off criticism as he sold or traded off any veteran of value while devoting his limited resources to try to speed up the development of the team's minor league prospects.

Shortly after taking over, Rickey had unveiled a five-year plan that targeted 1955, the last year of his contract, as the season the Pirates would blossom into a National League pennant winner. It quickly became obvious that the plan was grossly over-ambitious. Taking advantage of the even more inept Chicago Cubs, the Pirates clawed their way up to seventh place in 1951. But the next year they fielded one of the worst teams in major league history and took out an exclusive four-year lease on the National League basement.

Pittsburgh's First Black Players

One of the greatest, and the most puzzling, disappointments of Rickey's Pittsburgh days was his inability to find good black players for the team. When he took over, it was anticipated that the Pirates would immediately begin importing black players. But it wasn't until the fourth year of his reign that a black player appeared in a Pittsburgh uniform. Rickey detractors have criticized his failure to more speedily integrate the Pirates.[10] It's suspected that Negro League owners refused to deal with him because he'd never paid them for Robinson, Campanella, and Newcombe. The criticism included insinuations that maybe "The Great Emancipator" wasn't really that interested in the plight of black players now that they didn't come so cheap. In retrospect, Rickey probably would have been better off making token payments to the Negro League owners, but Rickey always eschewed tokenism. With the Dodgers, he did in fact pay a record price for Dan Bankhead's contract. By 1951, however, Negro League talent had been picked over, and the black leagues were no longer much of a factor.

The Pirates' lack of immediate success in uncovering top-flight black talent wasn't for lack of trying. Shortly after arriving in Pittsburgh, Rickey dispatched a memo to Branch Jr. that said, "I think that we will take all good colored players regardless of background, or age, or salaries. Everything hinges on ability."[11]

At the club's 1951 spring training camp, Ed "Santa Fe" Morris, a semi-pro pitching legend, became the first black player to don a Pirate uniform. He worked out with the club for a few weeks, but was not signed.[12] Early in the 1951 season, veteran hurler Roy Welmaker, winner of 16 games for San Diego the previous year, became the first black player of note to enter the Pirates system. Welmaker, who spent most of his Negro League career with the Homestead Grays, was acquired from San Diego by the Pirates' new Triple A affiliate, the Pacific Coast League Hollywood Stars.[13] He looked like a hot prospect when he opened the 1950 season with a string of victories for San Diego, but the parent Indians quickly lost interest when they discovered that he had had 36 birthdays rather than the 29 he claimed.[14] The aging lefty blew his chance for a Pirate call up with a disappointing Pacific Coast League performance. The first black player signed by the Pirates under Rickey's direction may have been catcher Valmy Thomas, who would eventually reach the majors with the New York Giants.[15] Later in the season, the organization signed their first black prospect who would someday become a Pirate, pitcher Bennie Daniels.[16]

One of the biggest obstacles facing many teams that wanted to integrate in the late 1940s and early 1950s was the location of minor league franchises, and the Pirates were no exception. With the Dodgers, Rickey had to luxury of being able to assign black prospects to teams in Canada and New England. But most of the Pirates' minor league affiliates were located in the Deep South when Rickey arrived, making the placement of black prospects problematic. The Pirates were still tied to McKinney's Indianapolis franchise as their Class AAA minor league affiliate, and while some American Association clubs had accepted black players by 1951, Indianapolis was not one of them.[17] The Pirates' Class AA franchise was the New Orleans Pelicans in the staunchly segregated Southern Association. The Charleston Rebels in the segregated South Atlantic League were their Class A affiliate. Their Class B farm clubs were Burlington in the segregated Carolina League and Waco in the segregated Big State League. Nor were the organization's Class C clubs located in Hutchinson, Kansas, and Modesto, California, or its Class D teams in Bartlesville, Oklahoma; Brunswick, Georgia; Eugene, Oregon; Mayfield, Kentucky; or Salisbury, North Carolina, hospitable spots for black players. Valmy Thomas spent his first season on loan to St. Jean in the Provincial League. Bennie Daniels, originally ticketed for Modesto, had to spend his first season on loan to Great Falls in the integrated Pioneer League. Gabe Patterson, who had begun his professional career in the Negro Leagues ten years earlier, became the first black player to take the field for the Butler, Pennsylvania, squad in the integrated Mid-Atlantic League.[18] He walked away after 31 games with a .337 lifetime average in Organized Baseball.

Rickey promptly took steps to address the farm club problem by entering into a working agreement with Hollywood. The next year, the Pirates contracted with the Denver Bears of the Western League, acquiring rights to several black players, including future major leaguers Curt Roberts and Bobby Prescott, as well as former Negro League star Ed Steele, in the process.[19] They also negotiated an agreement with Batavia of the Pennsylvania-Ontario-New York (PONY) League. This provided the Pirates with another spot to send young black prospects like Howard Jennings, the 1952 PONY League batting champ, and first baseman R.C. Stevens, who would eventually make it to Pittsburgh.[20] During the 1952 season, the organization reportedly had about a dozen black players scattered throughout their revamped farm system.[21]

After the conclusion of his first season in Pittsburgh, Rickey sent the following report to Galbreath who hopefully had become accustomed to the Mahatma's verbosity by that time:

> Our scouting program has been given considerable thought and we have planned to make a very systematic and expanded effort in the field on young Negro players in America. Also a plan in the field of commission scouting has for months been held up partly due to our financial situation. We believe the "commission scouting" will produce more players, and at less cost per player. But the overall scouting expense could within one year's time be considerably increased. If the "commission scouting" program were to develop as it could develop and as it should, it will eventually need for more manpower, more scouts. Therefore, we are holding up on it. We are going through with the program on Negro scouting, although that too could and might necessitate turning the matter of our present scouts into the field for half the summer, or perhaps all of it. The justification of this is quality, with comparatively little bonus problem. The fact is that the young American Negro scouting field has scarcely been touched at all by professional baseball. The work of the past year has, very largely, almost completely excluded Negro scouting.[22]

By the mid–1950s, Rickey employed 55 commissioned scouts, including 22 coaches of black colleges and high schools, but the gems seem to elude the Pirates.[23] Rickey was struck between a rock and a hard place. He didn't want marginal veterans, couldn't afford stars or expensive advanced prospects, and couldn't wait for raw talent to develop.

For example, superscout Howie Haak reportedly struck a deal to purchase the contract of young shortstop Ernie Banks from the Kansas City Monarchs for $6,500, but the transaction was vetoed for budgetary reasons.[24] Banks went to Chicago and enjoyed a Hall of Fame career with the Cubs. A few years later, Rickey claimed the Pirates had a chance to pick up a young outfielder named Hank Aaron from the Braves in a deal for infielder Danny O'Connell, but were forced to take veterans in a futile attempt to achieve immediate respectability instead.[25]

Before the 1952 season, Rickey attempted to acquire shortstop Jim Pendleton, a former Negro League star he'd recruited for the Dodgers several years earlier. Pendleton was stuck behind Pee Wee Reese in the Brooklyn system, but Rickey's former employers were extending no favors. Their exorbitant asking price was Pittsburgh ace Murry Dickson, a 20-game winner in 1951.[26]

The First Black Pirate?

Speedy switch-hitter Carlos Bernier joined the Pirates for the 1953 season and hit a meager .213 as their center fielder while leading the team in stolen bases. Bernier, who starred for Pacific Coast League Hollywood in 1952 after being acquired in the minor league draft, was Puerto Rican and is considered by many to be the club's first black major leaguer.

Since the "gentleman's agreement" by which black players were excluded from Organized Baseball was never recorded, it's impossible to determine if Bernier would have been permitted to participate in Organized Baseball before the color barrier fell. The informal criteria seemed to be simply that if someone in authority deemed a player to be black, he was black, and therefore ineligible to earn a living as a major league baseball player. Latin American players like Bernier were undoubtedly the bane of those individuals invested in maintaining the racial purity of Organized Baseball.

In the early days of baseball's integration, *The Sporting News* seldom failed to inform their readers of the ethnic classification of non–Caucasian players. American born players that the paper considered to be "Negro" (presumably using the same secret standard that Organized Baseball had developed) were thusly labeled. Hispanic players, on the other hand, were usually only classified by their native country, although it was sometimes considered necessary to identify a particularly dark-skinned Latino like Minnie Minoso as a "Cuban Negro." The lighter complexioned Bernier, however, was invariably identified simply as Puerto Rican. For example, a 1950 mention in *The Sporting News* makes no reference to Bernier as a Negro, yet references several other "Negro" players in the same article.[27] But confusion about Bernier's racial status evidently existed. After Bernier's rookie season with the Pirates, a reader wrote to the "Voice of the Fan" column in *The Sporting News* inquiring as to whether Bernier was the Pirates' first black player. The inconclusive answer was "Bernier is Puerto Rican."[28] Earlier, an article in *Ebony* magazine had named Bernier the Pirates' "best Negro prospect" for the 1953 season.[29]

Puerto Rican outfielder Carlos Bernier may have been the first black Pirate in 1953, though African American Curt Roberts, who debuted the next year, is often listed as the first (1954 Bowman card).

Bernier was 21 years old when he began his Organized Baseball career in 1948, which may be an indication that he wasn't able to "pass" earlier. He started with Port Chester in the Colonial League, one of the few circuits where black players were readily accepted at that time. In *Crossing the Line* by Larry Moffi and Jonathon Kronstadt, Bernier is profiled as one of the black players who debuted in the big leagues from 1947 through 1959.[30] But Jules Tygiel, author of *Baseball's Great Experiment,* did not consider him to be one of the first black players in Organized Baseball.[31] However, Larry Lester, co-founder of the Negro League Museum in Kansas City and author of several books on the Negro Leagues, regards him as a black player.[32]

The call on Bernier's racial heritage determines whether the Pirates can be considered the seventh major league team to integrate or if they fall to a ninth-place tie with the St. Louis Cardinals. For purposes of this publication, Bernier is considered to be black for no better reason than, in the author's opinion, Bernier (leading batter) looks darker-skinned than Ron Piche (leading pitcher) and Dewey Soriano (league president) on the Pacific Coast League page of the *1962 Baseball Guide*—a methodology that is probably no shakier than that used by Organized Baseball before integration.

Interestingly, Bernier may actually have been the first black player in the Pittsburgh organization. According to the record book, the Pirates picked him up in the minor league draft after the 1951 campaign. But two years earlier, in August 1949, the American Association Indianapolis Indians purchased Bernier's contract from Bristol of the Colonial League. At that time, Indianapolis was a Pittsburgh farm club owned by Frank McKinney, who also happened to own the Pirates, and managed by none other than Al Lopez. Bernier didn't last long with Indianapolis, appearing in only two contests before being returned to Bristol.[33] What's really interesting is that Indianapolis is generally not believed to have accepted black players before the 1952 season.[34] This may constitute proof that Bernier was not considered to be black, but there's also the distinct possibility that the brevity of his stay in Indianapolis may have been due to pigmentation of his skin.

To further cloud the "first black Pirate" issue, Mexican outfielder Felipe Montemayor debuted with the Pirates a week before Bernier made his first appearance in a Pittsburgh uniform. Acquired by the Pirates in the spring of Rickey's first season, Montemayor would appear in only 64 games for the Pirates in 1953 and 1955. He is generally not listed as a black player, yet he was not permitted to live with his white teammates in Florida during spring training.[35] Montemayor may have been dark-skinned enough to have been kept out of Organized Baseball when the color barrier was in force. But he played for the New Orleans Pelicans from 1951 through 1954, so evidently his skin tone wasn't too objectionable for the discriminating Southern Association.

On opening day of the 1954 season, second baseman Curt Roberts became the first African American to play for the Pirates. Roberts, who teamed with Ernie Banks to form the Kansas City Monarchs' double-play combination before entering Organized Baseball, was originally signed by the Boston Braves organization and came into the Pirates fold when they acquired an interest in the Denver Western League club in 1952. As the Pirates' regular second baseman in 1954, he sparkled in the field, but not at the plate. Roberts would never get another chance to play regularly for Pittsburgh or any other major league organization though he would star in Triple A for years. Former Boston Braves star Sam Jethroe, who Rickey originally signed for the Brooklyn Dodgers six years earlier, also began the 1954 season with the Pirates but lasted only two games. Later that season, veteran Negro League outfielder Luis Marquez received a brief trial. Meanwhile, Carlos Bernier spent the 1954 campaign

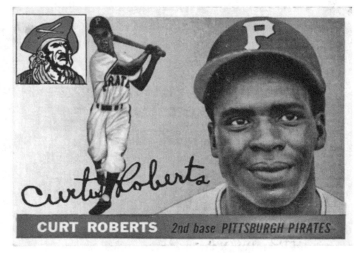

CURT ROBERTS 2nd base PITTSBURGH PIRATES

Second baseman Curt Roberts, an African American who debuted in 1954, is often listed as the first black Pirate (1955 Topps card).

back in Triple A where he would star for 11 more years without getting another big league shot.

The Acquisition of Roberto Clemente

In 1955, dividends were realized from the franchise's first foray into the Latino baseball market that had been initiated by an early Rickey directive to Howie Haak.[36] That year, a pair of Cuban players, veteran right-hander Lino Donoso and promising young outfielder Roman Mejias, debuted with the Pirates. Neither would have much of an impact in Pittsburgh, although Mejias would later have a couple of decent big league seasons with the Houston Colt 45s and the Boston Red Sox. The 1955 season also heralded the arrival of Puerto Rican outfielder Roberto Clemente, who would become the most famous Pirate player since Honus Wagner.

The story of Rickey's theft of Clemente from the Dodgers has become the stuff of legend. Clemente received a $10,000 bonus to sign with Brooklyn before the 1954 season, and under the bonus rules then in existence the Dodgers had to keep him on their big league roster all year or risk losing him to another club in the annual major league draft. The Dodgers elected to take a chance and assigned the 19-year-old outfielder to Montreal rather than sacrifice a precious roster spot — a decision that was undoubtedly affected by the fact that they already had five black players on the roster.

According to legend, the Dodgers concocted an elaborate plan to hide Clemente's talent by playing him sparingly under circumstances in which it would be difficult for him to excel. The depth to which the Dodgers' plan went and even the very existence of such a conspiracy is disputed.[37] Likewise, the details of Clemente's discovery vary, but the most common version of the story seems to be that Clyde Sukeforth stumbled across the young outfielder on a scouting expedition to check out pitcher Joe Black. Black had lost his touch after winning the 1952 Rookie of the Year award with the Dodgers and was trying to regain his form with Montreal. Sukeforth, who had been instrumental in choosing Jackie Robinson for the Dodgers before accompanying Rickey to Pittsburgh, was greatly impressed by the natural talent Clemente displayed in pregame practice and reported his find to Rickey. Subsequently, master scout Howie Haak was dispatched to double check Clemente's capabilities and also reported back positively.[38] However they actually managed to find out about Clemente, the last-place Pirates

Future Hall of Famer Roberto Clemente was "stolen" from the Dodgers organization in 1955 by none other than Branch Rickey (1964 Topps Giant Issue card).

had the first pick of the draft and used it to deftly pluck the future Hall of Famer from the Dodgers' grasp.

Of course, Clemente would go on to win four National League batting titles and be elected on the first-ballot to the Hall of Fame after his brilliant career ended when he died in an airplane crash on New Year's Eve 1972 while on a humanitarian relief mission. His last hit that September was the 3,000th of his career — all of them in a Pittsburgh uniform.

Rickey Steps Down

Rickey probably hated to shell out the $4,000 draft price to acquire Clemente, but he no doubt derived intense satisfaction from sticking it to his old nemesis O'Malley. But he wasn't able to fully enjoy the fruits of the Clemente acquisition while with the Pirates. His original contract was up at the end of the 1955 season, and he was shuffled off to the sidelines as a highly paid consultant per prior agreement with Galbreath. At the time, the Pirates had employed only seven players at the major league level whose complexion could have kept them out of Organized Baseball prior to the dismantling of the color barrier. Of the seven, only Clemente enjoyed success with the Pirates. In fact, Clemente would be the only black performer to play a major role with the franchise until 1962.

Rickey's successor was Joe L. Brown, son of comedian Joe E. Brown who had been a minor Pirate stockholder. The club soared to the dizzying heights of seventh place in Brown's first year, but fell back to the more familiar confines of the National League basement in 1957. In 1958, however, the Pirates surged to a shocking second place in the standings, and they finished fourth in 1959 before capturing the pennant and World Championship in 1960 — five years after the final year of Rickey's original five-year plan.

Though he received little credit at the time, every one of the major contributors on that 1960 squad could be linked to Rickey. Aces Vern Law and Bob Friend were inexperienced young hurlers when Rickey took over and developed under his tutelage. Clemente and relief ace Roy Face were both "pirated" from the Dodger system. Slugging first baseman Dick Stuart, future Hall of Fame second sacker Bill Mazeroski, 1960 National League Most Valuable Player Dick Groat, and all-star left-fielder Bob Skinner were all signed during Rickey's tenure. Third baseman Don Hoak, pitcher Harvey Haddix, and catcher Smoky Burgess were acquired in exchange for big Frank Thomas, who developed and made his major league debut during Rickey's reign. Center fielder Bill Virdon, lefty starter Wilmer Mizell, backup catcher and World Series hero Hal Smith, utility infielder Dick Schofield, and platoon outfielder Gino Cimoli were all acquired in exchange for players who had matriculated in the Rickey-built farm system.

Ironically, Clemente is the only black player on the list. In fact, the 1960 Pirates were probably the last team to compete in the World Series with only one black player in a significant role. Clemente was the only black player to get a hit for the Pirates, while their opponent, the New York Yankees, got tremendous performances from their two black players, Elston Howard and Hector Lopez.

With Brown occupying the general manager's seat, the Pirates auditioned pitchers Bennie Daniels and Al Jackson, first baseman R.C. Stevens, and Virgin Islander outfielder Joe Christopher from their farm system and acquired veterans Gene Baker, Jim Pendleton, and Harry Simpson from 1956 through 1959 — none of whom panned out for them.

The 1960s and Beyond

Despite a slow start, the 1960s would be a different story for the Pittsburgh franchise. In 1961, the Pirates made history when they named Gene Baker to manage their Batavia farm team, earning him the distinction of being the first black manager to be employed by a major league organization.[39] Baker, once an all-star second baseman with the Chicago Cubs, was acquired during the 1957 campaign. But early the next year he suffered a serious leg injury that ended his career as a front-line big leaguer. He would remain with the Pittsburgh organization as a fringe player, minor league manager, coach, and scout for more than 30 years. In 1963, Baker became the second black big league coach under manager Danny Murtaugh, and during the season he became the first black man to handle a big league team after Murtaugh was ejected from a late-season contest.[40]

Though the Pirates had only one pennant to show for the decade of the 1960s, they were a consistent contender and along with the Giants became the leading developer of black baseball talent. During that era, the club developed black stars Willie Stargell, Donn Clendenon, Al Oliver, Bob Veale, Al McBean, Dave Cash, Dock Ellis, Manny Sanguillen, and Gene Clines. They also traded for established black veterans like Maury Wills, Matty Alou, Manny Mota, and Jose Pagan. By 1967, five regulars and two top subs were black, as were the ace of the staff and two of the top relievers. Ironically, their manager for the first half of the season was Harry Walker, who had apparently developed a more enlightened attitude after encountering some problems with black players in a previous managerial tour with the St. Louis Cardinals.

The Pirates began the decade of the 1970s with three straight post-season appearances and a 1971 World Championship banner. On September 1, they fielded the first all-black starting nine in big league history to beat the Phillies, 10 to 7.[41] A little more than a month later, they opened the World Series with eight black players in the lineup.[42] The Pirates would capture National League Eastern Division Championships again in 1974 and 1975 but fail to advance to the World Series. They would end the decade as World Champions, however. The 1979 squad gained fame as "The Family" under the leadership of Willie Stargell, with black stars Dave Parker, Omar Moreno, Bill Madlock, Bill Robinson, Lee Lacy, Manny Sanguillen, Mike Easler, Jim Bibby, John Candelaria, and Grant Jackson also playing major roles.

The last twentieth-century hurrah for the Pirates came when they captured successive National League Eastern Division titles from 1990 through 1992 before black stars Bobby Bonilla and Barry Bonds opted for free agency.

Chapter 10

THE PHILADELPHIA/KANSAS CITY/OAKLAND ATHLETICS

For the first half century of the American's League's existence, Connie Mack was the owner, general manager, and manager of the Philadelphia Athletics. In fact, the team seemed to be referred to as "Connie Mack's Athletics" as often as the Philadelphia Athletics.

Mack built two baseball dynasties in Philadelphia. The first captured pennants in 1910, 1911, 1913, and 1914, and featured the famed $100,000 infield of Eddie Collins, Home Run Baker, Stuffy McInnis, and Jack Barry. The second dynasty, led by all-time greats Lefty Grove, Mickey Cochrane, Jimmie Foxx, and Al Simmons, broke the reign of the New York Yankees to win the American League flag each year from 1929 through 1931. But most of the intervening years were marked by second-division finishes and financial hardship.

By 1935, the ravages of the Great Depression had forced Mack to sell off the last vestiges of his 1929–31 powerhouse. From 1935 through 1946, the Athletics never rose higher than sixth place and finished dead last in the American League standings nine times, despite stiff competition for the basement from the St. Louis Browns and the Washington Senators. Mack's last hurrah came when his Athletics made a miraculous run at respectability from 1947 through 1949, peaking with a fourth-place, 84-victory effort in 1948. By 1950, however, they were back in the cellar as their once-loyal following shifted its affections to the Philadelphia Phillies' Whiz Kids, who won an exciting race for the National League pennant that year. After the season, the 87-year-old Mack finally stepped down as manager, turning the reins over to coach Jimmy Dykes, who was already pretty much running the team on the field. The old man still owned the team and remained a presence in the front office as his health permitted, but his sons Earle and Roy ran the club along with farm director Art Ehlers, who formally took over the general manager duties he had been unofficially handling for years.

Mr. Mack

Connie Mack was often described as courtly, gentlemanly, and even saintly. Almost everybody in baseball, including his players, called him Mr. Mack, and he was often referred to as the "Patriarch of the League." On the occasion of his death in 1956, famed columnist Red Smith described him as "tough and human and clever." Smith went on to write: "Many people loved him and some feared him, everybody respected him and, as far as I know, nobody ever disliked him in the 93 years of his life."[1]

But Mack was a staunch opponent of baseball integration, though not a publicly outspoken one. When called upon to comment on the news of Jackie Robinson's signing in late 1945, Mack tersely stated, "I'm not familiar with the news and don't know Robinson. I wouldn't care to comment."[2] Two years later, in the middle of Robinson's rookie season, "Mack was wary on the subject of Negroes in baseball; didn't want to be quoted," according to interviewer Ward Morehouse.[3]

Speaking about the integration of the franchise, long-time Athletics shortstop and manager Eddie Joost said, "I don't know why it took so long. But I know players and management didn't get together and decide to keep black players off the team. Connie Mack never mentioned the subject of integration."[4]

Sinister racist motives and actions have been attributed to the old man and his team. Mack's been accused of being "racist on principle" and willingly hurting the quality of his team by turning down opportunities to acquire black stars like Larry Doby, Minnie Minoso, and Hank Aaron.[5] In the early years of integration, he allowed black players to be prime targets for abuse by his Athletics. Coach Al Simmons rode Willard Brown particularly hard during Brown's brief stay with St. Louis in 1947.[6] Larry Doby claims that the Athletics engaged a professional heckler to torment him in Philadelphia and even paid the guy to follow him to New York.[7] Minoso remembers that Jimmy Dykes, who took over as Athletics manager in 1951, used to direct his pitchers to throw at him and called him every name in the book, including "black nigger so-and-so" and "black dog."[8]

Personally, however, Mack seemed to be a sophisticated segregationist rather than a racist redneck. He didn't appear to hate blacks though he was said to have worked hard to keep

Connie Mack, the patriarch of the American League who managed the A's from 1901 through 1950, quietly resisted the intrusion of black players (1961 Fleer card).

blacks out of his Germantown neighborhood.[9] He was always friendly and courteous to the Negro League stars of the pre-integration era, often publicly praising their talents and telling them what great major leaguers they would make if only.... "I'm sorry to say this, but I'd give half my ball club for a man like you," he told Webster McDonald of the Philadelphia Stars after watching him best Dizzy Dean two straight times in 1935 exhibition contests.[10]

Mack also enjoyed a close relationship with Negro League great Judy Johnson, a Philadelphia native who would eventually do some scouting for the Athletics after integration. He once admitted to Johnson, "If you were a white boy you could name your own price."[11] In an exchange recounted by Johnson years later in John B. Holway's *Blackball Stars,* Johnson asked Mack what he had meant by an earlier comment, "Judy, it's a shame you're a Negro." Mack's reply was, "If you want to know the truth, Judy, there are just too many of you to go in."[12]

This last statement probably best exemplifies Mack's attitude towards blacks in baseball. The old man may have simply been afraid of upsetting the established order that he'd done so much to create.

Mack and Washington Senators owner Clark Griffith represented the old guard of Major League Baseball, having been around since the inception of the American League. Both were firm traditionalists and were politically well connected inside and outside of baseball. They were supporters and contemporaries of Commissioner Mountain Kenesaw Landis and J.G. Taylor Spink, publisher of *The Sporting News*, who were also considered staunch segregationists.[13] According to the black press, Mack and Griffith considered integration a "Communistic plot to overthrow baseball — to create confusion between the races and finally, to overthrow the government."[14]

The success of baseball's first black players put old-timers like Mack and Griffith in an embarrassing position. The immediate recruitment of black players in large numbers would have constituted an admission of guilt by the baseball establishment, giving lie to their old friend Landis' preposterous position that blacks really weren't barred from Organized Baseball. As late as 1949, Mack maintained, "...the development of [Negro] players may be slow for I have been advised that there are not many Negro boys playing baseball."[15]

Whatever his true motives, Connie Mack took them to his grave with him. But the fact of the matter is that the Athletics didn't sign their first black player until he was no longer actively running the club. Even after the franchise finally acquired a few black minor leaguers, Wendell Smith wrote in 1953, "Owner Connie Mack has been steadfast in his position against Negro players."[16]

Apparently Mack, like his old friend Griffith, didn't have a problem with Latinos though, even some with darker-than-average skin tones. In 1902, he gave Columbian Louis Castro, one of the first Hispanic players of the 20th century, a shot at the Athletics' second base job. In 1918, Cuban outfielder Merito Acosta, whose brother played in the Negro Leagues, appeared in 49 games for the Athletics. During World War II, the Athletics employed Mexican hurler Jesse Flores and Cuban center fielder Bobby Estalella (see Washington Senators chapter). Later, Havana-born Mike Guerra spent four years handling a share of the club's catching duties, and Mexican League refugee Roberto Ortiz was given an audition.

The Organization Integrates

Shortly after Mack stepped down, Judy Johnson was put on the payroll as a scout.[17] Johnson is often identified as the first black scout associated with a major league organization, but John Donaldson had already signed several players for the White Sox before Johnson officially signed on with the A's. Johnson would later claim that he tried to get the Athletics to buy Hank Aaron's contract from the Indianapolis Clowns for $3,500, but the price was too high, and he was also unsuccessful in persuading them to acquire Ray Dandridge, who was stuck in the Giants farm system.[18]

Instead, the Athletics elected to take a more modest, and inexpensive, approach to integration. Before the 1951 season, they signed two 18-year-old local black prospects, Marion Scott and Clarence Wilford.[19] Scott would only pitch a few games in the Athletics' system while Wilford would never play for the organization. Prior to the 1952 campaign, the Athletics made a major move when they entered into a working agreement with St. Hyacinthe in the Class C Canadian Provincial League, acquiring the rights to several black players in the process. In the early 1950s, the Provincial League was a haven for displaced Negro League veterans, as well as one of the few lower leagues open to young black players entering Orga-nized Baseball. The next spring, the Athletics invited four former Negro Leaguers who played for St. Hyacinthe to camp: pitcher Bob Trice, infielder Alonzo Braithwaite, and outfielders Joe Cephus Taylor and Al Pinkston. Also receiving an invitation was a Panamanian shortstop named Hector Lopez, who had swiped 32 bases and led the Provincial League in runs scored for St. Hyacinthe.[20] Braithwaite was returned to the Canadian circuit for the 1953 season, but Trice and Pinkston were optioned to the franchise's Triple A Ottawa affiliate, and Taylor and Lopez, who would turn out to be the gem of the lot, were sent to Williamsport in the Class A Eastern League.

On September 13, 1953, the Athletics became the fourth American League team and eighth major league outfit to integrate when 27-year-old Bob Trice took the mound to face the St. Louis Browns. Trice, who toiled for the legendary Homestead Grays in their declin-ing years, had won 21 games for Ottawa and was named the 1952 International League MVP. He was impressive in three late-season starts and was counted on for the Athletics' starting rotation in 1954.

Manager Dykes and general manager Ehlers left Philadelphia to join the newly relocated Baltimore Orioles before the 1954 season. Veteran shortstop Eddie Joost was offered the man-agerial post with the Mack brothers sharing front-office duties. The Athletics began their last year under the ownership of the Mack family, as well as their last in Philadelphia, with two promising young black players who had captured Most Valuable Player awards in Triple A ball the previous year on their roster, Trice and Vic Power.

Power had been obtained from the New York Yankees in a big off-season trade. The ver-satile Puerto Rican had won the American Association batting title as well as the Most Valuable Player Award with Kansas City in 1953. But Power was simply too flamboyant and controversial for the stuffy Bombers and had never been given a chance with the parent club despite star-ring for the organization at the Triple A level for three years (see New York Yankees chapter).

Trice began the 1954 season in spectacular fashion, winning his first four starts with com-plete-game efforts, including a 1–0 shutout of the Yankees. But he lost his effectiveness and won only three of his next eleven decisions. The failures tormented the big pitcher, and he suffered psychologically. Even though he was leading the staff in victories at the time, he asked to be returned to Ottawa where he had been tremendously popular with the fans.

"I figure in the long run this is what's best for me," Trice said. "And since I cannot seem to win in my present frame of mind, the team shouldn't miss me. Maybe after a few weeks at Ottawa, I'll be able to come back and win."[21] By the time he returned, the Athletics had moved to Kansas City, and the big right-hander would never win another big league game.

Power also endured a difficult rookie season in Philadelphia. When he reported to spring training, batting coach Wally Moses confiscated his favorite 36-ounce bat that he'd hit .349 with the previous year in the American Association and forced him to use a lighter model.[22] He was also assigned to play center field, where he ran himself ragged covering for slow-mov-ing behemoths Gus Zernial and Bill Renna at the corners. As a consequence, Power hit only .255 in 1954, but he would catch fire in his sophomore campaign and star for the Athletics for another 3½ seasons before departing in a trade that brought Roger Maris to the Athlet-ics. Power would ultimately complete an impressive 12-year major league career with an excel-lent .284 career batting average and ownership of the first seven American Gold Glove awards issued for first-base play.

Power's tenure with the Athletics was not without racial problems. In his first spring training at West Palm Beach, he and Trice were quartered in the black section and had to

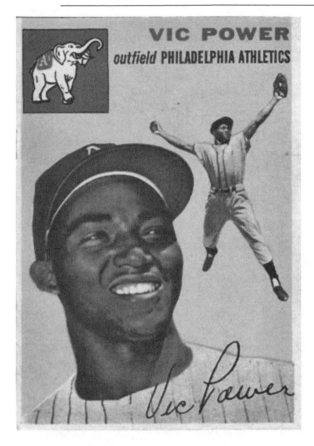

Flamboyant Vic Power was not considered the right type of player for the New York Yankees, but became a star with the Athletics (1954 Topps card).

walk two miles to practice because they couldn't get a cab. Eventually blacks were allowed to stay in the same hotel with their white teammates, but they were cautioned not to use the pool, look at white women, or eat in the hotel restaurant.[23] Even at the park, black players were discriminated against. They couldn't use the same bathroom as the white players or drink cold water from the fountain in the dugout. Instead, they had to hike to a fountain behind the center field fence for warm drinking water.[24]

After Trice's voluntary demotion, Joe Taylor was promoted from Ottawa to keep Power company, becoming the third black player to appear in a Athletics uniform. Taylor, a hard-hitting outfielder, would get trials with four major league clubs, but he would never establish himself in the big leagues despite excellent minor league credentials.

The Move to Kansas City

The 1955 season brought a change of ownership, a change of managers, a change of general managers, a change of scenery, and a change in the complexion of the team. Chicago industrialist Arnold Johnson purchased the franchise from the Mack family and relocated it to Kansas City. The move west was not seen as a good sign for the continued progress of integration. Power, in particular, was not looking forward to returning to the Midwest, where he had encountered hostility and discrimination while playing for the Kansas City Blues.[25] But the unpleasantness of the club's new venue was at least partially offset by the presence of new manager Lou Boudreau, who gained a reputation as a friend of black ballplayers while managing Cleveland (see Cleveland Indians chapter).

In training camp prior to the 1955 season, big Al Pinkston, who had captured the South Atlantic League batting crown the previous season, opened eyes with his lusty hitting.[26] According to Ernest Mehl's column in *The Sporting News*, "...there is a growing belief that this huge 220-pound Negro lad with the power of a bull may be a future major league great."[27] Pinkston seemed a cinch to make the squad, but shortly before breaking camp he was optioned to the International League. Apparently, while obliging the press with stories of his early days in black baseball, he inadvertently tipped the Athletics' brass to the possibility that he might be a tad older than he'd led them to believe. The "lad" was, in fact, much closer to age 40 than the 28 years he claimed, having started his Negro League career with St. Louis Stars back in 1936. Pinkston would go on to play 11 more years in the minors before finally hanging up his spikes at the age of 47 in 1965. Despite being 33 years old when he debuted in Organized Baseball, he finished with a remarkable .352 career batting average and six minor league batting titles to his credit — a total that tied him with Smead Jolley for the all-time record.[28]

Joe Taylor was also returned to the minors before the 1955 season started, and Trice was sent down early in the campaign. But on May 11, the Athletics acquired a pair of black players who would go on to have some excellent seasons in Kansas City, Harry "Suitcase" Simpson and Hector Lopez.

Simpson, a former Philadelphia Star in the Negro National League, is one of the few early black players to receive a second chance at the big leagues. Dubbed "The Tan Ted Williams," he joined the Indians in 1951 accompanied by considerable hype after a phenomenal campaign with San Diego in the Pacific Coast League. But the pressure of big expectations and the fact that the Indians chose to keep him rather than Minnie Minoso got to him. After three years of struggling in Cleveland, Simpson spent a lackluster 1954 campaign with their Indianapolis farm team. Playing under Lou Boudreau after his sale to Kansas City, he was finally able to relax and started blasting the ball. In 1955, he was one of four Athletics hitters to hit .300 and, the next year he earned a berth on the American League All-Star squad.

The same day Simpson was purchased from the Indians, the Athletics called up Hector Lopez from Ottawa. Playing third and second base, Lopez hit a productive .290 as a rookie in 1955. In four full seasons and part of a fifth with the Athletics, Lopez would stand out as one of the hardest hitting infielders in the league, but his lousy defense at either second or third base often attracted more attention than his potent bat. He managed to lead American League third baseman in errors in 1955 and 1956 despite spending considerable time at other positions, and he was saved from earning the distinction a third straight time in 1957 by an injury. In 1958, he moved over to second base and promptly laid claim to the error crown at his new address in only 96 appearances.

With Simpson and Lopez joining Power, who finished second in the league in batting, the Athletics 1955 lineup improved by 12 games over the previous year and moved up from last to sixth place.

By the mid–1950s, a tremendous gap in black talent had developed between the two major leagues. In 1956, the National League boasted 36 black players, at least 17 who could be classified as regular position players or front-line pitchers. The American League, on the other hand, fielded only 15 black performers — only eight of whom played in more than half their team's games or pitched more than a handful of innings. The Athletics were the only American League club with three black first-stringers and appeared to be the league's best hope for picking up the integration pace.

The Yankee Influence

But in those days it was best not to count on the Athletics for anything. Kansas City owner Arnold Johnson was a friend and business associate of Yankee owners Dan Topping and Del Webb, and his top aides George Selkirk and Parke Carroll also had deep personal ties to the Yankees.[29] Under their leadership, the Athletics devolved into little more than a puppet operation for the Yankees. Any decent player that came their way was available to the Yankees, and they even stored prospects like Clete Boyer and Ralph Terry on their roster until they were ready for pinstripes. "It must be great to have your own farm system in the same league," observed Cleveland general manager Hank Greenberg with more than a touch of sarcasm.[30] Unfortunately, Johnson and company seemed to share the views of their masters when it came to integration.

The Athletics remained the only team in the league with three black regulars until Simpson was swapped (to the Yankees, of course) during the 1957 season. They were also the only black players on the roster except for a brief appearance by former New York Cuban hurler Jose Santiago. Santiago had been purchased from Cleveland early in the 1956 season. Despite good minor league numbers, he had never been able to find a place on the vaunted Cleveland staff. Unfortunately, he couldn't crack the miserable Kansas City rotation either and was back in the minors after a disappointing 22-inning audition. After Santiago, almost five years would pass before another black Kansas City Athletic would be introduced.

Shortly after the Simpson trade, Harry Craft replaced Lou Boudreau as manager, and the Athletics ended the 1957 campaign with only two black players on their roster, Power and Lopez. They began the 1958 season the same way until the June 15 trade deadline when Vic Power was swapped to the Cleveland Indians and Simpson was reacquired from the Yankees — exactly a year after he'd been traded away. The 1959 season began with Simpson and Lopez as the only two black players on the Kansas City roster, but Simpson was soon dispatched to the Chicago White Sox, leaving Lopez as the team's only black player. A few weeks later, Lopez was also sent packing to join (who else?) the New York Yankees.

After the Lopez trade in early 1959 through the end of the 1960 season, no black player participated in a major league game for the Athletics. In fact, the 1960 Athletics are the last major league team to go an entire season without a black player on the roster. More than 90 black players appeared in the major leagues that year, but none wore a Kansas City uniform.

The Arrival of Charlie Finley

That situation was remedied when Charles Oscar Finley, a.k.a. Charlie O, purchased controlling interest in the franchise following Johnson's death. As hard as it is for baseball traditionalists to swallow, it was Finley who finally brought full integration to the Athletics, or A's as they came to be more commonly called, and in the process made the franchise respectable. Upon taking over prior to the 1961 season, Finley immediately cut off the Yankee pipeline and began promoting and acquiring young black players. Norm Bass, a 22-year-old righty, notched a team-leading 11 victories in 1961, veterans Bob Boyd, Wes Covington, and Ozzie Virgil spent time on the roster, and seasoned minor leaguers Bobby Prescott and John Wyatt were given trials.

Finley initially hired Frank Lane as his general manager, but the arrangement only lasted a matter of months. But the intrepid Joe Gordon's stint as manager was even shorter lived. Gordon was fired after only 59 games with the team in eighth place, on their way to a tie for ninth with the newly minted Washington Senators under Hank Bauer. Pat Friday settled in as general manager with Hank Peters serving as assistant GM and farm director, but Finley ran his own show.

The 1962 season was an integration bonanza in Kansas City as five black rookies earned regular jobs and the team employed more black players at the major league level than any other team in the American League. Rookie John Wyatt, who began his Organized Baseball career in the Cardinal farm system in 1954 after a stint in the remnants of the Negro Leagues, developed into as one of the top relief pitchers in baseball. Outfielder Manny Jiminez and third baseman Ed Charles were obtained from the Milwaukee organization and enjoyed excellent freshman campaigns as did outfielder Jose Tartabull and hurler Diego Segui. In addition, former Cincinnati prospect Orlando Pena nailed down a spot in the starting rotation after being picked up in mid-season. Norm Bass' promising career petered out, however, and he ended up pursuing a much more successful career as a safety in the National Football League. The 1962 A's won 11 more contests than they captured the previous year and finished the season in sole possession of ninth place.

Yet another old Yankee, Ed Lopat, replaced Bauer in 1963, and the A's moved up to eighth place. Thereafter, they dropped to tenth in three of the next four seasons under a succession of managers that included Mel McGaha, Haywood Sullivan, Al Dark, and Luke Appling. But the club was gradually forming a solid nucleus as budding black stars Bert Campaneris, Johnny "Blue Moon" Odom, and future Hall of Famer Reggie Jackson joined talented young white players like Catfish Hunter, also a future Hall of Famer, Dick Green, Chuck Dobson, Dave Duncan, Rick Monday, Sal Bando, and Joe Rudi.

Success in Oakland

The Athletics left Kansas City for Oakland in 1968 without ever posting a winning record in the Midwest. But in their first year on the West Coast, Bob Kennedy managed the franchise to their first winning season since 1952. The season also marked the debut of Rollie Fingers — another Hall of Fame-bound prospect.

In 1969, the Athletics became legitimate contenders, finishing second in the American League Western Division under the new six-team, two-division alignment. The managerial revolving door continued as Hank Bauer replaced Bob Kennedy. Bauer's second shot at managing the Athletics ended with a dozen games remaining in the season and the team in the same place it would finish under his successor, John McNamara. The season also witnessed the arrival of Vida Blue. In 1969, black pitcher Mike Cuellar of the Orioles tied Denny McLain of the Detroit Tigers for the Cy Young Award. Two years later, Blue would become the first black American League pitcher to win the award outright.

The Athletics finished second again in 1970. Highlights of the season included the addition of respected former National League star Felipe Alou; a late season no-hitter by Vida Blue, only his third big league victory; an American League earned run average title for Diego Segui after his return from a year in exile with the ill-fated Seattle Pilots; and a spectacular bullpen performance by seasoned veteran Mudcat Grant to recapture his status as the winningest black hurler in American League history. Grant left the American League after the 1967 season as the circuit's all-time leader with 117 wins. But during his two-year National League sojourn, runner-up Earl Wilson pulled within one win of Grant's total. Early in the 1970 season, Wilson forged into the lead and was a victory ahead, 120 to 119, when he was traded to the National League San Diego Padres. Grant won four more games after Wilson's departure to retake the lead. Wilson was through after the 1970 campaign while Grant added a final American League victory in 1971 to finish with 124.

Hall of Famer Dick Williams began the 1971 season in the Oakland managerial hot seat, Finley's 11th skipper in 11 seasons, if Hank Bauer is counted twice for his two stints. That year, the A's captured the Western Division championship behind the spectacular pitching of Vida Blue, but a post-season-tested Baltimore squad swept them in the League Championship Series.

A remarkable A's dynasty began in 1972 as they beat the Detroit Tigers for the American League title and then upset Cincinnati's mighty "Big Red Machine" to capture the world championship. Black players were well-represented on that first championship squad, with Vida Blue and Blue Moon Odom in the starting rotation and Bert Campaneris and Reggie Jackson starring in the field. Other notable black players on the championship roster were outfielder Angel Mangual, late-season pickup Matty Alou, and promising young slugger George Hendrick. The Athletics repeated as World Champions in 1973 with the same basic nucleus. Speedy center fielder Billy North was the most significant addition to the roster.

Sick of Finley's interference, Williams gave up the A's managerial post after the 1973 World Series. Finley, who invented the practice of recycling managers before anyone in the baseball world knew of George Steinbrenner, replaced him with Al Dark who had spent two years managing the club in the mid–1960s. Dark's religious fervor caused some dissention among the troops, but didn't prevent them from capturing a third-straight World Championship in 1974. Finley also brought in track star Herb Washington to serve as the baseball's first exclusive pinch runner. Washington would hang up his spikes two years later with the remarkable career stat line of 105 games played, 31 stolen bases, and a lifetime batting average of .000.

The disintegration of the three-time World Champion squad began before the 1975 season when an arbitrator awarded free-agent status to ace hurler Catfish Hunter and the Yankees scooped him up. Without Hunter anchoring the staff, the Athletics managed another division championship under Dark but succumbed to the Boston Red Sox in the League Championship Series.

During the 1975 campaign, Andy Messersmith of the Los Angeles Dodgers and Dave McNally of the Baltimore Orioles played out their option and were declared free agents through arbitration. For years Finley had underpaid his players, and free agency was the death knoll for his Oakland dynasty. Reggie Jackson signaled his intention to play out his option in 1976, and he was traded to Baltimore before the season started. New manager Chuck Tanner led the club to a surprising second-place finish, but after the season Bert Campaneris, Sal Bando, Joe Rudi, and Don Baylor, who was obtained in trade for Jackson, defected to other organizations.

Thus Charlie Finley, the man who did more for black players than anyone in the history of the franchise, followed in the footsteps of the venerable Connie Mack, the man who resisted integrated, by overseeing the erosion of an A's dynasty for lack of funds. Even the addition of Dick (formerly Richie) Allen in 1977 couldn't prevent the team from tumbling into the basement of the American League Western Division behind the new Seattle Mariner franchise.

Chapter 11

THE CHICAGO CUBS

It's probably no coincidence that the four clubs represented on the steering committee that produced the infamous 1946 "Race Question" report didn't lead the charge to integrate Major League Baseball. Their track record is especially deplorable considering that all four operated in cities where rival franchises integrated years ahead of them. The New York Yankees and the Boston Red Sox were notorious foot-draggers, with New York being the sixth American League franchise and thirteenth overall to integrate while Boston was the absolute last big league team to field a black player. The Chicago Cubs and St. Louis Cardinals were also among the latter half of the sixteen major league teams in order of integration, with Chicago becoming the ninth franchise in late 1953 and St. Louis the tenth at the beginning of the 1954 campaign.

The sixteen teams that comprised Major League Baseball during the integration era fall rather neatly into three categories corresponding closely to the order in which they introduced their first black players.

The first five teams to commit to integration — the Brooklyn Dodgers, Cleveland Indians, New York Giants, Boston Braves, and Chicago White Sox — were innovators. Technically, the St. Louis Browns were the third team to put a black player in their lineup, but their initial half-hearted attempt at integration in 1947 can hardly be considered a commitment. The innovators weren't afraid to take risks or alienate the rest of the baseball establishment to bolster their rosters. They greatly strengthened themselves by embracing integration, and as a result they were among the most successful franchises of the 1950s.

The Yankees, Red Sox, Philadelphia Phillies, and Detroit Tigers were the last four teams to integrate, and they fall into the obstructionist category. They were among the more successful teams of the immediate post-war era, but their stubborn resistance to the recruitment of black players eventually ended up costing them. The Cardinals also fit into this category prior to Gussie Busch's purchase of the franchise.

The third group consists of the St. Louis Browns, Chicago Cubs, Pittsburgh Pirates, Philadelphia Athletics, Cincinnati Reds, and Washington Senators. The signing of Satchel Paige midway through the 1951 season has to be considered the Browns' first true commitment to integration, and the other five integrated at the major league level during the 1953 and 1954 campaigns. This group can best be categorized as "feckless." Its members consistently ranked among the worst in the majors in terms of administration, performance, and attendance. They generally fielded second-rate teams when integration came about and continued to field lousy teams for a decade or more thereafter. For the most part, they didn't actively oppose integration. They were just slow to accept it and predictably ineffectual when they finally did. But this was their modus operandi, applying to their entire business of fielding a competitive big league baseball team rather than just integration. The Cubs of the late 1940s and early 1950s fit comfortably into this classification. They usually lost about 90 games a year and ranked near the bottom of the league in key hitting, pitching, and fielding categories.

Franchise History

In fact, the Cubs are the most notorious losers in baseball history. The 2008 baseball season began with masochistic Cub fans anticipating their 100th-straight world championship-free campaign, more than 40 years longer than the next worst performance. Likewise, their 62-year (and counting) absence from the World Series stage is also securely in the record books for the foreseeable future.

But the Chicago Cubs were a powerhouse in the first decade of the 20th century, capturing consecutive National League pennants from 1906 through 1908 and also winning the World Series the latter two years. They were led by shortstop Joe Tinker, second baseman Johnny Evers, and first baseman-manager Frank Chance, who would be forever immortalized in verse for their dazzling Tinker-to-Evers-to-Chance double plays, and a sensational pitching staff led by the fortuitously maimed "Three Finger" Brown.

Though they captured a somewhat tainted wartime pennant in 1918, the Cubs had been reduced to mediocrity by 1921 when minority stockholder William Wrigley purchased control of the franchise. Wrigley, founder of the Wrigley Chewing Gum empire, was an avid baseball fan who spent freely to restore the Cubs to their former greatness and was rewarded by a pennant in 1929. When he died in January 1932, he left his 37-year-old son Philip with a pretty good baseball club that would win the National League pennant that year and again in 1935 and 1938. But by the 1940s, the nucleus of the team had grown old, and it had become a losing outfit. The Cubs did win the 1945 National League flag, but it was primarily because they had so many veteran players who were too old or infirm to be called for military duty. After the war, the team faded quickly. From 1947 until 1961, they never landed in the first division, finishing fifth three times, sixth twice, seventh on six occasions, and dead last four times. When the National League expanded to ten teams in 1962, the Cubs became the first ninth-place club in modern National League history when the Houston Colts posted a better record in their very first year of existence. The Cubbies then proceeded to carry their record of futility through the mid–1960s under the leadership of Philip (or P.K.) Wrigley.

P.K. Wrigley

Fortunately, for the Wrigley estate, P.K. was better at selling chewing gum than producing a winning baseball team. Unlike his father, he was rather reclusive and avoided the limelight. P.K. just wasn't a die-hard baseball fan. He didn't seem particularly interested in running a major league team, keeping the Cubs primarily out of respect for his father's wishes.[1] After one particularly disastrous season, he even apologized for his inattention to the franchise.[2] P.K. often seemed more interested in having a beautiful, inviting stadium than a winning team. He insisted that the baseball operation be self-sustaining, refusing to use funds from his gum company or his vast personal holdings to improve the team, yet he had revenue-producing billboards that covered the outfield fences at Wrigley Field torn down and replaced with a lush growth of ivy. He also had more than half of the available tickets for every game set aside for walk-up patrons and eventually became something of a cult hero for his stubborn refusal to install lights that would enable the team to play lucrative night games.[3]

In comparison to the rest of the baseball establishment, P.K. was "an odd duck," described as "equal parts progressive and Paleolithic."[4] His aversion to night baseball and extensive farm systems was certainly old-fashioned, but he was often innovative — though hardly a maverick in the Bill Veeck mode. In fact, many of his ideas were simply ahead of their time. Early on, he pushed for relaxation of the reserve clause and improvement of player benefits.[5] He advanced the idea of a baseball school for young prospects long before the Kansas City Royals academy came into existence. He funded a study to analyze player's reflexes and other motor skills. He was the first to let the grass grow over the path between the mound and home plate. He was also the first to install loud speakers in the park, and the scoreboard at Wrigley field was the first to flash balls and strikes. And he was instrumental in the development of the players' pension plan and other benefits. His most famous innovation was the establishment of a "college of coaches" in the early 1960s to manage the Cubs on a rotating basis, an imaginative idea that would be devoid of enthusiasts and imitators.

The name Philip K. Wrigley listed as one of the sponsors of the infamous "Race Question" report" is something of a mystery. He certainly seemed to possess a much more enlightened perspective than most of his fellow owners. While he was developing Catalina Island in the 1930s, someone on his staff called him for guidance because a black man wanted to move there. "See if you can find a history book and read the Constitution of the United States," P.K. advised.[6] Almost a decade before Jackie Robinson's debut, he spoke of the inevitability of the integration of baseball and cautioned "there are men in high places who don't want it.[7] In 1943, he met with representatives of the Negro American League to discuss baseball's relations with the black player. According to reports, "Wrigley indicated that the Cubs would scout the Negro league next season in an effort to ascertain their relative merit with major league players."[8] Often described as modest, he supported many philanthropic and charitable organizations and undoubtedly didn't consider himself to be a bigot.[9]

In addition, the Cubs employed several Latino players before the color line was broken, including "swarthy" complexioned Puerto Rican hurler Hi Bithorn.[10] As a rookie in 1942, Bithorn teamed with Cuban catcher Sal Hernandez to form Major League Baseball's first all–Latino battery.[11] The next year, Bithorn was the ace of the Chicago staff, winning 18 games for the fifth-place 1943 squad and leading the league in shutouts. After spending the next two seasons in the military, he returned in 1946 with a sore arm and won only seven more big league games. In his 1977 autobiography, *Baseball as I Have Known It*, celebrated sportswriter Fred Leib claims that in the winter of 1946–47 he met one of the dancers in an all-black dance troupe who was pointedly introduced to him as a first cousin of Hi Blithorn.[12]

Tentative Steps Toward Integration

The Cubs, in fact, indicated an early willingness to integrate after the color line was crossed. Late in the 1947 season, they conducted a Wrigley Field tryout for catcher John "Hoss" Ritchey, who led the Negro American League in batting that year with the Chicago American Giants.[13] Ritchey, a San Diego native, would ultimately sign with his hometown Padres and become the Jackie Robinson of the Pacific Coast League in 1948. The next year, they held discussions with the Dodgers about the purchase of Don Newcombe, then with Montreal, before Rickey's reported $500,000 asking price scared them off.[14]

During the 1949 season, the Cubs became the seventh major league franchise to bring black players into its organization. At the beginning of the season, they extended a tryout to pitcher Alvin Spearman with their Janesville affiliate in the Class D Wisconsin State League, but didn't retain him.[15] Spearman would pitch for the Chicago American Giants for a few years before entering Organized Baseball and enjoying some success in the California League. Later, they signed three black prospects, pitcher Robert Burns, infielder Billy Hart, and former Dodger recruit Sammy Gee, all of whom played for the Cubs' Sioux Falls affiliate in the Class C Northern League.[16]

Yet, under Wrigley's direction, the Cubs were guilty of what is, arguably, the single most conspicuously prejudicial treatment of a black player since the color line was crossed. To the detriment of the team, Cubs' management refused to promote infielder Gene Baker who was clearly one of the top players in their organization. Baker would spend four seasons — the prime years of his career — starring in the Cubs' farm system rather than Wrigley Field.

So why did Wrigley end up being an obstacle to the integration movement rather than an earnest supporter?

In *Wrigleyville*, author Peter Golenbock writes at length of P.K.'s personnel management weakness. Among other faults, Wrigley is labeled as unpredictable and not caring enough about winning. He's also accused of not always hiring competent baseball people and not listening to the few able ones, like young Bill Veeck, who somehow managed to come under his employ. "[Wrigley] was not the type of man to hire a strong-willed baseball brain to make his team a winner. He could not have worked with a Branch Rickey or a Larry MacPhail. They would have overwhelmed him because Wrigley would have to do what they wanted rather than continue to make all the decisions himself."[17] Given the Cubs' track record, this sounds like a reasonable assessment.

In 1940, Wrigley hired newspaperman Jim Gallagher as general manager rather than a progressive executive with a solid baseball background who might have compensated for his own lack of experience, but might also have rocked the boat. Gallagher, only 36 years of age when he ascended to the general manager post, had apparently convinced P.K. that he had what it took to run a big league club with his handling of press arrangements during the 1938 World Series.[18] Gallagher quickly replaced Wrigley Field icon Gabby Harnett as manager and proceeded to make a series of poor trades that would cement the club's second-division status.

When the initial battles to break down color barriers were being fought in the late 1940s and early 1950s, the Cubs' managerial and front-office lineup presented a formidable obstacle.

The Cubs field manager in the late 1940's was Charlie "Jolly Cholly" Grimm, a former Cub first baseman in his second tour of duty as manager. Grimm was a likeable character, but hardly considered progressive. As manager of the Boston Braves in 1952 he would have problems with black outfielder Sam Jethroe, who he insensitively called "Sambo."[19] Later on, Charlie would tab rookie outfielder Hank Aaron with the nickname "Stepanfetchit" — "because he just keeps shuffling along."[20] Grimm, who invariably seemed to end up back in Chicago, was a Cub vice president when Wrigley's ill-fated rotating manager plan was implemented. He reportedly conspired to make sure that Buck O'Neill, whom the Cubs had hired to be the first black major league coach, never got a chance to sit in the manager's seat and become the first black man to pilot a major league club.[21]

Grimm's successor was Frankie Frisch, the manager of the Cardinals old "Gas House Gang," who was as old-school as they come. Frisch was canned in 1951 and replaced by Phil Cavaretta, who, as team captain in 1947, had reportedly led a team meeting in which the players voted to boycott Robinson.[22]

Long-time Dodger scout Wid Matthews replaced Gallagher, who was kicked upstairs in 1949 after a decade of mismanagement. In 1945, Branch Rickey had assigned Matthews to scout Jackie Robinson, supposedly for a spot on a new Negro League club Rickey was planning. According to Jules Tygiel, one of the foremost experts on baseball's integration, "[Matthews] would likely have resigned had he known Rickey's intentions." After observing Robinson, Matthews filed a report labeling him "strictly the showboat type."[23] Later, Matthews would advise Rickey not to sign Willie Mays because he couldn't hit a curveball.[24]

Another denizen of the Chicago front office in that era was Lennie "Boots" Merullo, who earned his nickname with a four-error inning while playing shortstop for the Cubs. In his last season as an active player, Merullo got into a scuffle with Jackie Robinson after the two got tangled up in play at second base, and he was subsequently labeled by the press as being antagonistic toward black players.[25]

As a Cub executive Charlie Grimm reportedly subverted Buck O'Neill's opportunity to become the first black to officially manage in the major leagues (1960 Topps card).

Nevertheless, the Cubs continued integrating their minor league system. Six Negro League veterans reported to the Haines City spring training base of their new Springfield International League affiliate before the 1950 season. Gene Baker, a 25-year-old shortstop, had been purchased from the Kansas City Monarchs. Slugging outfielder Bob Thurman and catcher Earl Taborn were acquired from the New York Yankees system. The contracts of pitcher Leroy Ferrell and infielder Jim "Junior" Gilliam had been conditionally purchased from the Baltimore Elite Giants.[26] And former Philadelphia Stars hurler Bill Ricks was also on hand.[27] Ferrell reportedly ate himself out of camp.[28] Taborn, Gilliam, and Ricks were also found wanting and returned to the Negro Leagues.

Baker and Thurman began the 1950 season with Springfield. Thurman spent the whole year with Springfield while Baker played only three games before being demoted to Des Moines in the Class A Western League. But Baker was back in Triple A with the Cubs' Pacific Coast League Los Angeles franchise after 49 games in Class A. The smooth-fielding shortstop would star for Los Angeles through the 1953 season, making the Pacific Coast League all-star team in each of his three full seasons, before finally getting a shot at the majors. Thurman wasn't so patient. After three seasons in the Chicago organization with no opportunity for advancement, he jumped his contract to join an outlaw league in the Dominican Republic. Later, he would reach the major leagues and become a valuable extra outfielder and pinch-hitter for the Cincinnati Reds.

Jim Gilliam was the most fortunate of the Cubs' first platoon of black players. Being rejected by the Cubs was the best thing that ever happened to him. After another season in Baltimore, Gilliam was acquired by the Brooklyn Dodgers organization. By 1953, Gilliam was handling second base for the pennant-winning Dodgers and capturing National League Rookie of the Year honors, while the older and more accomplished Baker was still languishing in the last-place Cubs' minor league system.

The Gene Baker "Monkey Business"

The list of black players who were treated unfairly in the decade following Jackie Robinson's debut is extensive. Many of the most flagrant cases are documented in these pages though hundreds more certainly occurred, especially in the minor leagues. Few can be fully appreciated, since the players involved rarely got a full chance to validate their talents at the major league level. Vic Power's tribulations with the New York Yankees (see Yankees chapter) garnered the most publicity, but the Baker travesty is the more egregious.

The circumstances were similar; both Power and Baker had excellent minor league batting stats, both were considered tremendous defensive talents, and both subsequently proved to be big league all-stars. Evidence that Power was probably the more talented player is balanced out by the fact that the older, more accomplished Baker was forced to waste four years in the Cubs system compared to Power's three-year sentence in the Yankee organization. On the other hand, criticism of Power's behavior and character must also be put aside, given the attitude of the times. What ultimately sets the two cases apart is that the Yankees didn't really *need* Power, while the lowly Cubs refused to promote Baker when they were desperate for a player of his talents. Power was trying to crack a Yankee roster that managed to capture the World Championship without him every year. Baker, on the other hand, couldn't buy an opportunity to earn a place on one of the worst teams in baseball — one that was particularly weak at the position where he excelled.

Baker, described as a flashy, acrobatic defender with a strong arm who covered lots of ground, had been regarded as one of the top defensive shortstops in the Negro Leagues.[29] After his first season in Organized Baseball, he gained a reputation as the best defensive shortstop in the Pacific Coast League. In a comparison with Oakland's star shortstop and former Negro League

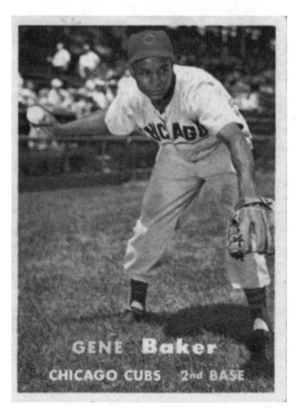

The Cubs' failure to promote talented Gene Baker to the majors until he was almost 30 years old was one of baseball's most flagrant cases of discrimination (1957 Topps card).

veteran Artie Wilson, *The Sporting News* conceded that Wilson was the better hitter, but gave Baker the nod on defense, citing his stronger arm and superior range.[30] In addition to his superlative defense, Baker showed speed on the bases and decent power at the plate for a middle infielder. The slender infielder also proved his durability by playing a record 420 straight games from July 8, 1950, through August 31, 1952, despite contending with base runners sliding into second base with spikes high — an especially perilous hazard for a black infielder at that time. Furthermore, Baker displayed a keen knowledge of the game. Pitcher/author Jim Brosnan, a former teammate, said, "Gene Baker was bright, knew the game well, the fundamentals."[31] In the latter stages of Baker's career with the Pittsburgh Pirates, manager Danny Murtaugh would observe, "[Baker] knows more baseball than fellows twice his age. He's one of the smartest I've ever met."[32]

Keeping an infielder of Baker's caliber in the minor leagues for four years might have been justified if Joe Tinker and Johnny Evers were still manning the Cubs' keystone area in the early 1950s. But during this period the Cubs' shortstop and second base positions were occupied by a collection of underachievers. The shortstop job was held by error-strikeout-and-injury-prone Roy Smalley, while the primary second baseman was light-hitting, fumble-fingered Eddie Miksis. The only comparison to their celebrated predecessors was an update of the famous "Tinker-to-Evers-to-Chance" refrain by Wrigley Field boo-birds to "Miksis-to-Smalley-to-Addison." Addison, of course, is the name of the street that borders Wrigley Field behind the first-base side — not the Cubbie first sacker of the era.[33]

Smalley took over as the Cubbies' regular shortstop in 1948 and led the league in errors in each of his first three seasons at the post. In 1950, he showed promise when he led National League shortstops in homers and runs batted in, but he hit only .230 and led the league in strikeouts. He also led his colleagues in assists, putouts, double plays, and total chances per game, but he was charged with 51 errors — a horrendous total that hasn't been topped in the major leagues since. To complement his penchant for clutch errors, Smalley further aggravated Chicago fans by failing to hustle out grounders on those infrequent instances when he actually made contact at the plate, and he became one of the most unpopular and raucously jeered players to ever wear a Cub uniform.[34]

Miksis came over from Brooklyn during the 1951 season in a trade for Wayne Terwilliger, who finished with the next-to-worst fielding stats in the league as Smalley's double-play partner in 1950. Miksis remained in the lineup through 1953, consistently challenging for the league lead in errors at second while also putting in some error-filled time at shortstop.

Early in the 1951 campaign, Smalley broke his ankle and was out of the lineup for more than two months. In the interim, the club struggled along with rookie Jack Cusick, who hit a woeful .177, and Bob Ramazzotti, a 34-year-old war veteran with a bad back, rather than giving Baker a chance. In fact, Smalley would also miss almost half of the next two seasons, yet the Cubs never took advantage of his prolonged absences to audition Baker at shortstop.

Injuries limited Smalley to 82 games at shortstop in 1952, but Baker remained down on the farm while Tommy "Buckshot" Brown, whose scatter arm accounted for his nickname, was given first shot at replacing Smalley. Brown committed 14 errors in 39 games at shortstop, a record that made even Smalley look good. Eventually Miksis, who was on pace to lead the league's second baseman in errors, was shifted to shortstop, depriving him of worst fielding honors at second. Meanwhile the Cubs rejected a $30,000 offer from San Francisco for Baker. "Not even $100,000 would get Baker's contract ... we're bringing him up in 1953 as the first Negro to wear a Cub uniform," were general manager Wid Matthews hollow words in *The Sporting News*.[35] After the season, the Cubs announced that Baker would have the honor of being the first black to attend their pre-season major league training camp the next spring. No reason was offered as to why he couldn't have been extended an audition during the 1952 campaign.[36]

In the spring of 1953, Cubs manager Phil Cavarretta pledged that Baker would get every chance to win the shortstop job. But shortly thereafter the front office announced that they were returning the 28-year-old shortstop to Los Angeles again "for further seasoning."[37] The move brought the black media's growing frustration with the Cubs' brass to a crescendo.

A week later, A.S. "Doc" Young began his column in *Jet* magazine by noting that "Phil Cavarretta, sophomore manager of the Chicago Cubs, virtually admitted that fans who have been calling shortstop Roy Smalley a bum for years were right, but added: 'Smalley is the best shortstop I have. So I have to play him.' Curiously Phil made this statement shortly after Gene Baker, the best shortstop the Cubs own, had won an exhibition game with a two-run homer." Young went on, "The prevailing opinion is that the Cub's just don't want a Negro player at Wrigley Field.... They say repeatedly that Baker is 'a year away' and continually harp on their doubt about his hitting ability. It appears that Gene, who's been on farms for three years now, will still be a year away when he's old and gray.... And what about Smalley, Cavarretta's 'best shortstop?' He hit a puny .222 last year, not to mention a plethora of horrendous errors." Young finished his article quoting an unnamed veteran baseball observer as saying, "I feel the same way about the Cubs that Jackie Robinson does about the Yankees. Smalley never was and never will be the shortstop Gene Baker has been for at least two years. But the Cubs don't want him."[38]

Even Wrigley was critical of the action. "I don't think the situation has been handled properly. It sounds like monkey business to me. I just returned from Los Angeles where I saw Baker play and he was sensational. I shall discuss the matter with Wid Matthews as soon as I return West [to the team's Catalina Island training camp]," he vowed.[39] Apparently the Cubs general manager was able to pacify his outraged boss or Wrigley felt powerless to do anything about what was going on in his front office. The decision to demote Baker stuck, and the season opened with the much-maligned Roy Smalley back at his old shortstop post.

The incident probably illustrates the reason the Cubs took so long to integrate. Despite good intentions, Wrigley apparently wasn't sure enough of his baseball instincts to confront his recalcitrant front office and cancel Baker's demotion.

Despite only appearing in 77 games, Smalley made 25 errors in 1953, almost managing to recapture the league error crown that he'd been forced to relinquish the previous two years due to time on the disabled list. He lost out to Solly Hemus of the Cardinals, a mere pretender to the throne, who required 150 games to botch 27 chances. Smalley's fielding average was an abysmal .932, but it was better than his backup Buckshot Brown's .903 mark. Rather than promote Baker, the Cubs again turned to Miksis, who held a comfortable lead in the second-base error competition at the time. Miksis committed 12 errors in 53 games at shortstop, but they didn't count in the second-base competition so he had to settle for a tie with Milwaukee's Jack Dittmer. Miksis, however, committed his 23 miscues in only 92 appearances at second while Dittmer needed 138 games.

That season Gene Baker batted a solid .284, slammed 20 homers, stole 20 bases, drove in 99 runs, scored 89 times, and drew 78 walks in 162 games for Los Angeles.

Management's Excuses

Cub management denied racism, of course. They were concerned that attendance might be compromised by the presence of a black player, ignoring the fact that attendance at

Comiskey Park increased dramatically after the White Sox acquired Minnie Minoso in 1951. And Satchel Paige's first appearance at Comiskey Park with the Indians in 1948 resulted in massive gridlock that brought traffic on the streets, as well as the sidewalks around the stadium, to a standstill. The official paid admission of just over 51,000 trailed the all-time record but would undoubtedly have surpassed it if the estimated 15,000 fans left standing at the gate had been admitted.[40] But Chicago was a very segregated city at the time. Blacks were largely confined to ghetto areas, which were among the worst slums in the country. The White Sox played on the south side of Chicago while Wrigley field was on the north side of the city where fewer blacks lived.[41]

In the midst of the Baker controversy, Jim Gallagher demonstrated that his promotion to vice president hadn't affected his judgment by engaging in a media debate with Branch Rickey over the merits of extensive farm systems versus minor league independence. "Fewer worthwhile players are coming up than ever before," Gallagher intoned.[42] It must have taken all of Rickey's self control to refrain from pointing out that Gallagher's statement was certainly accurate if a team insisted on leaving their best players in the minors. Rickey once observed, "This team [the Cubs] has to approach cooperative perfection to remain in the shadow of last place. There is artistry in ineptitude, too, you know."[43]

The Cubs Finally Integrate

Baker finally got his chance in Chicago late in the 1953 season and made good. But it wasn't at shortstop, and he wouldn't even get to be the first black player to grace the Cubs' lineup. Baker was nursing an injury when he was called up, so the distinction of being the first black man to appear in a Cub game went to Ernie Banks, whose contract had been acquired from the Kansas City Monarchs a few days after Baker was added to the parent roster. The Cubs reportedly shelled out $35,000 for the rights to Banks and a young pitcher named Bill Dickey. Banks performed well, so Baker was shifted to second base when he was ready to play. The duo finished out the 1953 season in impressive fashion and went on to form the Cubs regular double-play combination from 1954 through 1956. Despite management's apprehensions about black players being accepted by Cub fans, the duo became huge crowd favorites, inspiring the formation of a fan club whose monthly newspaper was called *Keystone Capers*.[44]

While Baker would develop into a fine

Ernie Banks, the last Negro League star to move directly from black baseball to the big leagues, would become known as "Mr. Cub" over the course of his Hall of Fame career (1959 Topps card).

major league second baseman, Banks was destined to become the best and most popular player in Chicago Cubs history. He would end his 19-year major league career in 1971 with 512 homers in 2,528 games — all with the Chicago Cubs. An 11-time all-star, he led the league in home runs and RBIs twice and captured two National League Most Valuable Player Awards. In 1977, he would become the fourth black player elected to the Baseball Hall of Fame.

It was serendipity, however, that Banks ended up with the Cubs. He hadn't made that much of an impression in his first tour of duty in the Negro National League at the age of 19, but he began to blossom while playing service ball and caught the attention of the Dodgers and Indians.[45] He was under contract to Kansas City, however, and wanted to return there. Back with the Monarchs in 1953, he proved to be a brilliant major league prospect and developed the confidence to give the big leagues a try.[46] The Monarchs reportedly offered his services to the Yankees, Pirates, White Sox, Cardinals, and Browns before making a deal with the Cubs.[47]

In *Wrigleyville*, Len Merullo asserts that one of the main reasons the Cubs obtained Banks was to provide someone to eat and room with Baker on the road.[48] For that era, $35,000 seems like a lot to pay for a traveling companion, but a year earlier the Cubs reportedly rejected a $30,000 offer from San Francisco for Baker. It may be that the Cubs really were lucky enough to pick up a future Hall of Famer when all they were looking for was a roomie for Baker. Another consideration that might have entered into the deal was that Banks reportedly refused to sign with anyone unless they agreed to bring him to the majors immediately, and the hapless Cubs were in a position to oblige.[49]

The Cubs opened the 1954 season with Baker at second and Banks at shortstop, and both were named to *The Sporting News* all-rookie team at the close of the campaign. Former Homestead Grays outfielder Luis Marquez also began the season with the Cubs. Marquez, who spent the 1951 season with the Boston Braves, again failed to hit and was soon dispatched to Pittsburgh.

In 1955, Clarence "Pants" Rowland, who had attempted to audition some black players for his Pacific Coast League Los Angeles club back in 1943, took over as club vice president.[50] Pitcher Sam Jones, another former Negro Leaguer, joined Banks and Baker on the Cubs roster, and all three represented the Cubs on the roster of the National League All-Star Team that year. Banks emerged as a superstar, placing a close third in Most Valuable Player balloting behind Campanella and Duke Snider of the pennant-winning Dodgers.

The next year veteran outfielder Monte Irvin was drafted from the Giants in the off-season, and speedy 25-year-old center fielder Solly Drake also made the club out of spring training. On April 20, 1956, they joined Baker and Banks in the lineup with Jones on the hill as the Cubs became only the second major league team in history to field a starting lineup with a majority of black players. They routed the Cincinnati Reds 12 to 1 as Jones went the distance, Banks and Irvin slammed homers, Baker collected three hits, and Drake went two-for-two, scored a pair of runs, and stole a base.

For much of the first half of the season, Baker, Banks, Irvin, and Drake were in the regular lineup with Jones in the starting rotation. In addition, the Cubs hired respected former Negro League player and manager Buck O'Neill, who had been instrumental in bringing Banks and others into the Cubs fold, as a scout.[51] Suddenly, it seemed that one of the laggards in the integration movement was turning into one of the leaders. But within months, the Cubs began reverting to form. Midway through the campaign, Drake was sent down to the American Association, even though the switch-hitter was leading the team in steals. Drake, one of the first amateur black prospects signed by the franchise, would never get another major league opportunity with the Cubs despite excellent performances in the minors. Curt Roberts of the Pittsburgh Pirates said, "Every time I hear the Cubs are looking for a center fielder I laugh, because all they have to do is let [Drake] play and there's no doubt he'll produce."[52]

A Step Back

Before the 1957 season, John Holland replaced Wid Matthews as general manager, and Bob Scheffing took over as field manager. Under the management of old Cub favorite Stan Hack, the club had finished seventh, sixth, and eighth from 1954 through 1956, and the brass apparently arrived at the conclusion that the number of black players were the cause of the club's dismal performance. Convinced that Jones was about worn out, they included the veteran hurler in an unfortunate off-season trade with the Cardinals. Then Irvin, who had performed well in a platoon role the previous year, was returned to the minors before the beginning of the season, leaving Baker and Banks as the only two black players on the roster.

Next, fault was found with the defensive efforts of the two black infielders. Apparently Cubs' management had embraced the commonly held perception of the time that black players didn't have the intangibles required for leadership positions like second base and shortstop. This prejudice led to the "stacking phenomenon," where black players were inevitably shifted to less-demanding defensive positions.[53] Baker began the 1957 campaign at third base before being swapped to the Pittsburgh Pirates in the opening weeks of the campaign. His replacement at third was none other than Ernie Banks. Throughout much of the first half of his career, the Cubs seemed determined to get Banks off shortstop. They couldn't say much when he made 34 errors as a rookie, since that total paled in comparison to his predecessor, Roy Smalley. As a sophomore, Banks led the National League in fielding, but the next year a sore arm affected his defense. During the 1957 campaign, he played 100 games at shortstop between various third-base experiments and finished second in fielding behind Cincinnati defensive whiz Roy McMillan. By 1959, Banks had reduced his errors to a mere 12 and posted the best fielding mark in the league. In 1960, he again led National League shortstops in fielding and captured a Gold Glove Award. Yet six weeks into the 1961 season, Banks found himself stationed in left field for 23 games followed by a trial at first base. He returned to shortstop for the remainder of the campaign and finished the year with the league's best total-chances-per-game figure and one of the best fielding averages in the league. But the shift to first base was made permanent for the 1962 campaign, and he never appeared at shortstop again.

The trade of Baker early in the 1957 season left Banks as the lone black player on the Cubs' major league roster, a situation that would exist throughout the remainder of the campaign.

The club improved to sixth place in 1958, Scheffing's second year at the helm, after finishing seventh in 1957. Cuban second baseman Tony Taylor joined the team, giving the Cubs two black players again. After struggling through a difficult rookie season, Taylor teamed with Banks to form a fine double-play combination in 1959. But in the early weeks of the 1960 season, he was swapped to the Philadelphia Phillies — another trade of a black player that backfired for the Cubs. By that time, however, some of Buck O'Neill's recruits were beginning to show up. Hard-hitting outfielder George Altman won a regular spot as a rookie in 1959 and would spend nine years in the major leagues before heading to Japan for a second career. O'Neill's contacts in the black baseball community also led to the signing of future

Hall of Famers Billy Williams and Lou Brock before he was rewarded with a position on the Cubs' coaching staff.

The 1960s and Beyond

In 1960, Banks and Altman were the only black players to remain on the Cubs roster all season. Solly Drake's little brother Sammy started the season with the Cubs as a utility infielder, the duo forming the first brother combination of black major leaguers (Matty Alou wouldn't join Felipe with the Giants until late in the season). Sammy, a speedy switch-hitter like his brother, would bat only .050 in brief trials with the Cubs before going to the New York Mets, where he would get a better chance to prove he couldn't hit big league pitching.

The next year, Billy Williams won the left field job and became the 10th black National League Rookie of the Year in the league's first 15 years of integration. Fortunately, the Cubs hung on to William's for fourteen more years while he put together a Hall of Fame career. Unfortunately, they wouldn't have the foresight to hang on to young Lou Brock, another future Hall of Famer, who debuted in the Cubs outfield late in the 1961 season. In 1962, the Cubs regular lineup included five black players: first baseman Banks, right fielder Altman, left fielder Williams, rookie Brock in center, and shortstop Andre Rodgers, who arrived the previous year from San Francisco. They were the only black players on the roster. In 1963, Altman was swapped to the Cardinals, but Ellis Burton took his place to keep the number of black regulars at five, but again they were the only black players on the team.

After two mediocre seasons in the Cubs outfield, Brock was traded to the St. Louis Cardinals early in the 1964 campaign in an extraordinarily lopsided deal for sore-armed pitcher Ernie Broglio. The young speedster spurred the Cardinals to the World Championship that year and would go on to break Maury Wills single-season stolen-base record as well as Ty Cobb's career mark, bang out more than 3,000 hits, and gain a first-ballot election to Cooperstown. The Cubs also returned Burton to the minors in 1964, leaving them with only four black players: Banks, Williams, Rodgers, and rookie pitcher Sterling Slaughter for most of the campaign — one of the lowest totals in the National League. In 1965, George Altman rejoined the team and Roberto Pena started the campaign at shortstop, but Rodgers and Slaughter departed to keep the Cubs near the bottom in terms of minority employment.

Through the mid–1960s, the Cubs maintained a solid black presence in terms of quality if not quantity. They steadfastly adhered to the practice of not keeping any more black players around than was necessary, using fewer black players than other National League teams. In fact, from the time Ernie Banks took his place in the Chicago lineup until the Cubs finally achieved a measure of respectability under Leo Durocher in 1967, the team had kept only three black performers as bench players or second-line pitchers for a complete season. Andre Rodgers spent 1961 as Banks' shortstop heir, veteran George Altman returned as a platoon outfielder for the 1965 and 1966 campaigns, and young pitcher Sterling Slaughter spent the 1964 campaign in the bullpen.

In 1966, the Cubs hit the jackpot in a deal that brought in two black regulars, outfielder Adolfo Phillips and right-hander Ferguson Jenkins, from the Phillies for a couple of aging veteran hurlers. Phillips was the man the club wanted to solve their center field problem, and he had some useful seasons. But Jenkins would post six straight 20-win seasons for the Cubs beginning in 1967 and would eventually end up in the Hall of Fame.

The Cubs' small but talented nucleus of black stars — Jenkins, Williams, and Banks —

helped turn them into pennant contenders in the late 1960s, although they never quite managed to bring home the flag. When Jenkins, the winningest black hurler in history, joined Banks, Williams, Brock, and Monte Irvin in Cooperstown in 1991, the Cubs became the first team to have had five black Hall of Famers wear their jersey.

Unfortunately, the Cubs had severed relations with Banks, "Mr. Cub," a decade earlier when the *Chicago Tribune* purchased the franchise from the Wrigley family. The new owners understandably sought to de-emphasize the team's losing legacy, although firing one of the few "winners" they'd ever had hardly seemed the way to go. Banks moved to Los Angeles, but when the *Tribune* recently expressed interest in selling, it was reported that Ernie Banks was part of a group of prospective buyers.[54]

Chapter 12

THE ST. LOUIS CARDINALS

The St. Louis Cardinals were the most successful team in the National League during the 1940s, but by the end of the 1950s they had degenerated into a second-division club due largely to their initial refusal to join the integration movement in Organized Baseball.

Thanks to the fertile minor league farm system built by Branch Rickey during his tenure as general manager, the Cardinals won 960 games from 1940 through 1949, 31 more than the powerful New York Yankees in the American League and 66 more than the Brooklyn Dodgers, the second most successful National League franchise of the decade. Led by the great Stan Musial and an ever-changing cast of topflight pitchers, the Cardinals captured the World Championship in 1942, 1944, and 1946, and nearly won in 1943 as well, losing to the Yankees in a hard-fought seven-game series.

The dynasty officially ended when the Brooklyn Dodgers clinched the National League pennant in 1947, Jackie Robinson's first year in the major leagues. But the beginning of the Cardinals' slide can be pinpointed to August 28, 1945, the day the Dodgers signed Robinson. It would be more than seven years before the Cardinals signed a black player, and their reluctance to avail themselves of the rich supply of black baseball talent while their National League rivals were stocking their rosters led to their downfall.

On April 13, 1954, the Cardinals became the sixth National League team to list a black player in their lineup, narrowly beating out the Cincinnati Reds for that lowly spot by a few days. But the Reds were actually way ahead of the Cards. In 1954, a young black prospect by the name of Frank Robinson was working his way up through the Cincinnati minor league chain. St. Louis, on the other hand, didn't have a solid black prospect in their system and had been forced to purchase their first black player, Tom Alston, from the Pacific Coast League in the off-season. Alston would flop miserably, while Robinson would end up with 586 home runs and a pair of Most Valuable Player Awards to show for 21 years as a major league star.

Franchise History

In 1919, Branch Rickey moved over from the front office of the St. Louis Browns to take over the dual role of field manager and general manager of the Cardinals. He inherited a second-rate outfit in terms of both talent and resources. The previous year, the Cardinals finished at the bottom of the National League in the standings and in attendance ranking. The Cards even took a back seat in their hometown, with the fifth-place Browns drawing almost 50 percent more fans per game.

But under Rickey's leadership, the Cardinals eventually won the "Battle of St. Louis." They achieved a measure of respectability under Rickey's field management before he turned the reins over to Rogers Hornsby in 1925, but his greatest contribution was assembling Organized Baseball's first extensive farm system. Prior to the advent of the farm system, major league teams were forced to acquire young players from independent minor league franchises. Since St. Louis was by far the smallest city to field two major league teams, the Cardinals couldn't hope to compete with the richer clubs in purchasing players. Under Rickey's plan, the Cardinals acquired control of minor league franchises where they could grow their own talent. Young prospects were signed in quantity and dispersed throughout the system to ripen into future Cardinal stars or be shopped to other teams. Critics dubbed it the Cardinals' chain, likening the setup to a chain gang, but it was a phenomenal success. The first wave of young stars from Rickey's system paid off with a World Championship in 1926, National League pennants in 1928 and 1930, and another championship in 1931. By 1934, the famous Gashouse Gang had been assembled, and they prevailed over the Detroit Tigers in the World Series with a roster that featured home-grown products Dizzy Dean and Paul Dean, Joe Medwick, Pepper Martin, Rip Collins, Wild Bill Hallahan, Tex Carleton, and Bill DeLancey. From 1926 through 1942, the Cardinals won seven pennants under Rickey's command, though they never drew more than 762,000 fans in a season.[1]

Sam Breadon had become the majority owner and president of the Cardinals shortly after Rickey came aboard. A tough, tight-fisted New Yorker who made his fortune in the automotive industry, Breadon was a self-made man. Naturally his relationship with the more loquacious and erudite Rickey was somewhat strained. He grew jealous of Rickey, who justifiably received the lion's share of the credit for the team's success. In the 1930s, Breadon sold his lucrative Pierce-Arrow dealership and began meddling in the day-to-day operations of the team. By the end of the 1942 season, Rickey had endured enough of Breadon's interference. After the Cards won 106 games to capture the pennant and prevailed over Joe DiMaggio's New York Yankees in the World Series, he resigned to take over the operations of the Brooklyn Dodgers while Breadon stepped in to run the Cardinals himself.[2]

Rickey left behind a youthful and extremely talented club led by managerial genius Billy Southworth, and a farm system brimming with top prospects. The Cardinals thrived during the war years when they suffered fewer player losses to military service than most teams. Despite the loss of Southworth, who left for a handsome multi-year contract to manage the Boston Braves after the 1945 campaign, they were heavy favorites to repeat in 1946, but they ended the regular season in a first-place tie with Rickey's Dodgers. The Cards won a one-game pennant playoff and went on to take the World Series from Ted Williams and the Boston Red Sox.

The Initial Years of Integration

In 1947, the Cards looked even stronger. Future Hall of Famers Stan Musial and Red Schoendienst manned first and second base while shortstop Marty Marion and third baseman Whitey Kurowski completed the best infield in the game. The outfield included Enos Slaughter, another future Hall of Famer, in right field and gifted Terry Moore, the team captain, in center. Young Joe Garagiola and Del Rice handled the catching duties and the pitching staff featured Howie Pollet, Harry Brecheen, Murry Dickson, and Al Brazle. All of the aforementioned were products of the fertile farm system. The promotion of rookie Jim Hearn and the return of Red Munger from military service further deepened the talented pitching staff, and the acquisition of slugging outfielder Ron Northey from the Philadelphia Phillies bolstered the batting order.

Yet the Dodgers, who'd dumped ace hurler Kirby Higbe and done little to improve their roster other than promote Robinson, easily took the pennant by a five-game margin over the second-place Cardinals.

The ominous turn of fortunes should have been a wakeup call for the Cards. It wasn't. Despite the wealth of their farm system, it would be almost two decades before the Cards would finish atop the National League standings again.

Team Culture

St. Louis, called the Gateway City, was the southernmost city to host a Major League Baseball team in 1947. Missouri was a border state that had tenuously remained part of the Union during the Civil War. But it was also a slave state, and southern sympathies ran so strong that a government in exile was formed and many Missourians fought on the side of the Confederacy. St. Louis was the city where Dred Scott unsuccessfully sued for his freedom, an event that may have led directly to the war.

Befitting their geographical location, the Old South was well represented on the Cardinal roster. Enos "Country" Slaughter was from North Carolina, captain Terry Moore from Alabama, Marty Marion from South Carolina, Murry Dickson from Missouri, Red Munger from Texas, Harry Brecheen and Al Brazle hailed from Oklahoma, and Howie Pollet and manager Eddie Dyer, who replaced Southworth, were from Louisiana

From the beginning, the Cardinals organization could be characterized as being "unsympathetic" — or, less charitably, "antagonistic" — toward the integration of Major League Baseball. Owner Breadon was firmly against the integration of the game. In the late 1930s, he flatly rejected a proposal by Rickey to bring black players to the Cardinals.[3] He also served on the committee that originated the 1946 "Race Question" report that advised against the immediate introduction of black players into the major leagues.

During Jackie Robinson's rookie season, the Cards competed with the Phillies for the distinction of being his greatest tormentor. In early May, the *New York Herald Tribune* broke the story that Cardinal players had plotted to strike before their first game against Robinson and the Dodgers in Brooklyn a few days earlier. According to reporter Stanley Woodward, the strike was narrowly averted by the actions of Breadon and National League president Ford Frick.[4] Breadon tried to play down the strike threat in the press, but intimated that he was concerned about "an accidental spiking or other incident at his own park which might lead to an unpleasant situation."[5] Old Sam turned out to be quite a prophet. In August, Enos Slaughter spiked Robinson while the rookie was covering first base — an act that was seen by many, including Dodger second baseman Eddie Stanky who was closest to the play, as intentional. Just two days earlier, Cardinals outfielder Joe Medwick had also opened a gash on Robinson's leg with his spikes.[6] Cardinal catcher Joe Garagiola reportedly almost tore one of Robinson's shoes off in yet another "accident" that year.[7]

Fred Saigh's Reign

After the 1947 season, Breadon, who was suffering from prostate cancer, sold his interest in the franchise to Bob Hannegan, the former U.S. Postmaster General, and a local criminal attorney named Fred Saigh, the son of a Syrian immigrant. The original plan called for

Hannegan to be the club president, but health problems soon forced him to turn the operation over to Saigh.[8]

Shortly after Saigh took over, Rickey approached him about putting a black player on the Cardinals, but the new owner put him off, claiming he needed to study the issue. Saigh's excuse for his reluctance to integrate the Cardinals was a familiar one. He claimed to fear for his investment, afraid that the Cards' southern fan base wouldn't support the team if a black man were on it.[9] Many years later, Saigh would insist that the Cardinals sold over $200,000 worth of tickets in 1951 solely because of their stance against integration.[10] But that old defense rang hollow. Although the St. Louis Browns' initial attempt at integration in 1947 didn't have the desired impact on gate receipts, the arrival of Satchel Paige midway through the 1951 campaign boosted attendance appreciably. In 1952, Paige's first full year with the Browns, attendance increased from less than 300,000 to almost 520,000 fans — more than the club had drawn when they won the American League pennant in 1944. In addition, among major league cities, St. Louis had one of the highest percentages of non-whites in its population.[11] The city had always been a big Negro League baseball venue, and local black fans streamed through the turnstiles alongside white fans to see Jackie Robinson compete against the Cardinals.

During his stint as club owner, Saigh became something of a mover and a shaker in baseball circles, helping to orchestrate the overthrow of Happy Chandler as Commissioner of Baseball in favor of Ford Frick.[12] Under Saigh's leadership, the Cardinals remained an all-white organization. After finishing second to the Boston Braves in 1948, they chased the Dodgers down the stretch before losing out on the last day of the 1949 season. That year, there could be no doubt that the Dodgers' black stars, Robinson, Campanella, and Newcombe, made the difference between the two clubs, but the Cardinals still weren't listening. From 1950 through 1952, they still stubbornly refused to recruit black players and faded into the middle tier of the National League, finishing fifth, third, and tied for third — never getting closer to the winner's circle than eight games. Among the black players the Cardinals snubbed was Elston Howard, who grew up in the shadow of Sportsman's Park and attended a Cardinal tryout before signing with the Kansas City Monarchs.[13] The franchise also passed on Minnie Minoso after looking him over at a Ridgefield, New Jersey, tryout.[14]

Before the 1953 season began, Saigh was forced to sell the franchise after being indicted for income tax evasion. He ended up doing jail time.

Near the end of the Saigh era, Wendell Smith, the first black journalist elected to the writer's wing of the Baseball Hall of Fame, fingered the Cardinals as the most prejudiced team in baseball, claiming they would "walk away with the title" if a competition were held. "The Cardinals are completely unreconstructed," wrote Smith. "They are as anti–Negro as they were back in 1947.... Just this past season [1952] the Dodgers charged [that] the Cardinals hurled racial epithets during a game in St. Louis." Cardinal manager Eddie Stanky reportedly defended his bench jockeys by insisting that he only heard words like "porter" and "shoeshine boy" used.[15]

The Busch Era Begins

Replacing Saigh as the new owner of the St. Louis Cardinals was beer baron August Anheuser Busch, Jr., heir to the Anheuser-Busch Brewing empire. Under the ownership of both Breadon and Saigh, the Cardinals had been an under-funded penny-pinching operation, kept competitive by the abundance of their vast farm system. The Cards didn't even have their own ballpark, leasing rundown Sportsman's Park from the Browns. It was obvious that St. Louis, one of Major League Baseball's smallest markets, couldn't adequately support two teams, and there were fears that Saigh intended to move the franchise to Milwaukee, leaving St. Louis to the Browns. Instead the arrival of the Busch fortune on the scene forced the Browns to leave town.

"Gussie" Busch, in his early fifties when he purchased the Cardinals, had a reputation as a hard-living playboy. Long-time St. Louis broadcasting icon Harry Caray described him as "a booze-and-broads man."[16] His great grandfather, Adolphus Busch, co-founded the Anheuser-Busch Brewing Company along with Eberhard Anheuser in 1865. After young Gussie's "resourcefulness" helped the Busch empire survive Prohibition, he headed up the conversion back to a legitimate beer-making enterprise and personally purchased the high-stepping Clydesdale horses that would become the company's signature. He ascended to the presidency of Anheuser-Busch in 1949 after the death of his older brother.[17]

Busch claimed to have purchased the Cardinals out of civic duty, but advertising opportunities for his product might also have had something to do with it. In fact, the natural combination of beer and baseball made the acquisition of the Cardinals a coup for both the brewing company and the team. Busch also acquired Sportsman's Park from the departing Browns and promptly re-named it Busch Stadium after an attempt to christen it Budweiser Park met with priggish disapproval from the baseball establishment.[18]

The lack of a baseball background — or even an abiding interest in the game — didn't prevent Busch from taking a hands-on approach to the operations of the team. Possibly influenced by the fact that African Americans were Anheuser-Busch consumers the same as white folks, he wanted a black player for the Cardinals and wanted one immediately. By that time, most major league teams in the majors had been signing young black players for their farm systems for a few years, even if they hadn't totally embraced integration at the top level. The Cardinals, however, didn't have a single black player in their organization when Busch took over.

Busch took it upon himself to de-segregate the club. When attempts to purchase established black performers failed, he decided the Cardinals needed to develop their own black stars.[19] Less than a year after Busch took control, Cardinals Chief Scout Joe Mathes told *The Sporting News*, "One of the first things Mr. Busch told us when he took over the club was that he wanted good ballplayers regardless of race, color, or creed. Now we have 13 colored boys among our 141 professional rookies."[20] Busch also hired former Negro League standout Quincy Trouppe as a scout. Trouppe's first move was to recruit the organization's first black prospect, Leonard Tucker, out of Fresno State University.[21] The Cardinals thought Tucker was of normal college student age when they signed him, but he'd already done a four-year military hitch and was at least 23 years old when he began his professional baseball career in 1953. His age became an issue with the Cardinals, and he never made it to the big time despite impressive power figures in the minors, including a 1956 Triple Crown season when he led the Southwestern League with a .404 batting average, 51 homers, and 181 runs batted in.[22]

The Cards Integrate

Before the 1954 season, Busch, acting almost independently, acquired the contract of black first baseman Tom Alston from the San Diego Padres of the Pacific Coast League for the then-princely sum of $100,000 and a couple of players, one of whom was former Philadelphia

Phillies hero Dick Sisler.[23] Although his intentions were commendable, the fact that Busch knew little about the game doomed his efforts.

Alston opened the 1954 season at first base for the Cardinals. But the lanky first sacker couldn't stand the combined pressure of breaking the Cardinals color barrier along with justifying his huge price tag.[24] He would end up being a colossal disappointment. The scouting reports tabbed Alston as a brilliant fielder with good speed and quickness and described him as bright and hardworking.[25] He'd enjoyed a good, though hardly sensational, 1953 campaign in the Pacific Coast League, but he couldn't handle big league pitching. Furthermore, he complained of an assortment of maladies, including a sore arm, bad back, thyroid condition, and chronic exhaustion.[26] Many suspected that he was a hypochondriac and that his problems were mental rather than physical.[27] In addition, Alston was several years older than the Cardinals thought. In mid-season, he was demoted to Rochester of the International League after playing in 66 games, and he would appear in only 25 more contests for the Cardinals over the next three seasons. He had often talked of quitting and after the 1957 season he walked away from the game for good. Despite a college education, he was never able to hold a job after baseball and ended up spending several years in mental institutions.[28]

But Gussie Busch and the Cardinals would ultimately come up with a black rookie star during the 1954 campaign, almost by accident. Early in the season, they took a brief look at Bill Greason, a former Negro Leaguer hurler and future preacher. Greason only got a four-inning trial, but his replacement, Brooks Lawrence, won 15 games and posted the second-highest winning percentage in the league despite spending the first two months of the season with the Cards' Columbus farm club. Lawrence, an unheralded 29-year-old right-hander, spent five years in the minors after signing with Cleveland in 1949 and was about to hang up his toe plate when St. Louis drafted him after the 1953 season.[29] The intelligent, articulate moundsman, who matriculated at Miami University of Ohio before beginning his professional career, could have served as a building block for the introduction of more black players to St. Louis. But Brooks never made it through his sophomore reason in Cardinal red.

The Cardinals also signed two other black prospects before the 1954 season who would eventually become solid major leaguers, but not for the Cardinals. Pitcher John Wyatt would develop into a relief ace in the American League, and Ruben Amaro would become a Gold Glove shortstop for the Philadelphia Phillies.

Emotional as well as physical problems contributed to the failure of Tom Alston, the first black St. Louis Cardinal (1955 Bowman card).

Manager Eddie Stanky

Frequent front office upheaval and managerial turnover marked Busch's first decade as owner of the Cards. Much of the franchise's failure to develop and retain good black players is due to their managerial selections. When Busch took control of the club, he inherited Eddie "The Brat" Stanky who would be on hand to welcome the Cardinals' first black players. Stanky, a teammate of Jackie Robinson in 1947, was thought to be one of the supporters of a Dodger player petition against Robinson and even told Robinson to his face that he didn't like him.[30] But he's also been given credit for courageously coming to Robinson's defense when the Philadelphia Phillies engaged in a vicious verbal assault on him.[31] After the 1947 campaign, Stanky was traded to make room for Robinson at second base, and in 1951 he was the regular second baseman for the New York Giants' pennant-winning team that featured black stars Monte Irvin, Hank Thompson, and Willie Mays. Apparently Stanky respected black players for their ability on the baseball field, but couldn't entirely overcome his biases.

During Lawrence's rookie season, Stanky was using him almost every day as both a starter and reliever. When a reporter asked the Cardinal manager if he wasn't afraid of abusing the hurler's arm, he replied, "I didn't know you could hurt one of them." It's little wonder that Lawrence developed ulcers during his rookie season and was hospitalized when they flared up during the winter. When the 1955 season began, he was still weak from his ordeal and pitched ineffectively.[32]

Stanky was fired as manager early in the 1955 campaign. He later managed the White Sox and then enjoyed a successful career coaching at the University of South Alabama before the Texas Rangers lured him back to the big time in 1977. He lasted only one game before becoming fed up with modern players. It may be merely coincidental that the Rangers had a healthy contingent of black players.

Harry "The Hat" Walker Takes Over

While Stanky's dismissal was not exactly a blow to Busch's on-going effort to integrate the St. Louis Cardinals, the hiring of Harry "the Hat" Walker as his replacement certainly was. Walker was born in Pascagoula, Mississippi, and grew up in Alabama. His father, a former major league pitcher, was nicknamed Dixie, and Harry probably would have carried the nickname too if it hadn't already been bestowed on his older brother — the Dodger outfielder who objected most strenuously to Robinson's presence. Harry Walker had been a member of the Cardinals' 1942, 1943, and 1946 pennant-winning squads. After a trade to the Phillies, he won the 1947 National League batting championship, combining with 1945 champ Dixie to become the first brother combo to win major league batting titles. He returned to the Cardinals in 1950 to finish out his playing career and stayed on as a coach and minor league manager.

Under Walker's management, Busch's plans for an integrated Cardinal powerhouse took a step backward. According to Lawrence, "[Walker] didn't like blacks. Walker didn't make any bones about it.... It wasn't any secret how he felt, so I just decided to stay out of his way, because I was the only black on the team at that time." Lawrence fell into disfavor when he failed to regain his touch and was dispatched to Oakland of the Pacific Coast League late in the season. It seems that Walker needed to get in some pension plan time as an active player, so the team's sole black representative was sent down to open up a roster spot — a move that returned the Cardinals to segregated status.[33]

A decade later, a reconstructed Harry Walker would be credited with turning light-hitting Dominican outfielder Matty Alou into a batting champion while the pilot of a heavily black Pittsburgh Pirates squad.

Frank Lane as General Manager

In 1953, the first season under Busch ownership, the Cardinals finished in a third-place tie with the Phillies. They slumped to sixth in 1954, and the slide continued in 1955 when they fell to seventh place — their worst finish since Branch Rickey's first year a manager of the team 36 years earlier. Initially Busch had appointed Anheuser-Busch executive Dick Meyer as general manager because he'd played some college baseball.[34] But the embarrassing 1955 campaign was enough to finally convince Busch to hire a general manager with a baseball background and entrust him with the authority to run things. That October, he hired Frank Lane who had had tremendous success with the Chicago White Sox before losing a power struggle with some members of the ruling Comiskey family.

"Trader" Lane lived up to his nickname. One of his first moves was to swap Lawrence and a minor league infielder to the Cincinnati Reds for lefthander Jackie Collum. At the time, the deal looked one-sided in the Cards' favor, but it backfired when Lawrence developed into Cincinnati's staff ace while St. Louis proved to be but a brief stop along Collum's nomadic career path that produced only seven more major league victories. After the season started, Lane dealt 1955 Rookie of the Year Bill Virdon to the Pirates for diamond gypsies Bobby Del Greco and Dick Littlefield, another trade that would hobble the franchise for years. Then he incurred the wrath of the Cards' faithful by trading gracefully aging favorite Red Schoendienst to the Giants for fast-fading Al Dark and tossing in promising outfielder Jackie Brandt to boot. Despite Lane's deals, the Cardinals moved back into the first division in 1956, finishing fourth under the solid leadership of new manager Fred Hutchinson.

With the exception of the Philadelphia Phillies, the Cardinals were the biggest losers in the baseball integration process. Ten years after the major league color barrier was pierced, the Cardinals still hadn't had a black player spend a full season with the club. In 1956, Lawrence was starring in Cincinnati while the Cards' contingent of black players, consisting of Tom Alston, rookie Charley Peete, and journeyman acquisition Chuck Harmon, spent most of the campaign in the minor leagues. For the entire 1956 season, the total contribution of black players to the Cardinals' fortunes consisted of only 10 hits in 69 at-bats — a miserable .145 average. Meanwhile, each of the Cardinals' National League rivals, except for the still-segregated Phillies, had at least one black future Hall of Famer on their roster. The Dodgers still had Robinson and Campanella on their pennant-winning squad. The fast-rising Braves featured young Hank Aaron in their outfield. The Giants had the great Willie Mays in center field. The Cubs had Ernie Banks patrolling shortstop and veteran Monte Irvin platooning in left field. The cellar-dwelling Pittsburgh Pirates were realizing their first dividends from the acquisition of Roberto Clemente the previous year. And Frank Robinson captured Rookie of the Year honors in Cincinnati. The Cardinals' poor luck with black players didn't even end with the regular season. In the off-season, Charley Peete, who won the 1956 American Association batting championship after an early season trial with the Cards was ruined by an injury, was killed in a plane crash en route to Venezuela for winter ball.

The irony of the Cardinals' situation is that their Rickey-built farm system continued to pump out quality products. Between 1953 and 1955, Cardinals got exceptional rookie seasons from no less than 13 freshmen players who would develop into solid major leaguers. First baseman Steve Bilko, third sacker Ray Jablonski, outfielder Rip Repulski, and pitcher Harvey Haddix came up in 1953. Outfielder Wally Moon, first baseman Joe Cunningham, catcher Bill Sarni, shortstop Alex Grammas, and Lawrence debuted in 1954. And outfielder Bill Virdon, third baseman Ken Boyer, and pitchers Larry Jackson and Luis Arroyo joined the club in 1955. But despite adding these young talents, they continued to slide in the standings. In 1956, the Cards debuted four more rookie stars, second baseman Don Blasingame, catcher Hal Smith, pitcher Lindy McDaniel and outfielder Jackie Brandt, but only moved up to fourth place.

Lane's trading acumen improved in 1957, and the Cards finished a surprising second behind the powerful Milwaukee Braves. Before the season, they acquired hurler Sam Jones, one of the few successful black pitchers in the majors at the time, from the Cubs. Jones fit nicely into the starting rotation and became the first black player to spend an entire season with the club. He was also the team's only black representative for most of the season. Alston was hospitalized after a mysterious loss of weight and strength, spending all but nine games on the disabled list, and Harmon was shipped to the Phillies early in the campaign. Late in the season, former Kansas City Monarch Frank Barnes made his major league debut at age 29.

After the season, "Frantic Frank" Lane arranged to send rising young star Ken Boyer to the Phillies for veteran Richie Ashburn, and he was working on moving Cardinal icon Stan Musial. When Busch got wind of it he cancelled the Boyer deal, aborted the Musial discussions, and fired Lane, replacing him with Bing Devine.[35]

The Promotion of Bing Devine

Branch Rickey was in charge back when Devine joined the Cardinals' front office out of college and began working his way up the club's executive hierarchy. After five years as the Rochester general manager, he returned to St. Louis in 1956 to assist Lane. Devine would lay the groundwork for three Cardinal pennants in the 1960s by engineering a series of outstanding deals that brought in a bevy of talented black players and reversed the team's fortunes.

Devine's first trade was a beauty. In a bold move that more than evened the score with Cincinnati for the disastrous Brooks Lawrence deal, he acquired 20-year-old outfielder Curt Flood from the Reds in exchange for mediocre reliever Willard Schmidt. Flood captured the regular center field job and along with Jones, who established a new team strikeout record, gave the Cardinals an unprecedented two black players on the roster for the entire season. In addition, four other black players also spent time on the roster in Devine's first year in the general manager's hot seat. Unfortunately, the Cards fell to sixth place, and manager Fred Hutchinson got the axe late in the campaign. The 1959 season began with feisty former Cardinal shortstop Solly Hemus, the seventh Cardinal manager of the decade, at the helm.

The efforts of Busch and Devine to fully integrate the Cardinals were finally starting to pay off, however. Seven black players spent time with the club in 1959, and for most of the season there were at least four black players on the roster. In addition to Flood, veteran first baseman George Crowe, who was acquired from Cincinnati in the off-season, and young outfielder/first baseman Bill White, who came over from the Giants in exchange for Sam Jones, spent the whole season with the Cards. Outfielder Joe Durham and pitcher Bob Gibson began the season with the team, but both were shipped out early. By the time Gibson was recalled in July, former Cincinnati Royals basketball-star-turned-pitcher Dick Ricketts had come and gone, and lefthander Marshall Bridges had joined the bullpen brigade. Ricketts and Durham would never resurface in the majors, but Bridges would develop into a dependable reliever. Crowe would establish a since-broken career record for pinch-homers before retiring. Flood, White, and Gibson would all go on to stardom with the Cardinals, but not without enduring a bumpy 2½ years under Solly Hemus first.

Manager Solly Hemus

Hemus had served as the Cardinals' regular shortstop from 1951 through 1953 and spent the next two seasons with the team as a utility infielder. After being swapped to the Phillies in 1956, Hemus impressed Busch with a fawning note expressing how much he loved being a Cardinal and asking for the chance to return if the circumstances were right.[36] Three years later, the Cardinals reacquired the little veteran and appointed him manager/utility-infielder. One of Hemus' first managerial moves was to bench Flood and let him know that he didn't think he'd make it as a major league hitter.[37] He also suggested to Gibson, once a star forward at Creighton University, that he might be better off pursuing a basketball career.[38] In addition, he insisted on playing White, an excellent defensive first baseman, in the outfield while keeping Musial, who was actually more comfortable in the outer garden, at first base.

Early in his first year at the Cardinal helm, Hemus stuck himself in the lineup in an attempt to spark the team and

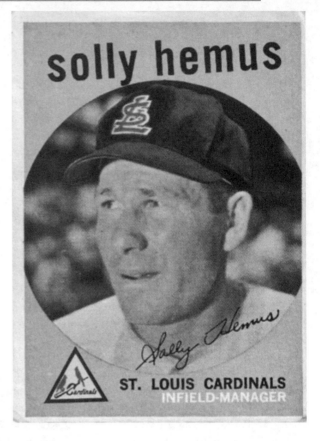

While managing the Cardinals feisty Solly Hemus was dubbed "Little Faubus" after Arkansas' segregationist governor (1959 Topps card).

promptly started a brawl with Pirate hurler Bennie Daniels. Afterward, he proudly reported in a team meeting with the several black Cardinals present that he called Daniels a "black son of a bitch."[39] Daniels, who hailed from Arkansas, reportedly dubbed Hemus "Little Faubus," likening him to Arkansas Governor Orville Faubus, who publicly vowed to close the state's public schools rather than integrate them.[40]

The 1960s and Beyond

The Cardinals actually made significant strides in the integration arena during Hemus' managerial term, although it was probably despite his influence. The 1960 season began with White doing a poor imitation of a center fielder while the gifted Flood warmed the bench alongside Gibson. Eventually Hemus moved White back to first base and reluctantly installed Flood in center field. Later, Julian Javier was acquired from the Pirates to play second base, giving the club three black regulars for the first time. But the careers of Flood and Gibson didn't really take off until Johnny Keane replaced Hemus midway through the 1961 campaign.

In light of the backward racial attitudes that the Cardinal organization of the integration era seemed to have, it's ironic that the Cards may have employed the first minority manager —

if not the first black manager. Mike Gonzalez remained with the Cardinals as a coach and scout for many years after his lengthy catching career ended, and he is widely credited with coining the wonderfully concise yet wholly informative "good field — no hit" scouting report.[41] Gonzalez, who some thought might have black ancestors, twice took over the reins as interim manager of the Cardinals, for 17 games in 1938 and six in 1940.[42] Of course, Branch Rickey was the Cards' general manager at that time.

By 1962, Gibson anchored the pitching staff, and the Cards' regular lineup included four black players — White, Flood, Javier, and rookie shortstop Julio Gotay. Veteran Minnie Minoso, acquired from the White Sox in the off-season, was supposed to be a fifth black regular until an early season injury derailed his campaign.

That spring, a momentous event in the baseball integration process occurred off the field. Housing arrangements for black players had always been a problem during spring training in the South. They were usually not allowed to stay with their teammates and often stayed in boarding houses or the private homes of black or Hispanic families in the area. Amazingly, the teams,

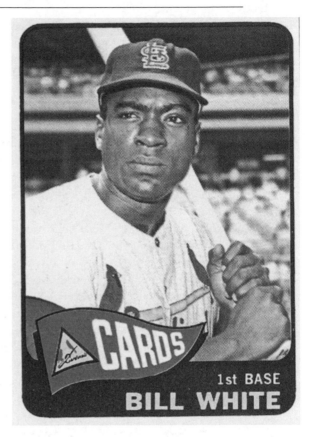

First baseman Bill White rose to stardom with the Cardinals and later became the first black man to hold the office of league president (1965 Topps card).

who carried considerable economic clout, did little to try to change the situation. In the spring of 1961, Bill White finally had had enough when he found out about a St. Petersburg Chamber of Commerce sponsored "Salute to Baseball" breakfast at a local yacht club that only white players were invited to attend. White went public with his objections. The issue of segregated facilities in Florida finally received national attention, and the Players' Association, under pressure from their growing black constituency, issued a resolution to the owners asking them to ensure that black players were properly housed at spring training. The Cardinals addressed the issue by canceling their luxury hotel accommodations and moving the team into a downscale non-segregated establishment. Team leaders Ken Boyer and Stan Musial, who normally stayed in beachfront condos, moved in with the team to show their support. Many veterans claimed the action brought the team together, and it forced the city to change their policies lest they lose major league business. Other teams followed suit, using their dollars to induce equality.[43]

The Cards captured the National League pennant in 1964, the franchise's first flag since the major leagues were integrated. The key to their success was Devine's acquisition of young black outfielder Lou Brock in a mid–June deal with the Cubs that exceeded the Flood trade in terms of one-sidedness. With Brock in left, Flood in center, White at first, Javier at second, and Gibson heading the pitching staff, the Cardinals triumphed over the New York Yankees in the World Series. Except for the replacement of White with Orlando Cepeda, this nucleus would stay intact to bring another World Championship to St. Louis in 1967 and add another pennant in 1968. In fact, the 1967 champs had nine black players making significant contributions. Unfortunately, the architect of the club's success, Bing Devine, was canned shortly after bringing Brock to St. Louis.

The first generation of black players changed the tempo of the game with a revolutionary blend of daring speed and slashing power, ironically a style that the Cardinal teams of the 1940s had pioneered. But while a steady stream of lithe, but powerful, black stars poured into the major leagues during the late 1940s and early 1950s, the Cardinals became obsolete. In 1953, the last year of the Cardinals' self-inflicted segregation, speedy hard-hitting black rookies Billy Bruton, Junior Gilliam, Al Smith, Jim Pendleton, Gene Baker, and Ernie Banks debuted in the major leagues. That same season, three rookies broke into the Cardinal lineup. But Bilko, Jablonski, and Repulski sounded like a meatpacking operation and resembled butchers in the field as well.

The Cardinals rebounded quickly from the effects of their early anti-integration policies. Their 1960s nucleus of black stars would leave a lasting impression on the baseball landscape. After a stellar career, White would go into baseball administration and eventually become president of the National League. Flood would pave the way for free agency and gain the lasting appreciation of future generations of major leaguers by challenging the reserve clause all the way to the Supreme Court. Brock, Gibson, and Cepeda would be inducted into the Hall of Fame after their fabulous careers were over. Ironically, Gibson is the only one of the distinguished group who was a product of the Cardinal farm system.

Chapter 13

THE CINCINNATI REDS

According to the history books, the Cincinnati Reds, baseball's oldest professional team, were laggards in the integration movement. They were the next-to-last 20th-century National League franchise and 11th major league team to put a black player in the lineup. Ironically, they may really have been the first.

The Reds were trailblazers in the recruitment of Hispanic baseball players. In the fall of 1908, they became the first American squad to barnstorm Cuba since the early 1890s. Dark-skinned Cuban ace Jose Mendez, known as "El Diamante Negro" or "The Black Diamond," was the star of the show, but the Reds were also impressed by some of the slightly lighter-skinned Cubans.[1] A few years later, they signed Rafael Almeida and Armando Marsans, who had competed against them on the island. Almeida and Marsans, who were moderately dark-complexioned, were passed off as part–Spaniard rather than part-black despite the fact that both had previously appeared in the American Negro Leagues. Third baseman Almeida played parts of three seasons with the Reds, but could never win a regular spot despite a good glove and decent batting average. Outfielder Marsans, however, played eight major league seasons. The two were initially greeted with some hostility in the "Queen City," but Marsans eventually became a crowd favorite with his daring base running and aggressive slides.[2]

Another Cuban who was suspected of having black ancestry, catcher Mike Gonzalez, got his first real big league chance with the Reds in 1914. Gonzalez, who also played some Negro League ball, enjoyed a 17-year National League career that included stops in Boston, New York, Chicago, and St. Louis as well as Cincinnati.[3]

A few years later, Dolf Luque, who was rumored to be at least part black, would become a mainstay of the Cincinnati pitching staff. From 1918 through 1929, he won 153 games for the Reds, peaking with a 1923 season in which he paced the National League with 27 wins and a 1.93 earned run average. Luque, who was called "The Pride of Havana," pitched for a couple of Negro League clubs and also put in time with the Braves, Dodgers, and Giants before beginning a 20-year major league career in 1914 that would see him rack up 193 victories, most of them in a Reds' uniform.[4]

In 1944, the Reds recruited veteran Cuban hurler Tommy de la Cruz to bolster their wartime pitching staff. The 32-year-old de la Cruz won a spot in the starting rotation and posted an earned run average well below the league norm in 1944, but the next year he was gone from the big league scene, never to return. Veteran scout Howie Haak, who combed the Caribbean for the Pittsburgh Pirates in the 1950s, claimed, "Tommy de la Cruz was as black as they come." Years later, a NBC documentary on the history of Latin American Players, *Baseball With a Latin Beat*, tabbed de la Cruz as baseball's first 20th-century black player.[5]

Franchise History

In 1869, the Cincinnati Red Stockings became the first professional baseball team — at least the first to publicly acknowledge their men were paid a salary to play. The club eventually gravitated to the American Association, then switched its allegiance to the National League in 1890. The Reds captured their first National League pennant in 1919. After defeating the Chicago "Black Sox" in the tainted 1919 World Series, the Reds remained contenders through the first half of the 1920s before entering a prolonged period of futility.

Larry MacPhail persuaded electronics magnate Powel Crosley, Jr., to purchase the financially bereft Cincinnati franchise in 1933 and install him as general manager. Crosley, who also owned the largest radio station in the world, was the most "hands-off" club owner of the era, preferring "to put the best available baseball men in charge and give them free reign."[6]

In the decade prior to World War II, the Reds were an innovative, winning team. MacPhail, who while in the army during World War I was reportedly involved in a plot to kidnap Germany's Kaiser Wilhelm, came

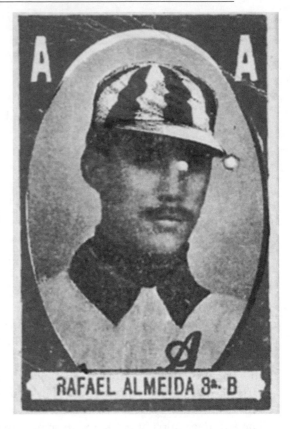

The 1911 debut of Cubans Rafael Almeida and Armando Marsans raised objections until the Reds produced "evidence" of Spanish ancestry (Cuban card).

to Cincinnati with a reputation for being a restless, daring and imaginative executive who loved turmoil and thrived on controversy.[7] Under his command, the Reds became the first team to travel by plane, and he helped pioneer regular radio broadcasts of games. He's even credited with introducing the ballpark organist to entertain the fans. In 1935, MacPhail introduced night baseball to the major leagues, a move which helped get the Reds back on sound financial footing. It's ironic that, as president and general manager of the mighty New York Yankees a decade later, MacPhail would be an outspoken defender of the status quo and an opponent of integration.

Before leaving the club in a flap over stock ownership after the 1936 season, MacPhail had also begun to get the team turned around on the field. By 1939, the Reds were in the winner's circle, with the departed MacPhail receiving more credit for building the pennant-winning team than his successor Warren Giles. They repeated as National League champs in 1940 and defeated the Detroit Tigers in the World Series. Under Giles' stewardship, the Reds remained a competitive squad through 1944 before descending into the depths of the National League standings. From 1945 through 1955, they would not finish higher than fifth place.

Giles, who began his career as a major league baseball executive under Branch Rickey in St. Louis, served as Cincinnati general manager through the 1951 campaign. The corpulent, silver-haired Giles was the ultimate insider, a power in behind-the-scenes baseball politics.

He was so popular with his fellow moguls he was almost elected to replace Happy Chandler as Commissioner of Baseball in 1951. He was deadlocked with Ford Frick in the balloting before graciously withdrawing for the good of baseball and the position of National League President.[8] In that capacity, he presided over an era in which the National League forged well ahead of their American League counterparts in integration, although there's little evidence to suggest that he personally helped the cause.

While still running the Reds in 1949, Giles mouthed the following politically correct (for the times) blather: "Recent performances by Negroes in the major leagues indicates that the outstanding Negro player can qualify for major league standard of play. As more of them develop, more will have an opportunity, although the ratio of Negro players to other players in the major leagues will probably be small for many years."[9] Like so many general managers of the era, Giles apparently couldn't find "outstanding Negro players" and wasn't interested in anything less, since the Reds made no move to integrate during his tenure.

The Reds didn't sign their first black player until long-time general manager Warren Giles resigned to become president of the National League (1959 Topps card).

Team Culture

In the early days of baseball's integration, Cincinnati, along with Philadelphia and St. Louis, was a place that black players wished to avoid.[10] Cincinnati is one of the more southerly major league cities. It's situated on the banks of the Ohio River across from Kentucky, a state that permitted slavery and was divided in its allegiance during the Civil War. The city has a long history of racial violence dating back to riots begun by whites to terrorize the free black community in 1829.[11] Even as the 21st century dawned, police killings of several young black males incited the Cincinnati Riots of 2001. To this day, the city's neighborhoods remain highly segregated.[12]

Cincinnati fans were merciless in their abuse of black players at cozy Crosley Field where the crowd sat close enough to personally share their most intimate biases. Hank Thompson of the New York Giants recalled, "The worst fans were in Cincinnati. Whenever there was a lull, some loudmouth would yell: 'Nigger' ... and you could hear it all over the place."[13] Most sources place Cincinnati as the site of the most celebrated incident of Robinson's first season. Legend has it that respected Dodger shortstop Pee Wee Reese, a Kentucky native, shocked a hostile Crosley Field crowd into submission by draping his arm around the rookie's shoulders in a courageous display of solidarity, although similar incidents undoubtedly occurred elsewhere.[14]

Five years later, Wendell Smith would write, "[Cincinnati fans] still seem to take delight in 'riding' Negro players from the stands."[15] The team itself was just as bad according to Smith, who would slot the Reds behind only the St. Louis Cardinals in his ranking of the most prejudiced National League teams. "The Cincinnati Reds have been almost as brutal on Negro players as the Cardinals," he wrote. "In 1947, for example, the Reds were particularly rough on Robinson. They called him everything they could think of from the bench."[16] In 1949, *The Sporting News* passively mentioned that "Cincinnati Reds' pitchers took turns putting the Giants two Negro players (rookies Monte Irvin and Hank Thompson) on the seats of their trousers."[17]

In late September 1951, hopes for a change in the Reds' racial climate got a boost when Giles left Cincinnati for the National League office, and his able long-time assistant Gabe Paul was elevated to the general manager position. Paul, who was Jewish and knew a thing or two about prejudice and discrimination, was not averse to integrating the Reds.

But during Paul's initial season in charge, death threats against Jackie Robinson necessitated the employment of armed bodyguards while the Dodgers were in Cincinnati.[18] Reds' bench jockeys helped keep racial tension high with a taunting rendition of "Old Black Joe" when Dodger hurler Joe Black took the mound against them.[19] And manager Luke Sewell did his part by warning black Boston Braves first baseman George Crowe that he would be badly hurt if he didn't learn to avoid tight pitches.[20]

Another obstacle to Paul's integration efforts was that the Reds' top farm clubs were located in Tulsa, Oklahoma, and Columbia, South Carolina, not exactly ideal spots for vulnerable, impressionable young black players. When Paul took over, the Reds didn't even have an exclusive Triple A affiliation, although they often assigned players to Charleston in the American Association.

Nevertheless, Paul forged ahead with a determined effort to integrate the Reds. Within months of his taking office, the organization hired black scouts Elwood Parsons and Alvah Caliman.[21] Before the 1952 season, five black prospects were signed for the organization's lower-level farm teams. Of the five, only shortstop Gilbert Jones, rated the best amateur player in the Pittsburgh area the previous year, and pitcher Jim Summers would ultimately play in the Cincinnati organization. Both were slated for the Reds' new Burlington, Iowa, farm club in the Class B Illinois-Iowa-Indiana (Three I) League but spent their only season in Organized Baseball with the Mattoon Indians in the Class D Mississippi-Ohio Valley League.[22]

The Burlington franchise did integrate in 1952, however. Before the season, the Reds acquired the contract of Chuck Harmon from Buffalo of the International League and assigned him to Burlington, where he led the league in stolen bases.[23]

Rogers Hornsby Appointed Manager

Unfortunately, Paul made another move his first year in office that probably set the course of integration in Cincinnati back at least a year. When he took over as general manager, he inherited easy-going Luke Sewell as his field manager. When Sewell resigned in the middle of the 1952 season, Paul, against sound advice from many quarters, hired batting legend Rogers Hornsby to take over the reins. Paul was convinced that Hornsby, who had just been fired by the St. Louis Browns, would be the firm taskmaster the Reds needed to break out of the doldrums.[24]

Hornsby was not the right man to oversee the introduction of a black player in Cincinnati. Upon the announcement of Robinson's signing with Brooklyn, he flatly predicted, "It won't work out." Hornsby felt that a "mixed baseball team differs from other sports because ball players on the road live much closer together. It's going to be more difficult for the Negro player to adjust himself to the life of a major league club, than for the white players to accept him."[25]

Blacks clearly understood where Hornsby was coming from. "The prospects for a better deal [for black players] in Cincinnati are far from bright," predicted Wendell Smith before the 1953 season, "The team is now managed by one of the most bigoted men in baseball, Rogers Hornsby."[26] The next spring, Willie Powell, a former Negro League pitcher trying to make the squad as a 35-year-old rookie, was being kidded by teammates for carrying a record player on a spring training trip. "You wouldn't be listening to that music if Hornsby were here," they chided. "From what I hear, if Hornsby were here, I wouldn't be," Powell retorted.[27]

A lot of white folks didn't seem to think much of Hornsby either. Columnist Earl Lawson, who covered the Reds for 34 years, called him, "one of the most prejudiced, uncouth, thoughtless individuals I've ever met." As a manager, he was hypercritical and totally insensitive to the feelings of his players.[28]

The Reds actually played winning baseball after Hornsby took over two-thirds of the way through the 1952 season, moving from seventh up to sixth place under his direction. But, as had happened in St. Louis, the crusty veteran ended up losing the respect of the team as well as a lot of games. He left with eight games remaining in the 1953 season when Paul refused to renew his contract. Years later, Hornsby confided to Earl Lawson that he thought he'd been let go because, unaware that Paul was Jewish, he'd complained to him about "Kikes" running down the neighborhood where he'd owned a apartment.[29]

A Poor Man's Jackie Robinson

With Hornsby gone, the way was clear for the Reds to join the growing majority of integrated major league teams in 1954. New manager Birdie Tebbetts, who had majored in psychology at Providence College, was the antithesis of his predecessor. Tebbetts, a longtime big league catcher, was a master storyteller who cultivated a good relationship with the press and was generally well liked by his players.

Much like Branch Rickey's choice of Jackie Robinson to integrate the Dodgers, Chuck Harmon was hand-picked by Gabe Paul to cross the color line in Cincinnati

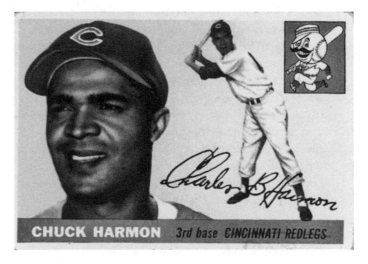

In 1954 former college basketball standout Chuck Harmon became the first African American to play for the Reds (1955 Topps card).

because of personal qualities as much as talent.[30] An old pro at busting color barriers, the 30-year-old Harmon was sort of a poor man's Jackie Robinson. He was one of the first 18 black players in Organized Baseball, beginning his career in 1947 as the first black player on the Gloversville-Johnstown Glovers, one of only two black players in the Canadian-American League. In 1949, he moved to Olean of the Pennsylvania-Ontario-New York League (PONY League), becoming one of that circuit's first black performers. A college basketball star, Harmon was invited to the Boston Celtics pre-season camp in 1950 and unsuccessfully vied with four other black players for the distinction of being the National Basketball Association's first black performer before returning to baseball. Before the 1952 season, Buffalo of the International League acquired him to break their color line, but he didn't make the team and was picked up by the Reds organization before the season began.[31] After his fine season with Burlington, the Reds assigned Harmon to Tulsa to integrate their Texas League affiliate along with Puerto Rican outfielder Nino Escalera, whose contract had been purchased from the Toledo franchise of the American Association during the 1952 season.[32]

Thanks, in part, to Paul running interference for him, Harmon enjoyed a decent rookie season for the 1954 Reds.[33] He became the first African American to play for the Reds, but he missed distinction of becoming the first black player to play for the Reds by a couple of pitches. In the third game of the season, Escalera, who was described as "visibly as dusky-toned as Chuck Harmon's," was inserted as a seventh-inning pinch-hitter, becoming the first acknowledged black player in Cincinnati Reds history.[34] The very next batter up was Harmon, also in a pinch-hitting role. Many, however, consider Harmon the first black Cincinnati Red since he was already in the organization when the Reds acquired Escalera's contract. In fact, Harmon was added to the parent roster after the conclusion of the 1953 Texas League season, but he wasn't brought up for late-season trial with the Reds with Hornsby still around.[35]

Neither Escalera nor Harmon could be considered top prospects. Escalera, who originally signed with the New York Yankees and spent four years in their system, had little power and batted only .249 in 1952, his only full season at the Triple A level. Harmon had never advanced beyond Class B before spending the 1953 season in Class AA with Tulsa. Harmon spent three full seasons and part of a fourth as a utility player in the majors, and earned the nickname "The Glove" because he carried around a different glove for each position he played—first base, third base, and outfield.[36] Escalera, however, didn't hit his weight (which was only 165 pounds) for the 1954 season, the only shot he'd get at major league pitching.

Prior to the 1953 campaign, the Reds signed a couple of promising young black prospects, infielder Chico Terry and outfielder Frank Robinson, and assigned them to their Ogden club in the Class C Pioneer League. Terry would enjoy some good seasons and advance as far as Triple A while Robinson would go on to become one of baseball's all-time greats. The Reds also obtained pitcher Brooks Lawrence from the Cleveland Indians' system early in the 1953 campaign, but lost him to the Cardinals in the minor league draft that winter after he won 18 games for Portsmouth in the Piedmont League. In addition, they acquired the rights to the aforementioned Willie Powell, who had had an excellent 1953 season at Charleston but wouldn't make the cut with the Reds.

The Reds' Mentor Corps

The Reds faced a serious dilemma when they finally began to pursue integration in earnest. Cincinnati had the fewest residents of any major league city at the time, making the

Reds a "small market franchise" long before the term came into vogue.[37] The club couldn't afford to buy established black stars or top prospects from other teams, and the Negro Leagues had already been picked clean of cheap ready-made talent. Furthermore, they didn't have any advanced black prospects in their system, since they hadn't recruited black players before Paul took over as general manager.

Paul realized that the Reds would have to develop their own black talent in the minor leagues to catch up with their National League rivals, while simultaneously preparing the right environment for young black players to flourish at the major league level. Therefore, the club was forced to turn to black veterans who hadn't been able to find a home in the big leagues with other organizations for immediate help. The Reds chose their first generation of black players judiciously, selecting respected veterans who were not only useful performers, but would serve as mentors for the succeeding generation of young black prospects. The players selected were generally well educated and were all veterans of military service as well. They'd paid their dues in black baseball as well as organized ball.

In 1955, the Reds dropped Escalera but added slugging outfielder Bob Thurman and pitcher Joe Black, both former Negro Leaguers. Former Philadelphia Stars infielder Milt Smith was also auditioned at third base, but he failed to stick.

By the beginning of the 1956 season, the Reds had assembled an impressive cast of veteran black players that included:

Chuck Harmon, who had played semi-regularly for the Reds the previous two seasons. In college, Harmon led the University of Toledo to the 1943 National Invitational Tournament finals in basketball.

Bob Thurman, who starred as a pitcher-outfielder for the legendary Homestead Grays alongside Josh Gibson and Buck Leonard. Thurman, who broke in as a 38-year-old rookie in 1955, was a former Yankee and Cub farmhand, who had been playing in an independent league in the Dominican Republic. Thurman had to purchase his release from the Chicago Cubs and petition Organized Baseball for reinstatement before he could join the Reds.

Former Rookie of the Year Joe Black, who was acquired from Brooklyn early in the 1955 campaign. Black was a graduate of Morgan State College, where he would later return for an advanced degree in psychology. After baseball, Black would become one of the country's highest-ranking executives with Greyhound Bus Lines.

Hard-hitting first baseman George Crowe, who came from the Braves in a trade for Bob "Hurricane" Hazle before the 1956 campaign. In high school, Crowe had been named the first Indiana "Mr. Basketball" before starring for Indiana Central College (later University of Indianapolis). His older brother Ray gained national fame when he coached Crispus Attucks (led by Oscar Robinson) to the Indiana high school state championship, the first black team to achieve that distinction.

Scholarly pitcher Brooks Lawrence, whose weighty reading material sometimes intimidated sportswriters.[38] Lawrence attended Miami University of Ohio and was so well read that he was accepted as a contestant on *The $64,000 Question*, the *Jeopardy* of the era. Unfortunately, the baseball schedule kept him from appearing on the show.[39]

The Reds' black veterans tried to make sure that open communications were maintained with the white players while running interference for the club's upcoming young black prospects. They discouraged congregating together and insisted that their lockers be interspersed among the white players. "If you keep huddled up, you're like a bunch of crabs in a barrel; we're not going to learn anything, and the people around us are not going to learn anything," argued Lawrence.[40]

They also took on the role of mentors for young black players coming up with the Reds and throughout the league. "Each new black kid who came up, we took him under our wing," explained Lawrence." We'd teach him the ropes. We'd set up a screen around him and say, 'No you can't do this type of thing. You can't go into these kinds of bars.'"[41]

Crowe emerged as the leader. Vada Pinson, who would star for a decade in a Cincinnati uniform, remembered when he first arrived, "[Crowe] took me under his wing. He came up to me and said, 'If there are any problems, you come to me. I'm your father, your big daddy up here.'" When asked about his role, Crowe responded, "I like to see everybody keep their nose clean. And when you have fellows who are coming along who are new to this, I'm glad to give guidance."[42]

According to Robert Boyle, author of "The Private World of the Negro Ballplayer," an insightful 1960 article that was featured in *Sports Illustrated*, "Crowe has a sense of responsibility as a 'race' man. If, for example, the players get an invitation to make a public appearance, he always tries to get a Negro player to attend. If no one can, he goes himself."[43]

The efforts seemed to work off the field. Thurman, who served as an informal traveling secretary for the club's black players, proudly exclaimed, "You talk about family. That's the greatest set of guys you ever want to be around. They don't think nothing about any color."[44]

The Reds' "mentor program" worked on the field too. After finishing fifth in 1954 and 1955, the 1956 squad was expected to end up in the second division for the 12th-straight season. But the Reds surprised with a strong run at the National League flag before finishing third, only two games behind the pennant-winning Dodgers. Eight black players suited up for the Reds that year, the most in the majors. Harmon was traded to the Cardinals early in the season, and 38-year-old rookie lefthander Pat Scantlebury was found wanting. But Lawrence developed into the ace of the staff, Black helped solidify the bullpen, Crowe and Thurman provided powerful bats off the bench, and rookie left fielder Frank Robinson won National League Rookie of the Year honors, contributing 38 homers to the team's record-tying season total of 221. In September, 18-year-old Curt Flood, who would later develop into a star with the St. Louis Cardinals, came up for a look.

Robinson was the first beneficiary of the Reds' enlightened policies. Recognizing the inevitable problems of loneliness and isolation that plagued young black players, management tried to counter by pairing them up with solid veteran role models when possible. They were richly rewarded for this sensitive and sensible approach when

Veteran George Crowe was a respected leader among black players in the 1950s and early 1960s (1957 Topps card).

the 20-year-old Robinson burst upon the big league scene and set a new rookie home run record. After marking himself as a future star in his first two seasons in the organization, Robinson spent a disappointing 1955 campaign with Columbia in the South Atlantic League nursing an injured throwing arm. His roommate was former Negro League star Marvin Williams, the third player who participated in the infamous Fenway Park tryout with Jackie Robinson and Sam Jethroe in 1945. Williams, whose own aspirations of major league stardom had been derailed by an arm injury, not only talked the dejected Robinson out of quitting baseball, he introduced him to a new batting stance that helped him better cover the outside corner of the plate.[45] Robinson would go on to tie the major league rookie home run record in 1956. Five years later, he would be named the National League Most Valuable Player, and five years after that, he would capture the American League Most Valuable Player Award, the only player to win the honor in both major leagues. Near the end of his magnificent playing career, he would have the distinction of becoming the first black man to manage a major league team and go on to a successful managing career.

Interestingly, the veteran black players the Reds picked up to staff their mentor program were all African Americans. In fact, only four of the 17 black players to appear in a Cincinnati uniform in the 1950s were of Hispanic heritage, and they had no impact. But that too would change. In 1955, Paul entered into an operating agreement with the Havana franchise in the International League that would prove to be an ideal proving ground for young Latino prospects until Fidel Castro intervened four years later.

The Reds slumped back into the middle of the pack from 1957 through 1960, but they continued to be among the leaders in number of black players. Joe Cephus Taylor, the old Philadelphia Athletic prospect, spent some time with the club in 1957, and former Dodger great Don Newcombe and future star Vada Pinson joined the Reds in 1958. Negro League veterans Jim Pendleton and Marshall Bridges were also with the club in 1959 and 1960 respectively. But most of the new black prospects joining the Reds around the turn of the decade were Latinos.

The 1960s and Beyond

Gabe Paul left Cincinnati after the 1960 season to help set up the expansion Houston Colts. But the new organizational culture he established would serve the Reds well into the future. In fact, the team Paul left behind captured the 1961 National League pennant with former St. Louis Browns executive Bill DeWitt in the general manager's seat.

Given their late start, the Reds may be the major leagues' most remarkable success story in the integration department. After Gabe Paul took over, the Reds added six farm teams and more than quadrupled the number of players in their system.[46] African American prospects Frank Robinson, Curt Flood, Vada Pinson, Joe Gaines, Jesse Gonder, Tommy Harper, and Lee May, as well as Latino youngsters Orlando Pena, Felix Torres, Mike Cuellar, Tony Gonzalez, Elio Chacon, Leo Cardenas, Chico Ruiz, Cesar Tovar, and Tony Perez were signed. The Reds weren't above taking a look at seasoned Hispanic prospects either. Lefties Pat Scantlebury, from Panama, and Diomedes Olivo, of the Dominican Republic, were both born before 1920. All of these players would make the major leagues. Unfortunately Flood, Pena, Gonzalez, Cuellar and Tovar would develop into stars with other teams. But Robinson and Pinson would lead the Reds to the 1961 pennant, finishing first and third respectively in National League Most Valuable Player balloting, while Cardenas, Harper, Perez, and May would also develop into key performers for the Reds.

By 1965, the Reds were regularly fielding a team with five black players. Robinson and Pinson remained the club's biggest stars while Cardenas took over as the regular shortstop in 1962 and Tommy Harper captured a first-string outfield job the next season. In 1965, future Hall-of-Famer Tony Perez came up to share first base with Gordy Coleman.

Before the 1966 campaign, Bill DeWitt, who acquired an ownership interest in the club when Powel Crosley died shortly after he'd come aboard as general manager, almost destroyed the franchise with a horrendous trade. He sent Frank Robinson to the Baltimore Orioles for pitcher Milt Pappas and a few fringe players. Robinson went on to lead the Orioles to the pennant, win the Triple Crown, and become the first player to earn MVP honors in both leagues while Pappas disappointed Cincinnati fans. It's been speculated that one of the reasons for the deal was that some in the Reds organization felt there were too many black players on the team, although DeWitt's personal dislike for Robinson may have had more to do with it.[47]

After the 1966 season, DeWitt sold the Reds to a syndicate headed by newspaper publisher Francis Dale. The Reds recovered from the Robinson debacle to capture the 1970 National League pennant, although they lost to Robinson's Baltimore Orioles in the World Series. Black stars Tony Perez and Lee May, who were signed by Gabe Paul, still starred for the Reds, as did Bobby Tolan who was acquired in a trade for Vada Pinson, another Paul signee. The emergence of young black stars Dave Concepcion, Wayne Simpson, and Hal McRae also contributed to the success of the first edition of the "Big Red Machine," as the Cincinnati powerhouse of the 1970s came to be known. Later, future Hall of Famer Joe Morgan, acquired in a trade for May, George Foster, and Dan Driessen would be among the black stars who would help maintain the dynasty.

Continuing Problems

But the Reds are one of those teams who would always seem to be haunted by racial problems.

After slugging outfielder George Foster, the 1977 National League Most Valuable Player, was traded to New York Mets in 1982, he accused the Reds of maintaining a double standard, claiming that he and other veteran black stars, like Dan Driessen and Ken Griffey Sr., didn't receive the treatment from the club that their accomplishments warranted.[48]

In 1984, Marge Schott, the first woman to purchase rather than inherit ownership of a big league club, took over. Schott spent the money to make the Reds a contender again and reached the height of popularity in Cincinnati in 1990 when the Reds led the National League from the outset and finished the season with a sweep of the favored Oakland Athletics in the World Series.

Two years later, former team controller Tim Sabo contested his 1991 firing, claiming that one of the reasons for his dismissal was his opposition to the franchise's unwritten policy of not hiring blacks. Testifying on Sabo's behalf, former marketing director Cal Levy stated in a court deposition that he'd heard Schott refer to star outfielders Eric Davis and Dave Parker as her "million-dollar niggers."[49] In *The New York Times*, a former Oakland Athletics executive assistant quoted Schott as saying, "I would never hire another nigger. I'd rather have a trained monkey working for me than a nigger."[50] Schott is also alleged to have made statements defending Adolf Hitler, who she believed was "good for Germany (in the beginning), but went too far."[51] The controversial owner's mouth got her suspended from day-to-day operations of the team, and she was eventually forced to sell her controlling interest in the franchise.

In 2004, the Reds' undistinguished racial past was again resurrected when an ESPN Sports Classic program about prejudice in baseball aired which suggested that Brooks Lawrence might have been intentionally denied the opportunity to win 20 games back in 1956 because he was black. Old box scores seem to indicate there's some merit to the charge. On September 15, Lawrence registered his 19th win of the season to bring the Reds to within two games of first place with two weeks and 13 games left to go in the season. He didn't get another start, making five relief appearances and pitching only four and two-thirds innings the rest of the year. Skeptics point out that after winning 15 of his first 17 decisions Lawrence was ineffective the last two months of the campaign and undeserving of a start in the midst of a tight pennant race. But the Reds were eliminated from contention with two games left in the season. Though they still had a shot at second-place money, they could have extended the well-rested Lawrence a chance to win number 20.

Two questions remain unanswered. First, was Lawrence's arm in condition to pitch? He had already made 49 appearances that season and had a history of arm trouble. Unfortunately, Lawrence, the only person who could have definitively answered that question, died in 2000. The second question assumes that Lawrence's arm was okay and that the Reds maliciously denied Lawrence an opportunity to join the exclusive 20-win club. Was he denied this chance because he was black?

Given the behavior so often displayed by the baseball establishment, both now and then, an equally plausible explanation is that it was done to deprive Lawrence of the advantage of a 20-win season in his portfolio when it came time to negotiate his 1957 contract.

Chapter 14

THE WASHINGTON SENATORS/MINNESOTA TWINS

Washington — First in War — First in Peace — Last in the American League. Alas, this popular takeoff on the city's patriotic motto was all too accurate. The original Washington Senators could generally be found in or near the American League cellar from 1934 to 1960. They were also a second-division outfit when it came to integration.

Ironically, before Branch Rickey and the Brooklyn Dodgers picked up the torch, many in baseball felt that the Senators would be the first team to integrate when Organized Baseball opened its doors to black players.[1] The nation's capital seemed like the natural place for the debut of major league baseball's first black player of the 20th century. In 1950, 23.5 percent of the District of Columbia's metropolitan area's population was non-white, a figure that is more than twice as high as the metropolitan area of the average big league city. Furthermore, 35 percent of the city of Washington's population were African Americans, and the percentage was growing fast. By 1960, the majority of the city's population would be black.[2]

Unlike most cities, the relatively affluent black population of Washington embraced the Senators before integration. Black fans even supported them over Negro League teams that attempted to establish a base in the nation's capital before World War II. In 1934, H. Scott of the *Washington Tribune* wrote, "For years we have been trying to fathom this mania Negroes have for white professional baseball. We believe it is spurred by the desire to see the best in the sport."[3]

In addition, Senators' owner Clark Griffith was thought to have a favorable attitude towards African Americans. He regularly made Griffith Stadium available to black public high schools in the area and rented it out for black sporting, religious, and social events.[4] The Homestead Grays, the elite team of the Negro Leagues, played their home games in the stadium, and their owner, Cum Posey, enjoyed a close, symbiotic working relationship with Griffith. Therefore, it was assumed that the Senators would have first call on players like future Hall of Famers Josh Gibson, Buck Leonard, and Cool Papa Bell and other Negro League stars who played for the Grays.

The Senators had also been the leading importer of Latin players since the early part of the century, some of whom had skin as dark as many Negro League players. And with legendary scout Joe Cambria already mining the area, the Senators were certainly familiar with the Negro League stars who played in the Latin American winter leagues, as well as darker-skinned Cuban natives.

Last, but not least, the Senators, or Nats (Nationals) as they were often called, were a terrible team that needed talented ballplayers badly and didn't have the means to acquire them through traditional channels. In 1934, they acquired Allen "Bullet Ben" Benson from the bearded House of David barnstorming squad. The next year, they signed Edwin "Alabama" Pitts, a convicted felon they had scouted in Sing Sing prison.[5] During World War II, they fortified their roster with off-duty New York City sanitation worker Ed Boland and wooden-legged hurler Bert Shepard.

But those who expected Washington to be a leader in this area grossly underestimated the prejudice or stubbornness of the "The Old Fox," as Griffith was often called. Instead of being first, the Senators would be the 12th major league team to integrate. Even old Connie Mack's Philadelphia Athletics were ahead of them by almost a full year in putting a black player on the field.

Franchise History

Clark Griffith was a star pitcher for notorious racist Cap Anson's Chicago National League team in the 1890s. When the American League was founded in 1901, he joined Charles Comiskey as player-manager of the new Chicago White Sox, leading the new franchise to the new league's first pennant. Later, he managed the New York Yankees (nee Highlanders) from 1903 to 1908 and the Cincinnati Reds back in the National League from 1909 to 1911 before moving to Washington in 1912. Griffith managed the Washington franchise for almost a decade, gradually accumulating ownership shares, before taking control in 1920. A short time later, he inherited a full family. A nephew and niece from his wife's side of the family, Calvin and Thelma Robertson, came to live with Uncle Clark in 1922 and took the Griffith name when their father died a year later. Their mother and five siblings also moved to Washington and came under the Griffith family umbrella, although they retained their birth name.[6]

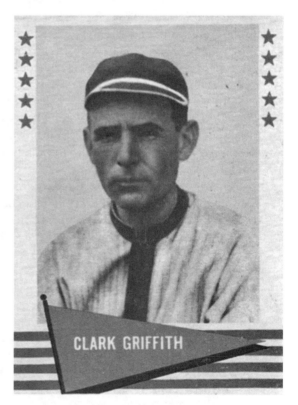

After the 1920 season, Griffith gave up the managerial reins to concentrate on rebuilding the roster. By 1924, he had put together a World Championship squad around aging pitching star Walter Johnson, young second baseman/manager Bucky Harris, hard-hitting outfielders Sam Rice and Goose Goslin, veteran shortstop Roger Peckinpaugh, and pitching aces Firpo Marberry, George Mogridge, and Tom Zachary. The Senators repeated as pennant winners in 1925 and remained competitive through the early 1930s. In 1933, they captured another pennant under the leadership of Joe Cronin, Griffith's manager, star shortstop, and son-in-law. In 1934, however, they

Long-time Washington owner Clark Griffith could never find an African American player with enough talent to play for his lowly Senators (1961 Fleer card).

tumbled to sixth place, and until World War II they only poked their heads out of the second division for a fourth-place finish in 1936. Financial pressures forced the sale of most of their stars, including Cronin who fetched a record price from the Boston Red Sox in 1935. The Senators managed to contend during the war years, but from 1947 until they pulled up stakes and moved to Minnesota after the 1960 season, they never ventured out of the second division. They finished in the cellar five times and in seventh place on four occasions during this period — no mean feat, considering the competition posed by the Athletics and Browns/Orioles.

Under Griffith, the Senators were chronically short of funds, which was not surprising considering almost the entire Griffith family drew salaries from the team. It seemed that everyone in the clan worked for the organization including nieces, nephews, cousins, and in-laws.[7] Nepotism was even practiced on the field. In addition to Cronin, pitcher Joe Haynes married into the family and subsequently moved into the administrative ranks when American League hitters forced him off the mound.[8] One of Griffith's nephews, Sherry Robertson, played for the Senators for ten years, despite an obvious lack of baseball talent. Robertson, of course, also moved into the front office after completing a less-than-illustrious playing career.[9]

The Pre-Integration Era

With Washington being the nation's capital and having such a large black population, Griffith and the Senators naturally came under more pressure to employ black players than other teams. The black press was well represented in the D.C. area and relentlessly pushed for action. For years, Griffith managed to put them off with tantalizing hints that integration was just around the corner.

In a 1937 interview with Sam Lacy, then with the *Washington Tribune*, Griffith predicted, "the time is not far off when colored players will take their places beside those of other races in the major leagues. However, I am not sure that time has arrived yet."[10] Unfortunately, Griffith would not conclude that the time had arrived until many years after it had become obvious to everyone else.

During World War II, pressure on the Senators to integrate intensified. Black soldiers were dying alongside whites on the battlefield, fueling demand for social change that was being led by the Washington press and black population. In addition, the Senators were hard hit by the military draft and badly needed an infusion of talent. Griffith apparently gave some thought to bringing in black players. After a Homestead Grays' game at Griffith Stadium in 1943, he reportedly summoned Josh Gibson and Buck Leonard to his office and asked them if they thought they could play at the big league level. When their answer was affirmative, he said, "The reason why we haven't got you colored baseball players on the team, the time hasn't come for you fellas to get on the team. The time hasn't come for you to be integrated."[11]

Instead, Griffith recruited 35-year-old Jake Powell, the "poster boy of baseball's racial bigotry," from the American Association.[12] While with the Yankees five years earlier, Powell endeared himself to black Americans by revealing that he kept in shape in the off-season by bashing the skulls of black citizens as a police officer in Dayton, Ohio (see Introduction). Upon Powell's first appearance in Griffith Stadium following his statements, black fans pelted him with bottles and miscellaneous debris. Griffith apparently either forgot about the incident himself or figured the memories of the black fans weren't too good. The super-patriotic Griffith also filled his war-ravaged roster with draft-proof Cuban ballplayers, courtesy of Joe

Cambria, rather than black citizens of the United States. During the 1944 campaign, many of the Cuban players went home rather than face possible service in the U.S. military, which further outraged the black population.[13]

Sam Lacy of the Baltimore *Afro-American*, Wendell Smith of the *Pittsburgh Courier*, and other representatives of the black press wrote about the embarrassment of fielding an all-white team in the capital of the free world. But it seemed that the more Griffith was pressured, the stronger his resolve to resist integration became. By the time the Dodgers signed Jackie Robinson, Griffith's stance had galvanized into his own separate-but-equal doctrine. He believed that the best hope for black players was a single professional, well-run Negro League that would operate alongside the two major leagues and eventually participate in a world championship series.[14]

The Homestead Grays

Of course, the new, improved Negro Major League envisioned by Griffith would also satisfy his dream — a healthy cash flow. More so than any other major league franchise, Griffith's Senators profited from Negro League baseball by renting out their stadium to the Homestead Grays. After the Grays shifted their base from Pittsburgh to Washington in 1940, they struggled mightily their first few years as the black community continued to support the Senators. But during World War II, the combination of better employment opportunities for black workers and the manpower drain on the major leagues turned things around. The Grays were a veteran team that lost few top players to military service. They became the best show in town, and black fans with a little extra spending money began to discover Negro League baseball. In fact, the Grays often drew bigger crowds than the Senators, with Griffith taking in 20 percent of the gate receipts, hiring out the services of the Senators' ushers and ticket takers, and pocketing the profits from concessions. It was suspected that Negro League baseball was the only thing keeping the Washington franchise out of bankruptcy. Griffith knew that integration of the major leagues would mean the end of Negro League baseball and his personal "Golden Goose."[15]

Branch Rickey put it bluntly when he said, "Don't let Mr. Griffith fool you. He's not interested in Negro baseball other than from the standpoint of financial gain. He's afraid he won't make the big hunk of money next year that he got this year from the Homestead Grays. Griffith's thinking more about his pocketbook than he is about the right and wrong in the thing."[16]

The Old Fox's opposition to integration for financial reasons showed a stunning lack of vision. The Senators undoubtedly could have recouped any revenues lost from the demise of the Negro Leagues by recruiting black players to attract black fans and fielding a decent team to increase attendance among both blacks and whites. Fans packed Griffith Stadium in 1947 when the hapless St. Louis Browns brought Hank Thompson and Willard Brown to the nation's capital for the first time.[17] A capacity crowd showed up to see Cleveland's Satchel Paige defeat the Senators on a Tuesday afternoon, August 30, 1948.[18] And the turnstiles hummed when Larry Doby and former Homestead Grays' slugger Luke Easter came to town with the Cleveland Indians in 1950.[19]

As the fiscal shock waves of integration spread through baseball in the wake of Jackie Robinson's debut, Griffith's worst fears were realized. The entertainment dollar of the black baseball fan was re-directed toward Major League Baseball and the already financially unstable

Negro Leagues began to founder. After the 1948 campaign in which they captured the Negro League World Championship, the Homestead Grays withdrew from the league and attempted to survive primarily as a barnstorming team. After 1950, they gave up the ghost and disbanded.[20]

Integration-Era Rhetoric

Still, Griffith refused to recruit black players for the Senators in the face of increasingly intense attacks from the mainstream press as well as black newspapers. The black writers like Sam Lacy had been patient with Griffith when he appeared to be one of the best hopes for integration, but they had come to recognize him as an adversary.[21]

"Yes, I've been convinced we may have overlooked an opportunity here and there to strengthen the Senators," Griffith admitted to Lacy on March 1949 in one of the most monumental understatements in baseball history. "And you can say I'm definitely interested in signing a good young colored player," Griff added, more than a dozen years after his "time not too far off" comment and more than five years before the Senators would actually bring an acknowledged black player to Washington.[22]

Rejecting suggestions that he sign available veteran Negro League stars like Buck Leonard of the Grays, Griffith claimed to be looking for a talented young black player who was good enough to bypass the team's southern-based minor league system and youthful enough to build a team around.[23] Of course, this mythical black phenom would also have to come dirt-cheap.

"The first black player to play for the Senators player will have to be great," Griffith often intoned, leaving one to wonder if anyone in the organization would even recognize such an unfamiliar level of talent.[24]

Before the 1952 season, the Senators finally signed their first acknowledged black players, Cuban infielders Juan Delis and Luis Morales, for their Danville affiliate in the Carolina League.[25] Though the 24-year-old Delis was immediately designated as the future first black Senator, the action did little to appease skeptics.[26]

The Senators also made noise about acquiring promising young black players like Harry Simpson and Vic Power, but deals never materialized.[27] As criticism mounted, Griffith responded by ranting, "Insinuations that the Washington club is opposed to playing Negroes on its team are lies. If I could find another Doby or Minoso, I would make a place on the Senators for him. But nobody is going to stampede me into signing Negro players merely for the sake of satisfying certain pressure groups."[28] About that time, Cleveland general manager Hank Greenberg proposed to swap Doby for Washington outfielder Jackie Jensen.[29] The Senators refused the offer, and a year later they swapped Jensen to the Red Sox for Tom Umphlett and Mickey McDermott, a couple of disappointing white players. It was the second time Griffith passed on Doby, a future Hall of Famer. A few years earlier, he had turned down an offer of Doby for outfielder Irv Noren, another white player of far lesser accomplishment.[30]

The Senators Finally Integrate

At the end of the 1953 season, there were only five players in the Senators system who the club considered to be black: Angel Scull, Julio Becquer, Juan Delis, Juan Visturer, Orlando Leroux. All of them were Hispanic.[31] Before the 1954 season, Scull, a speedy outfielder, was anointed the first black Senator. According to *The Sporting News*, the Cuban-born Scull was "assured of an outfield berth and will be the first Negro ever to play for the Nats."[32] He was considered such a lock to make the roster, in fact, that the Topps baseball card company included him in their 1954 set.

But trouble erupted when seven Cuban players at the Senators' Chattanooga farm club's minor league camp in Winter Garden, Florida, were ordered out of town by a city official. The Senators initially complied by sending the players to train with the Orlando club in the Class D Florida State League until the press got wind of the story. The city backed down when the FBI was brought in to investigate, but the Cuban players refused to return to Winter Garden. Griffith was upset and embarrassed over the incident. When reporters asked him why he didn't pull his farm clubs of out Winter Garden entirely, he righteously responded, "That would be as discriminatory as the people who started this in the first place. You don't solve anything by running away from it."[33]

The Sporting News reported that bitterness was expressed by unidentified Cuban players training with the parent club, which may well have led to the team's conclusion that Angel Scull was not "great enough" to wear a Senator

Cuban outfielder Angel Scull was touted as Washington's first black player in 1954, but was mysteriously banished to the minors before the season began (1954 Topps card).

jersey after all. He was optioned to Havana of the International League and would never get a big league opportunity, despite competing at the Class AAA level for ten years.[34]

In the closing weeks of the 1954 campaign, dark-skinned Cuban outfielder Carlos Paula debuted for the Senators. His arrival did little to placate the team's critics. In fact, Paula seemed to be exactly the type of talent that Griffin had consistently rejected — the type whose recruitment might be considered tokenism or "giving in to agitators."[35] A big right-handed hitter with a lousy glove and modest power for a man of his size, Paula was almost 27 years old and had never played at a higher level than Class A until he joined the Senators. It seemed that the franchise's "Anybody but a Negro" policy had evolved to "Anybody but an African-American."

Paula was unimpressive in his 1954 major league stint, but surprised everyone by starting off the 1955 campaign with a blazing bat. There was even some early talk of Rookie of the Year honors, but a tendency to swing at bad pitches soon had him on a steady diet of curveballs in the dirt. Despite tailing off in the second half, Paula finished the season with a .299 mark in 115 games, second best on the Senators. His work in the field, however, would be benevolently described as "crude," and he ended the year with the lowest fielding percentage among the league's outfielders by a considerable margin. Midway through the following season, he was back in the minor leagues for good.[36]

The Senators introduced three more black players during the 1955 season. Given the club's history, it was no surprise that they were also of Hispanic descent and also lacked big-time talent. Delis, the first black player signed by the organization three years earlier, quietly became the second black Senator. He would ultimately complete a 15-year career in Organized Baseball, but 1955 would be his only major league campaign. In September, Negro League veteran Vibert "Webbo" Clarke got a trial. Clarke, a Panamanian, was no doubt older than the 27 years he claimed, since he had been considered the ace of the Cleveland Buckeyes' staff almost a decade earlier. Clarke's 4.64 earned runs in seven appearances didn't look too bad compared Camilo Pascual's 6.14 mark, Ted Abernathy's 5.96, or Chuck Stobbs 5.00. But Webbo would never get another big league look while Pascual, Abernathy, and Stobbs would enjoy lengthy major league careers. Julio Becquer, a fancy-fielding Cuban first baseman with limited power, also appeared in 10 late-season games for the 1955 Senators. Becquer would later spend five seasons with the club, from 1957 to 1961, as a pinch-hitter and backup first baseman, twice leading the league in pinch-hits. Also in 1955, the Senators signed teenage catcher Clarence "Choo Choo" Coleman, who might be the first African American player signed by the organization. Choo Choo didn't go far in the Washington organization, but later gained a measure of notoriety as an original New York Met.

Griffith and the Senators were certainly slow to integrate, but they weren't the worst in town. Under the ownership of George Preston Marshall, the Washington Redskins of the National Football League adamantly refused to put a black player on their roster. Unlike Griffith, Marshall made no bones about it. "We'll start signing Negroes when the Harlem Globetrotters start hiring whites," he vowed.[37] Apparently no one informed him that the Globetrotters employed a white player, "Bunny" Leavitt, as far back as the 1930s.[38] The National Football League integrated in 1946, and in 1961 there were 83 black performers on league rosters.[39] The next year, the Redskins succumbed to legal and political pressure from the Kennedy administration and acquired superstar Bobby Mitchell from the Cleveland Browns.

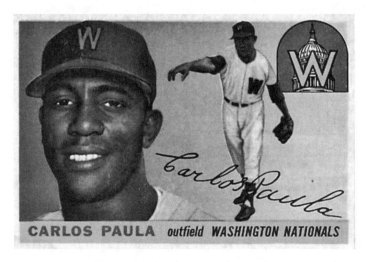

CARLOS PAULA   outfield WASHINGTON NATIONALS

Cuban-born Carlos Paula eventually became Washington's first "acknowledged" black player, though several other dark-skinned Hispanics played for the Senators prior to 1947 (1955 Topps card).

The Legacy of Clark Griffith

On October 27, 1955, Clark Griffith died at age 85 of complications from a stomach hemorrhage without ever finding an African American player who was good enough for his Washington Senators.

Originally Griffith had a reasonable, albeit selfish and shortsighted, financial motive for opposing integration. But the fact that he continued to resist long after the death knell sounded for the Negro Leagues is an indication that something else was at work. Griffith did not seem to be an overt racist like his former bosses Cap Anson and Charles Comiskey or his colleague George Preston Marshall. Griffith didn't seem to hate black people. But the Old Fox was already over 70 when the integration battle began heating up. A revolutionary thinker as a younger man, he'd developed into an archconservative as he aged and came to resist virtually every innovation that came along, from farm systems to night baseball.[40] Apparently an avid subscriber to contemporary McCarthyism, he railed against outside agitators and branded integration as a Communist plot to overthrow baseball.[41]

In a 1952 *Sporting News* puff piece marking Griffith's 50-year association with the American League (apparently everyone forgot about his years in Cincinnati), Griffith said, "My own position with regard to Negro players on the Washington club has come in for criticism and discussion which has not been fair to me." He went on to explain, "Several years ago, 'subversive' persons came to Washington from New York, and picketed our ballpark. I was accused of discriminating against Negro players. I appealed to prominent Negroes of the capital, explaining my side, showed them whence had come the picketers, and soon the excitement died out."[42]

After assuring readers that the Senators would welcome a black star and were still diligently scouring the landscape for qualified candidates, Griffith vowed, "I will not sign a Negro for the Washington club merely to satisfy subversive persons. I would welcome a Negro on the Senators if he rated the distinction, if he belonged among major league players."[43]

Aside from concerns about the "Red Menace," at least part of the problem may have been that Griffith perceived integration as a threat to the established order and didn't want any part of it. But the major cause of Griffith's continued self-destructive behavior in the face of all reason may just have been pure old mule-headed stubbornness. After years of lofty rhetoric, the Old Fox couldn't very well admit his original reason for fighting integration was primarily his own economic self interest — no matter how much it cost him.

Hispanic Senators

The funny thing is that the Senators were probably using black players more than 30 years before Jackie Robinson's Organized Baseball debut. While managing the Cincinnati Reds, Griffith helped pioneer the mechanism for qualifying suspiciously dusky-complexioned Hispanic players for the major leagues, a practice he would continue in Washington (see chapter 13).

In 1913, his second year as manager of the Senators, Griffith recruited 19-year-old Cuban outfielder Jacinto "Jack" Calvo. Calvo played in only 16 games that year and would return seven years later to appear in another 17 contests for the Senators. In between, he performed in the Pacific Coast League and the Negro Leagues, as well as in his native country. Though he contributed little to the Senators, Calvo was elected to the Cuban Baseball Hall of Fame in 1948.

The Senators employed a handful of Cuban players in addition to Calvo through the mid–1930s, none of whom had much of an impact. But as the team's fortunes declined, Griffith began to rely more heavily more on the cheap Latino labor supply. One of the most successful of Griffith's Cuban players was outfielder-third baseman Roberto "Bobby" Estalella, who played for the Senators from 1935 through 1939. According to *The Cultural Encyclopedia of Baseball*, Estalella was "arguably" the first black player in the Major Leagues in the 20th century "as he was far from white even by Cuban standards of ethnicity."[44] Nicknamed "El Tarzan" because of his strength and build, Estalella always denied having black heritage. But respected *Washington Post* columnist Shirley Povich described him as "swarthy" and regarded him as one of the players "I would characterize as black or seemed to me as black."[45] *Washington Star* reporter Burton Hawkins remembered, "Bobby Estalella definitely was black." The Latin players considered the stocky slugger from Cardenas, Cuba, to be a "mulatto"—a person with mixed black and white ancestry.[46]

Estalella's skin tone clearly worked against him. The Senators were the unquestioned leaders in the employment of Cuban players during the first half of the twentieth century. In fact, almost half of the Cubans who appeared in the major leagues during the segregation era played for the Senators. But Estalella arrived at a most prejudicial time in history, the mid–1930s, when the Washington roster was almost devoid of other Hispanic players.[47] He put up tremendous numbers in the minors and hit well in the big leagues when given a chance, but he couldn't seem to stick with the perennial second-division Senators. Estalella was eventually traded to the St. Louis Browns but returned to Washington during the war years to blend in with a plethora of new Cuban Senators. His best years were 1943 through 1945, after he was traded to the Philadelphia Athletics. At the age of 34 in 1945, Estalella recorded the fourth-highest batting average in the American League and also ranked among the league leaders in both on-base and slugging percentage. But he jumped to the Mexican League before the 1946 season and was suspended from Organized Baseball. He returned to the Athletics in 1949 when the ban was lifted, but he played only eight games before drifting back to the minor leagues.

After analyzing Estalella's career, statistics guru Bill James concluded, "[Estalella] was clearly a player who got a raw deal from baseball." James went on to say "Bobby Estalella ... was a fine player who could have had an excellent career ... somehow he slipped past the bouncer and got a chance to play. But not much of a chance."[48]

In 1953, Wendell Smith charged, "Clark Griffith ... has been a hypocrite on this subject for years. He has imported Latin players of Negro extraction for years and 'passed them off.'"[49]

Years later, Calvin Griffith, who took over control of the franchise after the death of his uncle, told his biographer, "There's no question that some of the ballplayers Mr. Griffith signed had black blood ... some of them were as black as your tape recorder."[50]

Under Calvin's leadership, the Senators' discriminatory practices continued. Delis, Clarke, and Becquer were back in the minors when the 1956 season began, and when Paula failed to duplicate his rookie success and was sent down in June, the Senators' roster returned to its familiar all-white status for the remainder of the season. Becquer re-emerged in 1957 to single-handedly integrate the Senators for most of the next two-and-one-half seasons. He was briefly joined by former Brooklyn Dodger star Joe Black, who was signed as a free agent late in the 1957 campaign after drawing his release from two minor league teams. In his last stint in Organized Baseball, Black became the first African American to wear the Washington Senators uniform.

Early in the 1959 season, the Senators acquired 26-year-old black outfielder Lenny Green from the Baltimore Orioles, and later that year dark-skinned Cuban shortstop Zoilo Versalles got his first taste of the big leagues. Green would become the club's regular center fielder and leadoff hitter from 1960 through 1962 while Versalles would develop into a topflight shortstop and man the post for the franchise from 1961 through 1967.

The 1960 season heralded the arrival of the team's first African American star, catcher Earl Battey from the Chicago White Sox, who helped the club improve by 10 games in the win column. Battey would rival Elston Howard of the Yankees as the American League's premier receiver for the first half of the 1960s, garnering three Gold Gloves and four All-Star

Game selections and catching more than 125 games every year before the heavy workload caught up with him. Washington's long-suffering black fans couldn't fully appreciate Battey's heroics, however, since the franchise relocated to the Minneapolis–St. Paul area and became the Minnesota Twins before the 1961 season.

Ironically, in their last season in the nation's capital, the Senators finally admitted an old Homestead Grays player into their organization. The Old Fox must have turned over in his grave when 43-year-old outfielder Bob Thurman, who would become a scout for the franchise two years later, joined their Charleston Triple A farm club.

The Move to Minneapolis

In 1962, the Twins blossomed into solid contenders largely due to the play of four black regulars, Battey, Green, Versalles, and veteran first baseman Vic Power, who was acquired from the Cleveland Indians before the season. In 1965, they captured the franchise's first pennant in 32 years, ending the Yankees' skein of five consecutive American League pennants. The ace of the staff was Jim "Mudcat" Grant, the first black twenty-game winner in American League history. The club's leading hitter was Tony Oliva, who had been the first black American League batting champion and rookie of the year in 1964, and captured the batting title again in 1965. Shortstop Zoilo Versalles captured American League Most Valuable Player honors that season, the second black player to win the award. And behind the plate was Earl Battey, enjoying the last productive season of his career at the age of 30.

The Twins closed out the decade of the 1960s with a Western Division Championship in 1969. Six black players performed in key roles for Minnesota that season. Oliva still starred in right field, although second baseman Rod Carew had supplanted him as the league's leading hitter. Former Dodger John Roseboro was behind the plate, and former Reds star Leo Cardenas manned shortstop while versatile Cesar Tovar handled center field and rookie left-hander Tom Hall helped solidify the pitching staff.

Amazingly, Hall was the first African American player developed in the Twins farm system to find success in Minnesota. The Twins employed about 25 black players before Hall's arrival, only nine of whom were American born. In fact, outfielder Pat Kelly, who didn't debut until late 1967, was the first African American graduate of the system to make the Twins' roster. Kelly would hit only .111 in limited action with the Twins, although he would establish himself in the big leagues after going to the Kansas City Royals in the 1969 expansion draft. The other eight African Americans — Joe Black, Lenny Green, Earl Battey, Ron Henry, Mudcat Grant, Walt Bond, John Roseboro, and Jim Holt — were acquired from other organizations.

The Minnesota Twins franchise and the Griffith family didn't really deserve the success they realized in the 1960s from the efforts of black players like Green, Power, Battey, Grant, Oliva, and Carew. Calvin Griffith certainly didn't have the charm of The Old Fox, though he did seem to have absorbed his racial attitudes and philosophies. Calvin once had the audacity to claim that his uncle refrained from integrating the Senators out of loyalty to the Homestead Grays. He also demonstrated his faith in the Old Fox's separate-leagues ideology by wistfully adding, "If he [Branch Rickey] hadn't signed Jackie Robinson there could have been in years to come, a challenge of the black to white."[51] Black catcher John Roseboro, who spent two forgettable seasons with the Twins after ten years as the Dodgers regular backstop, called Calvin, "The least likeable person I met in baseball."[52]

In 1958, Calvin had pledged to keep the franchise in Washington. "As long as I have any say in the matter ... the Washington Senators will stay here.... Next year, the year after, Forever," he promised.[53] Three years later, the club was in Minnesota. In a 1978 speech to a Minneapolis-area Lions Club, Calvin revealed the reason for the move: "It was when I found out you only had 15,000 black people here. Black people don't go to ball games, but they'll fill up a wrestling ring and put up such a chant it'll scare you to death. It's unbelievable. We came here because you've got good, hard-working, white people here." The Twins owner even threw in a gratuitous insult of the team's star player, calling Rod Carew a fool for signing a three-year $170,000 contract. Unfortunately for Calvin, a *Minneapolis Star Tribune* reporter in the audience diligently recorded and reported his comments.[54] Upon hearing of Calvin's comments, Carew responded, "I refuse to be a slave on his plantation and play for a bigot." He subsequently forced a trade to the California Angels where he played out his Hall of Fame career.

In truth, Calvin's revelation was no surprise, though many were incredulous that he was so foolish to brazenly admit it. But given the franchise history, that shouldn't have been a major shock either.

Just two years earlier, the Twins had been accused of allegedly helping Kansas City Royal star George Brett overtake black teammate Hal McRae to win the 1976 American League batting championship. The Royals had already clinched the Western Division Championship going into the final game of the regular season in Minnesota, with Brett and McRae locked in a battle for the batting crown. McRae held a microscopic lead when the Royals came to bat in the ninth inning. Brett needed a hit and got one when Twins' left fielder Steve Brye allowed his routine flyball to land untouched in front of him. When McRae, the next batter, followed with a groundout to shortstop, Brett had his first batting title. Afterward, McRae, a highly respected competitor who would later become one of baseball's first black managers, accused Brye of purposely letting Brett's ball drop in and charged the Twins and their manager Gene Mauch with racial bias.[55]

Under Calvin Griffith, the Twins continued to field a team with relatively few prominent African American players, and the number of Latinos petered out as well. The franchise's only African American superstar to date, Kirby Puckett, debuted in 1984, the year Griffith sold the franchise to billionaire Carl Pohlad. When the Twins captured their first World Championship in 1987, Puckett was the only frontline black performer on the squad. Under Pohlad's ownership, the Griffith legacy still lives on as, other than Puckett, black stars who come to Minnesota usually move on quickly.

It is truly a shame that the prejudice and stubbornness of the Griffith family probably deprived the nation's capital of major league baseball for 33 years. Calvin Griffith and the Senators were in a position to put some of the best baseball players in the country in Washington uniforms, increasing attendance and restoring the team to contender status with black stars. In 1960, the Senators installed Earl Battey and Lenny Green in the lineup, the first African Americans to play regularly in Washington. The result was a jump to fifth in the standings after three straight basement finishes and a 20 percent increase in attendance. But the city's black fans wouldn't get a chance to demonstrate how well they would support an integrated winner as the franchise fled for Minnesota's more Caucasian population. More African American players represented the expansion version of the Senators in their initial season than the original Senators fielded in their entire existence. Unfortunately, after years of losing, Washington fans didn't have the patience to wait for the new Senators to develop, and the franchise relocated to Texas after the 1971 season.

Chapter 15

THE NEW YORK YANKEES

Asked whether he thought "the Yankees are prejudiced against Negro players," Jackie Robinson replied, "I think the Yankee management is prejudiced. There isn't a single Negro on the team now and very few in the entire Yankee farm system." The unexpected question was spontaneously raised by a teenage panelist on the television show *Youth Wants to Know* in November 1952, shortly after another Dodger World Series loss to the Yankees.[1] At the time, Robinson had played six seasons in Brooklyn, and the New York Giants had been integrated for almost four years. Yet the New York Yankees, the wealthiest and most successful team in Major League Baseball, had been unable "to find a Negro player among the availables," according to their general manager George Weiss.[2]

At the outset, the Yankees organization aggressively opposed the integration of Major League Baseball. General manager and part owner Larry MacPhail presided over the committee that produced the infamous 1946 report and personally wrote the section entitled "The Race Question" that recommended against timely integration of the sport while taking potshots at "political and social-minded drumbeaters" who were "conducting pressure campaigns in an attempt to force major league clubs to sign Negro players."[3]

MacPhail left baseball after the 1947 World Series, but not before seeing Jackie Robinson run wild against his Yankees in that year's Fall Classic. His attitude about black players in Major League Baseball lived on in the Yankee front office, however. The Yankees would not put a black player on the field until 1955, the 13th major league organization to do so, and they would continue to field one of the whitest teams in the majors for more than a decade afterward.

Franchise History

The franchise that would become the most successful in baseball history began life in the American League as the Baltimore Orioles in 1901 under the leadership of John McGraw. Two years later, the not-so-unlikely partnership of gambling magnate Frank Farrell and former chief of police William Devery purchased the franchise and moved it to New York City.[4] The team, which was known as the Highlanders until adopting the "Yankees" name in 1913, was an also-ran for the first 20 years of its existence. In 1915, Jacob Ruppert, who had inherited a profitable brewery, and Tillinghast L'Hommendieu Huston, an ex-military man who made his fortune as an engineer in Cuba after the Spanish-American War, purchased the club. Ruppert, an officer in the National Guard, liked to be called Colonel, while Huston would actually work his way up to that rank in the army after re-enlisting before World War I.[5]

Before the 1920 season, the Yankees purchased Babe Ruth from the financially bereft Boston Red Sox and rode his thunderous bat to their first pennant the next year. From 1921 through 1943, the Yankees dominated the American League, capturing 14 pennants and 10 World Championships with rosters that featured future Hall of Famers Home Run Baker, Ruth, Waite Hoyt, Herb Pennock, Lou Gehrig, Earle Combs, Leo Durocher, Tony Lazzeri, Bill Dickey, Lefty Gomez, Red Ruffing, Joe Sewell, Joe DiMaggio, and Phil Rizzuto, as well as managers Miller Huggins and Joe McCarthy.

The Yankees, who were often referred to as the "Bronx Bombers," rose to prominence under the stewardship of general manager Ed Barrow. Barrow also served as president of the club after Ruppert's death in 1939 (Huston had sold out in the mid–1920s) until 1945, when Ruppert's heirs sold the franchise, including Yankee Stadium, to the triad of Del Webb, Dan Topping, and MacPhail for the bargain price of $2,850,000.

Del Webb, a high school dropout, was head of one of the largest contracting companies in the country. As a young man, he reportedly harbored dreams of being a big league player that were squashed by illness and injury. He turned to carpentry and built his company from the ground up, first taking advantage of the rapid growth of the Phoenix area then expanding to Los Angeles and Chicago before grabbing up more than $100 million in defense contracts during the war.[6]

Dan Topping took the more traditional road to wealth by inheriting his millions. His family had amassed a fortune in steel, tin, tobacco, railroads, and banking. Shortly after purchasing the Brooklyn Dodgers football team in 1934, he withdrew from the advertising firm of Lloyd and Topping to pursue a passion for sports administration. He was married six times and earned a reputation as a millionaire playboy.[7]

Larry MacPhail, who put the deal together, was responsible for the day-to-day operation of the club until his trademark flamboyant and erratic behavior became too much for his partners to bear. Negotiations to buy him out were already underway as the Yankees romped to the 1947 pennant. Originally, MacPhail was to stay on as general manager, but that plan disintegrated when, in a state of inebriation during the celebration of the team's World Series victory, he punched a sportswriter and publicly berated almost everyone else in the organization. Within 24 hours, a deal was struck whereby Topping and Webb purchased his share of the club for $2 million and the flamboyant MacPhail was out of baseball forever.

After MacPhail's departure, Webb served as the team's representative at league meetings while Topping became the hands-on managing partner. Farm director George Weiss, who had been fired by MacPhail at the infamous victory party, was retained and promoted to general manager.

The Beginning of the Integration Era

In the 1950s, the Yankees emerged as the main villains of the integration era, the primary focal point for anti-segregationist forces. They were not, however, the worst offenders. The Yankees became the 13th big league team to have a black player represent them when Elston Howard debuted on April 14, 1955. But five other franchises, the Athletics, Cubs, Cardinals, Reds, and Senators, only beat them out by slightly more than a season. Another two years would pass before the Philadelphia Phillies would become the 14th franchise to integrate at the big league level, and in the interim the Cardinals, Senators, and Baltimore Orioles would return to all-white rosters for a time.

Actually, the Yankees were one of the first organizations to recruit black players at the minor league level. They may have been justly accused of prejudice, but they hadn't maintained a baseball dynasty by being stupid. After witnessing the success of the newly integrated Dodgers in 1947 and Indians in 1948, they decided to get into the act. Monte Irvin, the Negro Leagues' top remaining star at the time, claimed in his autobiography that the Newark Eagles, who were in the process of disbanding, initially offered his services to the Yankees.[8] But after the neighboring Giants inked Irvin, the Yankees reported making offers to four veteran Negro League stars: shortstop Artie Wilson, outfielder Luis Marquez, slugger Luke Easter, and pitcher Ford Smith.[9] Shortly thereafter, the Yankees' acquisition of Marquez, the 1947 Negro National League batting champion, and Wilson, who won the 1948 Negro American League batting title, was announced in *The Sporting News*.[10] With these actions, they became only the fifth big league organization after the Dodgers, Indians, Browns, and Giants to sign a Negro League star.

Relations between the Yankees and their new black players quickly soured however, a condition that would plague the franchise for years. Though the Yankees had reached an agreement to purchase Wilson's rights from Birmingham conditioned on the shortstop's signing, they hadn't actually signed him. When Wilson subsequently balked at signing a minor league contract with the Yankees calling for significantly less than he'd made with the Birmingham club, Bill Veeck stepped in to negotiate the acquisition of Wilson's rights from the Black Barons and sign the player to a better deal with the Indians.[11] The Yankees vehemently accused Cleveland of tampering and filed a complaint with the commissioner's office. The Indians responded with a complaint of their own against the Yankees relating to the signing of Marquez. It seems that the Negro League rights to Marquez had been transferred to Baltimore when the Homestead Grays dropped out of the league after the 1948 season and that's who the Yankees negotiated the acquisition of the outfielder's services from. But Veeck had apparently purchased Marquez's contract from the Grays before the franchise withdrew from the Negro Leagues.[12] Forced to address the matter, Commissioner Chandler followed baseball tradition by ruling against the wishes and interests of both players. In May, he awarded Wilson, who was starring for the Indians' San Diego Pacific Coast League farm club, to the Yankees where he would be stuck behind Phil Rizzuto. Ownership of Marquez was transferred to the Indians, who already possessed a wealth of young outfield talent.[13] Yet a third casualty of the ruling was another former Negro League star, Frank Austin. When the Yankees thought they had both Wilson and Marquez, they had slotted the two black stars to play for their International League Newark Bears farm club. With the Negro League Newark Eagles folding after the 1948 campaign, the Yankees were hoping to entice black fans to see the freshly integrated Bears, replacing the revenue from the rental of the Newark stadium to the Eagles that they had lost.[14] But when the Wilson deal fell through, the Yankees turned to Austin of the Philadelphia Stars to replace him as the Newark shortstop.[15] Former Kansas City Monarch hurler Gene Collins was also with Newark in spring training, but he didn't make the cut.[16]

Both Marquez and Austin began the season in the Newark lineup until the commissioner's decision transferring Marquez to the Indians and awarding Wilson to New York left the Yankees with a dilemma. Everybody understood you had to have two black players on a squad so they could room together on the road, but now both of the organization's black players were shortstops. The club's solution was to send Wilson to Oakland of the Pacific Coast League, where black pals were available, and sell Austin to Portland where he would star for seven years without receiving a big league invitation.[17] "[Austin] was a victim of the parent

New York Yankees' back luck with Negro players," wrote *Newark Star Ledger* scribe Jim Ogle.[18] He wouldn't be the last.

Later that season, the Yankees recruited another pair of black players, outfielder Bob Thurman and catcher Earl Taborn, to keep the Newark fans happy.[19] Taborn failed to impress, but Thurman was a sensation before a hand injury slowed him down, and there was talk of an invitation to spring training with the parent club before the 1950 season.[20]

After the 1949 season, however, the Yankees sold the Newark franchise to the Chicago Cubs. No doubt aware that their remaining Triple A affiliate in Kansas City was no more ready for a black player than the Yankees themselves, the organization passed the contracts of Thurman and Taborn to the Cubs as part of the transfer. The Yankees' system remained re-segregated until 22-year-old hurler Frank Barnes and 21-year-old catcher/outfielder Elston Howard were purchased from the Kansas City Monarchs at the conclusion of the 1950 Negro League season. It appears that the Yankees became fed up with dealing with established Negro League stars after the Wilson affair and decided to invest in younger black players. Reporting the acquisition of Barnes and Howard, Dan Daniel wrote in *The Sporting News*, "Team's interest, 'aborted' after unpleasant experiences with Wilson and Marquez, has been revived." The report also mentioned that the Yankees had "dickered" with Easter but negotiations fell through because Weiss didn't like the "involvements" of Negro League contracts.[21] Apparently, the "unpleasantness" with Wilson and Austin left the Yankees reluctant to deal with all black shortstops because they passed on Howard's 19-year-old Monarch roommate Ernie Banks.[22] During the 1950 campaign, the Yankees also acquired outfielder Nino Escalera from Bristol of the Colonial League, and before the 1951 season they acquired versatile young Vic Power from Drummondville of the Canadian Provincial League. The following season, they went back to the Provincial League to sign pitcher Ruben Gomez of St. Jean.

After a lengthy apprenticeship, Elston Howard would eventually become the Yankees first black player while Wilson, Thurman, Barnes, Escalera, Power, and Gomez would all reach the major leagues with other organizations. Wilson captured the 1949 Pacific Coast League batting championship and enjoyed another fine year in Oakland before being sent to the New York Giants after the 1950 season. Thurman was buried in the Cubs' system for years before surfacing with the Cincinnati Reds in 1955. Despite winning 23 of 33 decisions in the Yankee chain, Barnes was sold to the St. Louis Browns during the 1951 season. He would eventually reach the big leagues for a few cups of coffee with the St. Louis Cardinals. The Yankees disposed of Escalera in 1952, and two years later he would become the Cincinnati Reds' first black player. Power and Gomez would both star in the major leagues after leaving the Yankees system in frustration.

Gomez, a flamboyant Puerto Rican right-hander, started the 1952 campaign with the Kansas City Blues, but soon grew disgusted and left early in the season to play in the outlaw Dominican Republic league.[23] Subsequently, he was allowed to purchase his release from the Yankees, who were undoubtedly delighted to get rid of the controversial young pitcher. Unfortunately for the Yankees, Gomez signed with the New York Giants as a free agent before the 1953 season and quickly won a spot in their rotation. In 1954, he contributed 17 victories to the Giants' pennant charge and posted another victory over the Cleveland Indians in the World Series with the Yankees gritting their teeth in the television audience. The acquisition of Gomez was a double coup for the Giants. In addition to getting a solid pitcher, the continued presence of Gomez in New York helped crank up the mounting criticism of the Yankees for their treatment of black players.

The Vic Power Affair

Criticism of the Yankees' racial attitudes reached a crescendo thanks largely to the obvious talent of Vic Power, who became the first young black player in their system to begin attracting widespread attention.[24] Power could play anywhere in the infield or outfield, but his favorite position was first base, one of the Yankees' few weaknesses at the time. In addition, Power was from Puerto Rico and would have been a natural drawing card for the large Puerto Rican population of New York. But Power was also flashy, a trait that didn't fit the Yankees' corporate image. He was outspoken and wasn't afraid to use his fists — traits the Yankee brass found unacceptable in a black player, though they were willing to overlook them in a white man.

"The first requisite of a Yankee is that he be a gentleman, something that has nothing to do with race, color, or creed," intoned Dan Parker, sports editor of the *New York Daily Mirror*.[25] For some reason, Parker didn't feel compelled to explain how feisty white Yankee veterans like Billy Martin and Enos Slaughter managed to pass that particular test. But the thing that probably distressed the Yankee brass the most was that Power was known to date white women. According to Roger Kahn, George Weiss told representatives of both the *New York Times* and the *Herald Tribune*, "Maybe he [Power] can play, but not for us. He's impudent and he goes for white women."[26]

After starring for Syracuse of the International League in 1951, Power enjoyed another banner year with the American Association Kansas City Blues in 1952. An early indication that something was amiss surfaced when the Yankees brought up third baseman Andy Carey and outfielder Bob Cerv rather than Power when the Blues' season ended. Carey and Cerv were both right-handed hitters who played positions that Power handled adeptly, and neither could match Power's hitting stats or versatility. Insult was added to injury when Power wasn't even invited to train with the parent club the next spring. The press castigated the club for blatant discrimination against Power, and protests by black and Puerto Rican youths occurred at Yankee Stadium, probably strengthening anti-minority sentiment in the front office.[27]

In the meantime, the Yankees seemed to have found an "acceptable Negro" in ex-marine Bill Greason, who had joined Oklahoma City of the Texas League after being discharged from the military and won nine of ten decisions. In what may have been little more than an attempt to distract attention from Power, the Yankees evinced keen interest in the 28-year-old former Negro Leaguer. *The Sporting News* dutifully reported that the Bombers offered $60,000, but, "It has been reported that [Oklahoma City owner] Humphries has set a price on Greason which indicates his desire to keep the Negro star for another season."[28] A four-inning stint with the St. Louis Cardinals in 1954 would comprise Greason's big league career.

Power returned to Kansas City for the 1953 season and led the American Association in batting, but once again he failed to receive a much-deserved summons to join the parent club when rosters were expanded late in the season. One of the prospects recalled instead of Power was slow-moving first baseman Gus Triandos from Birmingham of the Class AA Southern Association. When pressed, the Yankees claimed the decision was made because Triandos was able to catch, which really didn't seem to be a priority with competent veteran receivers Charlie Silvera and Ralph Houk already rotting on the bench behind iron man Yogi Berra.[29] The Yankees did drop one barrier during the 1953 campaign when they acquired light-hitting Cuban infielder Willie Miranda to caddy for aging Phil Rizzuto. Miranda is thought to be the club's first foreign-born Hispanic player since Armando Marsans finished his major league career with the Yankees in 1918.[30]

In the off-season, the Yankees transferred Power, along with Elston Howard, to their 40-man roster, to avoid losing him to another organization in the minor league draft. At the time, the Yankees had only six other black players in their chain, all performing in obscurity at lower minor league classifications. Always eager to defend the Yankees, Dan Daniel jumped the gun by crediting them as the 12th big league team, ahead of the Cardinals, Tigers, Red Sox, and Phillies, to open its roster to blacks. Apparently Daniel also credited the Senators with integrating by adding Angel Scull, who would never play in Washington, to their roster.[31]

But in December, the Yankees divested themselves of Power, packaging him in a massive ten-player deal with the Philadelphia Athletics. He would develop into an all-star with the Athletics and subsequent teams, always saving his best efforts for games against the Yankees.[32]

Winners of eight American League pennants and six world championships in the 1950s, the Yankees didn't really need much help, but both Power and Gomez would have come in handy. The versatile Power, who could play anywhere in the infield as well as the outfield, would have been a dream come true for Yankee manager Casey Stengel, who delighted in platooning and shifting players around. In addition, his steady right-handed bat would have helped address a weakness. Gomez would have undoubtedly strengthened a talented, but injury-prone, pitching staff. With the two Puerto Rican stars on the roster, the Yankees conceivably might have captured ten pennants in the decade.

In the wake of re-intensified criticism after the Power trade, the Yankees continued to hold fast to their contention that they were looking for just "the right type of Negro and weren't going to settle for anything less just to appease a bunch of troublemakers."[33]

Elston Howard Arrives

The Yankees image of "the right type of Negro" was becoming quite clear. Obviously he had to have talent. But equally important, he had to be someone who knew his place — not a hot dog like Power or a troublemaker like Jackie Robinson.[34] When and if they finally employed a black player, he would be a patient, gentlemanly, respectful black man. He would have to be willing to wait his turn without making waves and be grateful for any opportunity he was given.

During the 1953 season, that candidate had begun to emerge in the person of Elston Howard. The only problem was whether he had the talent.

After signing with the Yankees, Howard spent the last half of the 1950 season in the low minors before entering the military for two years of service. Following his discharge, he was assigned to Kansas City. An average defensive outfielder who could catch some, Howard ended the 1953 campaign with an unspectacular .286 average, 62 points lower than his teammate Power. Yet the Yankees began touting Howard as a better prospect. Owner Dan Topping told *The Sporting News*, "My information is that Elston Howard, Negro outfielder with Kansas City has a better chance to come up than Power."[35] It should be noted that Topping did not claim that Howard was considered a better ballplayer than Power.

Howard immediately became the organization's new black standard-bearer after Power was traded. In the spring of 1954, he and pitching prospect Eddie Andrews, who would never make the majors, became the first black players to train with the Yankees.[36] Howard had spent most of his career in the outfield, but the Yankees began grooming him as a catcher — despite the fact that incumbent Yogi Berra, already a two-time league MVP who would capture the honor a third time in 1954, had yet to celebrate his 30th birthday. Of course, many critics of the Yankees' track record on integration saw the attempt to convert Howard as merely a diversion. It was feared that he would be doomed to years in the minor leagues, polishing his skills while the Yankees put off contaminating their roster, all the while rebuffing critics by proudly pointing to their catcher of the future.[37]

But Howard ended up exceeding everyone's expectations. Catching for Toronto in 1954, he earned Most Valuable Player honors while leading the squad to the International League championship. His spectacular performance, plus the fact that the Yankees lost the pennant to Cleveland, the American League integration leader, made it impossible for the Bombers to farm him out again.

In the sixth inning of the second game of the 1955 season, Howard took over in left field after starter Irv Noren was ejected from the game.[38] The Yankees had finally found the "right kind of Negro." But even in their capitulation, the haughty franchise denied New York fans of color a moment of triumph. The Yanks just hadn't been able to work Howard into the lineup during a 19 to 1 opening day trouncing of the Senators in Yankee Stadium, so the momentous event had to take place in Boston's Fenway Park the following day. Howard rose to the challenge of being the first black Yankee with a fine rookie season as a platoon outfielder and backup catcher.

Impact of the Yankees' Integration

The impact of the integration of the Yankees cannot be overstated. They weren't merely the 13th major league team to lower their race barrier. The Yankees were Organized Baseball's flagship franchise, the most successful in the history of the game. Elston Howard's busting of the Yankees' racial barrier may have been the greatest event, symbolically at least, for the integration of Organized Baseball since Jackie Robinson crossed the major league color line in 1947. According to David Halberstam, "Robinson told Howard that in some ways what Elston was going through was as hard or harder than what he had endured. Robinson, at least, had always known that the front office was behind him, whereas Howard knew that the front office had brought him up reluctantly."[39]

The New York Yankees were one of baseball's last, and by far its most formidable, bastions of segregation. To the nation's black population, they symbolized the most objectionable elements of the white power structure. Despite representing the city with the largest population of black citizens in the country — a city that had already welcomed black players on its two National League franchises the previous decade — the Yankees stubbornly refused to allow a black player to wear their pinstripes for a full eight years after the color barrier fell. And, worse, they continued to win.

General Manager George Weiss

History has assigned the lion's share of the blame for the Yankees' foot-dragging on the integration front to George Weiss. Weiss served as the club's farm system director from 1933 until he succeeded Larry MacPhail as general manager in October 1947, a position he held through the 1960 World Series.

Weiss's profile in *The Ballplayers*, a publication that generally treats its subjects benignly, characterizes him as "a czar-like general manager" and as "a shy, colorless and humorless penny-pincher."[40] Bill Veeck delighted in addressing Weiss as "Old Pus Bag."[41] William Marshall, author of *Baseball's Pivotal Era*, describes Weiss as "cold and calculating ... both tight with the dollar and an outstanding administrator."[42] Notorious "trade-aholic" Frank Lane said, "I never made a single deal with him. He was too smart."[43]

When it came to racial attitude, Roger Kahn wrote, "personally Weiss didn't care for blacks and didn't trust them."[44] David Halberstam was less benevolent. In *October 1964*, he asserts, "[Weiss's] racism was an unfortunate reflection of both snobbery and ignorance: Weiss did not think that his white customers, the upper-middle class gentry from the suburbs, wanted to sit with black fans, and he did not think his white players wanted to play with blacks, and worst of all, he did not in his heart think that black players were as good as white ones. He did not think they had as much courage or that they played as hard."[45]

Weiss's own words regarding black players also convey his bias. In discussing Negro League stars Artie Wilson and Piper Davis in 1948, Weiss said, "They are both good ballplayers, [but] there isn't an outstanding Negro player that anybody could recommend to step into the big leagues and hold down a regular job.... These committees apply the pressure to hire one or perhaps two [black] players. If you hire one or two, they want you to hire another one."[46]

In *The Boys of Summer*, Roger Kahn recalls an incident that occurred during the 1952 World Series. According to Kahn, "the third highest executive [presumably Weiss], after three martinis, said he would never allow a black man to wear a Yankee uniform. 'We don't want that sort of crowd,' he said, 'It would offend boxholders from Westchester to have to sit with niggers.'"[47]

And George Weiss was definitely not a prospective member for the "Vic Power Fan Club." With Power hitting .355 in July 1952, he advised, "There are divergent opinions on his abilities." Then tearing a page from the Senators' owner Clark Griffith's book of rhetoric, he proclaimed, "We are eager to find a Negro player of Yankee class. But we are not going to have a Negro player merely as a concession to pressure groups."[48]

Team Culture

The unpopular Weiss makes an excellent target and no doubt deserves a good share of the blame, but the Yankees' stubborn refusal to accept black players in the face of intense national condemnation had to have had the backing of the entire organization. Had the term "institutional racism" been in vogue while the battle to integrate Major League Baseball was being waged, it certainly would have been applied to the Yankees.

Larry MacPhail fought hard to keep the Dodgers from introducing Jackie Robinson to the big leagues, and co-owners Del Webb and Dan Topping were not generally considered advocates for underprivileged minorities. According to Roger Kahn, "Between them, Dan Topping and Del Webb had no discernible social conscience. Topping was comfortable in an all-white, all-wealthy Southampton social world. Webb's construction company had built one of the concentration camps used to imprison Japanese Americans during World War II. With some drinks in him, Webb boasted that he had completed the concentration camp 'ahead of schedule.'"[49]

Topping liked to point to his Brooklyn Dodgers' recruitment of black football star Buddy

Casey Stengel (left) and George Weiss were the architects of the 1950s Yankees dynasty, which was accomplished with a predominantly white roster (National Baseball Hall of Fame, Cooperstown, N.Y.).

Young as evidence of his sympathy to the cause of integration. "Jim Crow, my eye," he cried in August 1953, "Who brought the first Negro football player into the All-America Conference? I did. I signed Buddy Young. How can anybody accuse any operation of which I am the head of Jim Crow." Later, in a statement disturbingly similar to his general manager's words of a year ago, Topping declared, "We are eager to get a Negro player on the Yankees. But we are not going to bring up a Negro just to meet the demands of pressure groups."[50]

Also manning the Yankees' front office in the early 1950s was Roy Hamey, assistant to Weiss. Before coming to the Yankees, Hamey was general manager of the segregated Pittsburgh Pirates until Branch Rickey's arrival after the 1950 season. Hamey would leave for the Philadelphia Phillies' general manager job in 1954, where he would preside over the only segregated team left in the National League for three years before integration was forced on them (see chapter 16).

Another occupant of the executive suite was farm director Lee MacPhail, who stayed on as the Yankees' farm director after his famous father left. After leaving the Yankees himself to take over as general manager of the Baltimore Orioles, MacPhail would oversee the further whitening of one of the palest teams in the major leagues (see chapter 5). Decades later, after he had ascended to the presidency of the American League, Lee MacPhail still wouldn't admit that there might have been a little prejudice in the Yankee organization. "I can't agree there was any racial bias there at all," he insisted, conceding only that "the Yankees may have perhaps dragged their feet a little bit."[51]

Of course, the incipient prejudice also existed in the lower ranks. Manager Casey Stengel was decidedly "old school" when it came to blacks. "When I finally get a nigger, I get the only one that can't run," he complained when he first saw Howard in action.[52] Stengel reportedly used to call Howard "eight ball" to his face.[53] But to his credit, "The Old Professor" came to recognize Howard's outstanding qualities and accepted him as a valuable member of the Yankees. Nevertheless, he refused to turn the regular catching job over to Howard even after it was generally conceded that he was a better receiver than Berra.

Before Howard joined the club, traveling secretary Bill McCorry reportedly vowed, "No nigger will ever have a berth on any train I'm running."[54] In a team meeting after Howard came up, Yankee scout Rudy York was sharing his secret for reading pitches from Orioles hurler Connie Johnson by watching his grip. "You know niggers have white palms, lighter than the backs of their hands," he revealed, oblivious to Howard's presence.[55] Ironically, Big Rudy, a Georgia native, had floored everyone a decade earlier when he greeted the news of Jackie Robinson's signing by saying, "I wish him all the luck in the world and hope he makes good."[56]

Amid the prevailing attitude in the Yankee executive suite, it's no wonder Yankee scouts had trouble recognizing the talents of black prospects. In 1947, Larry MacPhail told *The Sporting News* that his scouts "check[ed] both Negro Leagues and didn't find a player worth signing." According to the article, the Yankees looked at Larry Doby, Willard Brown, and Hank Thompson, and MacPhail predicted that "none of the three is good enough to stick in the big leagues."[57]

Certain elements of the press also helped the club to maintain the courage of their convictions and even swayed a few of the more gullible fans.

In January 1953 the New York Chapter of the Baseball Writers Association of America honored Dan Daniel of the New York *World-Telegram and Sun* for 30 years of contributions to the profession. That same week, Daniel came to the defense of the Yankees by informing readers of *The Sporting News*, "If Power were regarded as good enough to be that 'first,' Stengel would be only too glad to call him up. However, Yankee scouts refuse to give Vic that high rating which Weiss and Casey demand of the first Negro player to appear in a Yankee uniform."[58] Power, incidentally, had hit .331 and drove in 109 runs for the Yankees' Kansas City Blues farm club the previous year. Two years later, Daniel would ingenuously maintain that Elston Howard roomed alone his rookie year because he liked it that way.[59]

But Daniel didn't confine his absurd commentary on race matters to the Yankees. When the Indians signed Satchel Paige in 1948, he accused the veteran hurler of misrepresenting his age by 10 years.[60] The next year, a week after *The Sporting News* carried an item about Cincinnati headhunters taking aim at Monte Irvin and Hank Thompson of the Giants, Daniel disclosed, "The press box no longer discerns the color of the man at the plate. White players, once so conscious of a color line, now fail to discern the nature of a fellow hired man's skin pigment."[61] Apparently due to his color blindness, Daniel wasn't able to discern that only nine of the more than 500 men who appeared in a major league game in 1949 had dark skin. Nor did he realize that two of the three black hitters who played regularly that year ranked in the top five in the majors in being hit by pitches.[62] Furthermore, he hadn't heard that at least a quarter of the black hitters in Triple A ball were injured by wayward pitches that year.[63]

In his *Sporting News* column three years later, Daniel would outlandishly fantasize that boxing great Joe Louis, a top catcher as a Detroit schoolboy, "might have become the Tigers' first Negro player if he'd not gone in for fisticuffs." Ignored was the unfortunate fact that Louis was already 33 years old when the color line was broken, and at the time the article was written more than five years later, the notoriously prejudiced Tigers still weren't close to putting a black player in a Detroit uniform.[64]

Daniel, however, wasn't the only member of the press guilty of making excuses for the Yankees' discriminatory practices. In a July 1952 *Sporting News* article, correspondent Ernie Mehl explained that the Yankees' top farm club, the Kansas City Blues, didn't integrated earlier out of consideration for the old Kansas City Monarchs.[65]

Though prejudice seems to have pervaded the Yankee organization, sheer arrogance might have been an equally powerful dynamic. After all, the Bombers were the World Champions of baseball from 1949 through 1953, a record that's never been seriously threatened by anyone else. Why should they upset the status quo? "Why introduce a new product when the established one was working so well?" might have been the thinking of the management of the team whose approach was often likened to corporate America. The fact that the Yankees signed their first black players immediately after losing the pennant to the integrated Cleveland Indians in 1948 and didn't promote one to the big leagues until they lost another pennant to the Indians in 1954 is probably not purely coincidental.

The Next Black Yankees

Despite Howard's rookie success in 1955, there was no discernable change in the attitude or actions of the Yankee brass. Howard spent his first two-and-one-half years in the major leagues as the only black player on the Yankees roster, a circumstance that smacked of tokenism. Furthermore, the team signed few additional black players. Their stance seemed to defiantly assert, "Okay, we've got one. What more do you want?"

Howard's solitude was finally broken in 1957 when the Yankees acquired Harry Simpson from the Kansas City Athletics. But Simpson, a 1956 American League all-star, would be a huge disappointment in a Yankee uniform. At the time of the trade, he looked like just what the team needed, a lefty hitting outfielder/first baseman with speed and power who would be able to take advantage of the Stadium's friendly right-field fence. Unfortunately, the Yankees hadn't done their homework. Simpson had initially disappointed in Cleveland and would flop in New York six years later for the same reasons. Simpson was a sensitive man with a fragile ego whose confidence was easily shaken — not an ideal fit for the pressure-cooker atmosphere of the Big Apple. The fact that he was acquired in exchange for popular Billy Martin and was only the second black man to play for the Yankees didn't make things any easier. Another problem was that Simpson was not a dead-pull hitter like most of the left-handed hitters who had prospered in New York. He was a wrist-hitter who naturally hit straightaway with power and found the Yankee Stadium dimensions to be more of a hindrance than an advantage. Simpson maintained that his problems in Cleveland started when they tried to make him into a pull hitter. Added to this was the fact that the Yankees installed him in left field, a notorious "sun field" at Yankee Stadium, where he had to contend with the glare and tricky shadows while covering an enormous amount of real estate. A few early misfortunes soon cost him his confidence.[66] Exactly a year after acquiring him, the Yankees dispatched Simpson back to the more comfortable surroundings of Kansas City, and Howard was back in the familiar position of being the only black face in the team photo.

The arrival of the Yankees' third black player in 1959, almost a year after Simpson was sent packing, coincided with the team's first failure to win the American League pennant since 1954. Like Simpson, Hector Lopez arrived via the Kansas City–New York pipeline. Like Simpson, Lopez valiantly and often unsuccessfully battled Yankee Stadium's left-field sun. And also like Simpson, Lopez's offensive numbers suffered from the Stadium's daunting left-center field dimensions. Unlike Simpson, however, Lopez was able to hang in there, lasting almost eight years in a Yankee uniform, mostly as a hard-hitting backup outfielder, and collecting five World Series paychecks.

The Early 1960s

The Yankees began another string of American League pennants in 1960 that would last through 1964, but Weiss and Casey Stengel wouldn't be around for the duration. They were turned out to pasture after the Yankees lost the 1960 World Series to the Pittsburgh Pirates, replaced by Roy Hamey and Ralph Houk. The 1961 edition of the Bronx Bombers featured the Mickey Mantle/Roger Maris home run duo and is considered by many to be one of the finest teams of all time. They established a new major league record with 240 homers on their way to 109 victories and decisively bested the Cincinnati Reds in five games in the World Series. Howard and Lopez were the only two black players on the squad, as they had been since Lopez's arrival. In fact, with Marshall Bridges joining Howard and Lopez on the 1962 championship squad, the 1961 edition of the Yankees was left with the distinction of being the last major league team to win a championship with such a small minority presence on their roster.

In 1963, Howard became the first black player to capture the American League Most Valuable Player Award. From 1955 through 1959, he had backed up Berra behind the plate, platooned in left field, and filled in admirably at first base when necessary, and in 1960, he shared catching duties with Berra. Despite not being a full-fledged regular, he was selected to the American League All-Star team each year from 1957 through 1960. Howard really blossomed at the age of 32 when ex-catcher Ralph Houk took over for Stengel and installed him behind the plate full time. From 1961 until an injury reduced his production early in the 1965 season, he competed for recognition as the best catcher in baseball with Earl Battey of the Twins.

The Yankees repeated as American League pennant winners in 1963 and 1964 but lost both World Series to National League clubs with much stronger black-player contingents, the Dodgers and Cardinals.

The Fall of the Mighty Yankees

In 1965, the Yankees suddenly dropped to sixth place, and the next year they were dead last. Furthermore, they didn't finish higher than fifth place for the remainder of the 1960s and remained also-rans for the first few years of the 1970s before George Steinbrenner bought the franchise and started pouring millions into it.

To say the Yankees suffered from a shortage of black players in the integration era would be a difficult position to defend. After all, they captured 15 American League pennants and 10 World Championships in the 18 years after Jackie Robinson's debut. Even the popular belief that the failure of the Yankees to develop more top black players was the primary cause of franchise's abrupt collapse after their 1964 pennant-winning season is questionable. As pointed out in *The Decline and Fall of the New York Yankees*, which was released in 1967 before history could be properly revised, other critical factors were involved.[67] For example, the farm system was de-emphasized. In 1950, the Yankees had 15 farm clubs in their system, but by 1964, they were down to seven. Another major consideration was the team's reluctance to issue large bonuses. Before big money was to be had, the Bombers were able to rely on the magic of the Yankee name to tip the scales in their favor. Widely pursued prospects could hardly resist the lure of Yankee Stadium and those majestic pinstripes, until dollars began speaking loudly.

The Yankees' failure to bring black players to New York was a key component of their 1960s decline, but it didn't cause their downfall as much as it kept the franchise from maintaining its dominance over the rest of the clubs in the American League. During the 1950s, the Yankees weren't exactly hard-pressed to integrate in order to stay competitive with their league rivals. In fact, they seemed to set the tone for the entire American League. In 1954, the last year the Yankees remained segregated, there were only four black regulars in the American League: Larry Doby and Al Smith in Cleveland, Minnie Minoso in Chicago, and the Philadelphia Athletics' new acquisition, Vic Power. In contrast, the National League pennant-winning Giants alone had that many first-stringers, while the second place Dodgers had five (see chapters 2 and 6). Furthermore, six black National League rookies, including a couple guys named Aaron and Banks, won regular jobs that season.[68] In fact, five of the eight teams in the American League fielded all-white rosters for most of the 1954 campaign, while the Phillies were the only National League squad without at least one black player in a significant role.[69]

After Howard in 1955, the Yankee farm system didn't produce another successful black performer until 22-year-old southpaw Al Downing joined the rotation in 1963. But during that seven-year Yankee intermission, their American League rivals only introduced a dozen new black players who would ultimately hold a regular job in the majors for at least five seasons, with Minnesota's Tony Oliva the best of the lot. Meanwhile, the National League debuted eight future Hall of Famers (Frank Robinson, Orlando Cepeda, Willie McCovey, Bob Gibson, Billy Williams, Juan Marichal, Lou Brock, and Willie Stargell), in addition to a record-breaking base stealer (Maury Wills), a two-time batting champ (Tommy Davis), a Cy Young Award winner (Mike Cuellar), and a seven-time Gold Glove-winning center fielder (Curt Flood).

In total, the National League would introduce 17 future black Hall of Famers before the American League produced a black performer who would eventually gain entry based solely on his accomplishments on major league diamonds (assuming that Larry Doby's Negro League career and status as a integration trail blazer contributed to his selection). Jackie Robinson, Roy Campanella, Willie Mays, Ernie Banks, Hank Aaron, and Roberto Clemente debuted before the eight listed above, and Joe Morgan, Tony Perez, Ferguson Jenkins also debuted before Rod Carew joined the Minnesota Twins in 1967.

The American League's lethargic approach to integration in the 1950s and early 1960s reversed the lopsided balance of power between the two leagues. From 1903, the inception of the Fall Classic, through 1949, the American League won 29 of 46 match-ups (There was no series in 1904). The worm started to turn in the 1950s when the National League captured four of the last six series after the Yankees started the decade out with four straight championships. Then four different National League clubs combined for six championships in the 1960s as the Yankees faltered and the full impact of integration become obvious. In 1961, Giants' manager Al Dark matter-of-factly stated, "You know why the National League is better, because of the colored players."[70] Even American League president Lee MacPhail later admitted that a slow start in the acquisition of black players hurt his league.[71]

But American League clubs made great strides in acquiring black talent in the latter half of the 1960s and forged back ahead in the decade of the 1970s. After a Frank Robinson-led Baltimore club won in 1970, Charlie Finley's highly integrated Oakland Athletics took three straight championships from 1972 through 1974. Then after two years of dominance by Cincinnati's Big Red Machine, the New York Yankees found their way back to the winner's circle in 1977 after a 14-year absence and repeated in 1978.

Steinbrenner Takes Over

Following Steinbrenner's purchase of the Yankees in 1973, his "indiscriminate" spending brought in such top-notch black performers as first baseman Chris Chambliss, second baseman Willie Randolph, outfielders Mickey Rivers and Oscar Gamble, and pitcher Doc Ellis. In 1976, these guys helped bring the Yankees their first pennant in more than a decade — their longest drought since the 1910s. Also making a tremendous contribution was veteran outfielder Roy White who, along with Downing and second baseman Horace Clarke, was one of only three black players of note turned out by the Yankees' farm system in the decade of the 1960s. Steinbrenner's shopping spree finally culminated in back-to-back World Championships after the Yankees signed black super-slugger Reggie Jackson, the self-proclaimed "straw that stirs the drink."

The Yankees really deserved to suffer a bit for more their role in impeding the integration of baseball and their treatment of those black players who were unfortunate enough to come under their control during that era. They didn't seem bothered by the fact that Howard was the only black player to work himself through the Yankees' farm system and graduate to the big club until 1963 or that talented black players acquired from other teams didn't seem as productive in Yankee pinstripes. Nor did they seem concerned that Howard invariably ran into trouble finding decent housing in New York and didn't consider it a problem that he wasn't allowed to stay with his teammates at the team's hotel and had to board with black families in the area.[72]

Though they made Howard the first black coach in the American League after he retired as a player, the Yankees failed to give him a chance at the manager post for which he seemed eminently qualified. After his death in 1980, his wife Arlene said in an interview, "Elston wondered why he had to be better than everyone else, why he had to be superman to manage a baseball team. They wanted you to have a Ph.D. to manage if you were black, and about any white guy could manage. To Elston, it was like a slap in the face."[73]

Retrospectively commenting on the Yankees' attitudes and practices with regard to race during their heyday, Dan Daniel, one of the club's staunchest defenders admitted, "If the Yankees weren't guilty [of prejudice] as charged, they were certainly going out of their way looking for trouble."[74]

Chapter 16

THE PHILADELPHIA PHILLIES

In terms of wealth, market size, and talent, the last four major league teams to integrate were the elite franchises in the major leagues at the outset of the 1950s. The New York Yankees were owned by well-heeled partners Del Webb and Dan Topping, the Detroit Tigers were financed by Walter Briggs of Briggs-Stratton, and Tom Yawkey's millions kept the Boston Red Sox flush. These three clubs finished 1-2-3 in the American League race in 1950. In the National League, the 1950 pennant-winning Philadelphia Phillies were backed by the Carpenters' DuPont Company fortune. These franchises were situated in four of the most populous big league cities, and all placed among the top five clubs in the majors in attendance.[1]

To various degrees, these four teams ended up paying dearly for their resistance to integrating their rosters. But the Phillies, the last National League team to permit a black player to take the field in their uniform, paid the steepest price of all for their prejudice. In 1950, the Phillies captured the National League pennant with a talented young squad dubbed the "Whiz Kids" and in the process stole the hearts of Philadelphia fans from Connie Mack's Athletics. At the start of the second half of the 20th century, the Whiz Kids ruled the third-largest major league city and seemed poised on the brink of a dynasty.[2] But the unforgettable 1950 edition of the Phillies would be the last segregated team to win a National League pennant. While the Dodgers, Braves, and Giants — the three teams that would dominate the National League for the remainder of the decade — were stocking up on inexpensive black talent, the Phillies squandered a fortune on under-performing bonus babies. By the final years of the decade, they had taken out a long-term lease on the National League cellar that wasn't interrupted until the expansion New York Mets entered the league in 1962.

Franchise History

Before the emergence of the Whiz Kids, the Phillies hadn't fielded a decent team in more than 30 years. Prior to World War I, they took the 1915 National League pennant with the great Grover Cleveland Alexander heading the pitching staff and pre–Ruthian home run king Gavvy Cravath leading the offense. But financial uncertainty forced the franchise to sell Alexander and several other stars as the country was entering the war, and the franchise slid into a severe and lengthy decline. Between the onset of World War I and the end of World War II, the Phillies doggedly fought off the Boston Braves for recognition as the worst team in Major League Baseball. The competition was intense, but the Phils claimed the onerous distinction by virtue of finishing in the second division 27 times in the 28 years from 1918 through 1945, with only a miraculous fourth-place finish in 1932 breaking the skein. During that period, they finished dead last 16 times and next-to-last on eight occasions. In each of the ten years leading up to and including World War II, the Phillies lost more than 90 contests.

During the 1930s, Gerald Nugent assumed control of the financially strapped franchise. A furniture salesman whose mother was the team secretary under owner William F. Baker, Nugent was also an avid baseball fan and soon found himself working in the Phillies' front office. When Baker died, he left a share of the club to Nugent's mother, and Gerald took over as club president. A few years later, Mrs. Baker passed away, leaving her remaining shares to the Nugents.[3] Under Gerald Nugent's direction, continuing cash flow problems forced the team to eventually sell almost every quality player that fell into their hands, and he had to borrow funds from the National League to keep the Phillies afloat. In 1943, the league foreclosed on him and sold the franchise to lumber baron William Cox. But, within a year, Cox was forced out of the league for betting on his own team.[4] One could have argued that betting on the Phils was tantamount to charity rather than gambling, but the priggish Commissioner Landis forced Cox to sell his interests to multimillionaire Robert M. Carpenter Sr., one of the partners in the DuPont Corporation of Wilmington, Delaware.[5]

Carpenter purchased the Phillies as a civic gesture, as well as a means of keeping his 28-year-old son gainfully occupied. Sports-minded Bob Jr. had been an end on Duke's 1939 Rose Bowl team. He worked for DuPont before striking out on his own to try his hand at sports administration as a promoter, fight manager, men's and women's basketball team operator, and part-owner of the Wilmington minor league franchise in the Interstate League.[6]

The baseball world waited expectantly for the rich kid to choke on his silver spoon, but young Carpenter initially gave a surprisingly good account of himself. Baseball became his main business and his passion. He quickly hired respected former pitcher Herb Pennock as his general manager. Pennock had strong local ties. He was born in Kennett Square, just outside of Philadelphia, and eventually came to be referred to as "The Squire of Kennett Square." He began his playing career with the Philadelphia Athletics but achieved his greatest success with the powerful Yankee teams of the 1920s. He was the farm system director for the Boston Red Sox when Carpenter persuaded him to come home to Philadelphia.[7]

Pennock was the architect of the 1950 Whiz Kids, bringing most of the key players into the Phillies organization prior to his sudden death from a cerebral hemorrhage in January 1948 at the annual major league meeting in New York. He took full advantage of the only edge he had over his competitors — Carpenter's fabulous wealth — and plowed millions into signing the best young prospects he could find.[8]

Gradually, the plan came together. After losing 108 times in 1945, the Phils improved by 23 games in 1946 and managed a fifth-place finish under the field leadership of former New York Yankees star Ben Chapman. But the Phillies fell to a seventh-place tie in 1947 and were back in seventh again when 37-year-old Eddie Sawyer replaced Chapman midway through the 1948 season. Under Sawyer's direction, the Phillies clawed their way up to sixth place in the final standings; in 1949, the final pieces starting falling into place, and the youthful club moved up to third in the standings.

The Whiz Kids

The nucleus of the 1950 Whiz Kids squad consisted of farm-system products Robin Roberts, Curt Simmons, Bob Miller, and Bubba Church in the starting rotation, Granny

Hamner at shortstop, Willie Jones at third base, Richie Ashburn and Del Ennis patrolling the outfield, and Stan Lopata and Andy Seminick sharing catching duties. Except for the 29-year-old Seminick, none of these homegrown phenoms were older than 25 when the season started. A few thirty-somethings augmented the youthful talent. Thirty-three-year-old Jim Konstanty, who had been picked up off the minor league scrap heap two years earlier, was the ace of the bullpen. And 30-year-old first baseman Eddie Waitkus, making a miraculous comeback after being shot by an obsessed female fan the previous year, was the oldest regular position player.

The Whiz Kids took over first place on July 25, and hung on through a late-season slump and the loss of star lefthander Simmons to the military draft to prevail over the Brooklyn Dodgers on the last day of the season. Exhausted from the close pennant race, the young Phillies were swept by the veteran New York Yankees in what would be Major League Baseball's last all-white World Series.

With a cast of talented young players who had already been tested under fire, a brilliant young manager, and an aggressive, involved young owner with money to burn, the Phillies looked like the team to beat for the decade of the 1950s. But the seeds of the Phillies' downfall had already been sown.

Team Culture

In *To Every Thing a Season: Shibe Park and Urban Philadelphia*, Bruce Kuklick asserts, "As much as he could, Carpenter opposed a black presence in the Majors and certainly at Shibe Park," and charges that the Phillies "were racist on principle" and "willingly hurt the quality of their teams."[9]

During Jackie Robinson's rookie campaign, the Phillies rivaled the Cardinals as his most

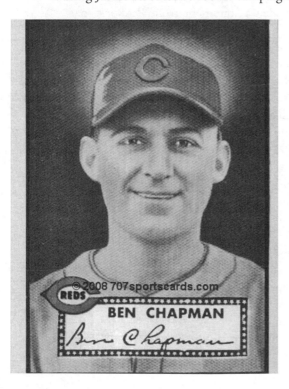

vicious antagonists. According to Dodgers' traveling secretary Harold Parrott, Phillies owner Bob Carpenter and general manager Herb Pennock called Rickey before the Dodgers' first trip to Philadelphia early in the 1947 season. Pennock told Rickey, "You just can't bring that nigger here with the rest of your team, Branch. We're just not ready for that sort of thing yet. We won't be able to take the field with your Brooklyn team if that boy Robinson is in uniform."[10]

Carpenter and Pennock backed down when Rickey called their bluff by agreeing to accept a forfeit, but when Robinson stepped on the field for the first game he was greeted with an unrelenting barrage of racial abuse from the Philadelphia dugout. The vicious attack was led by manager Ben

The Phillies under manager Ben Chapman mercilessly tormented Jackie Robinson during his rookie year (1952 Topps card).

Chapman, a native of Alabama whose racist views were well known from his playing days, and included vulgar references to Robinson's hygiene and genetic make-up as well as every possible derogatory name for a black man. Chapman even accused Robinson of sleeping with his teammate's wives and destroying the Dodgers with his mere presence.[11] Years later, Robinson would admit that the Phillies' insults brought him closer to the breaking point that any other incident.[12]

In the second game of the series, the Phillies continued their brutal verbal assault, finally driving Brooklyn second baseman Eddie Stanky, by no means an admirer of Robinson, to the rookie's defense. Stanky confronted Chapman and his raucous bench jockeys, calling them cowards and challenging them to pick on somebody who can answer back.[13]

The Phillies' conduct was so offensive that the press took up the cause, resulting in public condemnation of their actions and a reprimand from Commissioner Chandler. Chapman tried to dismiss his behavior as routine baptism of a rookie, no different than that afforded the likes of Hank Greenberg, Clint Hartung, Joe Garagiola, and Connie Ryan, players who apparently were frequent recipients of ethnic slurs.[14] And *The Sporting News* predictably downplayed the incident also, maintaining that Chapman was being criticized "for regarding Robinson as just another player, subject to the jockeying that any performer might receive."[15]

Although it apparently escaped Chapman, the Phillies' front office recognized the possibly of a public-relations nightmare and asked Rickey to persuade Robinson to participate in a media hatchet-burying on the Dodgers' next trip to Philadelphia. Robinson reluctantly, but graciously, agreed to pose for a photo with Chapman. Looking on in amazement, Chapman's old friend and former teammate Dixie Walker remarked, "I swear, I never thought I'd see Ol' Ben eat shit like that."[16]

With the help of *The Sporting News*, the Phillies even launched an embarrassingly transparent campaign to convince the readers of their pure racial motives. In July, a *Sporting News* item entitled "Phillies May Sign Negro" included a statement from Pennock that, "We're interested in any ballplayer of any race, color, or creed who can help the club" and implied it was possible that the Phils were dickering for one or two black players.[17] Two weeks later, the publication printed a rumor that the Phils were scouting Harlem Globetrotter star Goose Tatum, who spent his summers playing first base for the Indianapolis Clowns of the Negro American League.[18]

Despite the public relations effort, little changed in Philadelphia. Chapman survived the incident and was rehired for the 1948 campaign despite another seventh-place finish. Richie Ashburn, who debuted with the Phillies in 1948, remembered, "We had been told to slide hard into him [Robinson] as often as we could. We wanted to put him out of the game, and we thought that his legs had taken a lot of punishment."[19] According to Robinson, the Phillies were the only club to "dust him off consistently" during his 1947 rookie season.[20] Wendell Smith characterized the team as being "particularly resentful toward Negro players in 1947 and 1948."[21]

In a 1949 *Ebony* magazine survey, Carpenter would display his acute insight into the integration issue with the brilliant revelation, "the number of them [black players] in the major leagues will definitely increase." For some reason, the Phillies owner conveniently failed to append "but not in a Phillies uniform" to his statement.[22]

Long after Robinson and other black players had become established, the Phillies continued to carry the banner of prejudice. In May 1954, Robinson publicly warned Phillies pitchers to stop throwing at his head "or else."[23]

The City of Philadelphia

Nor was the "City of Brotherly Love" kind to all. As Wendell Smith would write about the city's acceptance of black players in 1953, "Slight improvement was noted past few years, but Philadelphia is still no paradise."[24]

Philadelphia ranked third among major leagues cities in both non-white and total population in 1950, but the city's percentage of non-whites was greater than its larger cousins, New York and Chicago.[25] Yet Philadelphia had a reputation as a racially segregated city.[26]

In addition, Philadelphia fans have long been considered among the worst in the world of sports. They once booed Athletics' outfielder Gus Zernial as he was being taken off the field on a stretcher after breaking his collarbone diving for a ball.[27] After being traded to the Cincinnati Reds before the 1952 season, outfielder Dick Sisler, one of the heroes of the 1950 Whiz Kids, labeled Philly fans "howling wolves." Sisler called them the "most vicious fans in the National League" and said Philadelphia was "the worst place I've ever played," claiming the fans affected the performance of several top Phillies players.[28]

Assigning the Blame

Herb Pennock, general manager of the Phils from 1944 until his death before the 1948 season, has received blame in some quarters for fostering a spirit of racial prejudice in the Phillies organization.[29] But few big league clubs were signing black players during Pennock's term as general manager, so there's not enough information to analyze his performance. Apparently, Pennock has already been judged to some extent for his racial attitudes. About fifty years after his death, a local attempt to erect a monument to the Squire of Kennett Square resulted in a minor scandal when some of his comments were recalled.[30] After Pennock's death, Carpenter took over the duties of general manager himself, although he continued to rely heavily on veteran baseball men for advice.

The Phillies' flush of success in 1950 probably cost them dearly in the long run by convincing club management that they could afford to ignore black players.

At least the Phillies didn't hand out the old bit about waiting for a black ballplayer who met their high standards, which would have been a hard to sell for the most unsuccessful franchise in major league history. Instead, the Phillies seemed to use their reputation for incompetence as a shield, trying to give the impression they were diligently, albeit futilely, trying to find black players.

The Phillies occasionally, however, had to feign interest in joining the integration movement to pacify those pesky agitators. In 1952, the club announced the signing of their first black player, 18-year-old Theodore Washington of the Philadelphia Stars. They also took credit for two other black players in the system, Gerry Jones and Chico Gerard, who were members of the Granby Canadian Provincial League that had recently affiliated with them. Washington was released without ever appearing in Organized Baseball, and Jones and Gerard were missing from the Granby roster the next year.[31]

The Last National-League Holdouts

After falling to fifth place in 1951, the Phillies rebounded to finish in the first division every year from 1952 through 1955, but they never seriously challenged for the pennant despite brilliant individual performances from future Hall of Famers Robin Roberts and Richie Ashburn. Before the 1954 campaign, Carpenter stepped down from the general manager's post and hired veteran baseball executive Roy Hamey to take over. Hamey was no stranger to segregation, having previously held the general manager's position for the all-white Pittsburgh Pirates from 1946 until Branch Rickey's arrival after the 1950 season and then serving as George Weiss's assistant with the New York Yankees before landing the Philadelphia job.

In 1956, the Phillies returned to the second division of the National-League standings, where they would remain for seven long years. Carpenter's reluctance to break up his old team had led to stagnation as the "Whiz Kids" had become the "Wheeze Kids." Roberts and Simmons still headed the pitching staff, although their pitches had lost a little sizzle, while Bob Miller had become a second-rate Jim Konstanty in the bullpen. Old "Puddin' Head" Jones still held down third base when his aching feet allowed, and Granny Hamner still roamed the middle of the diamond, living up to his nickname more and more. Richie Ashburn and Del Ennis still ranged the outfield, although they no longer ranged as far afield. Even old favorite Andy Seminick was back with the team after a Cincinnati odyssey, backing up his former understudy Stan Lopata.

From 1954 through 1956, the Phillies stood alone with the only segregated roster in the National League. Furthermore, they were the only sports team in the city without a black presence as the NFL Philadelphia Eagles introduced Willie Irvin in 1953 and the Philadelphia Warriors of the NBA recruited Jackie Moore for the 1954–55 season.[32] Even the Philadelphia Athletics in the American League had integrated with Bob Trice and Vic Power.

But while their rivals had been stocking their systems with black talent in the early 1950s, Carpenter's Phils had been lavishing another round of huge bonuses on young white prospects. Judicious bonus signings had been the key to the rise of the Whiz Kids. The attendance boom of the post-war years, however, had increased competition in the bonus sweepstakes. The second wave of Phillies bonus babies turned out to be "Fizz Kids" rather than "Whiz Kids" as expensive, highly touted prospects like Ted Kazanski, Mack Burk, and Tom Qualters left only a smudge on the record books.

When St. Louis and Cincinnati, the only other National League holdouts, introduced black players to their big league lineup at the beginning of the 1954 season, the Phillies still didn't even have a black prospect in their farm system. After the season, they finally took their first solid steps toward integration at the minor league level. They signed teenage phenom Charlie Randall, whose gaudy .351 rookie average with the Phils' Bradford affiliate in the PONY League in 1955 would earn him the distinction of being the first black player to wear a Phillies uniform at the club's training camp in the spring of 1956.[33] Randall, however, would never advance beyond Class A ball. Before the 1955 season, the Phils also quietly purchased the contracts of first baseman Pancho Herrera and pitcher Henry Mason from the Kansas City Monarchs, still struggling along in the last vestige of the old Negro Leagues. The 20-year-old Herrera and 23-year-old Mason had both starred in the East-West All-Star contest that summer.[34]

Among the stalwart black players the Phillies had passed on were Joe Black and Jim Gilliam, the 1952 and 1953 National League Rookies of the Year. The nearby Baltimore Elite Giants reportedly gave the Phils first crack at the pair for a mere $2,500 when shopping their contracts in 1950.[35] In the early 1950s, a Phillies official is said to have told one of their scouts, "if you keep talking about those Negro players you are going to find yourself working for Branch Rickey."[35] The Phillies could have had the great Roy Campanella, who grew up in Philadelphia. According to Campy, he requested a tryout with the Phillies during the war at the suggestion of manager Hans Lobert. Though he was well known as one of the top catchers in black baseball at the time, owner Gerald Nugent turned him down rather than challenge baseball's racial status quo.[36] Little had changed a decade later when black teenager Leon Wagner attended another Phillies' tryout camp. "You're a good prospect, but I want to be honest with you," said the scout in charge, "You won't have a real chance in this organization."[37] Wagner went on to sign with the Giants and develop into an all-star slugger.

By mid–1956, Ed Logan, starring in the nether regions of the Class D Midwest League, was being touted as possibly the Phillies' first black player, replacing Randall as the franchise's favored black prospect.[38]

Meanwhile, Herrera and Mason, both repeating solid seasons with Schenectady in the Class A Eastern League, were ignored. In fact, general manager Hamey had spent a week watching the Phillies' Schendectady and Syracuse farm clubs the year before and reported back "that on neither club was there any material that could help the Phils."[39] The fact that the Phillies continued to focus on black prospects in the lower minor leagues while neglecting more advanced prospects like Herrera and Mason seems an indication that they were still trying to put off integrating the big league roster. Herrera and Mason would eventually get a shot at the big time, but Logan, like Charlie Randall, would never see his name on a big league lineup card,

The Phillies Finally Integrate

In January 1957, shortly after Jackie Robinson's announcement of his retirement as an active player, he made the pointed comment, "If thirteen major league teams can come up with colored players, why can't the other three?"[40]

Whether jolted into action by Robinson's criticism or by shear desperation over their falling fortunes, the Phillies finally decided to get serious about integrating their big league roster. Unfortunately, they found themselves in the same spot that other resisters like the Cardinals and Reds had uncomfortably occupied years earlier — an absence of ready-for-prime-time black talent in their organization. Interestingly, there actually was a black hurler with a most impressive track record who'd posted an 11–4 won-lost record with a glittering 1.86 earned run average for the Phillies' Triple A Miami Marlins farm club. Ancient Satchel Paige had been signed by Bill Veeck, who was running the Marlins at the time, and his contract was the property of that minor league franchise. The Marlins, however, would certainly have been willing to make Paige available to the Phillies had his services been requested.

Instead, the Phillies turned to another former Negro Leaguer — one somewhat less celebrated than the legendary Paige. Infielder John Irvin Kennedy had shown up for a tryout during the 1956 campaign, and the Phillies invited him to their 1957 minor league training camp. But Robinson's retirement speech had ratcheted up the pressure to put a black player in Philadelphia candy-stripes, so when Kennedy impressed in the early stages of camp he immediately became the Phillies' "Great Black Hope." After 16 exhibition games, Kennedy was leading the team in hitting and had been tabbed as the probable replacement for Granny Hamner at shortstop.[41]

The Sporting News reported that Kennedy was 23 years old and had "never played a game in Organized Baseball."[42] The Phillies' new phenom was the talk of the Phillies camp, but the club's infatuation with their shortstop prospect waned when whispers that he might be a tad older than he'd claimed began.[43] It seems that Kennedy had neglected to include a few items on his resume, like his years as a star running back at Edwin Waters College around the turn of the decade, stints in the St. Louis Browns and New York Giants systems in the early 1950s, and a few years with Birmingham in the Negro American League. Kennedy had, in fact, been born back in 1926 and was six months older than the old Whiz Kid Granny Hamner!

Nevertheless, Kennedy made the opening day roster and is often identified as the Phillies' first black player. But the guy who officially made the Phils the 14th big league club to field a black player was Cuban Chico Fernandez, who opened the 1957 season at shortstop.

Many in the Philadelphia press didn't consider Fernandez to be black.[44] In fact, the announcement of his acquisition from the Dodgers for veteran outfielder Elmer Valo, four minor leaguers, and $75,000 a little more than a week before opening day made no mention of his racial heritage.[45] It wasn't until he bumped Kennedy aside to capture the regular short-stop job that Fernandez was referred to as a Negro.[46]

Chico Fernandez, who is described in *A History of Cuban Baseball, 1864–2006* as brown-skinned, probably had a dark enough complexion to have been excluded from Organized Baseball before the color barrier was breached. But like Carlos Bernier in Pittsburgh, Fernan-dez is often overlooked in identifying the first black players to perform for major league fran-

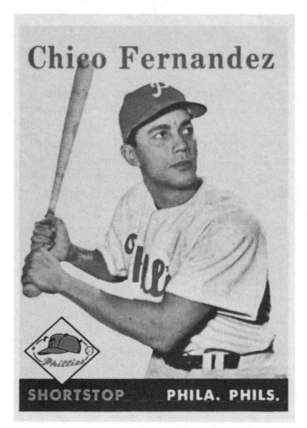

chise. Years after his retirement, he would complain, "I never got my full due as a black player when I stepped onto the field," al-though, he pointed out, "I was forced to live in the black section of town."[47]

Kennedy appeared briefly in five games for the Phillies, without getting a hit in two plate appearances or having a ball hit to him, before being quietly sent to the obscurity of the Class B Carolina League.[48] He would remain in the minors until 1961 without ever again rising above the Class A level. Veteran utilityman Chuck Harmon, who came over in a deal with the St. Louis Cardinals, imme-diately stepped into Kennedy's place as the second black player on the squad. Harmon found at least one familiar face in Philadel-phia. With Olean back in 1951, he had roomed with a young first baseman named Paul Owens.[49] In addition to being one of the first black-white roommate combos in Organized Baseball, they formed one of the most dynamic roomie duos of all time. Har-mon led the P.O.N.Y. league in runs batted in while finishing second in batting at .375, while Owens blasted the ball at a .407 clip to lead the league in hitting. An injury cut Owens' playing career short, and he joined the Phillies front office, working his way up to farm director and eventually becoming general manager.

Cuban-born Chico Fernandez was touted as the Phillies first black player after his acquisi-tion from Brooklyn, although the Dodgers did not list him as a black player (1958 Topps card).

Harmon performed well off the bench for the Phils in 1957, his final big league season, and Fernandez enjoyed a fine campaign as the Phillies' regular shortstop. But Fernandez would be the lone minority on the club for most of the 1958 season, and he endured a rough campaign. His batting average dropped more than 30 points, and he became a target for the ruthless Philadelphia boo-birds. Fernandez began the 1959 season at shortstop, teaming with rookie second baseman Sparky Anderson, but the talented 27-year-old had developed a reputation as being hard to handle and was benched in early June when the club elected to go with 29-year-old journeyman Joe Koppe.[50] In 1958, Fernandez had posted the second-best fielding mark among National League shortstops, more than 30 points above Koppe's average for the Braves' Wichita farm club in the American Association that year. Yet Fernandez languished on the bench for the rest of the 1959 campaign, while Koppe trailed the rest of the league's shortstops in fielding by a substantial margin. After the season, Fernandez was traded to the Detroit Tigers where he revived his career and became the first black regular shortstop in American League history.

The John Quinn Era Begins

In January 1959, respected and popular John Quinn was persuaded to give up the reins of the Milwaukee Braves, National League pennant winners the previous two years, to replace Roy Hamey as general manager of the hapless Phillies. Quinn had overseen the successful integration of the Braves during his tenure as their general manager, while Hamey had done little to bring in black talent in his four years with the Phillies. But in one of his last acts as general manager, Hamey consummated a horrendous trade with the Giants at the annual winter meetings to acquire a pair of black players. In exchange for veteran hurler Ruben Gomez and catcher Valmy Thomas, the Phils gave up pitcher Jack Sanford, the 1957 National League Rookie of the Year. Giant's coach Bill Posedel, who had been a member of the Phillies' staff the previous year, said, "It's the best deal the Giants could have made. I'm surprised Roy Hamey of the Phils went through with the deal."[51] Sanford went on to average 16 victories a year for the Giants over the next five seasons, while Gomez would win only five more major league games and Thomas would hit only .200 for the Phillies in 1959 and be out of the majors within three years. To his credit, Hamey also acquired dark-skinned Mexican shortstop Ruben Amaro from the Cards at the same meetings. Amaro would give the Phillies several years of topflight defense.

During Quinn's first season in Philadelphia, he brought in two more black veterans, acquiring former Cub outfielder Solly Drake from the Dodgers' system and ex–Brave hurler Humberto Robinson from Cleveland, neither of whom made much of an impact in Philadelphia. That year, the Phillies solidified their hold on the National League cellar with 90 losses.

When Quinn took over, there were only a handful of black players among the Phillies' farm hands, but by 1961 the number had jumped to 34 according to one source.[52] Included were future major leaguers Johnny Briggs, Alex Johnson, Larry Hisle, Ted Savage, Grant Jackson, Ferguson Jenkins, and brothers Richie and Hank Allen. All of these men were signed after Quinn took over. Under Quinn's color-blind leadership, the Phillies seemed to be making a sincere effort to erase all traces of the club's segregated past.

In fact, the Phils began the 1960 campaign with two black rookies in their opening day lineup. Spring-training sensation Tony Curry, one of the first Bahamians to make the major leagues, was in right field, while 6'3" 220-pound erstwhile first baseman Pancho Herrera found himself incongruously stationed at second base. Old Whiz Kid skipper Eddie Sawyer, who left the Phillies during the 1952 campaign, had been persuaded to leave his teaching post at his Ithaca College alma mater to return to the dugout during the 1958 season. Apparently the sight of Herrera lumbering around the keystone sack was more than the former professor could take, and he submitted his resignation after the team's opening day loss in Cincinnati. His simple explanation was, "I'm 49 — I want to live to be 50."[53]

Sawyer's replacement was 34-year-old Gene Mauch, a scrappy former utility infielder who had been managing Boston's Triple A farm club in Minneapolis. Fortunately, Mauch did not bring with him the attitude towards black players that seemed to prevail in the Red Sox system. Shortly after his arrival, the Phillies began a radical makeover of their roster. Among the first to go was Curt Simmons, leaving Robin Roberts as the last remaining Whiz Kid. Disappointing Ruben Gomez was also shown the door, but the club acquired two dark-skinned Cubans, second baseman Tony Taylor from the Cubs and outfielder Tony Gonzalez from the Reds, who moved into regular jobs. With incumbent Ed Bouchee going to Chicago in the deal to acquire Taylor, Herrera was mercifully shifted to first base, and Ruben Amaro soon took over the regular shortstop job, giving the new Phillies five young black regulars. And the quality was there. Taylor made the National League All-Star squad, Herrera finished second in National League Rookie of the Year voting to Dodgers outfielder Frank Howard, and Curry made the Rookie All-Star squad. Despite the influx of fine young players, however, the club lost five more games than the year before and again finished in last place.

Excluding starting pitcher Robin Roberts, the average age of Mauch's 1961 opening day lineup was less than 24 years of age, and the club featured five black players: Herrera at first base, Taylor at second, Amaro at shortstop, Gonzalez in center field, and Curry in left. The youth movement resulted in 107 losses, including a nightmarish 21-game losing streak, and a fourth-straight last-place finish. Curry was dispatched to the minors early in the year, but black veteran slugger Wes Covington was acquired during the season to provide a respected veteran presence as well as a solid bat.

In 1962, the National League expanded to ten teams, and Mauch led the youthful Phillies to seventh place with their first winning record since 1953. Taylor, Gonzalez, Amaro, Covington, and rookie Ted Savage gave the club a solid cadre of black regulars. But conspicuously absent from the mix was first baseman Pancho Herrera.

The Plight of Pancho Herrera

Herrera's experience typifies many of the problems encountered by black players trying to establish themselves in the major leagues in that era. He was 20 years old and had spent three seasons with the Monarchs when the Phillies purchased his contract along with pitcher Henry Mason's. Initially, they were both assigned to the Syracuse Chiefs, the Phillies' Triple A farm team. Herrera got off to a great start and was hitting over .300 after 18 games with the last-place Chiefs when he was demoted to the Class A Schenectady Bluejays. It seemed that Herrera and Mason had become virtually joined at the hip — forced to move through the Phillies organization in lockstep due to the perceived necessity of keeping black players in pairs for purposes of companionship, traveling arrangements, etc. Since there didn't seem to be room for Mason on the promising young Syracuse pitching staff that featured future major leaguers Dick Farrell, Jim Owens, and Seth Morehead, he was consigned to Schenectady, and Herrera had to accompany him.[54] Herrera's replacement was light-hitting Jimmy Westlake

The Phillies were slow to give Cuban first baseman Pancho "Frank" Herrera a big league chance and quick to discard him when he slumped after a fine rookie season (1961 Topps card).

who had hit five homers in the Pacific Coast League the previous year. At Schenectady, Herrera was stationed in the outfield due to the presence of favored white prospect Ed Bouchee at first base. Herrera and Mason both performed well for the Bluejays for the remainder of the 1955 campaign, but were not rewarded with promotions the next year. This time, Herrera appeared to be the stumbling block. The Miami Marlins had replaced Syracuse as the Phillies' top farm club, and the organization's Triple A first base job went to Bouchee. Since the Phillies didn't have a Class AA affiliate at the time, Herrera was returned to Schenectady for the 1956 campaign where he at least got a chance to play first base. He led the Bluejays in batting average and runs batted in while Mason won 15 games, but the duo had to wait until the next year before getting another Triple A opportunity.

Bouchee took over the Phillies' first base job in 1957, clearing the way for Herrera (and Mason) with the Marlins. Mason had a disappointing campaign, but Herrera led Miami in batting average, homers, and runs batted in. Yet he failed to get a late-season trial with the Phillies.

After enjoying an excellent rookie season as the Phillies' regular first baseman, Bouchee began the 1958 campaign undergoing psychiatric treatment at the Institute of Living in Hartford, Connecticut. During the off-season, he had been arrested for exposing himself before a six-year-old girl and pleaded guilty to indecent exposure.[55] Herrera began the season on the Phillies roster, but despite his excellent performance with Miami the preceding season, he wasn't given a full shot at the temporarily vacated first base job. In fact, he made only three scattered starts at first before being returned to Miami, leaving outfielders Harry Anderson and Dave Philley to man the post until Bouchee was welcomed back to the fold in July. Apparently the late 1950s was a more understanding era when it came to psychological disorders than racial heritage.

Herrera was recalled to Philadelphia late in the 1958 season and installed at third base, a new position for him, in place of injured veteran Willie Jones. Despite fielding well, only one error in 16 games at the hot corner, and posting a creditable .270 batting average, he was back in the International League for a third-straight season when the 1959 campaign opened. Apparently Bouchee's .257 batting mark after his reinstatement was considered good enough for him to keep the regular first job, and the franchise still couldn't bear to replace old "Puddin' Head" Jones at third base. Buffalo had replaced Miami as the Phillies' Triple A affiliate for the 1959 season, and Herrera enjoyed a tremendous season for the Bisons, winning the International League Triple Crown and leading the team to the league championship. He began the season playing third base due to the presence of popular veteran slugger Luke Easter, who'd slammed 38 homers for Buffalo the previous year. But early in the season, Easter was shipped to Rochester to make room for Herrera at first. Mason, who made an appearance with the Phillies at the end of the 1958 campaign after a mediocre performance in Miami, also performed brilliantly for the Bisons in 1959, posting the highest winning percentage in the International League. Yet neither received a late-season call-up.

Mason started the 1960 season in Philadelphia along with Herrera, but the combination was finally broken up when the pitcher was demoted to the minors early in the season, never to return. Based on his fine rookie campaign, Pancho "Frank" Herrera's image appeared on a Topps All-Star card when the company released its 1961 baseball card set. But the projected National League All-Star first baseman slumped after getting off to a quick start and was riding the bench by season's end. In the off-season, the Phils acquired veteran slugger Roy Sievers to handle first base, and Herrera found himself back in Buffalo where he once again reigned as the league home run and runs batted in king. Before the 1963 season, he was dispatched to the talent-laden Pittsburgh Pirates organization along with Ted Savage, another young black player who didn't immediately fulfill expectations with the Phillies, for veteran third baseman Don Hoak. Ironically, Herrera ended up emulating Luke Easter, the man he'd replaced in Buffalo years earlier, as he spent the next decade belting minor league homers without getting another major league shot.

The Arrival of Dick "Richie" Allen

Meanwhile, back in Philadelphia, the Phils finished a solid fourth in 1963. Before the 1964 campaign, they solidified their pitching staff with the addition of future Hall of Famer Jim Bunning and led the pack most of the way before blowing the pennant in the last week of the season. A key to the club's success was a young black slugger, then called Richie Allen, who won Rookie of the Year honors on the strength of a .318 batting average and 29 homers despite leading the league in errors at third base by a considerable margin. An irony of that ill-fated season is that the Phillies suffered from a pronounced weakness at first base throughout the year while Pancho Herrera toiled for Pittsburgh's Columbus farm team.

Seven black players made significant contributions to the 1964 Phillies. Allen, Taylor, Gonzalez, Amaro, Covington, and rookie outfielder Johnny Briggs spent the entire season on the roster, and another talented young outfielder, Alex Johnson, joined the club in late July and contributed a .303 average down the stretch. In addition, Adolfo Phillips, yet another black rookie outfielder, and veteran first baseman Vic Power also spent time with the club.

At the mid-point of the decade of the 1960s, the Phillies' brass undoubtedly thought their worst racial problems were behind them. They couldn't have been farther from the truth. Before the 1965 season, the team re-armed with the addition of slugging first baseman Dick Stuart, also known as "Dr. Strangelove," and playboy pitcher Bo Belinsky, two memorable characters who did little for the Phillies' cause. With the club wallowing in fourth place on July 3, Allen took offense to needling from veteran utility player Frank Thomas during pregame batting practice. Thomas referred to him as "Richie X," obviously alluding to controversial black leader Malcolm X, and the two went at each other. After Allen floored him with a punch, Thomas came up swinging a bat and connected with the young slugger's shoulder before teammates pulled them apart.[56]

Later, manager Gene Mauch would admit that both he and the front office mishandled the situation. Despite pleas from Allen to forget the incident, Thomas was immediately placed on waivers. Mauch explained to the press, "I had to choose between a 36-year-old veteran who was hitting .250 and a 23-year-old power hitter who was hitting .348." Naturally, the fans cast Thomas and Allen in the roles of victim and villain. The incident marked the turning point in Allen's relationship with the Phillies and the city of Philadelphia. Allen was labeled a troublemaker, the fans began booing him, and the press began scrutinizing his actions.[57]

Allen would come to symbolize the Phillies' racial problems as relationships between the club and their biggest star continued to deteriorate through the rest of the decade. His problems with the brass originally began when he was assigned to the Phillies' International League farm club located in Little Rock, Arkansas, for the 1963 season after pacing the club in homers during spring training. The 21-year-old prospect would be the first black man to play professional baseball in Arkansas since Uvold Reynolds and Joe Scott got trials with the 1954 Hot Springs Bathers in the old Cotton States League. On opening day, Arkansas's notoriously

racist governor Orval Faubus threw out the first pitch, and Little Rock fans welcomed Allen with signs that read "DON'T NEGRO-IZE BASEBALL" and "NIGGER GO HOME." Though he put together a successful season, leading the International League in homers and runs batted in before a late season call up, Allen resented the position management had put him in. Years later, he would say, "Maybe if the Phillies had called me in, man to man, like the Dodgers had done with Jackie, and said, 'Dick this is what we have in mind, it's going to be very difficult, but we're with you'—at least then I would have been prepared. I'm not saying I would have liked it. But I would have known what to expect."[58]

Desperately wanting out of Philadelphia as his relationship with the fans and management deteriorated, Allen embarked on a campaign to force a trade by flouting team rules and openly challenging management's authority, the only avenue open to him in the days before free agency.[59] He finally got his wish when he was traded to the St. Louis Cardinals after the 1969 season.

But the Phillies weren't out of the woods. The key player they received from the Cardinals in exchange for Allen was Curt Flood,

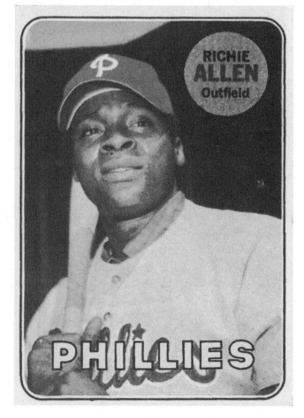

As a 21-year-old prospect, future superstar Dick "Richie" Allen was subject to racial harassment as the first black player for the Phillies' Little Rock, Arkansas, farm club (1969 Topps card).

a black all-star outfielder. Flood objected to being traded without his permission and refused to report to the Phillies. He decided to sit out the 1970 season and challenge baseball's jealously guarded reserve clause. Flood's actions were probably influenced by the distasteful prospect of playing for the racially troubled Phillies in a city he later described as the country's "northernmost southern city."[60] Flood returned to baseball in 1971, but only after a transfer to the Washington Senators was negotiated. His case was a precursor of free agency. Flood ended up losing, but the Phillies lost the services of a seven-time Gold-Glove-winning center fielder.

The Phillies' fortunes had declined precipitously after the 1964 disaster. By the time Major League Baseball expanded and adopted a divisional format in 1969, they were once again chronic losers. By 1974, however, they had regained respectability with the arrival of future Hall of Famers Steve Carlton and Mike Schmidt and were expected to contend in 1975. About a month into the new season, the Phillies shocked the baseball world when they reacquired Allen to handle first base. Allen had played single seasons with the Dodgers and Cardinals after leaving Philadelphia before seemingly finding a home with the Chicago White Sox. He won the American League Most Valuable Player Award with the Sox in 1972 and was leading the American League in homers when he suddenly "retired" with about 20 games left in the 1974 campaign. His contract was traded to the Braves in the off-season, but Allen had no intention of performing in Atlanta and remained in retirement until some of the Phillies players talked him into giving the "City of Brotherly Love" another shot.[61]

Allen's return to Philadelphia started out as a love-fest. The players, especially the team's new nucleus of black stars, welcomed him back with open arms, as did the fans. Allen was a good teammate and served as a mentor to young Mike Schmidt. Unfortunately, he was rusty from the layoff and lack of spring training and failed to hit as expected as the Phillies finished the season second in the National League East. He came back in 1976 and hit better, although still not up to his previous standard. The Phillies seemed to be coasting to the division championship, but as they began to falter down the stretch, problems began to crop up with Allen in the middle. He complained that black reserve outfielders Bobby Tolan and Ollie Brown were not getting enough playing time and argued with shortstop Larry Bowa, who was critical of Allen's defensive efforts.[62]

The Phillies righted themselves and went on to easily capture the division title, but controversy erupted again when the club decided to leave 40-year-old utilityman Tony Taylor, who had played sparingly, off the post-season roster. Allen threatened to boycott the playoffs if Taylor wasn't reinstated. The Phillies eventually agreed to take Taylor to the post-season as a coach, but the damage had been done. Subsequently, Allen requested and received permission to take the last series of the regular season off and the press chastised him for it.[63]

"I began to get booed, and the threats started coming to me in the mail," said Allen. "It was the 1960s all over again."[64]

Chapter 17

THE DETROIT TIGERS

The Detroit Tigers were the 15th of the 16 major league franchises in existence during baseball's integration era to put a black player in their lineup, trailed only by the Boston Red Sox. But the city of Detroit has the distinction of being the last major league outpost to be represented by a black baseball player, since Boston fans had the pleasure of watching Sam Jethroe and other black Boston Braves before that National League franchise left town. Even Milwaukee, Baltimore, Kansas City, Los Angeles, and San Francisco, where franchises had relocated during the 1950s, beat Detroit in the integration derby. Moreover, the Tigers were the last major league organization to let a black player perform in their farm system.

There was no good reason for the Tigers to bring up the rear in the employment of black players. In 1950, African Americans made up 11.8 percent of the Detroit metropolitan area's population, ranking fourth-highest below Washington, Philadelphia, and St. Louis among those metropolitan areas in the country that hosted Major League Baseball.[1] Most of the area's black citizens lived in the City of Detroit, and the number was growing fast. Over the next decade, the non-white population of the city would increase by 60 percent, while the white population declined more than 20 percent.[2] Furthermore, due to the highly unionized automobile industry, the black population of Detroit was relatively affluent, and there was less segregation than in other more ethnic northern cities. And Detroit's blacks were great baseball fans. In 1946, more than 300 black fans from Detroit booked a train to Montreal to see Jackie Robinson play.[3] In 1948, an erroneous rumor that Cleveland's Satchel Paige would start against the Tigers drew a record crowd to Briggs Stadium.[4]

Before the 1952 season, leading black columnist Wendell Smith nominated the Tigers for the title of most prejudiced team in the American League, ahead of (or is it behind?) the Red Sox. If the Tigers met their National League counterpart, the Cardinals, in "a World Series for possession of the 'Flag of Prejudice' it would be a battle royal," he wrote.[5] At the time, Gussie Busch was just beginning his efforts to integrate the Cardinals, while the Tigers were still years away from putting a black player in a Detroit uniform.

Walter Briggs

Blame for the franchise's terrible reputation and track record in the area of integration is usually placed squarely on the shoulders of longtime owner Walter O. Briggs, Sr. Briggs, a millionaire industrialist, was a self-made man who began working in a Michigan Central garage at the age of fifteen and worked his way up the ladder. In 1909, he founded the Briggs

205

Manufacturing Company, which eventually became the largest independent manufacturer of automobile bodies in the country and the leading supplier for Ford Motor Company.[6]

Briggs was a ruthless, cold-hearted employer, according to workers at his Briggs Manufacturing Company plants.[7] In the late 1920s, a fire at one of his plants killed 21 employees and critically burned many others. Briggs was publicly accused of ignoring unsafe working conditions.[8] The Briggs Company also had a sordid history in the area of labor relations. In 1933, at the height of the depression when jobs were scarce, 9,000 workers walked out because of poor working conditions. Briggs refused to negotiate and hired thugs to aggressively end the conflict.[9]

Briggs Manufacturing would become a frequent target of the United Auto Workers union (UAW) throughout the decade. Four years later, another major strike took place with 2,000 UAW members walking out after 200 of their fellow workers were laid off. Alexander Sarantos Tremulis, one of Briggs' designers at that time, recalled, "Briggs was becoming a hotbed for strikes.... I well remember the overturned Mack Avenue streetcars and walking through screaming picket lines to get to work. I also recall that when the temperature reached 90°, the workers walked off their jobs. One time when they walked off, the assembly line kept going and 40 or 50 [automobile] bodies dropped from the fourth floor to the ground. It made a fantastic sound."[10]

In 1945, strikebreakers beat union leaders outside the Briggs plant; the same year, a strike by 200,000 GM workers shut down plants for 113 days.[11] But Briggs' heavy-handed managerial methods made him plenty of money. In 1955, Briggs Manufacturing's revenue of $440.9 million ranked 65th in the first Forbes Fortune 500 listing.[12]

Franchise History

A genuine fan of the game, Walter Briggs bought his way into baseball by purchasing a 25 percent interest in the Tigers from Frank Navin in 1920. Navin had joined the Tigers' front office in 1903 and gradually acquired controlling interest. He ran the team personally and built the squad that captured three consecutive American League pennants from 1907 through 1909 with a team managed by Hughie Jennings that featured the great Ty Cobb manning the outfield alongside fellow Hall of Famer "Wahoo Sam" Crawford.

From 1910 through 1933, the Tigers were absent from post-season play despite consistently ranking among the top hitting teams in the league. In 1934, they acquired catching great Mickey Cochrane from the Athletics to take over in the dugout and behind the plate. Ably backed by first baseman Hank Greenberg, second baseman Charlie Gehringer, and outfielder Goose Goslin, who would all eventually join him in Cooperstown, the fiery Cochrane led the club to the 1934 pennant. The Tigers lost a hard-fought series to Dizzy and Paul Dean and the St. Louis Cardinals' Gas House Gang, but they were back the next year to beat the Chicago Cubs for the 1935 World Championship. A month after the World Series, Navin fell off a horse and died of heart failure. Briggs, who by that time had increased his stake in the club to about 50 percent but remained a behind-the-scenes partner, purchased the other half from Navin's heirs.

Briggs didn't hesitate to put his wealth behind the Tigers. His purchase of several quality veteran players to add to the club's core of homegrown talent led to an American League flag in 1940, the only break in a seven-year Yankee reign from 1936 through 1943. With Hal Newhouser and Dizzy Trout winning 56 games between them, the Tigers finished a game behind the St. Louis Browns in 1944. But in 1945 they captured the American League pennant and another World Championship. The biggest heroes were Most Valuable Player Newhouser and veteran slugger Greenberg, who made a dramatic mid-season comeback after 4½ years in the service to lead the offense.

The Yankees, Red Sox, and Tigers emerged from the war as the strongest franchises in the American League. In 1946 and 1947, the trio occupied the first three spots in the standings, with Detroit finishing second both years, first to the Red Sox, then to the Yankees. The arrival of Larry Doby and Satchel Paige, however, pushed Cleveland into the American League elite. While the integrated Indians were capturing the pennant in 1948, the Tigers dropped to fifth place in the standings.

Briggs, who desperately wanted to see his Tigers capture one more championship before he died, took no heed of Cleveland's success. A shrewd and innovative businessman, he let prejudice rule over his good business sense. Despite an influx of outstanding young players like George Kell, Fred Hutchinson, Hoot Evers, Vic Wertz, Art Houtteman, Johnny Lipon, and Johnny Groth, the Tigers couldn't capture another flag under his ownership.

After finishing fourth in 1949, the Tigers rallied to win 95 games and challenge the Yankees down the wire for the 1950 pennant. The next year, however, the Chicago White Sox acquired Minnie Minoso and fought their way into the first division, while the Tigers found themselves back in the lower tier of American League teams.

The Tigers' Racial Attitude

"The Detroit Tigers Baseball Club conjures up images of conservatism and dependability."[13] This statement certainly applied to the franchise under Briggs, especially the conservative part. He resisted virtually all innovations, including night baseball, radio and television coverage of games, and special events such as Ladies Day. Even routine advertising and public relations were ignored. When Doc Fenkell took over as public relations director for the team, he was told by his predecessor that his main job was to keep Briggs's name out of the paper.[14]

"Though no definitive Briggs quote on the subject ever saw the light of print, many black Detroiters believed Walter Briggs had vowed never to have black players on the roster so long as he was in charge of the club," according to author Michael Betzold.[15] Patrick Harrigan, author of *The Detroit Tigers: Club and Community, 1945–1995*, wrote, "Walter Briggs was both a sportsman and a racist."[16] Black columnist Wendell Smith, who grew up in Detroit, described Briggs as, "Oh so very prejudiced. He's the major league combination of Simon Legree and Adolf Hitler."[17] During Briggs' reign, "The saying around the Detroit clubhouse was 'no jiggs with Briggs.'"[18] Almost three decades after Briggs' death, Gates Brown, one of the first black Tigers, said, "Briggs.... The name doesn't set well in the black community. Say that name some places and you might get jumped on."[19]

The Tigers had no intention of signing black players and made no bones about it while Briggs was in charge. They made no pretense of looking for "the right kind" of black player. They didn't bother feigning concern for the plight of the Negro Leagues. They didn't rail about subversives and outside agitators. They didn't even bemoan the scarcity of black talent or even try to conceal the fact they weren't looking for it.

In a remarkably candid 1951 interview with the *Michigan Chronicle*, general manager Billy Evens readily admitted, "I know the Tigers are lagging but as I told the *Chronicle* two years ago, the question of hiring Negro ballplayers never bothered us. I think it would be unreasonable to say that the Tigers would be better if they had Negro players. The Tigers got along many years without Negro players.... In fact, all the teams in the majors got along without colored players." Evans closed the subject with the statement: "There are no plans at present that involve hiring of colored players."[20]

Yet the Tigers generally managed to fly under the anti-segregation radar in the early 1950s while the Yankees and Red Sox served as lightening rods. This was partly because they had become a second-rate team and partly because the accommodating mainstream Detroit press avoided the issue.[21] Only the city's black newspaper, the *Michigan Chronicle*, raised questions, but the Tiger brass effectively stonewalled them. Unlike their cohorts in the resistance effort, the club never claimed an interest in integration, so they couldn't be caught in a lie. There were never rumors of impending trades for black players or scouting reports on hot prospects to pique the public interest. And since the organization didn't have black players in their farm system, there were no incidences of mistreatment to rile sensibilities.

The death of Walter Briggs at age 84 in January 1952 spared the Tiger patriarch the heartbreak of witnessing the Tigers' embarrassing last-place finish that year — the first in the proud history of the franchise. Though confined to a wheelchair in his last years, he ran the club with an iron hand up until the very end. And true to his word, the Tigers did not have a single black player employed in their farm system at the time of his demise.

The Spike Briggs Era

Walter Owen Briggs, Jr., better known as Spike, took over the club upon his father's death. Much more social than his reclusive father, Spike was known to visit nightspots in Paradise Valley, Detroit's primarily black district.[22] But he apparently shared some of his father's attitudes. When a player's union representative proposed that a share of World Series receipts go to the player's pension fund, Spike responded, "Let's see whether he's in favor of the United States or some other country."[23] Still, black fans in Detroit and across the country, as well as white folks who wanted to see the best baseball possible, were hopeful. Unfortunately, Spike Briggs would disappoint them and just about everyone else. He would usher in an unprecedented era of turmoil in "Tigerland" that would see six different general managers and nine different field managers in the next dozen years.[24]

Still, the Tigers had it made in the "Motor City." The fourth most populous big league locale behind New York, Chicago, and Philadelphia, Detroit was by far the largest city to have only one major league team in the late 1940s and early 1950s.[25] And everybody agreed that it was a great baseball town. While a columnist for the *New Yorker,* noted author Roger Angell wrote, "Detroit in the 1930s had few visible economic virtues, but it may just have been the best baseball town in the country."[26] In 1949, V. G. Taylor Spink, editor of *The Sporting News*, also declared it "the best baseball city in the country."[27] Despite some awful seasons, the Tigers made a profit every year that the Briggs family owned the club, a trend that continued until the strike-shortened 1994 season.[28]

Injuries had ruined the 1951 season, and the Tigers tumbled to fifth place after finishing second in 1950. Young Art Houtteman, a 19-game winner the previous year, was injured in a car accident and missed the entire campaign. Arm problems limited Hal Newhouser to six victories, and a broken finger hampered Hoot Evers' batting stroke so severely that his average tumbled 99 points. But there was no cause for panic. Attendance still topped the one million mark, and the talented nucleus that had challenged for the pennant the year before was still around.

Under Spike Briggs, however, the once patient franchise wouldn't wait to see if the veteran nucleus could regroup. Briggs Sr. hadn't been in his grave six months when old favorites Hoot Evers, George Kell, Johnny Lipon, and Dizzy Trout were send to the Boston Red Sox in a huge trade.

The 1952 Tigers ended up losing 104 games. They fell into undisputed possession of last place on May 2 and never gave it up. But the franchise practice of excluding black players was only partly responsible for the stunning collapse. One reason offered is that Briggs had allowed the club to grow old and had neglected the farm system that his predecessor Frank Navin had built into one of the finest in the game, spending lavishly instead on under-performing bonus players like Dick Wakefield. The record, however, doesn't seem to bear this out. Catcher Aaron Robinson at 35 was the oldest regular position player on the 1950 squad with 31-year-old first baseman Don Kolloway the next oldest. The top five hitters, Kell, Evers, Lipon, Vic Wertz, and Johnny Groth, were all under 30. The only graybeard in the rotation was 35-year-old Dizzy Trout, while the big winner was 22-year-old Art Houtteman, and other starters included Newhouser (29), Fred Hutchinson (30) and Ted Gray (25). What's more, the young players who had entered the Detroit farm system under Briggs Sr. included future Hall of Famer Jim Bunning, Frank Lary, and Billy Hoeft, all of whom would become 20-game winners in Detroit, future American League batting champ Harvey Kuenn, pitcher Paul Foytack, center fielder Bill Tuttle, second baseman Frank Bolling, and catcher Frank House. Another product of the system, Billy Pierce, slipped through the Tigers' grasp and went on to become the winningest lefty in the American League for the decade of the 1950 in a Chicago White Sox uniform.

The immediate cause of the Tigers' dramatic downfall was the numerous ill-advised trades engineered by Spike Briggs. Technically the general manager is responsible for trades, but Spike Briggs, anxious to make his own mark on the franchise, was definitely a hands-on owner. During his first year in charge, the Tigers executed seven trades, most of them damaging, that sent 18 players packing. For instance, the trade of future Hall of Famer Kell along with shortstop Lipon, left fielder Evers, and veteran workhorse Trout netted fast-fading infielder Johnny Pesky, lumbering first baseman Walt Dropo, journeyman infielder Fred Hatfield, mediocre lefthander Bill Wight, and hard-hitting, slow-moving outfielder Don "Footsie" Lenhardt. All were disappointments. Six weeks later, slugger Vic Wertz was traded to the St. Louis Browns in a multi-player deal that landed pitcher Ned Garver. Wertz had three more 100 runs-batted-in seasons left. Garver, who had won 20 of the last-place Browns 52 victories in 1951, never showed such form with Detroit, but he was a decent starter for three years until he was sent to Kansas City in yet another lopsided Briggs trade.

After the 1952 season, general manager Charlie Gehringer "tried unsuccessfully to keep him away from Bill Veeck at the winter meetings, where Spike was drinking heavily."[29] He certainly must have been under the influence when he agreed to send veteran hurler Virgil Trucks, whose pair of no-hitters had been among the precious few bright spots of the dreadful 1952 campaign, to the Browns. The Tigers even threw in their leading hitter, center fielder Johnny Groth, for good measure. The only player of significance they received in return was defensively challenged outfielder Bob Nieman, who wouldn't be able to hold a regular job in Detroit. From February 1952 until new ownership took over late in the 1956 campaign, the Tigers negotiated more than 15 major league deals. A few turned out positive; most were detrimental to the club.

Yet, there was no such radical movement in the integration area. Despite reports that the Tigers made an offer for Cleveland's Larry Doby, the reigning American League home run champ at the winter meetings proceeding the 1953 season, no black players joined the organization in the first two years of Spike Briggs' reign.[30]

Spike Briggs did, however, officially discontinue his father's long-standing segregation policy and begin introducing young black players into the Tigers' farm system. The first black prospect the Tigers signed was 18-year-old outfielder Claude Agee, who would disappear after two minor league seasons.[31] Soon thereafter, they acquired 19-year-old pitcher Arthur Williams from Bakersfield of the California League.[32] Williams would post a fine 9–3 won-lost record in 1954, in his only season in the Detroit system before returning to the California League.

Before the 1955 season, the Tigers signed Bubba Morton, the first black prospect recruited by the organization who would eventually advance to the big leagues. In fact, Morton and pitcher Jim Proctor, who was purchased from the Negro League Indianapolis Clowns before the 1956 campaign, are the only two black players acquired under the Briggs family leadership to appear in a Detroit uniform.

Meanwhile, the Tigers continued to lavish money on white bonus prospects. The investment in future Hall of Famer Al Kaline paid off handsomely, but Jim Brady, Jim Small, Bob Miller, Reno Bertoia, George Thomas, and Frank House never became household names in Detroit. In 1958 alone, it was estimated that the franchise spent $250,000 on bonus players.[33] To put this amount in perspective, Tigers superstar Al Kaline was probably making about $50,000 at the time. In today's player market, this would be the equivalent of the Yankees shelling out $125 million annually for untried amateurs based on Alex Rodriguez's $25 million salary.

Although the Briggs fortune was estimated at more than $50 million at the time of Walter Sr.'s death, the family sold the franchise to an 11-man syndicate initially headed by Fred Knorr in October 1956.[34] Spike Briggs had attempted to put together his own group to purchase the team, but the effort unraveled when Henry Ford, an old friend of the family, withdrew his backing.[35] Thus, two generations of Briggs ownership ended without a black man in a Detroit Tiger uniform. The new syndicate included John Fetzer, who would gradually emerge as the leader of the group and eventually acquire controlling interest in the club. The original agreement called for Spike Briggs to stay on as general manager, but the arrangement didn't last long after Spike announced that he intended to continue running the team "his way."[36]

From 1953 through 1956, the Tigers were a mediocre outfit that generally loitered around the fringes of the first division, while the Indians and White Sox battled the Yankees for the pennant. Things didn't immediately change much under new ownership. The team maintained an indifferent level of performance on the field, as well as a pure-white major league roster. In 1956, the Tigers reportedly intended to make veteran Monte Irvin their first black player by drafting him from the Giants organization, but the Cubs grabbed him first.[37]

Pressure to Integrate

Critical remarks made by the retiring Jackie Robinson focused attention on the three remaining segregation diehards (see chapter 16). The Phillies quickly distanced themselves from the others when they began the 1957 season with Chico Fernandez at shortstop, leaving the Tigers and Red Sox twitching in the glow of the increasingly uncomfortable spotlight Robinson had directed their way.

The pressure intensified when the 1957 season passed without a black player donning a Tiger uniform. The franchise was finding itself more and more conspicuous in its segregation. The Detroit Lions, who had black players back in the 1940s, acquired black running back John Henry Johnson, who led them to the 1957 National Football League title.[38] The Ft. Wayne Pistons, who had relocated to Detroit for the 1957–58 National Basketball Association season, featured black stars Nat Clifton and Walter Dukes. Baseball fans could even see black ballplayers perform in Detroit uniforms, though not Tiger flannels. In 1958, the Detroit Clowns featured what has to be the strangest first-base combo in history with Harlem Globetrotter legend Goose Tatum sharing the bag with recently retired Piston star Clifton, a former Cleveland Indians farmhand.[39] The Detroit Stars had been a power in black baseball until Mack Park burned down in 1929. The fire killed Negro League baseball in Detroit by leaving the Stars with no place to play. In 1954, the Stars were resurrected to satisfy the void unfilled by the Tigers.[40] They were renamed the Clowns in 1958 after Tatum purchased the team and talked the 35-year-old Clifton into joining up.

As the 1958 campaign got underway without a black player on the roster, the Briggs Stadium boycott committee was formed. Initially, the committee set a deadline of May 7 for the Tigers to find a black player but pushed it back to June 1. General manager John McHale claimed the team was "willing" to field a black player, but "would not be pressured into it."[41] The Tigers had finally adopted the all-too-familiar mantra used by other integration resisters years earlier. Like their colleagues, the Tigers' brass were primarily interested in putting the best players they could find on the field — they just couldn't find any decent black ones. They weren't opposed to topflight black players who wouldn't cause trouble, but they were concerned about fan reaction, of course. And they weren't going to succumb to interference from rabble-rousing pressure groups.

In responding to the pressure groups, as they vowed they wouldn't, club officials revealed that there were 17 black players in their farm system. They also bragged that they had invested $75,000 in the development of colored players since 1954, a piddling amount considering the reported quarter of a million dollars they shelled out for bonus babies in 1958 alone.[42]

Ozzie Virgil to the Rescue

On June 6, 1958, the Tigers finally caved in to the pressure by inserting third baseman Ozzie Virgil into the lineup against the Senators in Washington. Like the Yankees with Elston Howard, the Tigers elected to downplay the debut of their first black player by introducing Virgil on the road. Despite McHale's denial that Virgil's promotion stemmed from picket threats by a "Detroit Negro organization," it was certainly pressure to integrate from outside the organization rather than the infielder's performance at Charleston that led to his promotion.[43] Future general manager Jim Campbell, the Tigers' farm director at the time of Virgil's debut, later admitted, "They were after my ass to bring up a black man but there was no one available that we liked."[44]

The Tigers had acquired the light-hitting, slick-fielding Virgil from the New York Giants before the season along with first baseman Gail Harris — the man they really wanted. At the time, they readily admitted that Virgil didn't fit into their plans.[45] He was immediately ticketed for the club's American Association Charleston farm team along with top black prospects in the Detroit system, future major leaguers Bubba Morton, Jake Wood, and Jim Proctor, as well as first baseman Wendell Antoine and outfielder Jackson Queen, who would never make it to the big time.[46]

Like the reaction of Senators' followers to Carlos Paula, Tigers' critics were not completely satisfied. According to the *Detroit Tigers Encyclopedia*, "He [Virgil] was never embraced by Detroit's African-American community, which always suspected that the Tigers had only selected Virgil because of his relatively light skin coloring."[47]

Furthermore, the dusky complexioned Virgil, who was born in the Dominican Republic, did not consider himself to be a Negro and reportedly didn't want to be regarded as such. "I'm not Negro; I'm Dominican; I'm Spanish," he complained in the Detroit dugout according to *Detroit News* reporter Joe Falls.[48] Bob Tighe, the son of Jack Tighe who was managing the Tigers when Virgil first came up, recalls his father telling him that Virgil maintained that he wasn't black and didn't want to be considered the first black Tiger.[49] A skeptic might even suspect that the Tigers didn't consider Virgil to be black when they traded for him, but conveniently changed their mind later. No mention of race was made in the announcement of his acquisition.[50]

Less than a week after Virgil's debut, Bill Norman, Virgil's manager at Charleston, replaced Tighe. Norman, who managed in the Cleveland Indians system for five years and spent two years as a coach with Bill Veeck's St. Louis Browns, seemed to have a good track record with black players. Long-time major league outfielder Al Smith, one of the first black players in the Eastern League, broke in under Norman with Wilkes-Barre back in 1948. "Fortunately, my manager, Bill Norman, was in my corner, so I didn't worry about anything," said Smith.[51]

Almost two weeks after being added to the roster, Virgil finally made his first appearance in Detroit on June 17. An impressive crowd of almost 30,000 fans showed up for Virgil's Briggs Stadium debut on a Tuesday night against the lowly Senators, and he rewarded them by lashing out five hits in five trips to the plate. Thereafter, Ozzie's hitting returned to its normal pedestrian level, and he eventually found himself warming the bench.

Virgil's debut earned him a double distinction, as he also became the first Latino to suit up for Detroit.[52] The Tigers were merely the next-to-last team to put a black player on their roster, but they were dead last when it came to Latinos by almost a full decade. That the Tigers didn't send any scouts to Latin America or the Caribbean may have had something

Dominican-born Ozzie Virgil is considered the Tigers' first black player despite his insistence that he was not a black man (1960 Topps card).

to do with the deficiency.[53] In fairness, however, both Cuban-born Luis Aloma and Venezuelan-born Alex Carrasquel toiled in the farm system in the late 1940s, although they never pitched for the Tigers. A footnote also goes to lefthander Hank Aguirre, who was on the roster when Virgil arrived. Aguirre was born in California, but was said to be of Mexican descent.[54]

The Disastrous Spring of 1959

Before the 1959 season, John McHale left for Milwaukee, and Rick Ferrell was named general manager. That spring, the Tigers made two disastrous moves involving black players that would haunt them for more than a decade. Apparently determined to find a recognizable African American player to put the race issue to rest for good, they acquired Larry Doby in a trade for Tito Francona during spring training. Almost 12 full years after becoming the first acknowledged black player to appear in the American League, Doby would gain the distinction of becoming the first African American to play for the Detroit Tigers. As with all matters related to integration, however, the Tigers were a little late. Doby was no longer the player the Tigers had supposedly pursued to break their color line several years earlier. By 1959, he was a pre-maturely aged 35-year-old with nagging physical problems. Moreover, the Tigers had no place for him to play. He wasn't going to displace future Hall of Famer Al Kaline or batting champ Harvey Kuenn, and the third outfield position was ably manned by a platoon of veteran sluggers, Charley Maxwell and Gus Zernial.

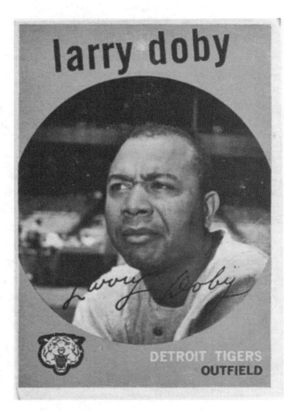

Meanwhile, the player the Tigers traded for Doby, Tito Francona, enjoyed a sensational campaign for Cleveland. The 25-year-old outfielder recorded the highest average in the league although he didn't have quite enough at-bats to qualify for the batting crown. Francona would go on to enjoy eleven more solid big league seasons for the Indians and several other teams.

But the worst was yet to come.

The acquisition of Doby eased the pressure on the club to find an African American player. Therefore, the Tigers didn't feel compelled to retain the young black infielder they had purchased from the Dodgers on a conditional basis.[55] The player, who they elected to return in order to clear the way for the eminently undistinguished Rocky Bridges at shortstop, was none other than Maury Wills. Wills would overcome the sting of Detroit's rejection and go on to break the all-time stolen base record of the greatest Tiger of them all, Ty Cobb. Before Wills' 14-year major league career was over, he would win the National

Slugging outfielder Larry Doby became the first African American to play for the Tigers almost twelve years after becoming the first black American Leaguer (1959 Topps card).

League Most Valuable Player award, lead the National League in steals six straight years, be named to five all-star teams, and play in four World Series — all for a team not named the Detroit Tigers.

Ozzie Virgil was returned to Charleston before the 1959 season, but the Tigers replaced him with another light-hitting, medium-complexioned Latino infielder who offered a variation on the spelling of the same first name — Ossie Alvarez. With Alvarez, a Cuban who had matriculated in the Washington Senators organization, and Doby, the Tigers began the campaign with two minorities on the roster. But Alvarez didn't last long, and Doby appeared in only 18 games for the Tigers before he was sold to the Chicago White Sox in mid–May. With Doby's departure, the Tigers reverted back to an all-white roster until 24-year-old Jim Proctor came up to pitch in two late-season games. Proctor, who began his baseball career as an Indianapolis Clown, was the first black player originally signed by the Tigers to don their flannels. He was bombed in his only start and would never get another big league opportunity despite winning 15 games in the Texas League the next year.

The 1960s and Beyond

Bill DeWitt was named president of the Tigers in November 1959, and a few weeks later Chico Fernandez was acquired from the Philadelphia Phillies. Fernandez, the first black player to play for the Phillies, would become the first black player to play regularly for Detroit as well as the first black regular shortstop in American League history. Early in the season, former Brooklyn World Series hero Sandy Amoros also joined the club, and later on Ozzie Virgil returned for another try at big league pitching.

DeWitt moved to Cincinnati after the 1960 season, but he left his mark in Detroit. The 1960 campaign was a turning point for the Tigers, aside from the integration improvement. The club finished a disappointing sixth, but key trades were made to acquire Rocky Colavito and Norm Cash.

The next year, the Tigers challenged the New York Yankees for the pennant, riding the powerful bats of Colavito, Cash, and Al Kaline and the stalwart arms of Frank Lary, Jim Bunning, and Don Mossi to 101 victories and a second-place finish. A contingent of four black players also contributed greatly to the team's success. Classy veteran center fielder Billy Bruton was acquired from the Milwaukee Braves to finally give the team an established African American star while rookie second baseman Jake Wood became the first black graduate of the Detroit farm system to capture a regular job. In addition, Bubba Morton, one of the team's first black recruits, contributed as a backup outfielder, and Fernandez handled shortstop duties. Bruton would give the club four solid seasons, helping to ease the way for future black stars in Detroit. Wood lost his starting spot the next year and never regained regular status, although he served as a valuable sub for several seasons. Morton would never crack the starting lineup but would spend seven years as a valuable reserve in the big leagues with the Tigers, Braves, and California Angels.

Over the next few seasons, the Tigers added several more black players who would play key roles. In 1960, Gates Brown was signed out of prison, and the next year Willie Horton was recruited off the mean streets of Detroit. Brown would go on to become one of the premier pinch-hitters in the game, while Horton would develop into the Tigers' first homegrown black star. During the 1966 season, the team traded for Boston hurler Earl Wilson, who while in a Detroit uniform would briefly hold the record for most career wins by a black American League pitcher.

Unfortunately, the City of Detroit had not made similar progress. The increase in black residents had resulted in the exodus of white residents to the suburbs, contributing to urban blight. Expressways had chopped up the city, ensuring easy access to Tiger Stadium, but creating enclaves of poverty. A Civil Rights Commission investigation into the city's police and fire departments revealed an extremely low ratio of black public servants in those areas, with only a single non-white representative in upper levels. After years of festering, one of the worst riots in the nation's history erupted in July 1967, resulting in the death of 43 people, the burning and ransacking of thousands of businesses, and the calling in of almost 5,000 federal troops to restore some semblance of order. Racial tensions continued to simmer after the withdrawal of the troops. White flight from the city intensified along with crime as the "Motor City" was re-dubbed "Murder City."[56]

Amazingly, the Detroit Tigers, encumbered by their notorious history of prejudice, stepped in to help ease the pressure. After their 1961 turnaround, the Tigers remained a first-division team without seriously contending for the pennant through 1966. But after losing out to the Boston Red Sox in one of the tightest pennant races in baseball history in 1967, the Tigers captured the American League pennant and the World Championship in 1968. Gates Brown, Willie Horton, and Earl Wilson were all key contributors along with veteran reliever John Wyatt, who was picked up during the season to help solidify the bullpen.

A sense grew that the championship brought the city together in the wake of the riots. Owner John Fetzer reportedly told manager Mayo Smith, "You've not only won the pennant and the series. You may have saved the city." This was certainly an exaggeration, but the championship couldn't have hurt the situation. Two decades later, Joe Falls would put it into better perspective when he wrote, "It would be foolish to say it cooled off the city in the spring of 1968, but they [the Tigers] gave us something else to think about."[57]

The Tigers failed to repeat in 1969, ending the 1960s as they had spent most of the decade with one of whitest rosters in the major leagues. Early in the campaign, Willie Horton walked out on the team for several days, reportedly in protest of the lack of opportunity extended to young black players in the Detroit system.[58] A few weeks later, one such player, rookie outfielder Ron Woods, was traded to the Yankees. His roster spot taken by 27-year-old rookie infielder Ike Brown, who became a footnote in the annals of baseball integration history as the last player the Negro Leagues would send to the majors.[59]

The following spring, Horton, Gates Brown, and rookie Elliott Maddox were fined for boycotting a youth-related team function because no black children were invited. The next year, tickets for the event were distributed to youths in the black community.[60]

Fortunately for the Tigers, the much slower introduction of black players in the American League kept junior-circuit integration laggards from suffering for their discriminatory practices as much as their National League brethren. But the Tigers definitely paid a price. For the entire decade of the 1950s, the Tigers got only 59 base hits out of black hitters and three ineffective innings out of black pitchers. Their three competitors who captured all of the American League pennants in the decade received much greater production. The Indians got almost 500 home runs from Larry Doby, Luke Easter, and company. The White Sox black-player contingent, primarily Minoso and Doby, slammed 186 homers and stole 167 bases. Even the Yankees got 75 homers out of Elston Howard, Hector Lopez, and Harry Simpson.

Throughout the latter half of the 1950s, the Tigers were considered a mystery team. Their lineup featured top performers Kaline, Kuenn, Ray Boone, Charley Maxwell, Bill Tuttle and

Frank Bolling, while their pitching staff included talented hurlers Bunning, Lary, Billy Hoeft, Don Mossi, and Paul Foytack. The team seemed to possess the talent to be a contender, but never achieved more than also-ran status. It was often said that the Tigers seemed to only be a player away from fulfilling their promise. That missing ingredient may have been just one talented black player.

Chapter 18

THE BOSTON RED SOX

In 1946, the Boston Red Sox won their first American League pennant since 1918. It would be another 21 years before they captured the flag again. The franchise's record of near-total futility from 1919 through 1966 is unmatched in the American League and equaled only by the hapless Philadelphia Phillies in the National League.

The primary reason for this lack of success is that the Red Sox failed to appreciate the value of the two most important baseball players of the 20th century, Babe Ruth and Jackie Robinson.

From 1914 through 1919, Babe Ruth played his home games in Boston's magnificent new Fenway Park. It took the club the better part of five years to realize that Ruth could help them more as an everyday player than a starting pitcher, but by 1919 he was playing the outfield on a regular basis between pitching assignments. That year, his 29 homers shattered the all-time major league record. The Red Sox, however, failed to recognize the drawing power, as well as the competitive benefit, of the long ball and sold his contract to the New York Yankees after the 1919 campaign to pay creditors.

The sale of Ruth was the last straw in the systematic destruction of a team that captured the World Championship in 1912, 1915, 1916, and 1918. Operating on a shoestring budget, they languished in the second division of the American League from 1920 through 1933, while the Babe was slamming 637 homers in a Yankee uniform.

Tom Yawkey Purchases the Sox

In 1933, millionaire Thomas Austin Yawkey arrived on the scene to rescue the Red Sox from their financial doldrums. A baseball fan and avid sportsman, Yawkey was a graduate of Yale — rumored to have played a little second base for the Eli. He was both the nephew and adopted son of Bill Yawkey, former majority owner of the Detroit Tigers before Frank Navin purchased the club. Bill Yawkey died when Tom was 16, leaving the teenager heir to a multi-million-dollar mining and lumber empire, which would be held in trust until he turned 30 years of age. Shortly after celebrating his 30th birthday, Yawkey purchased the Red Sox and began to put his wallet to work to turn the floundering franchise into a contender.[1]

The youthful Yawkey immediately brought in fellow Ivy Leaguer Eddie Collins, former star second baseman for the Philadelphia Athletics and Chicago White Sox, as vice president and general manager of the franchise. A year later, he purchased the contract of player-manager Joe Cronin from the Washington Senators. In 1933, Cronin had managed the Senators to the American League pennant while finishing runner-up to Jimmie Foxx in Most Valuable

Player voting. He rivaled Pittsburgh's Arky Vaughan as the best shortstop in baseball and was the son-in-law of Washington owner Clark Griffin, so the price was steep — a quarter of a million dollars and Boston's regular shortstop, Lyn Lary.

From 1933 through 1937, Yawkey and Collins would dig into the Yawkey fortune to acquire future Hall of Famers Rick Ferrell, Lefty Grove, Jimmie Foxx, Heinie Manush, in addition to Cronin. Other veteran stars, like Wes Ferrell, Mac Bishop, Rube Walberg, Doc Cramer, Bobo Newsom, Ben Chapman, Joe Vosmik, and Mike "Pinky" Higgins, were also added, but the Sox could never climb higher than fourth place in the American League standings.

Yawkey also sunk money into the development of a farm system, and by 1938 that investment was starting to pay off. Over the next five years, youngsters like Ted Williams, Bobby Doerr, Dom DiMaggio, Johnny Pesky, Jim Bagby, and Tex Hughson established themselves with the Red Sox. In 1938 and 1939 and again in 1941 and 1942, the Sox finished second behind the New York Yankees, but never less than 10 games behind. In fact, the 1940 season was the closest they would come to the Bronx Bombers during this period when a six-game gap separated the third-place New Yorkers from the fourth-place Bostonians.

With so many young stars of prime service age, World War II hit the Sox hard. A .500 record in 1944 was their best showing for the wartime seasons, but when the boys came home for the 1946 season, the Red Sox captured the American League flag. They finished 12 lengths ahead of the defending champion Detroit Tigers, before losing a hard fought seven-game battle for the World Championship to the St. Louis Cardinals.

The Integration Era

While the Red Sox were coasting to the 1946 pennant, Jackie Robinson was tearing up the International League with the Montreal Royals.

The previous year, under pressure from city councilman Isadore Muchnick, the Red Sox had reluctantly conducted a tryout for a trio of Negro League stars handpicked for the audition by black columnist Wendell Smith. Muchnick, a white politician who represented a largely black constituency, was threatening to withhold the annual permit for the Red Sox and Braves to play Sunday baseball unless the clubs made progress toward integration. The three players Smith rounded up were veteran Negro League stars Sam Jethroe of the Cleveland Buckeyes and Marvin Williams of the Philadelphia Stars, and Jackie Robinson, who was just beginning his first season in professional baseball with the Kansas City Monarchs.[2]

The Red Sox, of course, had no intention of violating the "gentlemen's agreement" barring black players from Organized Baseball. They were simply going through the motions to get the politician off their back. In fact, the workout was originally scheduled for April 14, but was postponed that day and the next, ostensibly due to the death and funeral of President Franklin Delano Roosevelt. It appeared the Sox were simply going to keep putting it off until the players got tired of waiting and rejoined the Negro League squads, but the black press had been eagerly anticipating the event and wouldn't let them off the hook.[3]

The workout, which consisted of shagging flies in the outfield and some batting practice, was supervised by 78-year-old coach Hugh Duffy. General manager Collins had another commitment, but Cronin was there, and Yawkey was also at the park. Afterward, the three Negro Leaguers were dismissed with an insincere promise to get back to them.[4]

Back at their hotel, the players laughed among themselves about the sham tryout, but

Robinson is purported to have told Smith, "It burns me up to come fifteen hundred miles to have them give me the runaround." Upon returning to the Buckeyes, Jethroe told teammates, "You just knew it was a farce because when the guys were out there, Joe Cronin didn't even bother to look. He was up in the stands with his back turned most of the time."[5]

Afterward, Red Sox officials took turns ducking responsibility before the black media. Yawkey said it was up to his baseball people, Cronin said it was up to Duffy to evaluate the players, and Duffy said he couldn't make a decision about their ability after only one workout. There wouldn't be a second one.[6] Muchnick and Smith had hoped to force the Braves to conduct a subsequent tryout, but discouraged by the Fenway Park fiasco, they abandoned that effort.

Instead of taking the opportunity that was literally being forced on them, the Sox became the last team to integrate their major league roster. It would be more than twelve years after Jackie Robinson broke the color barrier before the Red Sox trotted a 25-year-old black infielder named Pumpsie Green out to pinch run against the Chicago White Sox on July 21, 1959.

After the Sox slumped to third place in 1947, Collins passed the general manager baton to Cronin, and former Yankee skipper Joe McCarthy was lured out of retirement to take over as field manager. Boston ended the 1948 regular season tied for first place with the Cleveland Indians, the American League's only integrated team at the time, and lost a one-game playoff for the pennant. There's little doubt that the Red Sox would have captured the pennant outright if not for the contributions of Larry Doby and Satchel Paige to the Cleveland cause.

It was the first of many painful lessons that the management of the Red Sox would ignore — the first of several disappointments they would suffer for allowing their rivals to get the jump on signing black players. In 1949, the Red Sox were bridesmaids again, finishing a game behind the Yankees. Again, a Jackie Robinson would have easily made the difference.

In 1950, five years after participating in the infamous "non-tryout" at Fenway Park, Sam Jethroe won the Rookie of the Year award in a Boston uniform. Unfortunately for the Red Sox, who finished four games off the pace in third place, the uniform belonged to the Boston Braves. Although no incidents of violence marred Jethroe's arrival, he was crucified by the Boston press before he ever took the field in a big league game, and his presence failed to produce the anticipated boost in attendance at Braves' games (see chapter 7).

The Piper Davis/Willie Mays Connection

Actually, the Red Sox were not totally asleep at the wheel during the early days of integration. In reaction to Jethroe's much ballyhooed acquisition by the Braves, they moved to cover their bases by purchasing the contract of classy veteran Piper Davis from the Birmingham Black Barons on a conditional 30-day trial basis. At that time, half of the major league organizations had yet to sign their first black player.[7] The Red Sox owned the Southern Association Birmingham Barons as well as Rickwood Field in Birmingham, where the Black Barons were tenants. Thus, they were very familiar with the 32-year-old Davis, a speedy, versatile infielder who also managed the team. In 1948, he had led the Black Barons to the Negro American League pennant.

The Red Sox couldn't very well assign Davis to Birmingham. The Southern Association still fiercely clung to segregation when it disbanded in 1961. Besides, the city of Birmingham still had an ordinance barring blacks and whites from engaging in athletic competition. Boston's American Association franchise in Louisville, Kentucky, wasn't considered a viable option either, so the Sox sent Davis to the Scranton Miners of the Class A Eastern League. The veteran was leading the Miners in batting average and home runs when the deadline for the Red Sox to pick up their option on his services arrived.[8] Variously citing financial reasons and Davis's age, but probably influenced more by the unfriendly welcome the city of Boston had extended Jethroe, the Red Sox elected to return Davis to Birmingham.[9] Davis would eventually re-enter Organized Baseball, but he would never get a big league shot despite acquitting himself quite well at the Triple A level.

Boston's Birmingham connection also gave them an inside track on a Davis protégé who starred in the outfield for the Black Barons when his high school studies permitted. Legend has it that veteran scout Larry Woodall had been assigned to check out the teenage sensation. Woodall, who was not pleased with the assignment, grew impatient when bad weather forced a few postponements. "I'm not going to waste my time waiting for a bunch of niggers," he growled before heading home without ever seeing the youngster play.[10] Another account of the story has Boston scout George Digby filing wondrous reports on the same prospect only to have general manager Cronin reject them with the explanation, "We have no use for the boy at this time."[11] A few days after the Red Sox cut Davis, the young phenom signed with the New York Giants. Doubtlessly, the Sox's treatment of his mentor entered into the decision of young Willie Mays to pursue a career in Organized Baseball elsewhere, once again depriving the Red Sox of the services of one of baseball's all-time greats.

The Red Sox finished third again in 1951 behind the Yankees and Indians, but fell to sixth place in 1952. They landed in fourth place every year from 1953 through 1956 behind the Yankees, who integrated in 1955, and the Indians and White Sox, who had fielded black stars for years. When the Indians faltered, the Red Sox climbed up to third in 1957 and 1958, thanks to Ted Williams' consecutive batting titles and outstanding offensive production from Jackie Jensen, Frank Malzone, and Pete Runnels.

Who's to Blame

The man generally assigned the most blame for the Red Sox refusal to integrate is Mike "Pinky" Higgins, who managed the Sox from 1955 until he was replaced by Billy Jurges midway through the 1959 season. Higgins, who once called a Boston sportswriter a "nigger lover" for praising Minnie Minoso and later told reporter Al Hirshberg, "There will never be any niggers on this team as long as I have anything to say about it," is certainly a convenient target.[12] And, the fact is the Red Sox didn't introduce their first black player until a few weeks after Higgins was fired. But Higgins, an old hunting and drinking buddy, and close confidant of Yawkey, didn't single-handedly keep the Red Sox lily white, although he's certainly due a generous share of the discredit.[13]

In *Shut Out: A Story of Race and Baseball in Boston*, author Howard Bryant, a *Boston Herald* journalist, vigorously condemns the trio of Yawkey, Cronin, and Collins for the team's failure to integrate.

The day after the announcement of Robinson's signing, Collins ludicrously denied that a color barrier existed. "Of course they always have a chance to prove themselves in the minors," he said.[14] But the 60-year-old Collins retired as general manager after the 1947 season, although he stayed on as vice president for several more seasons. Therefore, like his old pal Herb Pennock, Collins' track record in the integration area is not sufficient for objective analysis. It does seem that Collins was at least willing to engage in discussions on the subject, even before the color line was crossed.[15]

Beloved Sox owner Yawkey is certainly due some blame. Yawkey, who generally wintered on his South Carolina plantation but could be found in Boston during baseball season, was extremely popular in baseball circles with executives, fans, and players alike. He was close to many of his Red Sox players, including Ted Williams, and in his younger days was occasionally spotted shagging flies and taking a few batting practice swings at Fenway Park. In fact, he often seemed to prefer the company of the clubhouse attendant and press steward to high society types.[16] Yet Yawkey rarely interfered with front office operations, depending on his general manager to run the team.[17] In 1980, four years after his death, he was named to the Baseball Hall of Fame, the first man to be honored strictly for his role as club owner.

Yawkey was a member of the committee that authored the infamous "Report" in 1946. Under his direction, discriminatory hiring practices were not limited to the Sox roster, but followed throughout Fenway Park.[18] He supported the openly prejudiced Higgins, bringing him back to manage the club in 1960 after he had been fired the previous season and then elevating him to general manager after the team again floundered under his field leadership.

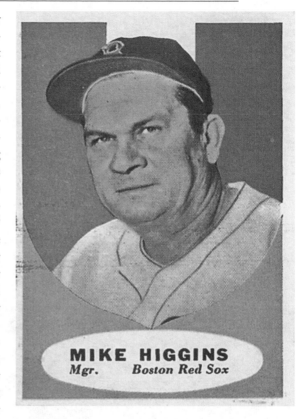

Mike "Pinky" Higgins of the Red Sox, the most overtly racist manager of his time, was rewarded with a promotion to General Manager (1961 Topps card).

According to Pulitzer-Prize-winning journalist David Halberstam, "Racism ... ran rampant through the Red Sox organization."[19] Halberstam characterized the Red Sox as exhibiting a "less refined racism" than the Yankees. "The top management of the Red Sox was mostly Irish, the most powerful group in Boston," he explained. "They had established their own ethnic pecking order, which in essence regarded WASPs with respect and grudging admiration and suspicion for being smart, perhaps a little too smart; and Italians by and large with disdain for being immigrants and Catholics, and yet failing to be Irish. Blacks were well below the Italians."[20]

The record seems to indicate that Yawkey was, at best, a compliant pawn of a racist element who wished to keep the Red Sox segregated or, at worst, a willing conspirator.

In the mid–1950s, black columnist Sam Lacy predicted, "The Red Sox will never have a colored player as long as Tom Yawkey is owner."[21] He was wrong. Yawkey was still in control when the Sox finally capitulated to integration. The club even kept black players after Pinky Higgins returned for a second term as manager and kept them when he was later elevated to general manager. But the Red Sox would never employ a black major leaguer while Joe Cronin controlled player movement.

The Cronin Legacy

Besides Yawkey himself, Joe Cronin was the team's only constant in the upper levels of management during the period when the Sox watched every other major league team integrate. Cronin was manager when the major league color barrier was broken in 1947 and general manager from 1948 through 1958 before leaving to take the job of President of the American League. Cronin was certainly in a position to have acquired a black player for the Sox if he had been so inclined. As American League president, Cronin would subsequently oversee the emergence of the National League as the dominant circuit as the disparity in black talent between the two leagues grew wider through the 1960s.

The politically savvy Cronin was popular with his bosses, the press, and the fans. "His smile and his manner place him rightfully in the blood royal of the Irish race" said one paper.[22] The men who played under him were not so enthusiastic, however.[23] Cronin had become a player-manager at age 26 and a general manager at age 42, only three years after his last plate appearance. He became the first former player to ascend to the position of league president, thanks to a strong recommendation from American League vice president Yawkey, who also happened to chair the selection committee.[24]

When Hall of Famer Joe Cronin ended his 11-year tenure as general manager of the Red Sox to become president of the American League, the Sox were still the only segregated big league team (National Baseball Hall of Fame, Cooperstown, N.Y.).

Cronin was too sharp to utter racist comments like Pinky Higgins. And like his predecessor Eddie Collins, he manipulated the press better than Yawkey. While Collins was general manager in 1947, *The Sporting News* dutifully reported that the Sox were "in the market for a couple of crack colored players."[25] During the Cronin era, encouraging rumors that the Red Sox were seriously pursuing black prospects continued. Before the 1953 season, they were supposedly bidding furiously against the Yankees for the contract of Texas League hurler Bill Greason.[26] After Vic Power's sensational 1953 performance for the Kansas City Blues, Dan Daniel identified the Red Sox and Reds as the most interested of several teams in acquiring the Yankee prospect.[27] A year later, they were reported to have offered the Dodgers $125,000 for Charlie Neal, billed as the highest offer for a minor leaguer in history, an offer that was later exaggerated to $250,000.[28] As late as 1957, *The Sporting News* managed to make it sound like the Sox were in the integration vanguard with the optimistic news flash, "Red Sox may ink Negro *in season or two.*"[29]

Somehow, Cronin managed to publicly appear sympathetic to integration, always right on the verge of taking a significant action. Of course, the local sportswriters were immensely helpful in this area. According to Howard Bryant, "A defining characteristic of the Boston press in those days would be never to challenge Yawkey directly to explain the team's racial direction, even when powerful city and state agencies would take an active role in challenging Yawkey to explain his hiring policies."[30]

Among the organizations challenging the Red Sox while the press ignored the issue were the Boston Ministerial Alliance, the NAACP, the American Veterans Committee of Massachusetts, and the Massachusetts Commission Against Discrimination.[31]

City of Boston

Ironically, it probably wouldn't have taken much to appease integration forces in the early-to-mid 1950s. Boston lacked a significant black media presence and had a small black population, especially as a percentage of the total population.[32] In addition, its black community was relatively prosperous and complacent. The city was often referred to as the "Cradle of Liberty" due to its rich abolitionist past as a safe harbor and popular destination for runaway slaves. Former slave Frederick Douglass came to prominence in Boston's anti-slavery movement. Massachusetts had eliminated segregation in public schools in the 1850s and was one of the first states to open its prestigious universities to black students. Blacks were allowed to serve on juries, railroad cars were not segregated, and public facilities such as operas, playhouses, and museums were open to blacks.[33] Due to its history, the city enjoyed a reputation for racial tolerance — though it was no longer deserved.

Black professional athletes had prospered in Boston long before the Red Sox integrated. The Boston Braves were one of the first major league teams to commit to integration. In addition to the aforementioned Sam Jethroe, three other black players performed for the Boston Braves from 1950 through 1952. The Boston Celtics broke the National Basketball Association color barrier in 1950, drafting Chuck Cooper of Duquesne with the first pick of the second round. Don Barksdale, the first black NBA all-star, joined Chuck Cooper on the Celtics in 1953. Three years later, Bill Russell, the NBA's first black basketball superstar, became a Celtic after leading the country to an Olympic Gold Medal, and by the late 1950s, the Celtics routinely put three black stars on the court. In 1966, Russell succeeded the legendary Red Auerbach, becoming the league's first black coach. Even the Boston Bruins beat the Red Sox to the punch when Willie O'Ree took the ice for the Boston Bruins in 1958 to become the National Hockey League's first black skater. Looking back at ancient history, the first black professional baseball player, Bud Fowler, debuted with a Lynn, Massachusetts, squad, and Cuban infielder Mike Herrera spent two seasons with the Red Sox between two Negro League stints in the pre–Yawkey 1920s.

Pumpsie Green: The "Last" First

The man selected by the Red Sox to carry on this proud legacy was a 25-year-old, switch-hitting infielder named Elijah "Pumpsie" Green, who was so dull he couldn't come up with a good story to explain the origins of his unique nickname.[34]

The Tigers' capitulation to integration during the 1958 campaign left the Sox as the lone segregated major league team on the eve of the 1959 season. Cronin's replacement as general manager, Bucky Harris, had no problem managing black players with San Diego back in 1949 and occupied the manager's seat when the Washington Senators finally integrated in 1954. He certainly understood the situation the Red Sox had put themselves in. But a severe shortage of black talent existed in the organization, which contained only a handful of black minor league prospects. A few years after the Piper Davis debacle, the Sox brass decided that they needed to get a few black players in their organization — at least for the sake of appearances. In 1953, they signed a big catcher by the name of Earl Wilson, who decided his future was on the mound after only 11 games behind the plate. Two years later, the contract of shortstop Pumpsie Green was acquired in a minor league deal. Gradually, this duo emerged at the top of a meager class of black prospects in the Red Sox system. Wilson had actually shown more promise before spending the 1957 and 1958 seasons pitching for the U.S. Marines. Meanwhile, Green had spent the 1958 campaign embellishing his good-field-no-hit reputation with the American Association Minneapolis Millers. But as the Red Sox began pre-season drills in Scottsdale, Arizona, he was the club's best hope for a black player to appease the franchise's growing swarm of critics.

Green responded to the intense scrutiny with a sensational performance in the early exhibition season and was selected the training camp's top rookie by Boston sportswriters.[35] Despite tailing off as the Sox barnstormed their way back east, he was still expected to make the squad. On April 9, three days before opening day, Harris said, "We now have 30 men (including Green) and can carry that many. We don't have to cut anyone from our squad for 30 days."[36] The very next day, manager Higgins made the surprise announcement that Green was being demoted back to Minneapolis for "more seasoning."[37] Obviously Higgins still had something to say about having a black player in a Red Sox uniform.

Though there were still legitimate doubts about Green's ability to hit big league pitching, a decade of lame excuses had left the black community with little faith in the integrity of the Red Sox brass. For example, a mini-scandal erupted when the press discovered that Green was staying fifteen miles away in Phoenix rather than with the team in Scottsdale. Rather than admitting that the hotel had barred Green from staying with his teammates, Sox management ingenuously claimed there was just not enough room for Green at the club's quarters.[38]

More than 12 years after Jackie Robinson broke the color barrier Pumpsie Green became the first black player to wear the Boston Red Sox uniform (1960 Topps card).

They also shamefully attempted to use Wilson to deflect criticism while under attack for sending Green down by claiming they would have already promoted the hurler to the big time if the military hadn't taken him first.[39] "The mealy-mouthed word of the Red Sox management notwithstanding," wrote Sam Lacy, "it is rather easy to conclude that the club has no desire to employ a colored ballplayer."[40]

The Sox got off to a terrible start both on and off the field when the 1959 season got under way. They were losing, and their error-prone shortstop Don Buddin, was being booed relentlessly.

In addition, protestors picketed Fenway Park carrying signs that said "Race Hate is Killing Baseball in Boston" and "We Want a Pennant, Not a White Team."[41] The Boston chapter of the NAACP, the American Veterans Committee of Massachusetts, and the Boston Ministerial Alliance banded together to file discrimination charges against the club, and the Massachusetts Commission Against Discrimination conducted an investigation to address the allegations. The commission cleared the team of misconduct, but exacted a public promise from the front office to make every effort to end segregation. Among the interesting findings of the investigation were that the Red Sox had only seven black players in their farm system and employed only one black worker at Fenway Park.[42]

Finally, the pressure became too much to bear. Apparently not wanting to make poor Pinky Higgins eat his racist words, the Red Sox fired him in early July with the team floundering in last place. After waiting a few weeks to make sure nobody got the impression they were giving in to outside agitators, the Sox put veteran second baseman Bobby Avila on waivers and promoted Green from Minneapolis to take his place. Of course, management wasn't about to give their detractors the satisfaction of allowing Green to make his debut at Fenway Park. Consequently, the initial appearance of a black man in Red Sox flannels occurred against the White Sox at Chicago's Comiskey Park, the first game of a two-week road trip.

But two weeks didn't blunt the desire of Boston's anti-segregation constituency to revel in their hard-won victory. About 20,000 extra fans showed up for Green's first appearance at Fenway Park. An area in deep center field was roped off to accommodate the overflow, and most of the spectators standing behind the ropes were black. Green rose to the occasion by slapping a triple off the Green Monster, Fenway's famous left-field fence, in his first at-bat in the old park.[43]

The Red Sox players didn't exactly welcome Green with open arms, but they accepted him much more readily than the brass. Boston icon Ted Williams went out of his way to put the rookie at ease by warming up with him before each game.[44] Seven years later, Williams would use his own Hall of Fame induction speech to petition for the recognition of former Negro League stars in the Hall.

Under the leadership of Higgins' replacement Billy Jurges, the Red Sox climbed from the cellar to fifth place. Green was the starting second baseman for much of the latter part of the season, and the Red Sox posted a .535 winning percentage with him in the starting lineup, compared to a .468 mark without him.

Green would spend the next three years backing up Boston regulars at shortstop and second base. But the club's second black player, Earl Wilson, who made his major league debut a week after Green, would eventually develop into a big league star. Wilson was haunted by control problems early in his career, a condition that seemed to mysteriously hinder most black pitchers trying to establish themselves in that era. He was 27 years old before the Sox finally gave him a real shot in their chronically weak rotation in 1962, but that year he become the first black American League hurler to throw a no-hitter. Wilson, who would enjoy his greatest success with the Detroit Tigers, would end his career with the second-highest American League win total accumulated by a black hurler.

The Early 1960s

When the Sox opened the 1960 season in Washington, Green was Boston's second baseman and leadoff man, as well as the only black player on the team, since Wilson had been optioned to Minneapolis. Apparently Green was held responsible for the Sox's embarrassing 10–1 loss, since he wasn't in the lineup the next day for the club's first home game of the year. Off to another bad start, the Sox dumped Jurges less than a third of the way through the 1960 schedule. Incredibly, Pinky Higgins, who had been lurking around the Red Sox front office since his firing the previous year, was brought back to manage the club. Fortunately, Sox general manager Bucky Harris managed to engineer a favorable deal for another black player days before Higgins was reinstalled, acquiring Willie Tasby in a trade with the Baltimore Orioles. Playing center field, the 27-year-old Tasby would be one of Boston's few bright spots on the way to a lackluster seventh-place finish. Inexplicably, he was left unprotected in the 1961 expansion draft, and the Red Sox first black regular was quickly snapped up by the new version of the Washington Senators. Green and veteran utility infielder Billy Harrell were the only two black players to appear in Boston uniforms in 1961, as Higgins brought the Red Sox home in sixth place in the new 10-team alignment. Harrell was gone in 1962, but Wilson reclaimed a roster spot and enjoyed a solid season in the Red Sox starting rotation. The team stumbled to eighth place, however, and Higgins, as reward for his managerial genius, was kicked upstairs to the general manager's post.

Pumpsie Green left Boston after the 1962 season to join the hapless New York Mets, but not before one last brush with fame. Midway through the season, he and teammate Gene Conley left the team bus, which was stuck in traffic on the way from Yankee Stadium to the Newark Airport. Conley allegedly needed to find a bathroom, and the ever-agreeable Green went along to keep him company. Their whereabouts remained a mystery for some time, no small feat considering that Conley, who played center for the Boston Celtics in the winter, stood 6'8" tall. Green caught up with the team the next day in Washington, and an inebriated Conley was apprehended a short time later attempting to purchase a ticket to fly to Israel for an impromptu visit to Bethlehem.[45]

In 1963, old Boston favorite Johnny Pesky tried his hand at managing the Red Sox, and they moved up to seventh place. As general manager, Higgins either didn't mind having black players in the dugout as long as he didn't have to be down there with them, felt compelled to convince the public he was no longer prejudiced, or really did turn over a new leaf. At any rate, he traded for Roman Mejias and Felix Mantilla, and for the first time the Sox started the season with three black players on the roster—an improvement, though still well below the major league average.

The Cuban-born Mejias was one of the first black players signed by the Pirates after Branch Rickey took over. Though he was never able to nail down a regular job with the Pirates, he was the expansion Houston Colts' best player in 1962. He spent the 1963 season in Boston platooning in center field and was gone after warming the bench in 1964. The Red Sox traded Pumpsie Green and pitcher Tracy Stallard, renowned for yielding Roger Maris's historic 61st homer, for Mantilla. Mantilla started his career in the Milwaukee Braves organization with a reputation as an outstanding defensive shortstop and spent six years on the Braves' bench waiting for a chance to play regularly. He finally got a shot at a full-time job when the Mets took him in the 1962 expansion draft, but somewhere along the line he had lost confidence in his defensive ability. Mantilla found Fenway Park's cozy left-field fence to his liking and turned into an offensive force in Boston, although he never recovered his former skill with the glove. In 1964, he had the fourth-highest home run percentage in the league, and the next year he led all major league second basemen in homers and runs batted in. Despite these accomplishments, Mantilla was constantly shifted around on defense and maligned by the front office and the press for his fielding. Before the start of 1966 season, the Red Sox traded the 1965 American League starting all-star second baseman to Houston for 34-year-old utility infielder Eddie Kasko.

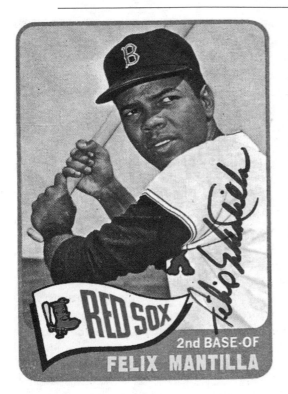

In 1965 second baseman Felix Mantilla became the first black Red Sox all-star, yet he was traded for an aging utility man at the end of the season (1965 Topps card).

Pesky was dismissed at the end of the 1964 season when the Sox fell back to eighth place, but when veteran Al Smith joined Wilson, Mantilla, and Mejias, it marked the first time the Red Sox roster included four black players. In 1965, Higgins pared the number of black Red Sox down to three, the second lowest representation in the majors, and the club ended up in ninth place under Billy Herman.

Late in the 1965 season, the hard-drinking Higgins was fired for excessively celebrating young Dave Morehead's no-hitter.[46] A few years later, an intoxicated Higgins would plow into a group of Louisiana state highway workers, killing one man and injuring several others. Adjudged guilty of negligent homicide and sentenced to four years in prison, he would serve only two months and die of a heart attack a few days after being paroled.[47]

General Manager Dick O'Connell

Veteran front office executive Dick O'Connell succeeded Higgins as general manager. O'Connell was not a favorite ex-player or another old crony of Yawkey. In fact, Glenn Stout, author of *Red Sox Century*, considers him to be the first member of the Yawkey upper-echelon to earn his title strictly on merit.[48] A native New Englander, O'Connell started at the bottom shortly after World War II and worked his way up through the Sox organization.

In 1966, O'Connell's first full season at the helm, the Red Sox more than doubled their contingent of black players. Mantilla was traded, but pitcher Jose Santiago (not the Jose Santiago who pitched for Cleveland and Kansas City in the 1950s), outfielder Joe Christopher, and second baseman George Smith, acquired from the A's, Mets and Tigers respectively, joined Wilson and veteran outfielder Lenny Green. In addition, freshmen George Scott at first base and Joe Foy at third made the starting lineup, giving the Sox seven black players to start the campaign. Though the Sox again ranked ninth in the final standing with Herman at the helm, they made a 10-game improvement in the won-lost column.

But old habits die hard. On June 13, the Red Sox made a trade to acquire two more black players, relief ace John Wyatt and speedy outfielder Jose Tartabull, from the Kansas City Athletics, bringing the club's number of black performers to nine. Upon hearing of the deal, Wilson joked with roommate Lenny Green that there were now too many blacks on the ball club. Sure enough, the next day, Wilson and Christopher were sent to the Detroit Tigers in a lopsided deal for outfielder Don Demeter, bringing the number of black players back down to seven again. Wilson would blossom into a 20-game winner with the Tigers, while Demeter would be of little use to the Red Sox.

For years, the Red Sox organization had been derisively referred to as "Crony Island."[49] Management was accused of maintaining a laid-back country club atmosphere where slow-moving, well-paid sluggers felt no urgency to actually win games as long as they kept their stats up. The era officially came to an end thanks to O'Connell's house-cleaning efforts and the selection of feisty Dick Williams to manage the squad in 1967. The arrival of the intense Williams coincided with breakthrough campaigns by outfielder Carl Yastrzemski and pitcher Jim Lonborg and the emergence of several young stars to create a pennant winner. The nucleus included seven black players in key positions. First baseman Scott, third sacker Foy, starter Santiago, relief ace Wyatt, and reserve outfielder Jose Tartabull were joined by rookie center fielder Reggie Smith at the start of the magical season, and veteran catcher Elston Howard was a crucial mid-season pickup.

Jackie Robinson was one of the few not enthralled with the Red Sox's "Cinderella season," however. Speaking at a dinner in upstate New York in the midst of the pennant race, he remarked, "Because of Boston owner Tom Yawkey I'd like to see them lose, because he is probably one of the most bigoted guys in baseball."[50]

After capturing the pennant on the last day of the season, the exhausted young Sox lost an exciting seven-game World Series to a veteran Cardinal outfit led by Bob Gibson. Boston's injury-riddled pitching staff was so thin they were forced to rely on untested rookies, and staff ace Lonborg started the deciding contest on two days rest. Ironically, if they hadn't parted with Earl Wilson to stay within their black player quota the previous year, the Sox probably would have had the pitching to bring the first world championship banner to Fenway Park in almost half a century.

Boston's defense of its long-awaited pennant got off to a bad start when Jim Lonborg suffered a broken leg in an off-season skiing accident and slugger Tony Conigliaro wasn't able to return from a serious beaning the previous season. In addition, a mysterious slump dropped slugger George Scott's batting average from .303, fourth highest in the league, to .171, next to the lowest. The Red Sox finished fourth with seven black players filling significant roles, but the next year, injuries, trades, and the expansion draft reduced the black front-liners to Reggie Smith and a resurgent George Scott. After introducing only two black players through 1959, the franchise came up with 19 new black players during the decade of the 1960s. This figure still put them near the bottom among all major league teams, but at least they were among the most improved.

The Sox captured another pennant in 1975 with pitcher Luis Tiant, slugging rookie outfielder Jim Rice, and hard-hitting first baseman Cecil Cooper as the top black players on the squad. The next year, Tom Yawkey died, and his widow Jean replaced Dick O'Connell with longtime assistant general manager Haywood Sullivan.

Under Sullivan's direction, the fabulously popular Tiant, who had become the winningest black pitcher in American League history with the Sox, was allowed to defect to the Yankees after the 1978 season. And slugging first baseman Bob Watson, who would eventually become Major League Baseball's first African American general manager, followed suit the next year. According to Howard Bryant, "When Watson walked out, that left Jim Rice as the only black player on the club," and "Rice remained the only black on the club for nearly four years."[51] This statement would be more accurate if the term "African-American" was used instead of "black." Rice was the only prominent American-born black on the squad until designated hitter Mike Easler was acquired in a trade and pitchers "Oil Can" Boyd and Al Nipper came of age in 1984. But Latinos Tony Perez, Mike Torrez, and Tony Armas graced the Sox roster during that period. Bryant also wrote, "During the 1980s, the Red Sox would field the fewest number of blacks of any major league team and would not sign a single black free agent."[52] This may well be true whether darker-complexioned Hispanics are included or not, but by the 1980s the widespread arrival of so many Caribbean players made any count problematic.

The fact that the Boston Red Sox were the last major league team to integrate may be ancient history, but throughout the 20th century, they consistently remained the franchise with the most glaring race relations problem.

In 1985, coach Tommy Harper, a former Boston outfielder, was fired for publicly objecting to a cozy, long-standing relationship between the club brass and the "exclusive" Elks Lodge in Winter Haven, where the Sox trained. The Winter Haven arrangement mirrored the situation that sparked protests from Bill White, Bob Gibson, and Curt Flood of the Cardinals in St. Petersburg almost a quarter of a century earlier. Harper won his suit filed with the Massachusetts Commission Against Discrimination, the same group that helped pressure the Sox to desegregate back in 1959, and the Equal Employment Opportunity Commission, but he was out of a baseball job.

Most of the organization's top black players fought with management or left under suspicious circumstances. The eminently gifted Reggie Smith was an early outspoken critic of team policies. Cecil Cooper would never get a chance to play regularly in Boston, but would blossom in Milwaukee. Future Hall of Famer Orlando Cepeda was unconditionally released after finishing among the top three on the club in batting, homers, and runs batted in. Another future Hall of Famer, Ferguson Jenkins, suffered through two of his worst years in Boston. Talented Oil Can Boyd self-destructed with the Red Sox. After a decade as one of the most fearsome hitters in the game, Jim Rice's declining years were filled with acrimony. He reportedly advised promising young Ellis Burks to "Get your six years in and then get the hell out of Boston."[53] It was advice that Burks would follow. After Mo Vaughn departed via free agency, Sean McAdam of the *Providence Journal* observed, "I don't know if it's racial — though I suspect that it is — but I've never seen a player leave here that was subject to so much *anger* as people directed toward Mo. I mean they took his leaving more personally than Fisk, Clemens, all of them."[54]

Although Jean Yawkey died in 1992, the franchise was owned by the Yawkey Trust until it was sold to a group led by John Henry, Tom Werner, and Larry Lucchino in 2002. Shortly thereafter, president and CEO Lucchino acknowledged on National Public Radio that "along with the team's positive traditions, the club's history has included 'an undeniable legacy of racial intolerance.'"[55]

At this time, the club's top hurler was Pedro Martinez and its best hitter was Manny Ramirez, both black Latinos. The only African American player of note was troublesome Carl Everett. The new ownership group quickly set about trying to improve the franchise image by obtaining three black American players of consequence. They acquired first baseman Tony Clark from the Detroit Tigers, traded Everett to the Texas Rangers for pitcher Darren Oliver, and signed all-time leading base stealer Rickey Henderson as a free agent. None of the three had good seasons, but the club improved its record by 11 wins.

By 2004, the Sox had rehabilitated their racial reputation enough that Ellis Burks returned as a free agent. That year, Martinez, Ramirez, and designated hitter David "Big Papi" Ortiz led them to their first World Championship since Babe Ruth pitched and batted them to the 1918 title. Finally, the "Curse of the Bambino" had been lifted.

Or was it the "Curse of Jackie Robinson?"

Chapter 19

THE 1960S EXPANSION TEAMS

After 60 years of operating with two eight-team leagues, the major leagues expanded to 20 teams in the early 1960s. The old Washington Senators moved to Minneapolis, and the American League gave one of the new franchises to Washington and also added the Los Angeles Angels. The National League introduced the New York Mets and Houston Colt 45's in 1962.

Though the situation had improved since the early days of baseball's integration era, marginality still existed, with white players usually retained as bench players or second-line hurlers rather than similarly talented black players. Due to this practice, black players dominated the minor leagues throughout the 1950s. But with 100 new roster spots opening at the major league level, many anticipated an influx of black minor leaguers to fill the new slots. They would be disappointed. Only 13 of the 103 players selected in the expansion draft were black. For the 1960 season, about 14 percent of the major league population was black, so the expansion clubs were starting out less than the average. Furthermore, the established clubs didn't immediately fill their vacated bench and bullpen slots with marginalized black minor leaguers. During the 1962 season, after the expansion teams were stocked, the percentage of black major leaguers was still about 14 percent, unchanged from the last pre-expansion campaign.

The Washington Senators

In their initial season, the new Senators introduced four African American players to Washington fans, more than the Griffith family had been able to find in the previous 14 years. On opening day of the 1961 campaign, Willie Tasby, nabbed from the Boston Red Sox in the expansion draft, became the first black player to take the field for the expansion Senators. Two games later, the new club started three African Americans, with pitcher Bennie Daniels and first baseman R.C. Stevens joining Tasby in the lineup. Daniels and Stevens, both Branch Rickey signees from his Pittsburgh stint, were acquired from the Pirates in a pre-season trade.

A month into the season, former Orioles farmhand Chuck Hinton, one of three black performers the Senators drafted, was called up from the minors to fill out the quartet. Later in the season, Cuban right-hander Hector Maestri, who was drafted from the original Senators, was called up.

The Senators were generally a bad ball club throughout the 1960s. Many of their promising black players failed to develop as expected. Tasby was traded early in the 1962 season, Bennie Daniels regressed after an excellent first season in Washington, and Chuck Hinton never reached the stardom predicted for him despite becoming Washington's first black all-star in

Chuck Hinton became Washington's first black all-star in 1964 — for the second edition of the Senators (1964 Topps Giant Issue card).

1964. The fabulous Minnie Minoso wasn't able to regain his form with the 1963 Senators after incurring a serious injury with the Cardinals the previous year, and hard-throwing Phil Ortega never panned out. The biggest success stories were Frank Valentine, who finally developed into a solid big league outfielder after hitting his thirties, and catcher Paul Casanova, one of the last Negro League players to graduate to the major leagues. In 1972, Washington was abandoned for the second time as the Senators relocated to Arlington, Texas.

The Los Angeles Angels

The Los Angeles Angels selected only one black player, Cuban Julio Becquer, in the expansion draft, but they acquired former Kansas City Monarch Lou Johnson from the Chicago Cubs before the season started. Neither was in the starting lineup, but both appeared in the Angels' first game. Becquer got the distinction of being the first black player to appear for the franchise when he entered the game for defensive purposes. Later, Johnson would pinch-hit to become the team's first African American player. Before he could get into another game, Johnson was swapped for Leon Wagner, in what would turn out to be a tremendous deal for the Angels. The next year, Wagner would become the team's first black player to make the American League all-star team.

In their second year of existence, the Angels mounted a surprising challenge for the 1962 American League pennant, thanks in large part to Wagner's bat and a fine performance by 30-year-old rookie third baseman Felix Torres, a dark-skinned Cuban. Unfortunately, the club's success was short-lived. In 1964, they traded Wagner, becoming one of the few teams of the era that the Cleveland Indians were able to best in a trade. Throughout the decade, the Angels maintained a minimal black-player presence.

The Houston Colts/Astros

The admission of Houston into the major leagues as part of the 1962 expansion of the National League had to cause integration proponents some consternation. The Texas metropolis would be the southernmost big league outpost, the major league's first old Jim Crow representative. But the Houston Buffs had been one of the first Texas League teams to integrate, welcoming former Negro League stars Bob Boyd and Willard Brown in 1954. After moving to the American Association as an affiliate of the Chicago Cubs in 1959, the Buffs continued to have a contingent of black players on their roster.

Former Pirate Roman Mejias and ex–Negro Leaguer Jim Pendleton were in the Colts' starting lineup for their inaugural season opener in right field and left field respectively. Mejias would lead the Colts in every major batting department in 1962 before being traded to the Red Sox for American League batting champion Pete Runnels. The versatile Pendleton, making a big league comeback at age 38 after a couple years in the minors, also enjoyed a decent season, helping out at six different positions. In mid-season, 28-year-old rookie J.C. Hartman, a former Kansas City Monarch, joined the club and took over the regular shortstop job for most of the last half of the season.

The Colts, who became the Astros when they moved to the Astrodome in 1965, became a top producer of black ballplayers. Among the young black stars they introduced during the 1960s are Hall of Fame second baseman Joe Morgan, center fielder Jimmy Wynn, pitcher Don Wilson, and a trio of hard-hitting first basemen, Bob Watson, John Mayberry, and Nate Colbert.

In 2005, the Astros became the first World Series team without an African American on their post-season roster. They did have six Hispanic players on the squad, a least three of whom wouldn't have had a chance of playing major league baseball before Jackie Robinson.

Second baseman Joe Morgan, who debuted with Houston in 1963, was the first black expansion player to make the Hall of Fame (1968 Topps card).

The New York Mets

A couple of familiar characters who most integration proponents probably considered adversaries resurfaced with the expansion New York Mets in 1962. Manager Casey Stengel and general manager George Weiss had been turned out to pasture by the New York Yankees after the Bombers lost the 1960 World Series to the underdog Pittsburgh Pirates, but they were quickly picked up to fill those roles with the Mets. Based on the Yankees' abysmal integration record, it is something of a surprise that seven of the 22 players selected by the Mets in the expansion draft were black. In fact, the Mets would employ six black players that first season, one of the top totals in the majors. Ex-Dodger Charlie Neal, ex–Red Elio Chacon, and ex–Brave Felix Mantilla were regulars in the infield. Ex-Pirate Al Jackson was the team's second best pitcher, and another ex–Pirate, Joe Christopher, was a semi-regular outfielder. And Choo Choo Coleman, an ex–Phillie, platooned behind the plate.

In *Once Upon a Time*, Leonard Shecter marveled, "Before their first season began, the Mets accomplished what the New York Yankees

Casey Stengel's original 1962 Mets expansion club featured more black players than he'd managed in 12 years with the Yankees (1965 Topps card).

could not do in thirty years — they integrated St. Petersburg, Florida."[1] And the Mets did it with none other than George Weiss in the general manager's chair.

The Mets were by far the worst of the early 1960s expansion teams, winning only 40 of 160 games in their first year and averaging more than 105 losses a year from 1962 through 1968. But they would also be the first expansion team to win a pennant. Stengel had kept everyone distracted until he stepped down in 1965 while Weiss assembled the core of a championship squad before he also retired in 1966. In 1969, they captured a surprise pennant and went on to post a shocking World Series victory over the heavily favored Baltimore Orioles. The Mets' farm system, however, produced only two topflight black players, Cleon Jones and Amos Otis, in the decade of the 1960s, and the club had become one of the whitest in baseball. The 1969 team had only three black players spend the entire season with the team, the lowest total in the National League. But Jones and Tommie Agee were the club's top position players, backup third baseman Ed Charles provided a solid veteran presence, and power-hitting first baseman Donn Clendenon was a tremendous mid-season addition.

Interestingly, the Mets are the flagship minority franchise in present times. Omar Minaya, who was born in the Dominican Republic, is the major league's first Hispanic general manager, and Willie Randolph, the Mets manager from 2005 to 2008, was one of baseball's few black managers. Under their leadership, the Mets assembled an impressive collection of minority talent that includes Carlos Beltran, Jose Reyes, Carlos Delgado, Ramon Martinez, Oliver Perez, and Johan Santana.

The 1969 Expansion

By the time the major leagues were ready to expand again before the 1969 season, the number of black major leaguers was up to more than 20 percent of the population, and the integration of baseball was no longer a major issue.

The Seattle Pilots, who would leave the Pacific Northwest for Milwaukee before a second season, featured two black players in their opening day lineup, second baseman and lead-off man Tommy Harper and number-three hitter, left fielder Tommy Davis. In addition, their most effective pitcher was veteran Diego Segui, but those three would be the only black players to play significant roles for the Pilots, and Davis would be traded to a contender late in the campaign.

The first Kansas City Royals lineup included four black players: catcher Ellie Rodriguez, shortstop Jackie Hernandez, third baseman Joe Foy, and right fielder Bob Oliver. These players would form a solid nucleus, along with speedy outfielder Pat Kelly and utilityman Juan Rios. Within five years, the club had made spectacular deals to add black stars Amos Otis, John Mayberry, and Hal McRae to their roster and developed into a pennant contender. By 1976, the club had captured its first Western Division title with Frank White, Al Cowens, and a white kid by the name of George Brett joining Otis, Mayberry, and McRae. From 1976 through 1985, the Royals made seven post-season appearances, collecting two American League pennants and a World Championship before the reality of small-market finances in the free-agent era began catching up with them.

The San Diego Padres also debuted with four black players in the starting lineup: Roberto Pena at second base, Rafael Robles at shortstop, and Tony Gonzalez and Ollie Brown in the outfield. In addition, the Padres' bench included future stars Nate Colbert and Cito Gaston, who would soon find themselves playing every day.

As befitting the city where Jackie Robinson debuted, the Montreal Expos were the early E.E.O. favorites among the 1969 expansion franchises. The Expos unveiled a squad that included black veterans Maury Wills, Mudcat Grant, Mack Jones, Donn Clendenon, and Manny Mota. They opened the season with Grant on the mound, Wills at shortstop, Jones in left field, and rookie Coco Laboy at third base. Less than two weeks into the season, six black players took the field against the Chicago Cubs with first baseman Clendenon and center field Mota joining the four opening day starters. Unfortunately, of the players mentioned, only Jones and Laboy were still with the club at mid-season.

The Expos never regained their status as an E.E.O. leader, but by the end of the 1970s, they had developed into a successful franchise with a solid contingent of black contributors. In 1994, they had the best record in baseball when the season was ended by a labor strike. The loss of revenue crippled the franchise, whose disgusted fans never returned in force. A decade later, the Expos ceased to exist as the team relocated to Washington, D.C.

Minority Management

After three more rounds of expansion, there were 30 major league teams entering the 2008 season, the 16 original franchises and 14 expansion franchises. It's amazing that 11 of the expansion franchises have employed dark-complexioned minority managers, as opposed to eight of the original franchises. Interestingly, the franchises who haven't happened upon a minority manager capable of leading their team includes many of the same outfits who couldn't seem to find worthy black players back in the first decade of baseball's integration era. The list includes the Boston Red Sox, New York Yankees, Philadelphia Phillies, St. Louis Cardinals, Minnesota Twins nee Washington Senators, and the Oakland Athletics formerly of Philadelphia and Kansas City — all of whom were equal opportunity foot-draggers. Also included are the Atlanta Braves, who were among the integration leaders while in Boston and Milwaukee. The franchise's move to Atlanta in 1966 undoubtedly discouraged the idea of having a black man as the public face of the organization, as has the longevity of current manager Bobby Cox. But the Braves were the first team to trust a black man, Bill Lucas, with top-level front office duties. The eighth original team to keep its managerial ranks lily white is the Los Angeles Dodgers — not to be confused with the Brooklyn Dodgers.

APPENDIX A:
POPULATION OF INTEGRATION
ERA MAJOR LEAGUE CITIES

From 1950 U.S. Census — Standard Metropolitan Areas

	Total Population	Non-white Population	Percent Non-white
Boston	2,369,986	55,725	2.4%
Chicago	5,495,364	605,238	11.0%
Cincinnati	904,402	95,656	10.6%
Cleveland	1,465,511	154,117	10.5%
Detroit	3,008,765	358,015	11.9%
New York	12,911,994	1,046,045	8.1%
Philadelphia	3,671,048	483,927	13.2%
Pittsburgh	2,213,236	137,261	6.2%
St. Louis	1,681,281	216,454	12.9%
Washington	1,461,390	343,140	23.5%

APPENDIX B:
FIRST BLACK AWARD WINNERS
AND LEAGUE LEADERS

Award/Title	*National League*	*American League*
Most Valuable Player	1949 — Jackie Robinson (Brooklyn)	1963 — Elston Howard (New York)
Cy Young	1956 — Don Newcombe (Brooklyn)	1969 — Mike Cuellar (Baltimore)*
Rookie of the Year	1947 — Jackie Robinson (Brooklyn)	1964 — Tony Oliva (Minnesota)
Batting Average	1949 — Jackie Robinson (Brooklyn) .342	1964 — Tony Oliva (Minnesota) .323
Home Runs	1954 — Willie Mays (New York) 51	1952 — Larry Doby (Cleveland) 32
Runs Batted In	1951 — Monte Irvin (New York) 121	1954 — Larry Doby (Cleveland) 126
Stolen Bases	1947 — Jackie Robinson (Brooklyn) 29	1951 — Minnie Minoso (Clev-Chic) 31
Hits	1956 — Hank Aaron (Milwaukee) 200	1960 — Minnie Minoso (Chicago) 184
Runs Scored	1956 — Frank Robinson (Cincinnati) 122	1953 — Larry Doby (Cleveland) 104
Slugging Average	1954 — Willie Mays (New York) .667	1952 — Larry Doby (Cleveland) .541
On Base Percentage	1952 — Jackie Robinson (Brooklyn) .440	1952 — Larry Doby (Cleveland) .442
Hit By Pitch	1948 — Jackie Robinson (Brooklyn) 7	1949 — Larry Doby (Cleveland) 7
Wins	1956 — Don Newcombe (Brooklyn) 27	1965 — Mudcat Grant (Minnesota) 21
Won/Lost Percentage	1955 — Don Newcombe (Brooklyn) .800	1965 — Mudcat Grant (Minnesota) .750
Earned Run Average	1959 — Sam Jones (San Francisco) 2.83	1968 — Luis Tiant (Cleveland) 1.60
Shutouts	1949 — Don Newcombe (Brooklyn) 5	1965 — Mudcat Grant (Minnesota) 6
Strikeouts	1951 — Don Newcombe (Brooklyn)† 164	1964 — Al Downing (New York) 217
Innings Pitched	1963 — Juan Marichal (San Francisco) 321	1979 — Dennis Martinez (Baltimore) 292

* Tied in voting with Denny McLain (Detroit)
† Tied for total with Warren Spahn (Boston)

Appendix C:
First Black Players in Various Minor Leagues[*]

1946	International League (AAA)	Jackie Robinson
1948	Pacific Coast League (AAA)	John Ritchey
1948	American Association (AAA)	Roy Campanella
1952	Texas League (AA)	Dave Hoskins
1954	Southern Association (AA)	Nate Peeples (2 games)
1948	Central League (A)	Dave Hoskins
1948	Eastern League (A)	Fred Thomas
1950	Western League (A)	Gene Baker
1953	Sally League (A)	Several including Hank Aaron
1946	New England League (B)	Roy Campanella & Don Newcombe
1947	Colonial League (B)	Six players with Samford
1949	Three I League (B)	Eugene Bremmer
1949	Western International League (B)	Art Pennington
1950	Inter-State League (B)	Willie Mays
1951	Florida International League (B)	Carlos Bernier & Roberto Vargas
1951	Carolina League (B)	Percy Miller
1952	Tri-State League (B)	Dave Mobley (4 innings)
1946	Canadian-American League (C)	Johnny Wright & Roy Partlow
1947	Sunset League (C)	Nate Moreland
1948	Mid-Atlantic League (C)	Josh Gibson, Jr.
1949	Pioneer League (C)	Eddie Moore
1949	Northern League (C)	Bob Burns
1949	Ohio-Indiana League (D)	Brooks Lawrence
1949	PONY League (D)	Chuck Harmon
1949	Miss-Ohio Valley League (D)	Quincy Smith

[*]Based on *The Sporting News* and player biographical accounts.

APPENDIX D:
ROSTER OF BLACK PLAYERS BY TEAM
(1947–1959)

Dodgers

Jackie Robinson	1947–56
Dan Bankhead	1947, 1950–51
Roy Campanella	1948–57
Don Newcombe	1949–58
Joe Black	1952–55
Sandy Amoros	1952, 1954–57, 1959
Jim Gilliam	1953–59
Charlie Neal	1956–59
Chico Fernandez	1956
Rene Valdez	1957
John Roseboro	1957–59
Bob Wilson	1958
Earl Robinson	1958
Solly Drake	1959
Maury Wills	1959
Tommy Davis	1959

Indians

Larry Doby	1947–55, 1958
Satchel Paige	1948–49
Minnie Minoso	1949, 1951, 1958–59
Luke Easter	1949–54
Harry Simpson	1951–53, 1955
Sam Jones	1951–52
Quincy Trouppe	1952
Dave Pope	1952, 1954–56
Dave Hoskins	1953–54
Al Smith	1953–57
Jose Santiago	1954–55
Billy Harrell	1955, 1957–58

Joe Caffie	1956–57
Larry Raines	1957–58
Mudcat Grant	1958–59
Vic Power	1958–59
Humberto Robinson	1959

Browns/Orioles

Hank Thompson	1947
Willard Brown	1947
Satchel Paige	1951–53
Jehosie Heard	1954
Joe Durham	1954,1957
Dave Pope	1955–56
Bob Boyd	1956–59
Connie Johnson	1956–58
Charlie Beamon	1956–58
Lenny Green	1957–59
Joe Taylor	1958–59
Willie Tasby	1958–59
Fred Valentine	1959

Giants

Hank Thompson	1949–56
Monte Irvin	1949–55
Willie Mays	1951–52, 1954–59
Ray Noble	1951–53
Artie Wilson	1951
Ruben Gomez	1953–58
Bill White	1956, 1958
Ozzie Virgil	1956–57

Giants *(continued)*

Andre Rodgers	1957–59
Valmy Thomas	1957–58
Willie Kirkland	1958–59
Orlando Cepeda	1958–59
Felipe Alou	1958–59
Leon Wagner	1958–59
Sam Jones	1959
Willie McCovey	1959
Jose Pagan	1959

Braves

Sam Jethroe	1950–52
Luis Marquez	1951
George Crowe	1952–53, 1955
Buster Clarkson	1952
Billy Bruton	1953–59
Jim Pendleton	1953–56
Hank Aaron	1954–59
Charlie White	1954–55
Roberto Vargas	1955
Humberto Robinson	1955–56, 1958
Wes Covington	1956–59
Felix Mantilla	1956–59
Juan Pizarro	1957–59
Lee Maye	1959

White Sox

Minnie Minoso	1951–57
Sam Hairston	1951
Bob Boyd	1951, 1953–54
Hector Rodriguez	1952
Connie Johnson	1953, 1955–56
Earl Battey	1955–59
Larry Doby	1956–57, 1959
Al Smith	1958–62
Harry Simpson	1959

Pirates

Carlos Bernier	1953
Curt Roberts	1954–56
Sam Jethroe	1954
Luis Marquez	1954
Roman Mejias	1955, 1957–59
Roberto Clemente	1955–59
Lino Donoso	1955–56
Jim Pendleton	1957–58
Gene Baker	1957–58
Bennie Daniels	1957–59
R.C. Stevens	1958–59
Joe Christopher	1959
Al Jackson	1959
Harry Simpson	1959

Athletics

Bob Trice	1953
Vic Power	1954–58
Joe Taylor	1954
Hector Lopez	1955–59
Harry Simpson	1955–59
Jose Santiago	1956

Cubs

Ernie Banks	1953–59
Gene Baker	1953–57
Luis Marquez	1954
Sam Jones	1955–56
Solly Drake	1956
Monte Irvin	1956
Tony Taylor	1958–59
Lou Jackson	1958–59
George Altman	1959
Don Eaddy	1959
Billy Williams	1959

Cardinals

Tom Alston	1954–57
Bill Greason	1954
Brooks Lawrence	1954–55
Chuck Harmon	1956–57
Charlie Peete	1956
Sam Jones	1957–58
Frank Barnes	1957–58
Curt Flood	1958–59
Joe Taylor	1958
Ruben Amaro	1958
Ellis Burton	1958
Bill White	1959
George Crowe	1959

Cardinals *(continued)*

Joe Durham	1959
Bob Gibson	1959
Dick Ricketts	1959
Marshall Bridges	1959

Reds

Nino Escalera	1954
Chuck Harmon	1954–56
Bob Thurman	1955–59
Joe Black	1955–56
Milt Smith	1955
Frank Robinson	1956–59
George Crowe	1956–58
Brooks Lawrence	1956–59
Pat Scantlebury	1956
Curt Flood	1956–57
Joe Taylor	1957
Vada Pinson	1958–59
Don Newcombe	1958–59
Danny Morejon	1958
Orlando Pena	1958–59
Jim Pendleton	1959
Mike Cuellar	1959

Senators

Carlos Paula	1954–56
Juan Delis	1955
Webbo Clarke	1955
Julio Becquer	1955, 1957–59
Joe Black	1957
Ossie Alvarez	1958

Zoilo Versalles	1959
Lenny Green	1959

Yankees

Elston Howard	1955–59
Harry Simpson	1957–58
Hector Lopez	1959

Phillies

Chico Fernandez	1957–59
John Kennedy	1957
Chuck Harmon	1957
Pancho Herrera	1958
Henry Mason	1958
Valmy Thomas	1959
Ruben Gomez	1959
Humberto Robinson	1959
Solly Drake	1959

Tigers

Ozzie Virgil	1958
Larry Doby	1959
Jim Proctor	1959

Red Sox

Pumpsie Green	1959
Earl Wilson	1959

APPENDIX E: BLACK PLAYER ALL-STAR SELECTIONS THROUGH 1969

National League

	Name	Year/Team	# Times
1	Jackie Robinson	1949–54 (Dodgers)	6
2	Roy Campanella	1949–56 (Dodgers)	8
3	Don Newcombe	1949–51, 1955 (Dodgers)	4
4	Monte Irvin	1952 (Giants)	1
5	Willie Mays	1954–69 (Giants)	16
6	Sam Jones	1955 (Cubs), 1959 (Giants)	2
7	Ernie Banks	1955–62, 1965, 1967, 1969 (Cubs)	11
8	Gene Baker	1955 (Cubs)	1
9	Hank Aaron	1955–69 (Braves)	15
10	Jim Gilliam	1956, 1959 (Dodgers)	2
11	Brooks Lawrence	1956 (Reds)	1
12	Frank Robinson*	1956–57, 1959, 1961–62, 1965 (Reds)	6
13	George Crowe	1958 (Reds)	1
14	John Roseboro*	1958, 1961–62 (Dodgers)	3
15	Charlie Neal	1959–60 (Dodgers)	2
16	Bill White	1959–61, 1963–64 (Cardinals)	5
17	Orlando Cepeda	1959–64 (Giants), 1967 (Cardinals)	7
18	Vada Pinson	1959–1960 (Reds)	2
19	Roberto Clemente	1960–67, 1969 (Pirates)	9
20	Tony Taylor	1960 (Phillies)	1
21	George Altman	1961–62 (Cubs)	2
22	Maury Wills	1961–63, 1965–66 (Dodgers)	5
23	Felipe Alou	1962 (Giants), 1968–69 (Braves)	3
24	Bob Gibson	1962, 1965–69 (Cardinals)	6
25	Billy Williams	1962, 1964–65, 1968 (Cubs)	4
26	Tommy Davis	1962–63 (Dodgers)	2
27	Juan Marichal	1962–69 (Giants)	8
28	Willie McCovey	1963, 1966, 1968–69 (Giants)	4
29	Julian Javier	1963, 1968 (Cardinals)	2
30	Curt Flood	1964, 1966, 1968 (Cardinals)	3
31	Leo Cardenas	1964–1966, 1968 (Reds)	4
32	Willie Stargell	1964–66 (Pirates)	3
33	Bob Veale	1965–66 (Pirates)	2
34	Dick Allen	1965–67 (Phillies)	3
35	Jim Ray Hart	1966 (Giants)	1

36	Joe Morgan	1966 (Astros)	1
37	Mike Cuellar	1967 (Astros)	1
38	Lou Brock	1967 (Cardinals)	1
39	Jim Wynn	1967 (Colts/Astros)	1
40	Tony Perez	1967–69 (Reds)	3
41	Ferguson Jenkins	1967 (Cubs)	1
42	Matty Alou	1968–69 (Pirates)	2
43	Cleon Jones	1969 (Mets)	1
44	Lee May	1969 (Reds)	1
45	Grant Jackson	1969 (Phillies)	1
46	Felix Millan	1969 (Braves)	1
Total		**National League**	**169**

American League

	Name	Year/Team	# Times
1	Larry Doby	1949–55 (Indians)	7
2	Minnie Minoso	1951–54, 1957, 1960 (White Sox), 1959 (Indians)	7
3	Satchel Paige	1952–53 (Browns)	2
4	Al Smith	1955 (Indians), 1960 (White Sox)	2
5	Vic Power	1955–56 (Athletics), 1959–60 (Indians)	4
6	Harry Simpson	1956 (Athletics)	1
7	Elston Howard	1957–65 (Yankees)	9
8	Earl Battey	1962–63, 1965–1966 (Twins)	4
9	Leon Wagner	1962–63 (Angels)	2
10	Juan Pizarro	1963–64 (White Sox)	2
11	Mudcat Grant	1963 (Indians), 1965 (Twins)	2
12	Zoilo Versalles	1963, 1965 (Twins)	2
13	Chuck Hinton	1964 (Senators)	1
14	John Wyatt	1964 (Athletics)	1
15	Tony Oliva	1964–69 (Twins)	6
16	Felix Mantilla	1965 (Red Sox)	1
17	Willie Horton	1965, 1968 (Tigers)	2
18	Frank Robinson*	1966–67, 1969 (Orioles)	3
19	Tommie Agee	1966–67 (White Sox)	2
20	George Scott	1966 (Red Sox)	1
21	Al Downing	1967 (Yankees)	1
22	Paul Casanova	1967 (Senators)	1
23	Rod Carew	1967–69 (Twins)	3
24	Jose Santiago	1968 (Red Sox)	1
25	Luis Tiant	1968 (Indians)	1
26	Bert Campaneris	1968 (Athletics)	1
27	John Odom	1968–69 (Athletics)	2
28	John Roseboro*	1969 (Twins)	1
29	Paul Blair	1969 (Orioles)	1
30	Roy White	1969 (Yankees)	1
31	Reggie Smith	1969 (Red Sox)	1
32	Reggie Jackson	1969 (Athletics)	1
33	Ellie Rodriguez	1969 (Royals)	1
34	Carlos May	1969 (White Sox)	1
Total		**American League**	**78**

* All-star selection in both leagues

CHAPTER NOTES

Introduction

1. Lawrence D. Hogan, *Shades of Glory* (Washington, D.C.: National Geographic, 2006), p. 18.
2. Burt Solomon, *The Baseball Timeline* (New York: DK Publishing, 2001), p 26.
3. Hogan, *Shades of Glory*, p. 6.
4. Hogan, *Shades of Glory*, p. 16.
5. James A. Riley, *The Biographical Encyclopedia of the Negro Baseball Leagues* (New York: Carroll & Graf, 1994), p. 294.
6. Hogan, pp. 50–53, p.70.
7. Hogan, *Shades of Glory*, p. 56.
8. Stefan Fatsis, "Mystery of Baseball: Was William White Game's First Black?" *The Wall Street Journal* 30 Jan. 2004, p. A1.
9. Hogan, *Shades of Glory*, p. 55.
10. Hogan, *Shades of Glory*, p. 53.
11. Hogan, *Shades of Glory*, p. 56.
12. Hogan, *Shades of Glory*, pp. 58–59.
13. Hogan, *Shades of Glory*, pp. 63–64.
14. Riley, *The Biographical Encyclopedia of the Negro Baseball Leagues*, p. 836.
15. Hogan, *Shades of Glory*, pp. 62–63.
16. Hogan, *Shades of Glory*, p. 47.
17. Hogan, *Shades of Glory*, p. 46.
18. Brad Snyder, *Beyond the Shadow of the Senators* (New York: Contemporary Books, 2003), p. 65.
19. John F. Steadman, "McGraw's Negro Second Baseman," *Baseball Digest* Oct.-Nov. 1962, pp. 65–66.
20. Jonathan Fraser Light, (Jefferson, NC: McFarland, 1997), p. 374; Joel Zoss and John Bowman, *Diamonds in the Rough* (New York: Contemporary Books, 1996), p. 144.
21. William Simon, ed., *The Cooperstown Symposium on Baseball and American Culture* (Jefferson, NC: McFarland, 2003), p. 64.
22. Tom Hawthorn, "The Rocky Saga of Vagabond 'Tribesman' Jimmy Claxton," in *Rain Checks: Baseball in the Pacific Northwest*, ed. Mark Armour (Cleveland: Society for American Baseball Research, 2006), pp. 44–45, 126.
23. Ibid.
24. Ibid.
25. Bill Kirwin, "Jim Crow in Canada," *The National Pastime* 19 (1999), pp. 38–42.
26. Peter C. Bjarkman, *A History of Cuban Baseball, 1864–2006* (Jefferson, NC: McFarland, 2007), p. 326.

27. Bjarkman, *A History of Cuban Baseball*, p.315.
28. Zoss and Bowman, *Diamonds in the Rough*, p. 149.
29. Jules Tygiel, *Baseball's Great Experiment* (New York: Oxford University Press, 1997), p. 25.
30. Bjarkman, *A History of Cuban Baseball*, p. 323.
31. Light, *The Cultural Encyclopedia of Baseball*, p. 374; Zoss and Bowman, *Diamonds in the Rough*, p. 148.
32. Tygiel, *Baseball's Great Experiment*, p. 25.
33. Robert Boyle, "The Private World of the Negro Ballplayer," *Sports Illustrated* 21 Mar. 1960, p. 17.
34. Tygiel, *Baseball's Great Experiment*, p. 33.
35. Light, *The Cultural Encyclopedia of Baseball*, p. 599.
36. Zoss and Bowman, *Diamonds in the Rough*, pp. 152–154.
37. Snyder, *Beyond the Shadow of the Senators*, p. 75.
38. Tygiel, *Baseball's Great Experiment*, p. 32.
39. Tygiel, *Baseball's Great Experiment*, p. 39–40; Robert W. Peterson, *Only The Ball Was White* (Englewood Cliffs, NJ: Prentice-Hall, 1970), p. 177.
40. *The Sporting News*, 23 Jul. 1942, p. 11.
41. Tygiel, *Baseball's Great Experiment*, pp. 30–31; *The Sporting News*, 6 Aug. 1942; John B. Holway, *Voices From the Great Black Baseball Leagues* (New York: Dodd, Mead, 1975), p. 11.
42. John McReynolds, "Nate Moreland: A Mystery to Historians," *The National Pastime* 19 (1999), pp. 57–58.
43. Snyder, *Beyond the Shadow of the Senators*, p. 192.
44. John B. Holway, *Black Diamonds* (Westport, CT: Meckler, 1989), p. 132.
45. Roy Campanella, *It's Good to Be Alive* (New York: Dell, 1959), p. 95; Peterson, *Only The Ball Was White*, p. 177.
46. Light, *The Cultural Encyclopedia of Baseball*, p. 374.
47. Peterson, *Only The Ball Was White*, p. 179.
48. Murray Polner, *Branch Rickey: A Biography* (New York: Atheneum, 1982), pp. 156–158.
49. Tygiel, *Baseball's Great Experiment*, pp. 43–44.
50. Eric Enders, "So Long, Sam," *EricEnders.com*, www.ericenders.com/jethroe.htm.
51. Tygiel, *Baseball's Great Experiment*, pp. 43–44.
52. Snyder, *Beyond the Shadow of the Senators*, p. 185.
53. *The Sporting News*, 6 Aug. 1942, p. 4.
54. Ibid.
55. Ibid.
56. *The Sporting News*, 21 May 1947, p. 14.

57. David Pietrusza, Matthew Silverman, and Michael Gershman, eds., *Baseball: The Biographical Encyclopedia* (New York: Total Sports, 2000), p. 635.

58. J. G. Taylor Spink, *Judge Landis and 25 Years of Baseball* (St. Louis: Sporting News, 1974), p. 36.

59. Spink, *Judge Landis and 25 Years of Baseball*, p. 35.

60. Pietrusza, Silverman, and Gershman, eds., *Baseball: The Biographical Encyclopedia*, p. 635.

61. Tygiel, *Baseball's Great Experiment*, p. 31.

62. Polner, *Branch Rickey*, p. 148.

63. *The Sporting News*, 23 Jul. 1942, p. 11.

Chapter 1

1. Polner, *Branch Rickey*, pp. 23–35.

2. Polner, *Branch Rickey*, pp. 36–46.

3. Polner, *Branch Rickey*, pp. 46–63.

4. Farm team count obtained from the Professional Baseball Players Database, Old-Time Date, Inc. (version 6.0).

5. Tim Cohane, "A Branch Grows in Brooklyn," *Look Magazine* 19 Mar. 1946, p. 70.

6. Woody Strode and Sam Young, "The Goal Dust Gang" in *The Jackie Robinson Reader*, ed. Jules Tygiel (New York: Penguin, 1997), p. 27.

7. Harvey Frommer, *Rickey and Robinson* (New York: Macmillan, 1982), pp. 29–31.

8. Tygiel, *Baseball's Great Experiment*, p. 61.

9. Frommer, *Rickey and Robinson*, p. 33.

10. Zoss and Bowman, *Diamonds in the Rough*, p. 102; Tygiel, *Baseball's Great Experiment*, p. 92.

11. Jim Kreuz, "Tom Greenwade and His '007' Assignment," *The National Pastime* 27 (2007), pp. 96–100.

12. Ibid.

13. Tygiel, *Baseball's Great Experiment*, p. 66.

14. Tygiel, *Baseball's Great Experiment*, p. 76.

15. *The Sporting News*, 1 Nov. 1945, p. 12.

16. Tygiel, *Baseball's Great Experiment*, p. 76.

17. *The Sporting News*, 23 Apr. 1947, p. 16.

18. Tygiel, *Baseball's Great Experiment*, p. 77.

19. *The Sporting News*, 1 Nov. 1945, p. 12.

20. Tygiel, *Baseball's Great Experiment*, p. 7.

21. Polner, *Branch Rickey*, pp. 188–189.

22. *The Sporting News*, 25 Feb. 1948, p. 2.

23. Polner, *Branch Rickey*, p.188.

24. *The Sporting News*, 23 May 1946, p. 19.

25. *The Sporting News*, 13 Dec. 1945, p. 18.

26. *The Sporting News*, 14 Mar. 1946, p. 20.

27. William Marshall, *Baseball's Pivotal Era: 1945–1951* (Lexington: University Press of Kentucky, 1999), p. 135.

28. David Craft and Tom Owens, *Redbirds Revisited* (Chicago: Bonus Books, 1990), p. 113.

29. *The Sporting News*, 17 Aug. 1947, p. 3. The players are former Negro Leaguers Al Preston, Fred Sheppard, Andres Pullize, Carlos Santiago, and Roy Lee and amateur free agent Johnny Haith.

30. *The Sporting News*, 20 Aug. 1947, p. 1.

31. *The Sporting News*, 21 May 1947, p. 14.

32. *The Sporting News*, 16 Jul. 1947, p. 16.

33. *The Sporting News*, 13 Aug. 1947, p. 9; *The Sporting News*, 20 Aug. 1947, p. 12.

34. *The Sporting News*, 25 Feb. 1948, p. 12.

35. *The Sporting News*, 14 Jul. 1948, p. 8.

36. *The Sporting News*, 22 Feb. 1961, p. 7.

Chapter 2

1. *The Sporting News*, 14 Jan. 1948, p. 15.

2. Mark Ribowsky, *A Complete History of the Negro Leagues: 1884–1955* (Secaucus, NJ: Carol Publishing, 1995), p. 283.

3. Marshall, *Baseball's Pivotal Era: 1945–1951*, p. 131.

4. Tygiel, *Baseball's Great Experiment*, p. 87.

5. *The Sporting News*, 14 Jan. 1948, p. 15.

6. Andrew O'Toole, *Branch Rickey in Pittsburgh* (Jefferson, NC: McFarland, 2000), p. 117

7. *The Sporting News*, 18 Feb. 1948, p. 5.

8. Ibid.

9. Peterson, *Only The Ball Was White*, p. 203.

10. Larry Moffi and Jonathan Kronstadt, *Crossing the Line* (Jefferson, NC: McFarland, 1994), p. 11; Peterson, *Only The Ball Was White*, p. 203.

11. Roger Kahn, *The Era: 1947–1957* (New York: Ticknor and Fields, 1993), pp. 246–247.

12. Tygiel, *Baseball's Great Experiment*, p. 213; *The Sporting News*, 27 Aug. 1947, p. 16; *The Sporting News*, 9 Feb. 1949, p. 6.

13. Monte Irvin with James A. Riley, *Nice Guys Finish First* (New York: Carroll & Graf, 1996), pp. 118–120; Tygiel, *Baseball's Great Experiment*, p. 245; *The Sporting News*, 29 Dec. 1948, p. 27.

14. Frommer, *Rickey and Robinson*, pp. 154–155.

15. *The Sporting News*, 8 Feb. 1950, p. 15.

16. Peter Golenbock, *Bums* (New York: Putnam's, 1984), p. 198.

17. *The Sporting News*, 24 Mar. 1948, p. 22.

18. *The New York Age* 20 May 1950, p. 24.

19. Kahn, *The Era: 1947–1957*, p. 261.

20. Marshall, *Baseball's Pivotal Era: 1945–1951*, pp. 207–208.

21. Danny Peary, *We Played the Game* (New York: Hyperion, 1994), p. 254.

22. Tygiel, *Baseball's Great Experiment*, p. 307.

23. *The Sporting News*, 28 Jul. 1954, p. 17.

24. Kahn, *The Era: 1947–1957*, pp. 265–268.

25. *The Sporting News*, 23 Jul. 1955, p. 18.

26. Ibid., p. 23.

27. Tygiel, *Baseball's Great Experiment*, p. 172.

28. Polner, *Branch Rickey: A Biography*, p. 204.

29. Frommer, *Rickey and Robinson*, pp. 195–196.

30. John Roseboro with Bill Libby, *Glory Days with the Dodgers* (New York: Atheneum, 1978), pp. 110–121.

31. Ibid., p. 73.

32. *The Sporting News*, 12 Jul. 1950, p. 56.

33. *The Sporting News*, 25 Feb. 1953, p. 5.

34. Golenbock, *Bums*, p. 422.

35. Roseboro with Libby, *Glory Days with the Dodgers*, p. 100

36. Maury Wills and Mike Celizic, *On the Run* (New York: Carroll & Graf, 1991), p. 156.

37. Leonard Shechter, "Can't Anyone Here Use Kanehl," *Sports Illustrated* 8 Aug. 1966, p. 65.

38. Moffi and Kronstadt, *Crossing the Line*, p. 73.

39. Zoss and Bowman, *Diamonds in the Rough*, p. 188.

40. Light, *The Cultural Encyclopedia of Baseball*, p. 599.

41. Ibid.

42. Joseph Thomas Moore, *Pride Against Prejudice* (Westport, CT: Praeger, 1988), p. 35.

43. *The Sporting News*, 20 Apr. 1987, p. 12.

44. Kahn, *The Era: 1947–1957*, p. 261.

45. Kahn, *The Era: 1947–1957*, p. 327.

46. *The Sporting News*, 20 Apr. 1987, p. 12.

Chapter 3

1. Bill Veeck with Ed Linn, *Veeck — As in Wreck* (New York: Bantam, 1962), p. 40.

2. Veeck with Linn, *Veeck — As in Wreck*, p. 76.

3. Jack Torry, *Endless Summers* (South Bend, IN: Diamond Communications, 1996), p. 4.

4. Tygiel, *Baseball's Great Experiment*, p. 212.

5. Gerald Eskenazi, *Bill Veeck: A Baseball Legend* (New York: McGraw-Hill, 1988), p. 66; Tygiel, *Baseball's Great Experiment*, p. 228.

6. David Jordan, Larry Gerlach, and Joe Rossi, "A Baseball Myth Exploded," *The National Pastime* 18 (1998), pp. 3–13.

7. Jules Tygiel, "Revisiting Bill Veeck and the 1943 Phillies," *The Baseball Research Journal* 35 (2007), pp. 109–114.

8. *The Sporting News*, 12 May 1948, p. 16.

9. *The Sporting News*, 20 Oct. 1948, p. 2.

10. Eskenazi, *Bill Veeck*, pp. 40–42.

11. Tygiel, *Baseball's Great Experiment*, p. 217.

12. Moore, *Pride Against Prejudice*, p. 69.

13. *The Sporting News*, 14 Jul. 1948, p. 8.

14. David Gallen, ed., *The Baseball Chronicles* (New York: Carroll & Graf, 1991), p. 225.

15. "Fred Thomas," University of Windsor website, Alumni Sports Hall of Fame, www.uwindsor.ca/units/alumni/sportsHall.

16. *The Sporting News*, 14 Jul. 1948, p. 6.

17. *The Sporting News*, 13 Apr. 1949, p. 13.

18. *The Sporting News*, 14 Mar. 1951, p. 14.

19. *The Sporting News*, 26 Apr. 1950, p. 5.

20. Tygiel, *Baseball's Great Experiment*, p. 80.

21. Tygiel, *Baseball's Great Experiment*, p. 169.

22. Irvin with Riley, *Nice Guys Finish First*, p. 118.

23. Veeck with Linn, *Veeck as in Wreck*, pp. 180, 184.

24. Ribowsky, *A Complete History of the Negro Leagues*, p. 305.

25. Moore, *Pride Against Prejudice*, p. 39.

26. Ribowsky, *A Complete History of the Negro Leagues*, p. 303.

27. Moore, *Pride Against Prejudice*, p. 101.

28. Russell Schneider, *The Boys of the Summer of '48* (Champaign, IL: Sports Publishing, 1998), p. 46.

29. *The Sporting News*, 8 Feb. 1950, p. 15.

30. Tygiel, *Baseball's Great Experiment*, p. 229.

31. Peary, *We Played the Game*, p. 339.

32. Danny Peary, "Interview with Vic Power," in *Cult Baseball Players*, ed. Danny Peary (New York: Simon and Schuster, 1990), p. 360.

33. Wes Singletary, *Al Lopez: The Life of Baseball's El Senor* (Jefferson, NC: McFarland, 1999), p. 220; A. S. "Doc" Young, *Jet* 19 Dec. 1957.

34. Moore, *Pride Against Prejudice*, p. 116.

35. Peary, *We Played the Game*, p. 168.

36. Singletary, *Al Lopez*, p. 222.

37. Peary, *We Played the Game*, p. 201.

38. Peary, "Interview with Vic Power," pp. 363–364; Peary, *We Played the Game*, p. 480.

39. Singletary, *Al Lopez*, pp. 213–226.

40. Zoss and Bowman, *Diamonds in the Rough*, p. 185; Tygiel, *Baseball's Great Experiment*, pp. 307–308.

41. *The Sporting News*, 12 Nov. 1947, p. 10.

42. Tygiel, *Baseball's Great Experiment*, pp. 216–217.

43. Moore, *Pride Against Prejudice*, p. 140.

Chapter 4

1. Tygiel, *Baseball's Great Experiment*, p. 219.

2. Marshall, *Baseball's Pivotal Era: 1945–1951*, p. 146.

3. Marshall, *Baseball's Pivotal Era: 1945–1951*, p. 147.

4. *The Sporting News*, 23 Jul. 1947, p. 8; Tygiel, *Baseball's Great Experiment*, p. 219.

5. Tygiel, *Baseball's Great Experiment*, p. 220.

6. Holway, *Black Diamonds*, p. 113.

7. *The Sporting News*, 30 Jul. 1947, p. 11.

8. *The Sporting News*, 26 Nov. 1947, p. 5.

9. Tygiel, *Baseball's Great Experiment*, p. 221; Bill James, *The New Bill James Historical Abstract* (New York: Simon and Schuster, 2001), p. 683.

10. Holway, *Black Diamonds*, p. 108.

11. Riley, *The Biographical Encyclopedia of the Negro Leagues*, p. 780.

12. Gene Karst and Martin Jones, Jr., *Who's Who in Professional Baseball*, p. 862; Arnold Hano, "Exclusive! Ex-World Series Star in Jail," *Sport* Dec. 1965.

13. *The Sporting News*, 23 Jul. 1947, p. 8.

14. 1950 United States Census (see Appendix)

15. *The Sporting News*, 30 Jul. 1947, p. 33.

16. Satchel Paige with David Lipman, *Maybe I'll Pitch Forever* (Lincoln: University of Nebraska Press, 1993), p. 238.

17. *The Sporting News*, 19 Apr. 1950, p. 40.

18. Holway, *Voices from the Great Black Baseball Leagues*, pp. 130, 272.

19. *The Sporting News*, 21 Jul. 1951, p. 32.

20. *The Sporting News*, 5 Sep. 1951, p. 22.

21. *The Sporting News*, 9 Apr. 1952, p. 29.

22. *The Sporting News*, 2 Jul. 1952, p. 28.

23. Brent Kelley, *Voices from the Negro Leagues* (Jefferson, NC: McFarland, 1998), pp. 176–180.

24. *The Sporting News*, 25 Feb. 1953, p. 31.

25. Moffi and Kronstadt, *Crossing the Line*, p. 109.

26. Peter Golenbock, *The Spirit of St. Louis* (New York: HarperCollins, 2000), p. 355.

27. Gallen, ed., *The Baseball Chronicles*, p. 216; Charles Einstein, *Willie's Time* (New York: Berkley Books, 1980), pp. 60–61.

28. Charles C. Alexander, *Rogers Hornsby: A Biography* (New York: Henry Holt, 1995), p. 261,

29. Alexander, *Rogers Hornsby*, p. 258.

30. *The Sporting News*, 20 Aug. 1947, p. 13.

31. *The Sporting News*, 16 May 1951, p. 21.

32. Peary, *We Played the Game*, p. 195.

33. Alexander, *Rogers Hornsby*, p. 266.

34. *The Sporting News*, 15 Aug. 1951, p. 15.

Chapter 5

1. *The Sporting News*, 3 Feb. 1954, p. 15.
2. Tygiel, *Baseball's Great Experiment*, p. 122.
3. Marshall, *Baseball's Pivotal Era: 1945–1951*, p. 133.
4. John Eisenberg, "The Quiet Pioneer," *Baltimore Sun* 23 Apr. 2004.
5. John Petkovic, "The Negro Leagues: Dave Pope," *Scam City*, http://www.scamcity.com/index.php?story_id=7.
6. *The Sporting News*, 25 Dec. 1965, p. 11.

Chapter 6

1. Polner, *Branch Rickey*, pp. 149–150.
2. Marshall, *Baseball's Pivotal Era: 1945–1951*, p. 190.
3. Leo Durocher with Ed Linn, *Nice Guys Finish Last* (New York: Simon and Schuster, 1975), p. 288; Marshall, *Baseball's Pivotal Era: 1945–1951*, p. 190.
4. Durocher with Linn, *Nice Guys Finish Last*, p. 297.
5. Durocher with Linn, *Nice Guys Finish Last*, p. 290.
6. Durocher with Linn, *Nice Guys Finish Last*, p. 13.
7. Durocher with Linn, *Nice Guys Finish Last*, p. 289.
8. Marshall, *Baseball's Pivotal Era: 1945–1951*, p. 190.
9. Noel Hynd, *The Giants of the Polo Grounds* (New York: Doubleday, 1988), pp. 343, 358.
10. Tygiel, *Baseball's Great Experiment*, p. 58.
11. Tygiel, *Baseball's Great Experiment*, p. 245.
12. *The Sporting News*, 14 Apr. 1948, p. 20; Ribowsky, *A Complete History of the Negro Leagues*, p. 311; Kahn, *The Era*, p. 188.
13. *The Sporting News*, 16 Mar. 1949, p. 27.
14. Irvin with Riley, *Nice Guys Finish First*, p. 125.
15. *The Sporting News*, 20 Jul. 1949, p. 13.
16. *The Sporting News*, 15 Mar. 1950, p. 30.
17. *The Sporting News*, 10 May 1950, p. 30.
18. *The Sporting News*, 14 Jun. 1950, p. 28.
19. *The Sporting News*, 5 Jul. 1950, p. 41.
20. Tygiel, *Baseball's Great Experiment*, p. 260.
21. *The Sporting News*, 2 May 1951, p. 15.
22. Eric Enders, "The Last .400 Hitter," *EricEnders.com*, www.ericenders.com/artiewilson.htm.
23. *The Sporting News*, 3 Aug. 1949, p. 24.
24. Irvin with Riley, *Nice Guys Finish First*, p. 142.
25. Light, *The Cultural Encyclopedia of Baseball*, p. 379.
26. John B. Holway, *Blackball Stars* (Wesport, CT: Meckler, 1988), p. 370; Zoss and Bowman, *Diamonds in the Rough*, p. 186.
27. Holway, *Blackball Stars*, p. 371.
28. Marty Appel, *Yesterday's Heroes* (New York: William Morrow, 1988), p. 101.
29. "Valmy Thomas," AOL Hometown, members.aol.com/vibaseball/Thomas.html.
30. Mike Shatzkin, ed., *The Ballplayers* (New York: Arbor House, 1990), p. 1123.
31. *The Sporting News*, 8 Nov. 1961, p. 20.
32. Pietrusza, Silverman, and Gershman, eds., *Baseball: The Biographical Encyclopedia*, p. 263.
33. *The Sporting News*, 22 Aug. 1964, p. 9.
34. Pietrusza, Silverman, and Gershman, eds., *Baseball: The Biographical Encyclopedia*, p. 263.
35. Durocher with Linn, *Nice Guys Finish Last*, pp. 204–205.
36. Durocher with Linn, *Nice Guys Finish Last*, pp. 290–296.
37. Golenbock, *Bums*, p. 145.
38. *The Sporting News*, 17 Mar. 1948, p. 30.
39. Willie Mays with Lou Sahadi, *Say Hey* (New York: Simon and Schuster, 1988), p. 45; *The Sporting News*, 5 Jul. 1950, p. 41.
40. Tygiel, *Baseball's Great Experiment*, p. 270, p. 279; *The Sporting News*, 29 Aug. 1951, p. 34.
41. Tygiel, *Baseball's Great Experiment*, p. 278.
42. Roer Kahn, *The Era*, p. 188.
43. Milton Gross, *New York Post* 1954, from correspondence with Norman Macht 22 Feb. 2008.

Chapter 7

1. Zoss and Bowman, *Diamonds in the Rough*, pp. 162–163; O'Toole, *Branch Rickey in Pittsburgh*, pp. 116–117.
2. Ed Fitzgerald, *The National League* (New York: Grossett and Dunlap, 1959), p. 101.
3. Ibid.
4. *The Sporting News*, 22 Dec. 1948, p. 13.
5. *The Sporting News*, 16 Feb. 1949, p. 24.
6. *The Sporting News*, 15 Jun. 1949, p. 32
7. *The Sporting News*, 18 May 1949, p. 47; *The Sporting News*, 17 Aug. 1949, p. 12.
8. Tygiel, *Baseball's Great Experiment*, p. 243.
9. Howard Bryant, *Shut Out* (Boston: Beacon Press, 2002), p. 29.
10. Golenbock, *Bums*, p. 145.
11. Bryant, *Shut Out*, p. 27.
12. Holway, *Blackball Stars*, p. 350; Zoss and Bowman, *Diamonds in the Rough*, p. 101
13. Roland Hemond. Interview. 19 Nov. 2007.
14. Moffi and Kronstadt, *Crossing the Line*, p. 51.
15. *The Sporting News*, 28 Jun. 1950, p. 30.
16. Moffi and Kronstadt, *Crossing the Line*, p. 51.
17. Riley, *The Biographical Encyclopedia of the Negro Baseball Leagues*, p. 176.
18. Moffi and Kronstadt, *Crossing the Line*, p. 76.
19. "George Crowe — Our First Mr. Basketball," *Indiana Basketball Hall of Fame*, www.hoopshall.com/inductees/1976/crowe.html.
20. *The Sporting News*, 20 Aug. 1952, p. 13.
21. *The Sporting News*, 26 Jul. 1950, p. 26.
22. *The Sporting News*, 19 Apr. 1950, p. 46; *The Sporting News*, 3 May 1930, p. 38.
23. Moffi and Kronstadt, *Crossing the Line*, p. 88
24. Enders, "So Long, Sam."
25. Boyle, "The Private World of the Negro Ballplayer," p. 76.
26. Hank Aaron with Lonnie Wheeler, *I Had a Hammer* (New York: HarperCollins, 1991), pp. 216–217.
27. Aaron with Wheeler, *I Had a Hammer*, p. 251.
28. *The Sporting News*, 31 Mar. 1954, p. 17; *The Sporting News*, 14 Apr. 1954, p. 25.
29. *The Sporting News*, 28 Apr. 1954, p. 31.
30. Tygiel, *Baseball's Great Experiment*, p. 276.

31. Aaron with Wheeler, *I Had a Hammer*, p. 252.
32. Aaron with Wheeler, *I Had a Hammer*, p. 267.
33. Aaron with Wheeler, *I Had a Hammer*, pp. 269–271.
34. Donald Dewey and Nicholas Acocella, *The Biographical History of Baseball* (Chicago: Triumph, 2002), pp. 361–362.

Chapter 8

1. Richard Lindberg, *Who's on Third?* (South Bend, IN: Icarus Press, 1983), p. 52.
2. Lindberg, *Who's on Third?*, p. 64.
3. *The Sporting News*, 21 Jul. 1948, p. 12.
4. Tygiel, *Baseball's Great Experiment*, p. 223.
5. "Baseball's Fastest Player," *Ebony* Oct. 1950, pp. 55–56.
6. Bob Vanderberg, *Minnie and The Mick* (South Bend, IN: Diamond Communications, 1996), p. 14.
7. 1950 United States Census (see appendix).
8. Peter Golenbock, *Wrigleyville* (New York: St. Martin's, 1999), p. 346.
9. *The Sporting News*, 6 Aug. 1947, p. 19.
10. *The Sporting News*, 5 Jan. 1949, p. 10; *The Sporting News*, 19 Jan. 1949, p. 10.
11. *The Sporting News*, 15 Jun. 1949, p. 22.
12. *The Sporting News*, 6 Jul. 1949, p. 34; correspondence with Jim Sandoval, Co-chair SABR Scouts Committee.
13. *The Sporting News*, 21 Mar. 1951, p. 23; Walter Dunn Tucker, "How Old Is That Guy, Anyway?" *The Baseball Research Journal* 36 (2007), pp. 94–98.
14. James, *The New Bill James Historical Baseball Abstract*, p. 176.
15. Bjarkman, *A History of Cuban Baseball, 1864–2006*, p. 55.
16. Minnie Minoso with Herb Fagen, *Just Call Me Minnie* (Champaign, IL: Sagamore, 1994), pp. 79–80.
17. *The Sporting News*, 19 Sep. 1951, p. 14.
18. Bob Vanderberg, *Sox* (Chicago: Chicago Review Press, 1984), pp. 241–242.
19. Lindberg, *Who's on Third?*, p. 85.
20. Lee Heiman, Dave Weiner, and Bill Gutman, *When the Cheering Stops* (New York: Macmillan, 1990), pp. 153–154.
21. Peary, *We Played the Game*, p. 168.
22. Minoso with Fagen, *Just Call Me Minnie*, p. 56.
23. *The Sporting News*, 28 Mar. 1956, p. 22.
24. Tygiel, *Baseball's Great Experiment*, p. 187.
25. Paige with Lipman, *Maybe I'll Pitch Forever*, p. 260; Minoso with Fagen, *Just Call Me Minnie*, p. 99.
26. Moore, *Pride Against Prejudice*, p. 111.
27. Veeck with Linn, *Veeck — As in Wreck*, pp. 350–351; Eskenazi, *Bill Veeck*, p. 131.
28. Minoso with Fagen, *Just Call Me Minnie*, p. 121.
29. Veeck with Linn, *Veeck — As in Wreck*, p. 351; Eskenazi, *Bill Veeck*, p. 131.
30. Durocher with Linn, *Nice Guys Finish Last*, p. 203.
31. Irvin with Riley, *Nice Guys Finish First*, p. 129.
32. Irvin with Riley, *Nice Guys Finish First*, p. 147.
33. Wendell Smith, "The Most Prejudiced Teams in Baseball," *Ebony* May 1953, p. 15.
34. John McReynolds, "Nate Moreland: A Mystery

to Historians," *The National Pastime* 19 (1999), pp. 57–58.
35. *The Sporting News*, 28 Mar. 1956, p. 22; Frederick A. Hurst, "Bobby Knight: Full Court Genius," *An Afro-American Point of View*, http://www.afampointof view.com/POV%20Archives/2005/January_2005/Jan_ Bobby%20Knight%20Full%20Court%20Genius/Bobby Knight_jan2005.htm.

Chapter 9

1. Tygiel, *Baseball's Great Experiment*, pp. 39–40.
2. Snyder, *Beyond the Shadow of the Senators*, p. 192.
3. Holway, *Black Diamonds*, p. 132.
4. *The Sporting News*, 11 Jan. 1950, p. 9.
5. Snyder, *Beyond the Shadow of the Senators*, p. 53; 1940 United States Census.
6. 1950 United States Census (see appendix).
7. O'Toole, *Branch Rickey in Pittsburgh*, pp. 12–13.
8. O'Toole, *Branch Rickey in Pittsburgh*, pp. 91–95.
9. O'Toole, *Branch Rickey in Pittsburgh*, pp. 68.
10. Ribowksy, *A Complete History of the Negro Leagues: 1884–1955*, p. 310.
11. O'Toole, *Branch Rickey in Pittsburgh*, p. 119.
12. *The Sporting News*, 14 Mar. 1951, p. 31; *The Sporting News*, 4 Apr. 1951, p. 11.
13. *The Sporting News*, 16 May 1951, p. 21.
14. *The Sporting News*, 2 May, 1950, p. 38.
15. "Valmy Thomas," AOL Hometown, members. aol.com/vibaseball/Thomas.html.
16. *The Sporting News*, 1 Aug. 1951, p. 32.
17. *The Sporting News*, 24 Oct. 1951, p. 24.
18. *The Sporting News*, 6 Jun. 1951, p. 35.
19. *The Sporting News*, 5 Mar. 1952, p. 16.
20. *The Sporting News*, 1 Oct. 1952, p. 60.
21. O'Toole, *Branch Rickey in Pittsburgh*, p. 119.
22. O'Toole, *Branch Rickey in Pittsburgh*, p. 50.
23. O'Toole, *Branch Rickey in Pittsburgh*, p. 160.
24. O'Toole, *Branch Rickey in Pittsburgh*, p. 120n.
25. O'Toole, *Branch Rickey in Pittsburgh*, pp. 128–129.
26. *The Sporting News*, 26 Mar. 1952, p. 25.
27. *The Sporting News*, 1 Feb. 1950, p. 22.
28. *The Sporting News*, 11 Nov. 1953, p. 14.
29. Wendell Smith, "The Most Prejudiced Teams in Baseball," *Ebony* May 1953, p. 18.
30. Moffi and Kronstadt, *Crossing the Line*, pp. 87–88.
31. Tygiel, *Baseball's Great Experiment*, p. 293.
32. Correspondence with Larry Lester, 30 Jul. 2007.
33. *The Sporting News*, 31 Aug. 1949, p. 24.
34. *The Sporting News*, 24 Oct. 1951, p. 24.
35. O'Toole, *Branch Rickey in Pittsburgh*, p. 150.
36. O'Toole, *Branch Rickey in Pittsburgh*, p. 5.
37. Stew Thornley, "Clemente's Entry into Organized Baseball," *The National Pastime* 26 (2006), pp. 61–71.
38. O'Toole, *Branch Rickey in Pittsburgh*, pp. 140–141; Thornley, "Clemente's Entry into Organized Baseball," p. 65.
39. "The Most Important Negro in Baseball," *Ebony* Oct. 1961, pp. 59–62.
40. *The Sporting News*, 5 Oct. 1963, p. 31.
41. The Pirates' all-black lineup on 1 Sep. 1971 in-

cluded Dock Ellis p, Manny Sanguillen c, Al Oliver 1b, Rennie Stennett 2b, Dave Cash 3b, Jackie Hernandez ss, Willie Stargell lf, Gene Clines cf, and Roberto Clemente rf.

42. The Pirates' World Series Game One lineup (9 Oct. 1971) featured Ellis p, Sanguillen c, Bob Robertson 1b, Cash 2b, Jose Pagan 3b, Hernandez ss, Stargell lf, Clines cf, and Clemente rf; Robertson was the only white player.

Chapter 10

1. Red Smith, "Connie, As Ever Was," in *To Absent Friends* (New York: Atheneum, 1982), p. 29.
2. Tygiel, *Baseball's Great Experiment*, p. 80.
3. *The Sporting News*, 27 Aug. 1947, p. 3.
4. Peary, *We Played the Game*, p. 228.
5. Bruce Kuklick, *To Every Thing a Season* (Princeton, NJ: Princeton University Press, 1991), p. 146; Holway, *Blackball Stars*, p. 163.
6. Marshall, *Baseball's Pivotal Era: 1945–1951*, p. 147.
7. Moore, *Pride Against Prejudice*, p. 90.
8. Minoso with Fagen, *Just Call Me Minnie*, p. 71; Peary, *We Played the Game*, p. 207.
9. Kuklick, *To Every Thing a Season*, p. 146.
10. Holway, *Voices From the Great Black Baseball Leagues*, p.87.
11. Shatzkin, ed., *The Ballplayers*, pp. 533–534.
12. Holway, *Blackball Stars*, p. 163.
13. Snyder, *Beyond the Shadow of the Senators*, pp. 177–178.
14. Snyder, *Beyond the Shadow of the Senators*, p. 180.
15. "How Owners of 16 Major Clubs Size Up Prospects for Colored Players," *Ebony* May 1949, p. 34.
16. Smith, "The Most Prejudiced Teams in Baseball," p. 18.
17. *The Sporting News*, 7 Feb. 1951, p. 19.
18. Holway, *Blackball Stars*, pp. 370–371.
19. *The Sporting News*, 7 Mar. 1951, p. 29.
20. *The Sporting News*, 24 Sep. 1952, p. 33.
21. *The Sporting News*, 21 Jul. 1954, p. 31.
22. Peary, "Interview with Vic Power," p. 360.
23. Peary, "Interview with Vic Power," p. 357.
24. Peary, *We Played the Game*, p. 266
25. Larry Moffi, *This Side of Cooperstown* (Iowa City: University of Iowa Press, 1996), pp. 99–100.
26. *The Sporting News*, 16 Mar. 1955, p. 15.
27. *The Sporting News*, 23 Mar. 1955, p. 16.
28. Shatzkin, ed., *The Ballplayers*, p. 538.
29. Light, *The Cultural Encyclopedia of Baseball*, pp. 395–396.
30. Shatzkin, ed., *The Ballplayers*, p. 1154.

Chapter 11

1. Golenbock, *Wrigleyville*, p. 240; Marshall, *Baseball's Pivotal Era: 1945–1951*, p. 193.
2. Marshall, *Baseball's Pivotal Era: 1945–1951*, p. 193.
3. Golenbock, *Wrigleyville*, pp. 265–271.
4. John Helyar, *Lords of the Realm* (New York: Ballantine Books, 1994), pp. 57–58.

5. Pietrusza, Silverman, and Gershman, eds., *Baseball: The Biographical Encyclopedia*, p. 1259.
6. Golenbock, *Wrigleyville*, p. 347.
7. Peterson, *Only The Ball Was White*, p. 179.
8. *The Sporting News*, 23 Dec. 1943, p. 16.
9. Pietrusza, Silverman, and Gershman, eds., *Baseball: The Biographical Encyclopedia*, p. 1258.
10. Bjarkman, *A History of Cuban Baseball*, 1864–2006, p. 323.
11. Bjarkman, *A History of Cuban Baseball*, 1864–2006, p. 328.
12. Fred Lieb, *Baseball As I Have Known It* (New York: Grossett and Dunlap, 1977), p. 313.
13. *The Sporting News*, 1 Oct. 1947, p. 16.
14. *The Sporting News*, 27 Oct. 1948, p. 14; *The Sporting News*, 13 Oct. 1948, p. 13.
15. *The Sporting News*, 4 May 1949, p. 41.
16. *The Sporting News*, 8 Jun. 1949, p. 42; *The Sporting News*, 24 Aug. 1949, p. 38.
17. Golenbock, *Wrigleyville*, pp. 269, 271–272.
18. Golenbock, *Wrigleyville*, p. 278.
19. Enders, "So Long, Sam."
20. Aaron with Wheeler, *I Had a Hammer*, pp. 117–118.
21. Light, *The Cultural Encyclopedia of Baseball*, p. 95.
22. Golenbock, *Wrigleyville*, p. 343.
23. Tygiel, *Baseball's Great Experiment*, p. 59.
24. Jackie Robinson with Charles Dexter, *Baseball Has Done It* (New York: Lippincott, 1964), p. 205.
25. Golenbock, *Wrigleyville*, p. 343.
26. *The Sporting News*, 1 Mar. 1950, p. 30.
27. *The Sporting News*, 3 May 1950, p. 32.
28. Riley, *The Biographical Encyclopedia of the Negro Baseball Leagues*, p. 279.
29. A. S. "Doc" Young, "Inside Sports," *Jet* 9 Apr. 1953, p. 53; Golenbock, *Wrigleyville*, p. 347.
30. Frank Finch, "Shortstop Aces," Oct. 1950 — article from Gene Baker's Hall of Fame file — publication unknown.
31. Golenbock, *Wrigleyville*, p. 347.
32. Moffi and Kronstadt, *Crossing the Line*, p. 84.
33. "BR Bullpen — Eddie Miksis," *Baseball-Reference.com*, www.baseball-reference.com/bullpen/Eddie_Miksis.
34. Peary, *We Played the Game*, p. 113.
35. *The Sporting News*, 25 Jun. 1952, p. 14.
36. *The Sporting News*, 22 Oct. 1952, p. 18.
37. "Wrigley Hits 'Monkey Business' in Gene Baker Shift," *Jet* 2 Apr. 1953, p. 51.
38. A. S. "Doc" Young, "Inside Sports," *Jet* 9 Apr. 1953, p. 53.
39. "Wrigley Hits 'Monkey Business' in Gene Baker Shift," p. 51.
40. *The Sporting News*, 28 Aug. 1948, p. 4.
41. Golenbock, *Wrigleyville*, pp. 346–347.
42. O'Toole, *Branch Rickey in Pittsburgh*, p. 107.
43. Golenbock, *Wrigleyville*, p. 280.
44. Moffi and Kronstadt, *Crossing the Line*, p. 84.
45. Golenbock, *Wrigleyville*, p. 349.
46. Peter C. Bjarkman, *Ernie Banks* (New York: Chelsea House, 1994), p. 23.
47. Tygiel, *Baseball's Great Experiment*, p. 244; O'Toole, *Branch Rickey in Pittsburgh*, p. 120; Holway, *Black Diamonds*, p. 102; Art Rust, Jr., *Get That Nigger*

Off the Field (New York: Shadow Lawn Press, 1992), p. 122; Golenbock, *The Spirit of St. Louis*, p. 355.

48. Golenbock, *Wrigleyville*, pp. 347–348.

49. Aaron with Wheeler, *I Had a Hammer*, p. 130.

50. *The Sporting News*, 29 Dec. 1954, p. 1.

51. Dewey and Acocella, *The Biographical History of Baseball*, p. 315.

52. Moffi and Kronstadt, *Crossing the Line*, p. 147.

53. Arthur R. Ashe, Jr., *A Hard Road to Glory* (New York: Amistad, 1993), pp. 55–56.

54. Gregory Meyer, "Mr. Cub Steps Up to the Plate," *Crain's Chicago Business*, 6 Aug. 2007, chicagobusiness.com/cgi-bin/mag/article.pl?id=28207.

Chapter 12

1. Marshall, *Baseball's Pivotal Era: 1945–1951*, p. 199.

2. Ibid.

3. Polner, *Branch Rickey*, p. 146.

4. Tygiel, *Baseball's Great Experiment*, pp. 185–186; *The Sporting News*, 14 May 1947, p. 13.

5. *The Sporting News*, 21 May 1947, p. 4.

6. *The Sporting News*, 27 Aug. 1947, p. 4.

7. Smith, "The Most Prejudiced Teams in Baseball." p. 15.

8. Marshall, *Baseball's Pivotal Era: 1945–1951*, p. 200; Golenbock, *The Spirit of St. Louis*, pp. 388–389.

9. Golenbock, *The Spirit of St. Louis*, pp. 390–391.

10. Tygiel, *Baseball's Great Experiment*, p. 286.

11. 1950 United States Census (see appendix).

12. Marshall, *Baseball's Pivotal Era: 1945–1951*, pp. 375–396.

13. Kahn, *The Era*, p. 233; Tygiel, *Baseball's Great Experiment*, p. 225.

14. *The Sporting News*, 30 Jun. 1948, p. 38.

15. Smith, "The Most Prejudiced Teams in Baseball, " p. 15.

16. Golenbock, *The Spirit of St. Louis*, p. 399.

17. Golenbock, *The Spirit of St. Louis*, pp.403–404.

18. Golenbock, *The Spirit of St. Louis*, p. 405.

19. Golenbock, *The Spirit of St. Louis*, p. 407.

20. *The Sporting News*, 27 Jan. 1954, p. 2.

21. *The Sporting News*, 3 Jun. 1953, p. 4.

22. *The Sporting News*, 11 Mar. 1959, p. 13.

23. Golenbock, *The Spirit of St. Louis*, p. 408.

24. Golenbock, *The Spirit of St. Louis*, p. 413.

25. Moffi and Kronstadt, *Crossing the Line*, p. 108.

26. Craft and Owens, *Redbirds Revisited*, pp. 9–15.

27. Golenbock, *The Spirit of St. Louis*, p. 408; and Rob Rains, *The St. Louis Cardinals: 100th Anniversary History* (New York: St. Martin's, 1992), p. 140.

28. Craft and Owens, *Redbirds Revisited*, pp. 13–14; Kelley, *Voices from the Negro Leagues*, p. 253.

29. Golenbock, *The Spirit of St. Louis*, p. 411.

30. Durocher with Linn, *Nice Guys Finish Last*, p. 203, p. 206.

31. David Falkner, *Great Time Coming* (New York: Simon and Schuster, 1995), p. 164; Polner, *Branch Rickey*, p. 198.

32. Golenbock, *The Spirit of St. Louis*, pp. 412–414.

33. Golenbock, *The Spirit of St. Louis*, pp.414–415.

34. Golenbock, *The Spirit of St. Louis*, p. 415.

35. Golenbock, *The Spirit of St. Louis*, pp. 417–418.

36. Brad Snyder, *A Well-Paid Slave* (New York: Viking, 2006), p. 53,

37. Golenbock, *The Spirit of St. Louis*, p. 435.

38. Ibid.

39. Snyder, *A Well-Paid Slave*, p. 53.

40. Boyle, "The Private World of the Negro Ballplayer," p. 78.

41. Shatzkin, ed., *The Ballplayers*, p. 1154.

42. Zoss and Bowman, *Diamonds in the Rough*, p. 149.

43. Snyder, *A Well-Paid Slave*, pp. 56–59.

Chapter 13

1. Bjarkman, *A History of Cuban Baseball, 1864–2006*, p. 137.

2. Bjarkman, *A History of Cuban Baseball, 1864–2006*, pp. 326–327.

3. Riley, *The Biographical Encyclopedia of the Negro Leagues*, p. 326; Zoss and Bowman, *Diamonds in the Rough*, p. 149.

4. Riley, *The Biographical Encyclopedia of the Negro Leagues*, p. 498; Zoss and Bowman, *Diamonds in the Rough*, p. 149.

5. Bjarkman, *A History of Cuban Baseball, 1864–2006*, p. 328; Zoss and Bowman, *Diamonds in the Rough*, p. 149.

6. Marshall, *Baseball's Pivotal Era: 1945–1951*, pp. 191–193.

7. Shatzkin, ed., *The Ballplayers*, p. 651.

8. Marshall, *Baseball's Pivotal Era: 1945–1951*, p. 395.

9. "How Owners Of 16 Major Clubs Size Up Prospects For Colored Players," p. 35.

10. Bryant, *Shut Out*, p. 71.

11. John Kiesewetter, "Civil Unrest Woven into City's History," *Cincinnati Enquirer* 15 Jul. 2001.

12. Kevin Sack, "Despite Report After Report, Unrest Endures in Cincinnati," *New York Times* 16 Apr. 2001.

13. Tygiel, *Baseball's Great Experiment*, p. 304.

14. Marshall, *Baseball's Pivotal Era: 1945–1951*, p. 142.

15. Smith, "The Most Prejudiced Teams in Baseball," p. 16.

16. Ibid.

17. *The Sporting News*, 10 Aug. 1949, p. 14.

18. Zoss and Bowman, *Diamonds in the Rough*, p. 179; Tygiel, *Baseball's Great Experiment*, p. 304.

19. Moffi and Kronstadt, *Crossing the Line*, p. 74.

20. *The Sporting News*, 2 Jul. 1952, p. 11.

21. Correspondence with Jim Sandoval, Co-Chair SABR Scouts Committee 15 Sep. 2007; *The Sporting News*, 13 Feb. 1952, p. 30.

22. *The Sporting News*, 27 Feb. 1952, p. 20; *The Sporting News*, 12 Mar. 1952, p. 27.

23. *The Sporting News*, 8 Apr. 1953, p. 30.

24. Earl Lawson, *Cincinnati Seasons* (South Bend, IN: Diamond Communications, 1987), p. 93.

25. Tygiel, *Baseball's Great Experiment*, p. 77.

26. Smith, "The Most Prejudiced Teams in Baseball," p. 16.

27. Lawson, *Cincinnati Seasons*, p. 100.

28. Lawson, *Cincinnati Seasons*, p. 93, pp. 96–103.

29. Lawson, *Cincinnati Seasons*, pp. 106–107.
30. Mike Bass, "Reds Harmon Broke Color Barrier Back In 1954," *Chuck Harmon: Major League Baseball Player*, 1 Mar. 1997, *www.chuckharmon.org/Scrips HowardStory.doc.*
31. *The Sporting News*, 24 Oct. 1951, p. 21.
32. *The Sporting News*, 22 Oct. 1952, p. 26. (
33. Bass, "Reds Harmon Broke Color Barrier Back In 1954."
34. Bjarkman, *A History of Cuban Baseball, 1864–2006*, p. 328.
35. Kelley, *Voices from the Negro Leagues*, p. 230.
36. Moffi and Kronstadt, *Crossing the Line*, p. 112.
37. 1950 United States Census (see appendix).
38. "Classics Reading Pitcher Brings New Hope to Cards," *Jet* 2 Aug. 1954, p. 55.
39. Golenbock, *The Spirit of St. Louis*, p. 409.
40. Tygiel, *Baseball's Great Experiment*, pp. 310–311.
41. Ibid.
42. Boyle, "The Private World of the Negro Ball player," p. 74.
43. Ibid.
44. Tygiel, *Baseball's Great Experiment*, p. 304.
45. Brent Kelley, "Marvin Williams: One of the Negro Leagues' Greatest Hitters Had Early Look by the Red Sox," *Sports Collectors Digest* 19 Dec. 1999, pp. 146–147.
46. Torry, *Endless Summers*, p. 87.
47. Al Hirshberg, *Frank Robinson: Born Leader* (New York: Putnam's, 1973), p. 102.
48. Lawson, *Cincinnati Seasons*, p. 144.
49. John Erardi, "'Bookkeeper Started It All: Sabo Suit Exposed Schott's Slurs," *Cincinnati Enquirer* 25 Oct. 1998.
50. Murray Chass, "Ex-A's Employee Cites Schott Racial Remarks," *The New York Times* 26 Nov. 1992.
51. Murray Chass, "Giving a Tongue a Rest," *The New York Times* 16 Jun. 1996.

Chapter 14

1. Snyder, *Beyond the Shadow of the Senators*, p. 59; Holway, *Voices From the Great Black Baseball Leagues*, p. 252.
2. 1950 and 1960 U.S. Census Reports (District of Columbia and City of Washington).
3. Snyder, *Beyond the Shadow of the Senators*, pp. 12–15.
4. Snyder, *Beyond the Shadow of the Senators*, pp. 12–13, p. 59, p. 63.
5. Snyder, *Beyond the Shadow of the Senators*, p. 73.
6. Snyder, *Beyond the Shadow of the Senators*, p. 67.
7. Snyder, *Beyond the Shadow of the Senators*, p. 282.
8. Shatzkin, ed., *The Ballplayers*, p. 455.
9. Snyder, *Beyond the Shadow of the Senators*, p. 282; Shatzkin, ed., *The Ballplayers*, p. 923.
10. Snyder, *Beyond the Shadow of the Senators*, p. 75.
11. Hogan, *Shades of Glory*, p. 307; Holway, *Voices From the Great Black Baseball Leagues*, p. 252.
12. Snyder, *Beyond the Shadow of the Senators*, p. 78.
13. William B. Mead, *The 10 Worst Years of Baseball* (New York: Van Nostrand Reinhold, 1978), p. 229; Snyder, *Beyond the Shadow of the Senators*, p. 190.
14. Snyder, *Beyond the Shadow of the Senators*, p. 75, p. 181.
15. Snyder, *Beyond the Shadow of the Senators*, p. 108, p. 220, pp. 232–233.
16. Snyder, *Beyond the Shadow of the Senators*, p. 232.
17. Snyder, *Beyond the Shadow of the Senators*, p. 262.
18. Snyder, *Beyond the Shadow of the Senators*, p. 263.
19. Snyder, *Beyond the Shadow of the Senators*, p. 266.
20. Dick Clark and Larry Lester, eds., *The Negro Leagues Book* (Cleveland: SABR, 1994), p. 28.
21. Snyder, *Beyond the Shadow of the Senators*, p. 287.
22. Snyder, *Beyond the Shadow of the Senators*, p. 279.
23. Snyder, *Beyond the Shadow of the Senators*, p. 279.
24. Tygiel, *Baseball's Great Experiment*, p. 287.
25. *The Sporting News*, 2 Apr. 1952, p. 25.
26. *The Sporting News*, 16 Apr. 1952, p. 16.
27. *The Sporting News*, 23 Jul. 1952, p. 12; *The Sporting News*, 28 Oct. 1953, p. 13.
28. Snyder, *Beyond the Shadow of the Senators*, p. 285.
29. Moore, *Pride Against Prejudice*, p. 99; Snyder, *Beyond the Shadow of the Senators*, p. 285; *The Sporting News*, 1 Apr. 1953, p. 20.
30. *The Sporting News*, 28 Oct. 1953, p. 13.
31. *The Sporting News*, 28 Oct. 1953, p. 2.
32. *The Sporting News*, 28 Oct. 1953, p. 13.
33. *The Sporting News*, 31 Mar. 1954, p. 17.
34. Ibid.
35. Snyder, *Beyond the Shadow of the Senators*, p. 285.
36. Moffi and Kronstadt, *Crossing the Line*, p. 116.
37. Alan Howard Levy, *Tackling Jim Crow* (Jefferson, NC: McFarland, 2003), p. 120.
38. "All-Time Harlem Globetrotters Roster," *The Association for Professional Basketball Research website*, members.aol.com/bradleyrd/trotters.html.
39. Levy, *Tackling Jim Crow*, p. 126.
40. Snyder, *Beyond the Shadow of the Senators*, p. 63.
41. Snyder, *Beyond the Shadow of the Senators*, p. 180.
42. *The Sporting News*, 23 Jul. 1952, p. 12.
43. Ibid.
44. Light, *The Cultural Encyclopedia of Baseball*, p. 374.
45. Snyder, *Beyond the Shadow of the Senators*, p. 70.
46. Snyder, *Beyond the Shadow of the Senators*, p. 71.
47. Bjarkman, *A History of Cuban Baseball, 1864–2006*, p. 446.
48. James, *The New Bill James Historical Baseball Abstract*, p. 196.
49. Smith, "The Most Prejudiced Teams in Baseball," p. 18.
50. Snyder, *Beyond the Shadow of the Senators*, pp. 72–73.
51. Snyder, *Beyond the Shadow of the Senators*, p. 283.
52. Roseboro with Libby, *Glory Days with the Dodgers*, p. 229.
53. Snyder, *Beyond the Shadow of the Senators*, p. 288.

54. Snyder, *Beyond the Shadow of the Senators*, p. 289.

55. *The Sporting News*, 16 Oct. 1976, p. 31.

Chapter 15

1. *The Sporting News*, 10 Dec. 1952, p. 3.

2. Tygiel, *Baseball's Great Experiment*, p. 294.

3. "The Race Question" 27 Aug. 1946 appears in Polner, *Branch Rickey*, pp. 188–191.

4. Ed Fitzgerald, *The American League* (New York: Grossett and Dunlap, 1959), p. 4.

5. Fitzgerald, *The American League*, pp. 9–11.

6. Marshall, *Baseball's Pivotal Era: 1945–1951*, p. 204.

7. Marshall, *Baseball's Pivotal Era: 1945–1951*, p. 205.

8. Irvin with Riley, *Nice Guys Finish First*, p. 120.

9. *The Sporting News*, 2 Feb. 1949, p. 24.

10. *The Sporting News*, 9 Feb. 1949, p. 1.

11. *The Sporting News*, 23 Feb. 1949, p. 18.

12. *The Sporting News*, 25 May 1949, p. 18.

13. Ibid.

14. Tygiel, *Baseball's Great Experiment*, p. 244.

15. *The Sporting News*, 9 Mar. 1949, p. 33.

16. *The Sporting News*, 9 Mar. 1949, p. 33; *The Sporting News*, 24 Aug. 1949, p. 21.

17. *The Sporting News*, 1 Jun. 1949, p. 21.

18. *The Sporting News*, 1 Jun. 1949, p. 24.

19. *The Sporting News*, 10 Aug. 1949, p. 31.

20. Tygiel, *Baseball's Great Experiment*, p. 295; *The Sporting News*, 31 Aug. 1940, pp. 33, 36.

21. *The Sporting News*, 26 Jul. 1950, p. 29.

22. Tygiel, *Baseball's Great Experiment*, p. 244.

23. *The Sporting News*, 3 Nov. 1954, p. 12.

24. *The Sporting News*, 20 Feb. 1952, p. 14.

25. Moffi and Kronstadt, *Crossing the Line*, p. 134.

26. Kahn, *The Era*, p. 189; Peary, *We Played the Game*, p. 303.

27. Tygiel, *Baseball's Great Experiment*, p. 296; Moffi and Kronstadt, *Crossing the Line*, p. 118; *The Sporting News*, 21 Oct. 1953, p. 10.

28. *The Sporting News*, 7 Jan. 1953, p. 20.

29. *The Sporting News*, 12 Aug. 1953, p. 8.

30. Jack Mann, *The Decline and Fall of the New York Yankees* (New York: Simon and Schuster, 1967), p. 86.

31. *The Sporting News*, 21 Oct. 1953, p. 10.

32. Peary, "Interview with Vic Power," pp. 359–360.

33. Tygiel, *Baseball's Great Experiment*, p. 297; *The Sporting News*, 23 Dec. 1953, p. 9.

34. Jess Bentert, "Elston Howard: The First Black Yankee," *Champion Yankees.Com*, http://www.angelfire.com/ny5/yankeeswebpage/elston.html.

35. *The Sporting News*, 19 Aug. 1953, p. 4.

36. *The Sporting News*, 6 Jan. 1954, p. 19.

37. Tygiel, *Baseball's Great Experiment*, p. 298.

38. *The Sporting News*, 27 Apr. 1955, p. 23.

39. David Halberstam, *October 1964* (New York: Villard Books, 1994), p. 235.

40. Shatzkin, ed., *The Ballplayers*, p. 1154.

41. Pietrusza, Silverman, and Gershman, eds., *Baseball: The Biographical Encyclopedia*, p. 1165.

42. Marshall, *Baseball's Pivotal Era: 1945–1951*, p. 203.

43. Pietrusza, Silverman, and Gershman, eds., *Baseball: The Biographical Encyclopedia*, p. 1207.

44. Kahn, *The Era*, p. 189.

45. Halberstam, *October 1964*, p. 231.

46. Eric Enders, "The Last .400 Hitter," *EricEnders.com*, www.ericenders.com/artiewilson.

47. Roger Kahn, *The Boys of Summer* (New York: Harper and Row, 1971), p. 160.

48. *The Sporting News*, 30 Jul. 1952, p. 2.

49. Kahn, *The Era*, p. 189.

50. *The Sporting News*, 19 Aug. 1953, p. 4.

51. Tygiel, *Baseball's Great Experiment*, p. 298.

52. Tygiel, *Baseball's Great Experiment*, p. 305.

53. Bentert, "Elston Howard: The First Black Yankee."

54. Tygiel, *Baseball's Great Experiment*, p. 294.

55. Tygiel, *Baseball's Great Experiment*, p. 305.

56. Tygiel, *Baseball's Great Experiment*, p. 27.

57. *The Sporting News*, 6 Aug. 1947, p. 19.

58. *The Sporting News*, 7 Jan. 1953, p. 20.

59. *The Sporting News*, 3 Aug. 1955, p. 5.

60. *The Sporting News*, 21 Jul. 1948, p. 12.

61. *The Sporting News*, 17 Aug. 1949, p. 12.

62. Doby tied for the American League lead while Robinson tied for second in the National League. Campanella was also plunked much more often than the average hitter

63. *The Sporting News*, 8 Jun, 1949, p. 30; *The Sporting News*, 29 Jun. 1949, p. 22; *The Sporting News*, 10 Aug. 1949, p. 24; Daniel Cattau, "So, Maybe There is Really Such a Thing as 'The Natural,'" *The Smithsonian* Jul. 1991.

64. *The Sporting News*, 13 Aug. 1952, p. 10.

65. *The Sporting News*, 30 Jul. 1952, p. 27.

66. Mann, *The Decline and Fall of the New York Yankees*, pp. 70–71.

67. Mann, *The Decline and Fall of the New York Yankees*, pp. 163–189.

68. List — Aaron, Banks, Gene Baker, Brooks Lawrence, Curt Roberts, and Sandy Amoros.

69. The Yankees, Tigers, and Red Sox had not integrated. The Senators' first black player, Carlos Paula, debuted 6 Sep. 1954, and the Orioles were segregated between Jehosie Heard's last appearance on 28 May 1954 and Joe Durham's first appearance on 10 Sep. 1954.

70. Mann, *The Decline and Fall of the New York Yankees*, p. 180.

71. Tygiel, *Baseball's Great Experiment*, p. 336.

72. Halberstam, *October 1964*, p. 237; Moffi and Kronstadt, *Crossing the Line*, p. 135.

73. Moffi and Kronstadt, *Crossing the Line*, p. 135.

74. Tygiel, *Baseball's Great Experiment*, p. 295.

Chapter 16

1. 1950 United States Census (see appendix). The 1950 attendance leaders were the Yankees, Tigers, Indians, Red Sox, and Phillies.

2. 1950 United States Census.

3. James P. Quirk and Rodney D. Fort, *Pay Dirt* (Princeton, NJ: Princeton University Press, 1997), p. 397; Shatzkin, ed., *The Ballplayers*, p. 813.

4. Fitzgerald, *The National League*, pp. 153–154.

5. Marshall, *Baseball's Pivotal Era: 1945–1951*, pp. 195–196.

6. Ibid.

7. Shatzkin, ed., *The Ballplayers*, p. 853.
8. Marshall, *Baseball's Pivotal Era: 1945–1951*, p. 196; Peter C. Bjarkman, ed., *The Encyclopedia of Major League Baseball Team Histories: National League* (Westport, CT: Meckler, 1991), p. 411.
9. Kuklick, *To Every Thing a Season*, p. 146.
10. Tygiel, *The Jackie Robinson Reader*, p. 137; Polner, *Branch Rickey*, p. 197.
11. Falkner, *Great Time Coming*, pp. 163–165; Frommer, *Rickey and Robinson*, pp. 136–137; Tygiel, *The Jackie Robinson Reader*, pp. 139–140; Polner, *Branch Rickey*, pp. 197–198.
12. Frommer, *Rickey and Robinson*, p. 136.
13. Falkner, *Great Time Coming*, p. 164; Polner, *Branch Rickey*, p. 198.
14. Tygiel, *Baseball's Great Experiment*, p. 183.
15. *The Sporting News*, 21 May 1947, p. 14.
16. Light, *The Cultural Encyclopedia of Baseball*, p. 599.
17. *The Sporting News*, 9 Jul. 1947, p. 25.
18. *The Sporting News*, 23 Jul. 1947, p. 19.
19. Zoss and Bowman, *Diamonds in the Rough*, pp. 165–166.
20. *The Sporting News*, 5 May 1954, p. 14.
21. Smith, "The Most Prejudiced Teams in Baseball," pp. 17–18.
22. "How Owners Of 16 Major Clubs Size Up Prospects For Colored Players," p. 35.
23. *The Sporting News*, 5 May 1954, p. 14.
24. Smith, "The Most Prejudiced Teams in Baseball," p. 18.
25. 1950 United States Census (see appendix).
26. William C. Kashatus, "Dick Allen, the Phillies, and Racism," *NINE: A Journal of Baseball History & Culture* 9.2 (2001), p. 151.
27. Peary, *We Played the Game*, p. 266.
28. *The Sporting News*, 13 Feb. 1952, p. 2
29. Bryant, *Shut Out*, pp. 43–44.
30. Bryant, *Shut Out*, p. 5.
31. *The Sporting News*, 1 Oct. 1952, p. 20.
32. Levy, *Tackling Jim Crow*, p. 98; Ron Thomas, *They Cleared the Lane* (Lincoln: University of Nebraska Press, 2004), p. 252.
33. *The Sporting News*, 7 Mar. 1956, p. 27.
34. *The Sporting News*, 1 Sep. 1954, p. 15.
35. Tygiel, *Baseball's Great Experiment*, p. 286.
36. Roy Campanella, *It's Good to be Alive* (New York: Dell, 1959), pp. 96–97; Holway, *Voices From the Great Black Baseball Leagues*, p. 12.
37. Robinson with Dexter, *Baseball Has Done It*, pp. 194–195.
38. *The Sporting News*, 25 Jul. 1956, p. 12.
39. *The Sporting News*, 18 May 1955, p. 10.
40. *The Sporting News*, 13 Feb. 1957, p. 24.
41. *The Sporting News*, 3 Apr. 1957, p. 14.
42. *The Sporting News*, 13 Mar. 1957, p. 17.
43. *The Sporting News*, 3 Apr. 1957, p. 14.
44. Bjarkman, *A History of Cuban Baseball, 1864–2006*, p. 341.
45. *The Sporting News*, 10 Apr. 1957, p. 11.
46. *The Sporting News*, 17 Apr. 1957, p. 24.
47. Bjarkman, *A History of Cuban Baseball, 1864–2006*, pp. 340–341.
48. *The Sporting News*, 15 May 1957, p. 35.
49. Moffi and Kronstadt, *Crossing the Line*, p. 112.
50. *The Sporting News*, 16 Dec. 1959, p. 20.
51. *The Sporting News*, 10 Dec. 1958, p. 20.
52. Kashatus, "Dick Allen, the Phillies, and Racism," 151–191.
53. Dewey and Acocella, *The Biographical History of Baseball*, p. 376.
54. *The Sporting News*, 18 May 1955, p. 34.
55. Dan Gutman, *Baseball Babylon* (New York: Penguin, 1992), p. 35.
56. Kashatus, "Dick Allen, the Phillies, and Racism," 151–191.
57. Ibid.
58. Ibid.; Andrew O'Toole, *The Best Man Plays* (Jefferson, NC: McFarland, 2003), p. 79.
59. Kashatus, "Dick Allen, the Phillies, and Racism," 151–191.
60. Snyder, *A Well-Paid Slave*, p. 13.
61. Kashatus, "Dick Allen, the Phillies, and Racism," 151–191.
62. Ibid.
63. Ibid.
64. Ibid.

Chapter 17

1. 1950 United States Census (see appendix).
2. 1950 and 1960 U.S. Census for Detroit urban area.
3. Patrick Harrigan, *The Detroit Tigers: Club and Community, 1945–1995* (Toronto: University of Toronto Press, 1997), p. 61.
4. *The Sporting News*, 18 Aug. 1948, p. 30.
5. Smith, "The Most Prejudiced Teams in Baseball," p. 14.
6. Marshall, *Baseball's Pivotal Era: 1945–1951*, p. 191.
7. Harrigan, *The Detroit Tigers*, p. 66.
8. Harrigan, *The Detroit Tigers*, p. 61.
9. Harrigan, *The Detroit Tigers*, p. 45.
10. "Briggs Manufacturing Co.—1909–1954," *Coachbuilt*, www.coachbuilt.com/bui/b/briggs/briggs.htm.
11. Harrigan, *The Detroit Tigers*, p. 47.
12. "Briggs Manufacturing," *Fortune 500 website*, http://money.cnn.com/magazines/fortune/fortune500_archives/snapshots/1955/281.
13. Morris Eckhouse, "The Detroit Tigers Baseball Club Conjures Up Images of Conservatism and Dependability," in *The Encyclopedia of Major League Baseball Team Histories: American League*, ed. Peter C. Bjarkman (Westport, CT: Meckler, 1991), p. 140.
14. Harrigan, *The Detroit Tigers*, p. 57.
15. Harrigan, *The Detroit Tigers*, p. 59.
16. Harrigan, *The Detroit Tigers*, p. 5.
17. Tygiel, *Baseball's Great Experiment*, p. 286.
18. Harrigan, *The Detroit Tigers*, p. 59.
19. Harrigan, *The Detroit Tigers*, p. 61.
20. Harrigan, *The Detroit Tigers*, p. 60.
21. Harrigan, *The Detroit Tigers*, pp. 60–61.
22. Harrigan, *The Detroit Tigers*, p. 83.
23. Harrigan, *The Detroit Tigers*, p. 79.
24. "Baseball America Executive Database," *Baseball America*, http://www.baseballamerica.com/execdb/.
25. 1950 United States Census (see appendix).

26. Harrigan, *The Detroit Tigers*, p. 49.
27. Ibid.
28. Harrigan, *The Detroit Tigers*, p. 6.
29. Harrigan, *The Detroit Tigers*, p. 69.
30. *The Sporting News*, 7 Jan. 1953, p. 20.
31. *The Sporting News*, 2 Sep. 1953, p. 21.
32. *The Sporting News*, 7 Oct. 1953, p. 11.
33. Harrigan, *The Detroit Tigers*, p. 80.
34. Marshall, *Baseball's Pivotal Era: 1945–1951*, p. 191.
35. Harrigan, *The Detroit Tigers*, p. 74.
36. Harrigan, *The Detroit Tigers*, p. 77.
37. Irvin with Riley, *Nice Guys Finish First*, p. 189; *The Sporting News*, 7 Dec. 1955, p. 6.
38. Levy, *Tackling Jim Crow*, p. 97.
39. Lyle K. Wilson, "The Last Negro League Baseball Game," *http://www.geocities.com/Colosseum/Field/1538/lastgame.html*.
40. Hogan, *Shades of Glory*, p. 249.
41. Harrigan, *The Detroit Tigers*, pp. 83–84.
42. Tygiel, *Baseball's Great Experiment*, pp. 328–329.
43. *The Sporting News*, 11 Jun. 1958, p. 10.
44. Harrigan, *The Detroit Tigers*, p. 85.
45. *The Sporting News*, 5 Feb. 1958, p. 25.
46. *The Sporting News*, 12 Feb. 1958, p. 8.
47. Harrigan, *The Detroit Tigers*, p. 93.
48. Harrigan, *The Detroit Tigers*, p. 84.
49. Correspondence with Bob Tighe, 26 Feb. 2008.
50. *The Sporting News*, 5 Feb. 1958, p. 25.
51. Peary, *We Played the Game*, p. 76.
52. Larry Lester, "First Latinos in Major League Baseball," *The Courier* (September 2007), p. 4.
53. Harrigan, *The Detroit Tigers*, p. 90.
54. Harrigan, *The Detroit Tigers*, p. 85.
55. *The Sporting News*, 22 Oct. 1958, p. 20; Wills and Celizic, *On the Run*, pp. 88–89.
56. Harrigan, *The Detroit Tigers*, pp. 100–101.
57. Harrigan, *The Detroit Tigers*, pp. 123–124.
58. Harrigan, *The Detroit Tigers*, p. 113.
59. Wilson, "The Last Negro League Baseball Game."
60. Harrigan, *The Detroit Tigers*, p. 113.

Chapter 18

1. Fitzgerald, *The American League*, pp. 121–124; Marshall, *Baseball's Pivotal Era: 1945–1951*, pp. 190–191.
2. Tygiel, *Baseball's Great Experiment*, pp. 43–44.
3. Falkner, *Great Time Coming*, p. 102; Tygiel, *Baseball's Great Experiment*, p. 44.
4. Tygiel, *Baseball's Great Experiment*, p. 44.
5. Falkner, *Great Time Coming*, p. 102.
6. Enders, "So Long, Sam."
7. The Chicago White Sox, Cincinnati Reds, Detroit Tigers, Philadelphia Athletics and Phillies, Pittsburgh Pirates, St. Louis Cardinals, and Washington Senators were still completely segregated.
8. *The Sporting News*, 24 May 1950, p. 38.
9. Kelley, *Voices from the Negro Leagues*, pp. 128–129.
10. Bryant, *Shut Out*, p. 45.
11. Bryant, *Shut Out*, pp. 46–47.
12. David Halberstam, *The Summer of '49* (New York: William Morrow, 1989), p. 186; Bryant, *Shut Out*, p. 45.

13. Bryant, *Shut Out*, p. 44, p. 62.
14. Tygiel, *Baseball's Great Experiment*, p. 80.
15. Bryant, *Shut Out*, p. 29.
16. Pietrusza, Silverman, and Gershman, eds., *Baseball: The Biographical Encyclopedia*, p. 1265; Marshall, *Baseball's Pivotal Era: 1945–1951*, p. 191.
17. Marshall, *Baseball's Pivotal Era: 1945–1951*, pp. 191–193; Bryant, *Shut Out*, p. 43.
18. Bryant, *Shut Out*, p. 88.
19. Halberstam, *The Summer of '49*, p. 186.
20. Halberstam, *The Summer of '49*, p. 184.
21. Bryant, *Shut Out*, p. 48.
22. Pietrusza, Silverman, and Gershman, eds., *Baseball: The Biographical Encyclopedia*, pp. 249–250.
23. Pietrusza, Silverman, and Gershman, eds., *Baseball: The Biographical Encyclopedia*, pp. 249–250; Eldon Auker with Tom Keegan, *Sleeper Cars and Flannel Uniforms* (Chicago: Triumph, 2001), pp. 160–164.
24. Bryant, *Shut Out*, p. 51; "The 1958 Year in Review," *Official Baseball Guide 1959*, p. 105.
25. *The Sporting News*, 2 Jul. 1947, p. 1.
26. *The Sporting News*, 24 Dec. 1952, p. 9.
27. *The Sporting News*, 21 Oct. 1953, p. 10.
28. *The Sporting News*, 15 Dec. 1954, p. 23; *The Sporting News*, 4 May 1960, p. 13.
29. *The Sporting News*, 16 Jan. 1957, p. 18.
30. Bryant, *Shut Out*, pp. 6–7.
31. Bryant, *Shut Out*, p. 7.
32. 1950 United States Census (see appendix).
33. Bryant, *Shut Out*, pp. 14–15.
34. Moffi and Kronstadt, *Crossing the Line*, pp. 210–211.
35. *The Sporting News*, 15 Apr. 1959, p. 16.
36. Tygiel, *Baseball's Great Experiment*, p. 331.
37. Moffi and Kronstadt, *Crossing the Line*, p. 226; Tygiel, *Baseball's Great Experiment*, p. 331.
38. *The Sporting News*, 4 Mar. 1959, p. 8.
39. Moffi and Kronstadt, *Crossing the Line*, p. 226.
40. Tygiel, *Baseball's Great Experiment*, p. 331
41. Tygiel, *Baseball's Great Experiment*, p. 331.
42. Bryant, *Shut Out*, p. 7; Tygiel, *Baseball's Great Experiment*, p. 332.
43. Moffi and Kronstadt, *Crossing the Line*, p. 212,
44. Bryant, *Shut Out*, p. 55.
45. Moffi and Kronstadt, *Crossing the Line*, p. 212.
46. Bryant, *Shut Out*, p. 64.
47. Pietrusza, Silverman, and Gershman, eds., *Baseball: The Biographical Encyclopedia*, p. 500.
48. Bryant, *Shut Out*, p. 67.
49. Bryant, *Shut Out*, p. 49.
50. Bryant, *Shut Out*, p. 88.
51. Bryant, *Shut Out*, p. 139.
52. Bryant, *Shut Out*, p. 153.
53. Bryant, *Shut Out*, p. 173.
54. Bryant, *Shut Out*, p. 249.
55. "The Boston Red Sox and Racism," *National Public Radio*, *http://www.npr.org/programs/morning/features/2002/oct/redsox/*.

Chapter 19

1. Leonard Shechter, *Once Upon a Time: The Early Years of the New York Mets* (1970; rpt. New York: Dial Press, 1983), p. 25.

BIBLIOGRAPHY

Aaron, Henry, with Lonnie Wheeler. *I Had a Hammer: The Hank Aaron Story*. New York: HarperCollins, 1991.

Alexander, Charles. *Rogers Hornsby: A Biography*. New York: Henry Holt, 1995.

Appel, Marty. *Yesterday's Heroes: Revisiting the Old-Time Baseball Stars*. New York: William Morrow, 1988.

Ardolino, Frank. "Jackie Robinson and the 1941 Honolulu Bears." *The National Pastime* 15 (1995): 68–70.

Ashe, Arthur, Jr. *A Hard Road to Glory: The African-American Athlete: Baseball*. New York: Amistad, 1993.

Auker, Elden, with Tom Keegan. *Sleeper Cars and Flannel Uniforms: A Lifetime of Memories from Striking Out the Babe to Teeing It Up with the President*. Chicago: Triumph, 2001.

Baseball: The Biographical Encyclopedia. Ed. Matthew Silverman, Michael Gershman, and David Pietrusza. New York: Total Sports, 2000.

The Baseball Chronicles. Ed. David Gallan. New York: Galahad Books, 1994.

"Baseball's Fastest Player." *Ebony* Oct. 1950.

Bayne, Bijan C. *Sky Kings: Black Pioneers of Professional Basketball*. Danbury, CT: Franklin Watts, 1997.

Bjarkman, Peter C. *Ernie Banks*. Baseball Legends series. New York: Chelsea House, 1994.

_____. *A History of Cuban Baseball, 1864–2006*. Jefferson, NC: McFarland, 2007.

_____, ed. *The Encyclopedia of Major League Baseball Team Histories: American League*. Westport, CT: Meckler, 1991.

_____, ed. *The Encyclopedia of Major League Baseball Team Histories: National League*. Westport, CT: Meckler, 1991.

Boyle, Robert. "The Private World of the Negro Ballplayer." *Sports Illustrated*. 21 Mar. 1960.

Bryant, Howard. *Shut Out: A Story of Race and Baseball in Boston*. Boston: Beacon Press, 2002.

Campanella, Roy. *It's Good to Be Alive*. New York: Dell, 1959.

Cattau, Daniel. "So, Maybe There is Really Such a Thing as 'The Natural.'" *The Smithsonian* Jul. 1991.

Chass, Murray. "Ex-A's Employee Cites Shott's Racial Remarks." *The New York Times* 26 Nov. 1992.

_____. "Giving a Tongue a Rest." *The New York Times* 16 Jun. 1996.

Clark, Dick, and Larry Lester, eds. *The Negro Leagues Book*. Cleveland: Society for American Baseball Research, 1994.

"Classics Reading Pitcher Brings New Hope to Cards." *Jet* 2 Aug. 1954.

Cohane, Tim. "A Branch Grows in Brooklyn." *Look Magazine* 19 Mar. 1946.

Craft, David, and Tom Owens. *Redbirds Revisited: Great Memories and Stories from St. Louis Cardinals*. Chicago: Bonus Books, 1990.

Deane, Bill. *Award Voting*. Cleveland: Society for American Baseball Research, 1988.

Dewey, Donald, and Nicholas Acocella. *The New Biographical History of Baseball*. Chicago: Triumph, 2002.

Durocher, Leo, with Ed Linn. *Nice Guys Finish Last*. New York: Simon and Schuster, 1975.

Einstein, Charles. *Willie's Time*. New York: Berkley Books, 1979.

Eisenberg, John. "The Quiet Pioneer." *The Baltimore Sun* 23 Apr. 2004.

The Encyclopedia of Major League Baseball Team Histories. Ed. Peter C. Bjarkman. 2 vols. Westport, CT: Meckler, 1991.

Erardi, John. "Bookkeeper Started It All: Sabo Suit Exposed Schott's Slurs." *Cincinnati Enquirer* 25 Oct. 1998.

Eskenazi, Gerald. *Bill Veeck: A Baseball Legend*. New York: McGraw-Hill, 1988.

Falkner, David. *Great Time Coming: The Life of Jackie Robinson from Baseball to Birmingham*. New York: Simon and Schuster, 1995.

Fatsis, Stefan. "Mystery of Baseball: Was William White Game's First Black?" *Wall Street Journal* 30 Jan. 2004.

Finch, Frank. "Shortstop Aces." Unidentified clipping from the Baseball Hall of Fame. Oct. 1950.

Fitzgerald, Ed. *The American League*. New York: Grossett and Dunlap, 1959.

_____. *The National League*. New York: Grossett and Dunlap, 1959.

Frommer, Harvey. *Rickey and Robinson: The Men Who Broke Baseball's Color Barrier*. New York: Macmillan, 1982.

Gallen, David, ed. *The Baseball Chronicles*. New York: Carroll & Graf, 1991.

Gibson, Bob, with Lonnie Wheeler. *Stranger to the Game: The Autobiography of Bob Gibson*. New York: Penguin, 1994.

Golenbock, Peter. *Bums: An Oral History of the Brooklyn Dodgers*. New York: Putnam's, 1984.

_____. *The Spirit of St. Louis: A History of the St. Louis Cardinals and Browns*. New York: HarperCollins, 2000.

_____. *Wrigleyville: A Magical History Tour of the Chicago Cubs*. New York: St. Martin's, 1999.

Gross, Milton. "I'm No Quitter." *Saturday Evening Post* 9 Mar. 1957.

Gutman, Dan. *Baseball Babylon: From the Black Sox to Pete Rose, the Real Stories Behind the Scandals that Rocked the Game*. New York: Penguin, 1992.

Halberstam, David. *October 1964*. New York: Villard Books, 1994.

_____. *Summer of '49*. New York: William Morrow, 1989.

Hano, Arnold. "Exclusive! Ex-World Series Start in Jail." *Sport* Dec. 1965.

Harrigan, Patrick. *The Detroit Tigers: Club and Community, 1945–1995*. Toronto: University of Toronto Press, 1997.

Hawthorn, Tom. "The Rocky Saga of Vagabond 'Tribesman' Jimmy Claxton." In *Rain Checks: Baseball in the Pacific Northwest*, ed. Mark Armour, 44–45, 126. Cleveland: Society for American Baseball Research, 2006.

Heiman, Lee, Dave Weiner, and Bill Gutman. *When the Cheering Stops: Former Major Leaguers Talk About Their Game and Their Lives*. New York: Macmillan, 1990.

Heylar, John. *Lords of the Realm: The Real History of Baseball*. New York: Ballantine Books, 1994.

Hirshberg, Al. *Frank Robinson: Born Leader*. New York: Putnam's, 1973.

Hogan, Lawrence D. *Shades of Glory: The Negro Leagues and the Story of African-American Baseball*. Washington, D.C.: National Geographic, 2006.

Holway, John B. *Black Diamonds: Life in the Negro Leagues from the Men Who Lived It*. Westport, CT: Meckler, 1989.

_____. *Blackball Stars: Negro League Pioneers*. Westport, CT: Meckler, 1988.

_____. "Dandy at Third: Ray Dandridge." *The National Pastime* 1 (1982): 7–11.

_____. *Voices from the Great Black Baseball Leagues*. New York: Dodd, Mead, 1975.

Honig, Donald. *Baseball America: The Heroes of the Game and the Times of Their Glory*. New York: Barnes and Noble, 1997.

_____. *Baseball in the '50s: A Decade of Transition*. New York: Crown, 1987.

_____. *Baseball When the Grass Was Real: Baseball from the Twenties to the Forties, Told by the Men Who Played It*. New York: Coward, McCann and Geoghegan, 1975.

Horgan, Tim. "Jimmy Piersall." In *Cult Baseball Players*, ed. Danny Peary, 276–83. New York: Simon and Schuster, 1990.

"How Owners of 16 Major Clubs Size Up Prospects for Colored Players." *Ebony* May 1949.

Hynd, Noel. *The Giants of the Polo Grounds: The Glorious Times of Baseball's New York Giants*. New York: Doubleday, 1988.

Irvin, Monte, with James A. Riley. *Nice Guys Finish First: The Autobiography of Monte Irvin*. New York: Carroll & Graf, 1996.

James, Bill. *The New Bill James Historical Baseball Abstract*. New York: Simon and Schuster, 2001.

Jordan, David, Larry R. Gerlach, and John P. Rossi. "A Baseball Myth Exploded." *The National Pastime* 18 (1998): 3–13.

Kahn, Roger. *The Boys of Summer*. New York: Harper and Row, 1971.

_____. *The Era, 1947–1957: When the Yankees, the Giants, and the Dodgers Ruled the World*. New York: Ticknor and Fields, 1993.

Karst, Gene, and Martin J. Jones, Jr. *Who's Who in Professional Baseball*. New Rochelle, NY: Arlington House, 1973.

Kashatus, William C. "Dick Allen, the Phillies, and Racism." *NINE: A Journal of Baseball History & Culture* 9.2 (2001): 151–191.

Kelley, Brent. "Marvin Williams: One of the Negro Leagues' Greatest Hitters Had Early Look By the Red Sox." *Sports Collectors Digest* 19 Dec. 1999.

_____. *Voices from the Negro Leagues: Conversations with 52 Baseball Standouts of the Period 1924–1960*. Jefferson, NC: McFarland, 1998.

"A Kid and an Old Timer." *Ebony* Jun. 1957.

Kiersh, Edward. *Where Have You Gone, Vince DiMaggio? Where Did They Go When the Cheering Stopped?* New York: Bantam, 1983.

Kiesewetter, John. "Civil Unrest Woven into City's History." *Cincinnati Enquirer* 15 Jul. 2001.

Kirwin, Bill. "Jim Crow in Canada: The Mysterious Case of Dick Brookins." *The National Pastime* 19 (1999): 38–43.

Koppett, Leonard. *Koppett's Concise History of Major League Baseball*. New York: Carroll & Graf, 2004.

Kuklick, Bruce. *To Every Thing a Season: Shibe Park and Urban Philadelphia, 1909–1976*. Princeton, NJ: Princeton University Press, 1991.

Kreuz, Jim. "Tom Greenwade and His '007' Assignment." *The National Pastime* 27 (2007): 96–100.

Lawson, Earl. *Cincinnati Seasons: My 34 Years with the Reds*. South Bend, IN: Diamond Communications, 1987.

Lester, Larry. "First Latinos in Major League Baseball." *The Courier* (SABR) Sep. 2007.

Levy, Alan Howard. *Tackling Jim Crow: Racial Segregation in Professional Football*. Jefferson, NC: McFarland, 2003.

Lieb, Fred. *Baseball As I Have Known It*. New York: Grossett and Dunlap, 1977.

Light, Jonathan Fraser. *The Cultural Encyclopedia of Baseball*. Jefferson, NC: McFarland, 1997.

Lindberg, Richard. *Who's on Third?: The Chicago White Sox Story*. South Bend, IN: Icarus Press, 1983.

Mann, Jack. *The Decline and Fall of the New York Yankees*. New York: Simon and Schuster, 1967.

Marazzi, Rich, and Len Fiorito. *Aaron to Zuverink*. New York: Avon Books, 1982.

Marshall, William. *Baseball's Pivotal Era, 1945–51*. Lexington: University Press of Kentucky, 1999.

Mays, Willie, and Charles Einstein. *Willie Mays: My Life In and Out of Baseball*. New York: Dutton, 1966.

Mays, Willie, with Lou Sahadi. *Say Hey: The Autobiography of Willie Mays*. New York: Simon and Schuster, 1988.

McReynolds, John. "Nate Moreland: A Mystery to Historians." *The National Pastime* 19 (1999): 55–64.

Mead, William B. *The 10 Worst Years of Baseball: The Zany, True Story of Baseball in the Forties*. New York: Van Nostrand Reinhold, 1978.

Minoso, Minnie, with Herb Fagen. *Just Call Me Minnie: My Six Decades in Baseball*. Champaign, IL: Sagamore, 1994.

Moffi, Larry. *This Side of Cooperstown: An Oral History of Major League Baseball in the 1950s.* Iowa City: University of Iowa Press, 1996.

_____, and Jonathan Kronstadt. *Crossing the Line: Black Major Leaguers, 1947–1959.* Jefferson, NC: McFarland, 1994.

Moore, Joseph Thomas. *Pride Against Prejudice: The Biography of Larry Doby.* Westport, CT: Praeger, 1988.

"The Most Important Negro in Baseball." *Ebony* Oct. 1961.

The Negro Leagues Book. Ed. Dick Clark and Larry Lester. Cleveland: Society for American Baseball Research, 1994.

Obojski, Robert. Bob Thurman Profile. *Sports Collectors Digest* 11 Oct. 1991.

_____. *Bush League: A History of Minor League Baseball.* New York: Macmillan, 1975.

_____. Sam Jethroe Profile. *Sports Collectors Digest* 27 Sep. 1991.

O'Toole, Andrew. *The Best Man Plays: Major League Baseball and the Black Athlete, 1901–2002.* Jefferson, NC: McFarland, 2003.

_____. *Branch Rickey in Pittsburgh.* Jefferson, NC: McFarland, 2000.

Overfield, Joseph M. "Easter's Charisma, Remarkable Slugging Captivated Fans." *Baseball Research Journal* 13 (1984): 14–16.

Paige, Leroy (Satchel), with David Lipman. *Maybe I'll Pitch Forever.* Lincoln: University of Nebraska Press, 1993.

Peary, Danny. "Interview with Vic Power." In *Cult Baseball Players,* ed. Danny Peary, 352–373. New York: Simon and Schuster, 1990.

_____. *We Played the Game: 65 Players Remember Baseball's Greatest Era, 1947–1964.* New York: Hyperion, 1994.

Peterson, Robert W. *Only the Ball Was White.* Englewood Cliffs, NJ: Prentice-Hall, 1970.

Polner, Murray. *Branch Rickey: A Biography.* New York: Atheneum, 1982.

"Problem Child." *Our Sports* Jun. 1953.

Quirk, James P., and Rodney D. Fort. *Pay Dirt: The Business of Professional Team Sports.* Princeton, NJ: Princeton University Press, 1997.

Rains, Rob. *The St. Louis Cardinals: The 100th Anniversary History.* New York: St. Martin's, 1992.

Ribowsky, Mark. *A Complete History of the Negro Leagues, 1884 to 1955.* Secaucus, NJ: Carol Publishing, 1995.

Riley, James A. *The Biographical Encyclopedia of the Negro Baseball Leagues.* New York: Carroll & Graf, 1994.

Robinson, Jackie, as told to Alfred Duckett. *I Never Had It Made.* New York: Putnam's, 1972.

Robinson, Jackie, with Charles Dexter. *Baseball Has Done It.* New York: Lippincott, 1964.

Roseboro, John, and Bill Libby. *Glory Days with the Dodgers and Other Days with Others.* New York: Atheneum, 1978.

Rosenthal, Harold. *The 10 Best Years of Baseball: An Informal History of the Fifties.* Chicago: Contemporary Books, 1979.

Rust, Art, Jr., *Get That Nigger Off the Field: The Oral History of the Negro Leagues.* New York: Shadow Lawn Press, 1992.

Sack, Kevin. "Despite Report After Report, Unrest Endures in Cincinnati." *The New York Times* 16 Apr. 2001.

Schneider, Russell. *The Boys of the Summer of '48.* Champaign, IL: Sports Publishing, 1998.

Shatzkin, Mike, ed. *The Ballplayers.* New York: Arbor House, 1990.

Shechter, Leonard. "Can't Anybody Here Use Kanehl?" *Sports Illustrated* 8 Aug. 1966.

_____. *Once Upon a Time: The Early Years of the New York Mets.* 1970; rpt. New York: Dial Press, 1983.

Simon, William, ed. *The Cooperstown Symposium on Baseball and American Culture.* Jefferson, NC: McFarland, 2000.

Singeltary, Wes. *Al Lopez: The Life of Baseball's El Senor.* Jefferson, NC: McFarland, 1999.

Smith, Red. *To Absent Friends from Red Smith.* New York: Atheneum, 1982.

Smith, Wendell. "The Most Prejudiced Teams in Baseball." *Ebony* May 1953.

Snyder, Brad. *Beyond the Shadow of the Senators: The Untold Story of the Homestead Grays.* New York: Contemporary Books, 2003.

_____. *A Well-Paid Slave: Curt Flood's Fight for Free Agency in Professional Sports.* New York: Viking, 2006.

Solomon, Burt. *The Baseball Timeline.* New York: DK Publishing, 2001.

Spatz, Lyle. *The SABR Baseball List & Record Book.* New York: Scribner's, 2007.

Spink, J. G. Taylor. *Judge Landis and 25 Years of Baseball.* St. Louis: Sporting News, 1974.

_____. *Official Baseball Guide: 1959 Edition: The 1958 Year in Review.* St. Louis: Sporting News, 1959.

Steadman, John F. "McGraw's Negro Second Baseman." *Baseball Digest* 21.9 (Oct.-Nov. 1962).

Thomas, Ron. *They Cleared the Lane: The NBA's Black Pioneers.* Lincoln: University of Nebraska Press, 2004.

Thornley, Stew. "Clemente's Entry into Organized Baseball." *The National Pastime* 26 (2006): 61–71.

Torry, Jack. *Endless Summers: The Fall and Rise of the Cleveland Indians.* South Bend, IN: Diamond Communications, 1996.

Tucker, Walter Dunn. "How Old Is That Guy, Anyway?" *Baseball Research Journal* 36 (2007): 94–98.

Tygiel, Jules. *Baseball's Great Experiment: Jackie Robinson and His Legacy.* New York: Oxford University Press, 1997.

_____. *Extra Bases: Reflections on Jackie Robinson, Race, and Baseball History.* Lincoln: University of Nebraska Press, 2002.

_____. "Revisiting Bill Veeck and the 1943 Phillies." *Baseball Research Journal* 35 (2006): 109–114.

_____, ed. *The Jackie Robinson Reader: Perspectives on an American Hero.* New York: Penguin, 1997.

Vanderberg, Bob. *Minnie and the Mick: The Go-Go White Sox Challenge the Fabled Yankee Dynasty, 1951 to 1964.* South Bend, IN: Diamond Communications, 1996.

_____. *Sox: From Lane and Fain to Zisk and Fisk.* Chicago: Chicago Review Press, 1984.

Veeck, Bill, with Ed Linn. *Veeck—As in Wreck.* New York: Bantam, 1962.

Westcott, Richard. *Diamond Greats: Profiles and Interviews with 65 of Baseball's History Makers.* Westport, CT: Meckler, 1988.

Wheeler, Lonnie. "Lawrence, Reds' Silent Giant Dies." *Cincinnati Post* 28 Apr. 2000.

Wilbert, Cynthia J. *For the Love of the Game: Baseball Memories from the Men Who Were There*. New York: Morrow, 1992.

"Will Bankhead Be Retained by the Brooklyn Dodgers or Will He Be Peddled Elsewhere to Keep the Negro 'Quota' at the Right Number in Ebbets Field?" *New York Age* 2 May 1950.

Williams, Jack. "John Ritchey, 80; 'Johnny Baseball' Was First Black in the PCL." *San Diego Union-Tribune* 21 Jan. 2003.

Wills, Maury, and Mike Celizic. *On the Run: The Never Dull and Often Shocking Life of Maury Wills*. New York: Carroll & Graf, 1991.

Wilson, Walt. "Willard Brown: A Forgotten Ballplayer." *The National Pastime* 24 (2004): 24.

"Wrigley Hits 'Monkey Business' in Gene Baker Shift." *Jet* 2 Apr. 1953.

Young, A. S. "Doc." *Negro Firsts in Sports*. Chicago: Johnson Publishing, 1963.

_____. "Inside Sports." *Jet* 9 Apr. 1953.

_____. "Inside Sports." *Jet* 11 June 1953.

Zoss, Joel, and John Bowman. *Diamonds in the Rough: The Untold History of Baseball*. New York: Contemporary Books, 1996.

Statistical Sources

The Baseball Encyclopedia. 10th ed. New York: Macmillan, 1996.

Daguerreotypes. 8th ed. St. Louis: Sporting News, 1990.

Minor League Baseball Stars. Vol. 2. Cleveland: SABR, 1985.

Minor League Baseball Stars. Vol. 3. Cleveland: SABR, 1992.

The Minor League Register. Baseball America, 1994.

The Sporting News Baseball Register. St. Louis: Sporting News. Various years.

The Sports Encyclopedia. New York: St. Martin's, 1993.

Total Baseball. 6th ed. Kingston, NY: Total Sports, 1999.

Who's Who in Baseball. Who's Who in Baseball Magazine Company. Various years.

Web Sites

"All-Time Harlem Globetrotters Roster," *The Association for Professional Basketball Research website*, members.aol.com/bradleyrd/trotters.html.

"Baseball America Executive Database," *Baseball America*, http://www.baseballamerica.com/execdb/.

Bass, Mike. "Reds Harmon Broke Color Barrier Back In 1954." *Chuck Harmon: Major League Baseball Player* 1 Mar. 1997.www.chuckharmon.org/Scrips HowardStory.doc.

Bentert, Jess. "Elston Howard: The First Black Yankee." *Champion Yankees.Com*. http://www.angel fire.com/ny5/yankeeswebpage/elston.html.

"The Boston Red Sox and Racism," *National Public Radio*. http://www.npr.org/programs/morning/features/2002/oct/redsox/.

"BR Bullpen — Eddie Miksis," *Baseball-Reference*, www.baseball-reference.com/bullpen/Eddie_Miksis.

"Briggs Manufacturing," *Fortune 500 website*, http://money.cnn.com/magazines/fortune/fortune500 archives/snapshots/1955/281.

"Briggs Manufacturing Co.—1909–1954," *Coachbuilt*. www.coachbuilt.com/bui/b/briggs/briggs.htm.

"David Taylor Hoskins." *Negro League Baseball Players Association*. http://www.nlbpa.com/hoskins_david.html.

Doyle, Pat. "Luke Easter: Myth, Legend, Superstar." *Baseball Almanac*. http://www.baseball-almanac.com/minor-league/minor9.shtml

Enders, Eric. www.ericenders.com.

"George Crowe — Our First Mr. Basketball," *Indiana Basketball Hall of Fame*, www.hoopshall.com/inductees/1976/crowe.html.

Hurst, Frederick A. "Bobby Knight: Full Court Genius." *An Afro-American Point of View*. http://www.afampointofview.com/POV%20Archives/200 5/January_2005/Jan_Bobby%20Knight%20Full%2 0Court%20Genius/BobbyKnight_jan2005.htm.

Meyer, Gregory. "Mr. Cub Steps Up to the Plate," *Crain's Chicago Business* 6 Aug. 2007. chicagobusiness.com/cgi-bin/mag/article.pl?id=28207.

Petkovic, John. "The Negro Leagues: Dave Pope." *Scam City*. http://www.scamcity.com/index.php?story_id=7.

Rives, Bob. "Bob Boyd." *The Baseball Biography Project*. http://bioproj.sabr.org/.

"Sam Jethroe." *Historic Baseball*. http://www.historicbaseball.com/players/j/jethroe_sam.html.

The Sporting News. www.paperofrecord.com.

"Thurman Dead in Wichita at 81." *The Deadball Era*. http://thedeadballera.com/Obits/Thurman.Bob.Obit.html.

Usen, Mark. "Cooperstown Confidential — Brooks Lawrence." *Big Bad Baseball*. www.bigbadbaseball.com.

"Valmy Thomas." AOL Hometown, members.aol.com/vibaseball/Thomas.html.

White, John. "Sam 'The Jet' Jethroe." *BaseballLibrary.com*. http://www.baseballlibrary.com/baseballlibrary/submit/White_John1.stm.

Wilson, Lyle K. "The Last Negro League Baseball Game." http://www.geocities.com/Colosseum/Field/1538/lastgame.html.

INDEX